Lecture Notes in Computer Science 11913

More information about this series at http://www.springer.com/series/7407

Sergei N. Pozdniakov · Valentina Dagienė (Eds.)

Informatics in Schools

New Ideas in School Informatics

12th International Conference on Informatics in Schools:
Situation, Evolution, and Perspectives, ISSEP 2019
Larnaca, Cyprus, November 18–20, 2019
Proceedings

Springer

Editors
Sergei N. Pozdniakov
Saint Petersburg Electrotechnical University
Saint Petersburg, Russia

Valentina Dagienė
Data Science Institute
Vilnius University
Vilnius, Lithuania

ISSN 0302-9743 ISSN 1611-3349 (electronic)
Lecture Notes in Computer Science
ISBN 978-3-030-33758-2 ISBN 978-3-030-33759-9 (eBook)
https://doi.org/10.1007/978-3-030-33759-9

LNCS Sublibrary: SL1 – Theoretical Computer Science and General Issues

This Springer imprint is published by the registered company Springer Nature Switzerland AG
The registered company address is: Gewerbestrasse 11, 6330 Cham, Switzerland

Preface

This volume contains the papers presented at the 12th International Conference on Informatics in Schools: Situation, Evolution, and Perspectives (ISSEP 2019). The conference was held at the University of Cyprus, November 18–20, 2019.

ISSEP is a forum for researchers and practitioners in the area of informatics education, in both primary and secondary schools (K12 education). It provides an opportunity for educators to reach the goals and objectives of this subject based on its curricula and various teaching/learning paradigms and topics, possible connections to everyday life, and various ways of establishing informatics education in schools.

This conference also has a focus on teaching/learning materials, various forms of assessment, traditional and innovative educational research designs, the contribution of informatics to the preparation of individuals for the 21st century, motivating competitions, and projects and activities supporting informatics education in schools. The ISSEP series started in 2005 in Klagenfurt, with subsequent meetings held in Vilnius (2006), Torun (2008), Zurich (2010), Bratislava (2011), Oldenburg (2013), Istanbul (2014), Ljubljana (2015), Münster (2016), Helsinki (2017), and St. Petersburg (2018). This 12th ISSEP conference was hosted by the University of Cyprus.

The conference received 55 submissions. Each submission was reviewed by up to four Program Committee members and evaluated on its quality, originality, and relevance to the conference. Overall, the Program Committee wrote 116 reviews and 90 reviews were prepared by external reviewers. The committee selected 23 papers for inclusion in the LNCS proceedings, leading to an acceptance rate of 40%. The decision process was made electronically using the EasyChair conference management system.

As at previous ISSEP conferences, much attention in the articles is devoted to the training of informatics teachers and to the teaching of informatics at different levels of school education. At the same time, increasing attention to the primary level should be noted. A feature of ISSEP 2019 is the interest of school education in contemporary computer science ideas that were previously studied only at universities: big data, machine learning, artificial intelligence, cybersecurity, and others.

We would like to thank all the authors who responded to the call for papers, the members of the Program Committee, the external reviewers, and last but not least the members of the Organizing Committee and Prof. George A. Papadopoulos – general and organizing chair of the local Organizing Committee.

September 2019

Sergei Pozdniakov
Valentina Dagienė

Organization

General and Organizing Chair

George A. Papadopoulos	University of Cyprus, Cyprus (george(at)cs.ucy.ac.cy)

Steering Committee

Andreas Bollin	University of Klagenfurt, Austria
Valentina Dagiene	Vilnius University, Lithuania
Yasemin Gulbahar	Ankara University, Turkey
Juraj Hromkovič	Swiss Federal Institute of Technology Zurich, Switzerland
Ivan Kalas	Comenius University, Slovakia
George A. Papadopoulos	University of Cyprus, Cyprus
Sergei Pozdniakov	Saint Petersburg Electrotechnical University, Russia

Program Committee Chair

Sergei Pozdniakov	Saint Petersburg Electrotechnical University, Russia

Program Committee

Erik Barendsen	Radboud University Nijmegen and Open Universiteit, The Netherlands
Andrej Brodnik	University of Ljubljana, Slovenia
Christian Datzko	SVIA-SSIE-SSII, Switzerland
Ira Diethelm	Oldenburg University, Germany
Michalis Giannakos	Norwegian University of Science and Technology, Norway
Bruria Haberman	Holon Institute of Technology, Israel
Peter Hubwieser	Technical University Munich, Germany
Petri Ihantola	Tampere University of Technology, Finland
Mile Jovanov	Ss. Cyril and Methodius University, Macedonia
Dennis Komm	Pedagogical University Chur, Switzerland
Mark Laanpere	Tallinn University, Estonia
Peter Micheuz	University Klagenfurt and Gymnasium Völkermarkt, Austria
Mattia Monga	Università degli Studi di Milano, Italy
Ralf Romeike	University Erlangen (FAU), Germany
Giovanni Serafini	Swiss Federal Institute of Technology Zurich, Switzerland
Maciej M. Syslo	Nicolaus Copernicus University, Poland

Additional Reviewers

Veljko Aleksić
Grillenberger Andreas
Cristian Bernareggi
Hans-Joachim Böckenhauer
Sona Ceretkova
Sébastien Combéfis
Andrew Paul Csizmadia
Vladimiras Dolgopolovas
Fabian Frei
Walter Gander
Daina Gudoniene
Bruria Haberman
Urs Hauser
Djordje Herceg
Metodija Janceski
Tatjana Jevsikova
Mile Jovanov
Filiz Kalelioglu
Peter Larsson
Inggriani Liem
Violetta Lonati
Dario Malchiodi
Anna Morpurgo
Mārtiņš Opmanis
Tauno Palts
Arnold Pears
Serena Pedrocchi
Rein Prank
Mareen Przybylla
Noa Ragonis
Ana Isabel
Frances Rosamond
Jacqueline Staub
Xinogalos Stelios
Seiichi Tani
Nicole Trachsler
Ausra Urbaityte
Peter Waker

Contents

Contemporary Computer Science Ideas in School Informatics

Teaching Informatics: From High School to University Level

Contests, Competitions and Games in Informatics

Teacher Education in Informatics

Empowering the Teachers with the NAPOJ - A Grassroots Movement Towards Computing Teachers Community of Practice

Andrej Brodnik[1,2](✉) and Matija Lokar[3]

[1] Faculty of Computer and Information Science, University of Ljubljana, Ljubljana, Slovenia
Andrej.Brodnik@fri.uni-lj.si
[2] Faculty of Mathematics, Natural Sciences and Information Technologies, University of Primorska, Koper, Slovenia
[3] Faculty of Mathematics and Physics, University of Ljubljana, Ljubljana, Slovenia
Matija.Lokar@fmf.uni-lj.si

Abstract. Computing is a relatively new area in high school education, not only in Slovenia but worldwide. Therefore, there is lack of qualified Computing teachers. However, even the existing ones often feel isolated and consequently insecure. The latter often stems from lack of trust in their own teaching practices. These feeling can be alleviated through participation in a Community of practice (CoP).

The article describes activities taken in a project NAPOJ to form an active community of practice for Slovene Computing teachers. NAPOJ started as a grassroots movement in a group of high school teachers and few higher education teachers involved in various activities (in-service teacher training, programming competitions, ...). The main goal of the project NAPOJ is to involve teachers in an active building of their competencies and improve cooperation among them, such as exchange of study materials, and good practices.

We started building the community by gathering the necessary materials and tools for teaching programming, an area where the idea of necessary cooperation occurred. Three systems that teachers use in teaching were connected: e-textbook, web classroom and a system for automated testing of program correctness. In the second year, we added physical computing as a motivational element. In the ongoing third year, the main emphasis is on supporting the programming competition preparations and on the exchange of good practice examples among teachers. The core activity is the formation of the community portal and regular monthly video conferences where certain, mostly didactic, topics in Computing are discussed.

Keywords: Community of practice · Computer Science teaching · Computing teaching · Motivation · Teaching programming

S. N. Pozdniakov and V. Dagienė (Eds.): ISSEP 2019, LNCS 11913, pp. 3–14, 2019.
https://doi.org/10.1007/978-3-030-33759-9_1

1 Introduction

Computing education is a relatively new area in high schools, not only in Slovenia but worldwide. Therefore, we are faced with many challenges regarding the method of teaching itself. Brodnik et al. [25] state that in Slovenia Computing is a compulsory subject in only one year in high school and an elective subject in the other three years, which differs a lot from the current practice elsewhere in Europe and the World-wide. Fortunately, the curriculum is very open and covers all four years, which gives the teachers a freedom when it comes to deciding on the selection of topics. This openness permits changes towards a better quality of Computing education [22,29]. Furthermore, we can observe a common awareness that a significant part of Computing lessons should be the teaching of programming skills. In particular as programming (not coding) is considered a natural technique to teach Computational Thinking. This confirms also an overview of contemporary recommendations for curricula (like CSTA in [16], IEEE in [19], the current UK curriculum in [17]), which shows the importance of basic computer programming skills in contemporary education. In Slovenia this awareness is evident in the new e-textbook for the subject [2,22] and certain changes in the Matura exam [1].

However, changing the emphasis from one part of the curriculum (digital literacy) to another (core concepts of Computing) and changing methods of teaching, required and expected substantial changes. The changes raised certain amount of resistance and disagreement among the teachers. A large amount of literature in this field shows [14,15,23,26,27,31] one of the possible methods to overcome the initial teachers' reluctance is to establish a strong and active community of practice. The article reports on the attempted establishment of such a community in Slovenia.

2 Learning Communities

As reported by Barber and Mourshed in [6] investment in the teachers is the key factor that determines the rise in the quality of the education system. The aforementioned authors state: "The quality of an education system cannot exceed the quality of its teachers."

Computing teachers frequently feel lonely in their field ([23]), which often goes hand in hand with the lack of trust in their own teaching practices. This is confirmed by Sentance and Humphreys in [26]. Establishing communities of practice can help the teachers to overcome this feeling of loneliness.

The Wenger-Trayners in [31] define a learning community as "... a group of people who share common academic goals and passions, and achieve self-improvement in the field through activity in the group". Beside the common academic interest, an important ingredient of a learning community is the fact, that the members are active practitioners who share experiences, stories, tools, and ways of addressing problems. Thus Fincher and Tenenberg in [28] and in [18] report on Disciplinary Commons project, within which a group of Computing teachers meet monthly and share study materials, teaching experiences and document their teaching practice. Ni and his co-authors in [23] report on how a self-organized local group of teachers proved to be a successful attempt at establishing a high school Computing teachers' community of practice. One of the most important results of the project was that practically all of the teachers reported that they felt community affiliation. The affiliation made it possible for the teachers to assess their work appropriately and to gain self-confidence as Computing teachers. A very successful community was founded within the Computing at School (CAS) movement in Great Britain. The CAS movement does not only take care of the learning community, but also provides support for the community, which is at the core of activity of the whole movement. CAS actually functions as the cover learning community that unites and directs the activities of a whole bunch of local communities of practice. The local communities mostly formed individually as a reflection of the needs of a local group of Computing teachers. As Sentence and Humphreys report in [26], the CAS project focuses on formation of local communities of practice and thus supports the teachers trying to implement the new curriculum into the lessons.

Therefore, the large and most importantly continuous growth of the number of members of the communities as reported by Berry in [8] should not be considered particularly surprising.

3 NAPOJ Project

For the project aimed at achieving better cooperation among computing teachers, especially concerning the exchange of study materials and teaching experiences, we were assigned funds within the Google CS4HS[1] call. Consequently, teachers had all their expenses for participation covered. Initially we concentrated on Gymnasium[2] high school teachers, but later expanded to all high school Computing teachers. Furthermore, as also primary school teachers of elective Computing subjects showed interest, we included them in the project as well.

The project was called NAPOJ in Slovene which translates to English as *potion*[3]. Because the main ingredient of the project was preparation of materials that could be used in teaching programming, we included in the project the textbook, a Moodle classroom, and a system for checking the correctness of programs. This also reflected in the logo in Fig. 1.

[1] Computer Science for High School.

[2] In Slovenia children enter primary school at age 6. The primary school has 9 grades and high school has 4 grades. Gymnasium is vaguely said a general high school offering students (aged 15–18) extension of the knowledge gained in primary schools. Upon its completion students undertake state wide external examination (Matura), which allows them to enrol into any type of tertiary education course.

[3] NAPOJ in Slovene stands for ***N****ačrtovanje poučevanja* ***A****lgoritmov in* ***P****rogramiranja ter* ***O****rganizaci****J****a skupnosti*, which translates in English as *Planning of Teaching Algorithms and Programming, and Organization of the Community.*

3.1 Goals

In the preceeding analysis we noticed the teachers felt they lacked the knowledge and confidence to teach beginners programming. Therefore the main goal of the first year of the NAPOJ project was to establish an active community of practice for Computing teachers and as a secondary goal to equip teachers with the necessary material and tools for teaching of programming basics. In the project we tried to show teachers that active participation in learning communities can give them the confidence and improve their knowledge they felt they lacked.

Fig. 1. The NAPOJ project logo reflecting the potion ingredients from left: system for checking the correctness of programs TOMO, textbook, a Moodle classroom SiO.

For this purpose three steps were performed. First, different study materials for teaching programming were connected. Next, we choose a group of master teachers (more on that in Sect. 3.2) and held a four day workshop for them. During the workshop we developed a set of study materials that could be used in class during programming lessons. The main goal of this step was to show that joint development and exchange of study materials can be a lot more effective than relying on own resources. Finally, master teachers held a series of regional workshops. These workshops disseminated the material and notion of CoP and tried to serve the needs of the local communities, and to establish stronger ties among the teachers within individual region.

3.2 Master Teachers

The first target group when establishing CoP were all teachers of Informatics. According to different authors [18,23,26,28] and partly following the model used in the 1995 project [7] called *Računalniško opismenjevanje* (eng. *Computing Literacy*), we used the *Master teachers model* discussed in [13,27].

Master teachers are teachers who are experts in the field of teaching Computing, and have a wish and ability to convey their knowledge to other teachers. The model focuses on the transfer of knowledge at local and personal levels within a particular field. Master teachers educate other teachers in their local environment and provide support for the local teacher community. This is also cost-effective as everything is happening locally. What is even more important such localized operation fosters personal contact among the participants.

A study by Boylan and Willis in [9] shows that the Master teachers model plays an important role in the process of introducing Computing at all levels of education in England following the reform of a new curriculum [17].

According to [9] in recognizing and choosing master teachers it is very important to achieve a level of certain diversity among the master teachers on professional, age, and personal levels. Of course, that is rather harder in Slovenia due to the small number of Computing teachers, than in England.

As reported in [25] there are approximately 140 teachers of subject Informatics (Computing) in high schools. As the coordinators of the project were for several years engaged in various activities such as professional development, organization of Computing competitions, various country wide projects on Computing education, national committee on Matura exam in Informatics, etc., they were aware of Computing teachers individual competencies and their previous activities. Furthermore, we wanted to achieve a good regional coverage as well. Consequently, we divided Slovenia into four regions each having an approximately the same number of gymnasia. Initially we invited 30 teachers and 26 of them attended the first one-day workshop. Although we focused on gymnasia teachers, following [9] regarding diversity of community members, we also involved some other high schools teachers as Master teacher candidates. Some primary school teachers joined as well. This proved as a big asset in the planned expansion of the community over the primary school teachers. During the workshop they were presented with a number of tasks, mostly connected with the preparation of learning resources to be accopmlished during summer months.

Based on candidates activities and the quality of their work during the summer and satisfying regional coverage, the final group of 14 candidates was chosen to become master teachers. Ratio 1:10 (1 master teacher on 10 teachers of Informatics) seemed appropriate. As the chosen group clearly diverged in their effort, no additional crirteria for selection was necessary. The chosen teachers attended the 4-day workshop at the end of the Summer. All their expenses were covered and their effort was recongized through their professional developement and professional seniority.

3.3 Materials and Tools

The Slovenian education space saw the emergence of several web services that can be used for teaching Computing and for programming courses. The first one important for the project NAPOJ is an interactive e-textbook [2] jointly published by all Slovenian Computer Science faculties. It is a group effort of several authors and used *de facto* an official textbook for Computing in high schools. More on the e-textbook and on the reasons for its creation in [21].

The second one is the web service TOMO [20,24,30], a tool for teaching and learning programming. It was developed by the University of Ljubljana, Faculty of Mathematics and Physics. TOMO allows on one side the learner to get an instant feedback about the correctness of programming exercise, and on the other hand permits teacher to monitor his/her progress. The service proved to be an effective tool in lab programming exercises.

Both services were augmented by Moodle LMS, providing the system for accessing and exchanging the material, for spreading information and for providing tools necessary for communication within the CoP. We prepared a Moodle classroom called NAPOJ in SIO (*Slovensko izobraževalno omrežje*, *Slovenian Education Network*), which is already known and used by the Slovenian teachers. The Moodle clasroom is organized based on educational units, and each of them includes several lesson plans, a link to the related chapter in the e-textbook, and a link to an appropriate exercises in the TOMO system.

Next, at the end of August the chosen 14 master teachers attended a workshop. Besides building CoP, the main purpose of the workshop was to prepare lesson plans for the educational units: *Basic concepts of programming*, *Writing independent programs and if statements*, *Loops*, *Tables*, *Functions*, and *Strings*. These units are only a smaller part of an e-textbook [2] and are related to programming. The other chapters follow mostly the standards in [16]. Each educational unit in SIO also contains a forum for the discussion on teaching of the unit. Unfortunately, forums have not yet fully taken off, which shows that building an active CoP will require still more effort.

Besides links to e-textbook and TOMO each educational unit also contains a sample lesson plan, which participants are encouraged to supplement with their own lesson plans. The inclusion of lesson plans permits also teachers with a lower self confidence in topic to go to the class and teach it.

Unfortunately, the analysis of the website activity shows that it has not really been widely accepted among the Computing teachers. An analysis in the form of an interview has shown that Computing teachers do not feel community affiliation yet. Among the reasons for this, teachers mostly mention fear to share their own lesson plans. Statements such as "what if there is something wrong in my lesson plan", or "I believe that my lesson plans are not good enough" show that more attention must be given to the establishment of community itself and to the spreading the awareness that cooperation and joint effort on the material contribute to personal development, as well as to the progress in teaching of Computing.

Following the August workshop master teachers themselves organized workshops in their local communities. The topics followed the ones previously encountered by the master teachers with a total participation of 51 teachers of Computing. During the first workshop, the participants were presented the tools (e-textbook, TOMO and the web classroom) and introduced the lesson plans. In the second workshop, that followed a two- or three-week period, during which the participants taught with the help of the prepared lesson plans, they evaluated the tools mostly considering a student motivation. Most regional workshop participants believed that this manner of teaching significantly contributes to the better knowledge of the students. The ready-made lesson plans help the teachers to overcome their reluctance to teach programming.

The dissemination of the environment was semi-successful. Indeed, the teachers started more boldly teaching programming, but the there was no significant response back to the community.

4 NAPOJ2

The successful completion of the NAPOJ project prompted us to re-apply for the Google call, that is for the 2017/18 period. The project itself was prepared in collaboration with Zavod 404 [33], that supplied the necessary experience and skills, and contributed to the workshops.

4.1 Goals

The main goals to foster CoP and to aid teaching programming remained the same with a move toward students. Reflecting the evaluation of project NAPOJ this time we targeted the motivational issue at the students at programming lectures. We wanted to increase student motivation by using *physical computing*. Consequently we wanted to equip teachers with the necessary environment and material they can use at lectures on programming.

Similarly as at NAPOJ we prepared a Moodle classroom with sample lesson plans. The lecture plan included the same educational units as at NAPOJ, but adapted for the physical computing. Finally, in collaboration with Zavod 404 we prepared RaspberyPi kits that included RaspberyPi, protoboard, necessary connection cables and a selection of actuators and sensors. Zavod 404 made kits available to schools at non profit price. The choice to go with RaspberyPi and not by Arduino or some other smaller processor was made because one can natively programme it in Python which was also the programming language of the original e-textbook.

4.2 Activities

General framework of activities followed the same pattern: August workshop for master teachers, where the material was prepared, followed by regional workshops organized by master teachers. However, there were two changes made. First the in the regional workshops the teachers were asked to bring also a few students. The reason for this was that application of teaching can be done more directly. The second difference was that at the end a general presentation of accomplished projects was offered by Zavod 404 at a local *Maker Faire*.

At the August workshop a number of materials were developed, some of which were put into a new e-textbook [5]. It consists of two parts. The first one brings instructions on how to put together the RaspberyPi kit that computer becomes operational. The second part brings a number of activities and suggestions for projects. Each of them is tied to the educational units mentioned in Sect. 3.3 (see columns in Fig. 2). Consequently teacher can enrich individual educational unit by a physical computing project. Of course, in the e-classroom the educational

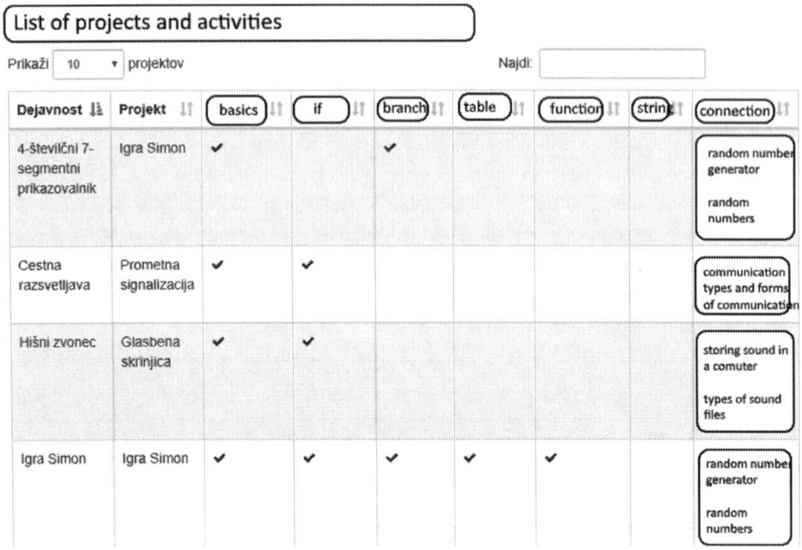

Fig. 2. Part of the projects list (partially translated).

units offered a possibility of extenting the list of projects and/or preparing one's own lesson plan.

Because in the NAPOJ2 at the regional workshops were also contributing the students (including some from primary school), Computing teachers were informed in advance about the material on physical Computing. The teachers were also invited to prepare projects that would then be upgraded and presented at regional workshops. This provided the regional workshops with an interesting mix of different experiences and knowledge in the field of programming physical systems. We enhanced it with two separate hands-on lectures for beginners and for advanced students. There were 4 regional workshops and with a participation of approximately 30 at each one.

The final evaluation showed that students like the teachers the notion of physical computing. However the teachers mentioned the complications with setting up the environment every hour. The problem might be overcome by using pre-assembled environment.

5 NAPOJ3

In the third year the project NAPOJ got a new source of support, the EU Social Funds financed *SKOZ project* (*Središče Karierne Orientacije Zahod*, *Centre of Career Orientation West*). The main goal of the national SKOZ project is to support specially talented students. Consequently the project was extended into this direction. The extension also required a broader consortium, which included all Computer Science faculties in Slovenia, Zavod 404 and ACM Slovenia.

5.1 Goals

The goals of the project represent three pillars with a common basis. The basis represents CoP, while the pillars are: competetive programming, research projects, and, the one related to this paper, support of curricular and extracurricular activities. The competitive programming activities were coordinated by former successful participants of international olympiads, while for the research projects were designated research assistants from the Computer Science faculties.

Further, in the previous years we learned, that teachers in schools would appreciate additional help not only in material and resources, but also in teaching help. As NAPOJ3 is to be run for two years we made for the first year a plan to proceed with work with (master) teachers in CoP, while at the same time try to involve university students as a help in teaching activities. Therefore we set up two goals, to foster CoP through a series of regular monthly web-conference meetings, and for the newcoming students start adapting the material that they can use in class. In the second year we want to bring both groups together.

5.2 Activities

The foremost concern was how to achieve a substantial growth in the number of active members of CoP. The well-established model of the August workshop with master teachers was followed this year, too. The workshop included presentations of different sources of materials and information regarding the teaching of Computing. Thus certain blogs on Computing didactic were presented, along with a selection of portals containing materials, examples of active communities, and important conferences and magazines on Computing didactic. The main purpose of these presentations was that teachers realize that cooperation is vital, even when the discovery of materials and following information about the field are concerned. The core part of the workshops therefore consisted of presentations of some articles, read and prepared by master teachers in pairs. This serves as the basis for the activities in the following year. The core activity during the year were regular monthly web conferences run using ARNES VOX system. During the conferences teachers presented interesting articles (like at the August workshop) and report about good materials and useful information.

Besides concern for upholding the CoP in the August workshop the third set of material for teaching programming was presented. In previous years the chosen programming language was Python. This is reasonable decision in particular if the students had any Computing education in primary school. Since this is not the case in Slovenia and to decrease the cognitive load [32], we prepared a new set. It is based on e-textbook *Slikovno programiranje* (*Visual programming*) [3] which follows the same sequence of educational units as it is used [2] (cf. Sect. 3.3). It replaces Python with Blockly. To support the automatic correctness verification we adapted the French system *Algorea*. The new system is called *Pišek* (*Chicklet*) and is available at http://pisek.acm.si/. The system is used in a similar way as TOMO service for Python.

Since the project is not over yet here are only some preliminary figures. In the competitive programming pillar 26 students participated. Unfortunatelly no student worked on a research project. Further, there were 8 web-conferences attracting 29 participants vast majority of which were Computing teachers – this represents approximately one fifth of community. Extracurricular activities were organized on 11 schools with approximate participation of 100 students.

6 Conclusion

Slovenia needs an active CoP of Computing teachers to substantially improve the quality of teaching (cf. CAS in Great Britain, CS4All in the USA, and others). Unfortunately, the first two years of the project have shown, that even the master teachers require a lot of encouragement to actively participate while other teachers are even harder to motivate to cooperate. This seems to be general trend we noted also in a well established CoP of mathematics teachers.

To overcome the difficulties we started to perform activities more regulary and there seems to be some progress. However, there is still a lot of room for improvement, especially considering well established communities like *Computing at school* in Great Britain (https://community.computingatschool.org.uk/). Nonetheless, beside the web meetings in person meetings are reported also to be of big importance in establishing communities [14,15,18,23,26–28].

For the future development of CoP we have to carefully consider [9] that analyzes the status of CoP in UK. The report presents a number of important suggestions and approaches to establish a solid and sustainable Computing teachers community. Cambridge et al. in [12] present an interesting diagram of development of CoP over the time (see Fig. 3). Slovenian Computing teachers CoP is currently at a *Launch* phase, and it is of utmost importance not follow the direction indicated by the red dashed line. Undoubtedly, the coordinators of the project have an important support role in this, but the key role to establish a sustainable CoP have teachers themselves with their master teachers. This is the essence of a grassroots movement.

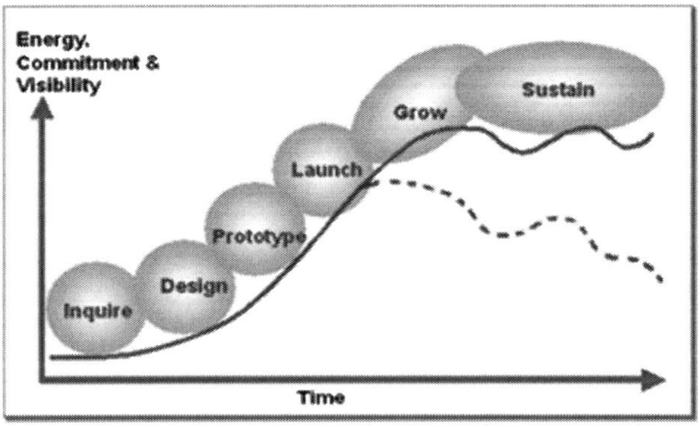

Fig. 3. Development of the community (adapted from [12]).

Acknowledgements. The NAPOJ and NAPOJ2 projects were financially supported by Google within *Computer Science for High School*. NAPOJ3 project was partly included in the SKOZ project. The work was also partially supported by the Slovenian Research Agency programme *P2-0359 Pervasive computing*.

References

1. Anželj, G., et al.: PIK: Predmetni izpitni katalog za splošno maturo 2017 - informatika (2017). http://www.ric.si/mma/2017M-INF-2017/2015083113004713
2. Anželj, G., et al.: Računalništvo in informatika v2.12; E-učbenik za informatiko v gimnaziji (2018). https://lusy.fri.uni-lj.si/ucbenik/book/index.html
3. Anželj, G., Brank, J., Brodnik, A., Fürst, L., Lokar, M.: Slikovno programiranje; E- učbenik za uvod v programiranje (2018). https://lusy.fri.uni-lj.si/ucbenik/prog/index.html
4. Anželj, G., Brodnik, A., Lokar, M.: NAPOJ - proti aktivni skupnosti učiteljev računalniških predmetov. Vzgoja in izobraževanje v informacijski družbi - VIVID 2017 : zbornik referatov. VIVID, Ljubljana (2018)
5. Anželj, G., Brodnik, A., Capuder, R., Lokar, M.: Malina in piton. E- učbenik za uvod v fizično računalništvo (2018). https://lusy.fri.uni-lj.si/ucbenik/rpi/index.html
6. Barber, M., Mourshed, M.: How the World's Best-Performing Schools Systems Come Out on Top. McKinsey Company, New York (2007)
7. Batagelj, V., Rajkovič, V.: Namen, cilji in smernice programa Računalniško opismenjevanje - RO (1995). http://www.educa.fmf.uni-lj.si/ro/izomre/novice/doc/vizija.htm
8. Berry, M.: A Cohernet Computing curriculum? (2018). http://bit.ly/csta2018
9. Boylan, M., Willis, B.: Independent Study of Computing At School Master Teacher programme. Sheffield Hallam University, Centre for Education and Inclusion Research (2017). https://www.computingatschool.org.uk/data/uploads/noe/cas-master-teacher-report-sheffield-hallam.pdf
10. Brodnik, A., Capuder, R., Lokar, M.: NAPOJ-3 - MU: Gradnja skupnosti (2018). https://moodle.lusy.fri.uni-lj.si/course/view.php?id=59
11. Brodnik, A., Lokar, M., Mori, N.: Activation of computer science teachers in Slovenia. In: Tatnall, A., Webb, M. (eds.) WCCE 2017. IAICT, vol. 515, pp. 658–662. Springer, Cham (2017). https://doi.org/10.1007/978-3-319-74310-3_67
12. Cambridge, D., Kaplan, S., Suter, V.: Communities of practice design guide, step-by-step guide for designing and cultivating communities of practice in higher education (2005). https://library.educause.edu/resources/2005/1/community-of-practice-design-guide-a-stepbystep-guide-for-designing-cultivating-communities-of-practice-in-higher-education
13. CAS Master Teachers. Network of Excellence Computer Science Teaching (2018)
14. Chalmers, L., Keown, P.: Communities of practice and professional development. Int. J. Lifelong Educ. **25**(2), 139–156 (2006)
15. Corso, M., Giacobbe, A.: Building communities of practice that work: a case study based research. In: The Sixth European Conference on Organizational Knowledge, Learning, and Capabilities. Bentley College, Waltham (2005)
16. CSTA: CSTA K-12 Computer Science Standards (2017)
17. Department of Education, Gov.UK: National curriculum in England: Computing programmes of study (2013)

18. Fincher, S., Tenenberg, J.: Warren's question. In: Proceedings of the Third International Computing Education Research Workshop, pp. 51–60. ACM (2007)
19. IEEE Curriculum and Accreditation Committee: IEEE Professional Educational Activities Board. Curriculum and Accreditation Committee (2013). https://www.computer.org/cms/peb/docs/CS2013-final-report.pdf
20. Jerše, G., Lokar, M.: Uporaba sistema za avtomatsko preverjanje nalog Projekt Tomo pri učenju programiranja. Vzgoja in izobraževanje v informacijski družbi - VIVID 2017 : zbornik referatov. Ljubljana (2018)
21. Mori, N., Lokar, M.: A new interactive computer science textbook in Slovenia. In: Brodnik, A., Tort, F. (eds.) ISSEP 2016. LNCS, vol. 9973, pp. 167–178. Springer, Cham (2016). https://doi.org/10.1007/978-3-319-46747-4_14
22. Mori, N., Brodnik, A., Lokar, M.: Development of CS curriculum for secondary schools through changes in external examination and textbooks. In: Proceedings of the IFIP TC3 Joint Conference Stakeholders and Information Technology in Education. Guimares: University of Minho (2016). http://saite2016.dsi.uminho.pt/wp-content/uploads/2016/06/Book-of-Abstracts.pdf
23. Ni, L., Guzdial, M., Tew, A. E., Morrison, B., Galanos, R.: Building a community to support HS CS teachers: the disciplinary commons for Computing educators. Proceedings of the 42nd ACM technical symposium on Computer Science education (SIGCSE 11), pp. 553–558. ACM (2011)
24. Pretnar, M., Lokar, M.: A low overhead automated service for teaching programming. In: Proceedings of the 15th Koli Calling International Conference on Computing Education Research. Koli, Finland: Proceedings of the 15th Koli Calling Conference on Computing Education Research (2015). https://doi.org/10.1145/2828959.2828964
25. RINOS: Snovalci digitalne prihodnosti ali le uporabniki? https://fri.uni-lj.si/sl/novice/novica/uporabniki-ali-snovalci-digitalne-prihodnosti (2018)
26. Sentance, S., Humphreys, S.: Online vs face-to-face engagement of computing teachers for their professional development needs. In: Brodnik, A., Vahrenhold, J. (eds.) ISSEP 2015. LNCS, vol. 9378, pp. 69–81. Springer, Cham (2015). https://doi.org/10.1007/978-3-319-25396-1_7
27. Sentance, S., Humphreys, S., Dorling, M.: The network of teaching excellence in CS and master teachers. In: Proceedings of the 9th Workshop in Primary and Secondary Computing Education, pp. 80–88. ACM (2014)
28. Tenenberg, J., Fincher, S.: Opening the door of the computer science classroom: the disciplinary commons. In: Proceedings of the 38th SIGCSE Technical Symposium on Computer Science Education, pp. 514–518. ACM (2007)
29. Tomažin, M., Brodnik, A.: Učni cilji pouka računalništva v osnovni šoli - slovenski in ACM K12 kurikulum. Organizacija: revija za management, informatiko in kadre, A173–A178 (2007)
30. UL FMF: Projekt Tomo. Projekt Tomo (2010–2019). https://www.projekt-tomo.si
31. Wenger-Trayner, E., Wenger-Trayner, B.: Introduction to Communities of Practice. A Brief Overview of the Concept and Its Uses. Wenger-Trayner, Grass Valley (2015)
32. Wilson, G. (ed.): Teaching Tech Together - Cognitive Load. (Lulu.com) (2018). http://teachtogether.tech/en/load/
33. Zavod 404: Mladinski tehnološko-raziskovalni center (2018). https://404.si/

An Exploration of Teachers' Perspective About the Learning of Iteration-Control Constructs

Emanuele Scapin and Claudio Mirolo(✉)

University of Udine, Udine 33100, Italy
scapin.emanuele@spes.uniud.it, claudio.mirolo@uniud.it

Abstract. A number of studies report about students' difficulties with basic flow-control constructs, and specifically with iteration. Although such issues are less explored in the context of pre-tertiary education, this seems to be especially the case for high-school programming learning, where the difficulties concern both the "mechanical" features of the notional machine as well as the logical aspects connected with the constructs, ranging from the implications of loop conditions to a more abstract grasp of the underlying algorithms.

As part of a project whose long-run goal is identifying methodological tools to improve the learning of iteration constructs, we interviewed 20 experienced upper secondary teachers of introductory programming in different kinds of schools from a large area in the North-East of Italy. In addition, a sample of 164 students from the same schools answered a survey which included both questions on their subjective perception of difficulty and simple tasks probing their understanding of iteration.

The interviews were mainly aimed at ascertaining teachers' beliefs about major sources of issues for basic programming concepts and their approach to the teaching and learning of iteration constructs. Each interview was conducted according to a grid of 20 questions, informed by related frameworks to characterize teachers' pedagogical content knowledge and to design concept inventories. In essence, data from teachers and students confirm that iteration is a central programming concept and indicate that the treatment of conditions and nested constructs are major sources of students' difficulties with iteration.

Keywords: Informatics education · Programming learning · High school · Teacher interviews · Iteration constructs · Novice programmers

1 Introduction

Students appear to struggle with programming, as witnessed, e.g., by the high drop out rates in tertiary education, which are a well known issue for Computer Science [10,12]. This may be ascribed to different causes, such as a lack of problem solving skills, or the peculiar study method required to learn programming;

S. N. Pozdniakov and V. Dagienė (Eds.): ISSEP 2019, LNCS 11913, pp. 15–27, 2019.
https://doi.org/10.1007/978-3-030-33759-9_2

indeed, according to some educators, programming requires "not a single, but a set of skills" [9,10].

Several works report about students' difficulties with basic flow-control constructs, and specifically with iteration. Kaczmarczyk et al. [11], for instance, identified "a number of misconceptions all related to an inability to properly understand the process of while loop functioning" and Cherenkova et al. [5] found that "students have significant trouble with conditionals and loops, with loops being particularly challenging". These issues are still little explored for pre-tertiary education, but at least anecdotal evidence seems to suggest that high-school students' difficulties range from the "mechanical" features of the underlying computation model to the more abstract aspects in connection with the algorithmic function of a construct.

For these reasons, we are working on a project aimed at identifying methodological tools to enhance a comprehensive understanding of the iteration constructs, the main steps being:

1. Interviewing a pilot sample of instructors about their approach to the teaching of iteration and their perception of students difficulties;
2. Collecting information about students' perception on the topic through a short survey;
3. Based on the outcome of steps 1 and 2, designing a survey to collect related information and good practices from a larger sample of teachers;
4. Figuring out some methodological approach to the teaching of iteration and building a catalogue of significant program examples to support students' learning;
5. Experimenting the instructional strategies in class to investigate on their effectiveness.

The methodological tools implied by step 4 should be intended to improve students' level of abstraction while dealing with programming constructs, rather than to focus on a stepwise analysis of how the code works (tools of the latter type are more widespread, see e.g. the paragraphs on program visualization in [15]). Source of inspiration in this respect may be the pedagogical work that elaborate on the concept of *loop invariant* [1,7,21].

Within this framework, the first two steps outlined above are the subject of this paper. More specifically, we conducted face-to-face interviews of 20 experienced upper secondary teachers of introductory programming in different kinds of high schools. The interviews were meant to ascertain teachers' thoughts about basic programming concepts, the importance they attach to the understanding of iteration within their curricula, as well as their strategies to teach iteration, to assess the learning of this concept and to enhance students' awareness and motivation. In addition, we administered a survey to a varied sample of 164 students from the same schools, in order to know also their viewpoint on the matter and to relate it to the perspective of their teachers. The student survey included both questions on their subjective perception and tiny problems addressing different features of the application of iteration constructs.[1]

The rest of the paper is organized as follows. In Sect. 2 we outline the background of this work. The Sects. 3 and 4 are about the methodology and the outcome of our investigation. Finally, in Sect. 5 we discuss the results and some future perspective.

2 Background

As mentioned before, the long-term objectives of our work are motivated by the crucial role of *iteration* in the learning of programming, an issue that has been investigated by several authors, e.g. [5,6,11].

In order to accomplish the tasks involved in steps 1 and 2, we had to devise a protocol to interview the teachers as well as a survey for their students. Interviewing teachers or students have become a popular way of data-collection in STEM fields, in particular in mathematics and physics education.

As far as teachers' instructional experience and practice are concerned, the usual reference framework is that of Pedagogical Content Knowledge (PCK), originally proposed by Shulman [20] to characterize the "blending of content and pedagogy into an understanding of how particular aspects of subject matter are organized, adapted, and represented for instruction". In this respect, the Content Representation (CoRe) format is an instrument to investigate teachers' PCK of a specific topic [13,16] through 8 standard questions, which are meant to capture teachers' knowledge about key ideas in connection with the topic. Although this approach has been mainly applied in science education research, there have also been a few attempts to exploit it to investigate on the teaching of programming [2,3,18].

If, on the one hand, the information from teachers could be collected through long and carefully conducted face-to-face interviews, on the other hand for the students we needed a short survey with sharp closed-ended questions, so that they did not get bored while answering them. Thus, to get insight on their subjective perception of "learning difficulties", we decided to provide a few lists of concepts among which to choose (plus an open "other" field).

To identify small sets of basic programming-related concepts we have drawn from some "validating" work on Concept Inventories for computer science [8,19] and introductory programming [4], as well as from the review analysis in [14]. The list in [4], for instance, covers the following concepts: function parameter use and scope; variables, identifiers, and scope; recursion; iteration; structures; pointers; Boolean expressions; syntax vs. conceptual understanding.

Finally, as to the "tiny" problems included in the questionnaire administered to the students, we chose to test the three learning dimensions addressed in [17], namely the understanding of the computation model underlying iteration, the ability to establish relations between the components of a loop and the statement

[1] Complete English versions of the interview questions and of the student survey are available online at: nid.dimi.uniud.it/additional_material/iteration_project.html.

of a problem, the ability to interpret the program structures in connection with iteration constructs.

1. Course organization (5 questions)	
programming languages, key programming concepts, related lesson plan, how much time for each concept, extra-computing prerequisites	
2. Introductory programming in general (6 questions)	
2.1. teaching	Are the tasks assigned to students simple variations of those dealt with in class? Or do they cover unfamiliar situations as well? What are your more frequent suggestions to students for improving their programming performance?
2.2. learning	What is the major learning obstacle that students face before being introduced to object-oriented programming?
2.3. assessment	How do you assess a working solution if it is inefficient, or convoluted, or somehow at odds with what you expected? While trying to achieve the assigned tasks, do you expect your students to apply the models introduced in class? Or do you also appreciate "creative" solutions? Are the different solutions by students compared in class? How?
3. Focus on iteration (5 questions)	
3.1. teaching	Can you show some of your favorite examples to make students learn how to apply the iteration constructs? In your teaching, do you cover the mappings between different iteration constructs (for, while, do-while/repeat-until)?
3.2. learning	In your experience, to what extent can students master the termination condition of a loop? Which features of the iteration constructs are usually understood by (most) students, and which are more difficult to them?
3.3. assessment	How do you usually assess an incorrect termination condition? And oversights about the first or last iteration?
4. General educational issues (3 questions)	
strategies to motivate students, manage different learning styles, deal with students' criticisms	
5. Other thoughts (1 question)	
Any other issues you deem important to consider about the teaching/learning of programming?	

Fig. 1. Structure of the teacher interview protocol.

3 Methodology

3.1 Instruments

To begin with, the structure of the interview protocol, partly inspired by the approaches to eliciting the PCK presented in the literature, is outlined in Fig. 1, where the most significant questions are reported verbatim. A set of questions (point 1) is aimed at framing iteration within the general context of introductory programming and the related prerequisites. Other questions (2) attempt to ascertain how central is the learning of iteration in the teacher's perspective, but without mentioning this topic explicitly (the wording of question 2.2 being meant to prevent discussion of issues arising with object-orientation, when covered in an introductory course). Then, the focus moves specifically to the teaching, learning and assessment of iteration (3). Some questions about more general educational issues (4) and a final open question (5) to collect further ideas not covered in the previous points conclude the interview session.

The survey addressed to students includes 11 questions, three of which ask to solve tiny problems by analyzing either small flow charts or short code fragments based on iteration. The main features of the questionnaire are shown in Fig. 2. Here there is not enough room to be more specific about the assigned problems, which will be discussed in more depth elsewhere, but we can note that they are quite simple and address the three learning dimensions mentioned above: the ability to grasp the connections between a loop's component (specifically, its condition) and the statement of a problem (3.1), the mastery of the "mechanics" of iteration (3.2), a more comprehensive understanding of the combination of program structures (3.3). Of course, the three small tasks were not meant to assess students' mastery of iteration, but just to get some insight about the alignment between subjectively perceived and actual difficulties.

---

1. Course organization (3 questions)
favorite programming languages, poor understanding of mathematical/logic prerequisites, accordance of the subject with personal expectations

2. Introductory programming in general (3 questions)
Do you think it would be needed to spend more time on some programming concepts? Which ones? (range of options or open "other" field)
Which kind of errors has been most penalizing for your grading? (open question)
Are you usually successful in solving unfamiliar programming problems? (Likert scale of 4 levels)

3. Focus on iteration (1 question and 3 tiny problems)
What do you find most difficult when trying to use a loop? (range of options)
Problem 3.1: Given the statement of a simple problem being solved, choose the correct *loop condition* in a flow chart. (4 options available)
Problem 3.2: Given a while loop with a composed condition and a nested conditional, determine the number of iterations for a given input. (6 options)
Problem 3.3: Given 5 code fragments involving nested construct with simple conditions, identify the functionally equivalent ones.

4. Other thoughts (1 question)
Do you have any suggestion to make learning informatics more interesting?

Fig. 2. Structure of the student survey.

3.2 Data Collection

We conducted accurate face-to-face interviews with 20 experienced high school teachers of informatics, working in 10 technical institutes and lyceums from a large area in the North-East of Italy. Each such session lasted one to two hours and was audio-recorded and (partly) transcribed with the interviewee's agreement. The survey was administered to 164 students attending classes on introductory programming in the same schools, mostly at the end their third or second year, depending on the kind of school.

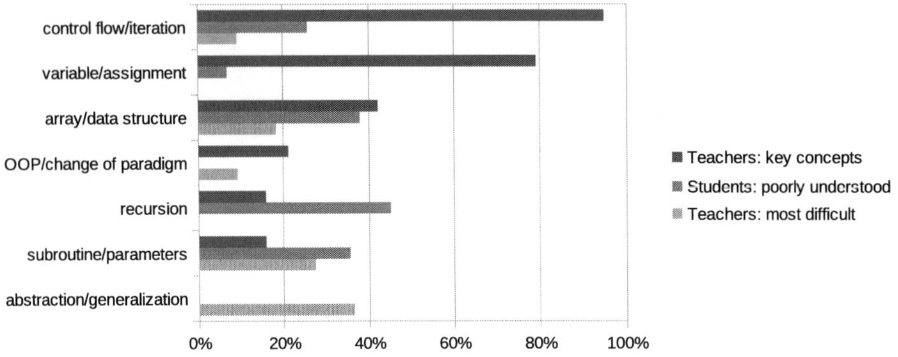

Fig. 3. Key programming concepts for teachers and their difficulty in the students' and teachers' perception. The absence of a visible bar means 0%.

4 Results

To present the main results of our investigation we follow the general structure outlined in Fig. 1 and, for the most part, mirrored in Fig. 2.

Course Organization. The most significant insight from this general section of the interviews is the (weighted) list of key concepts identified by the teachers. In the chart of Fig. 3, where tightly related concepts have been aggregated, the percentage of teachers indicating concepts in a certain area is represented by the length of dark-red bars. In the same chart, the "weights" of concepts are contrasted to their perceived difficulty for students and teachers, which pertain to the second section of the interviews and of the survey (see Figs. 1 and 2), and will be discussed later. What emerges clearly from the data in Fig. 3 is that almost all the teachers mention precisely control flow and *iteration* among the most important concepts of introductory programming—the second most popular choice being variables and assignment.

As to the adopted (by teachers) vs. the favorite (by student) programming languages there is a fairly high correlation, with C, C++ and C# at the top of the ranking, the only difference being the slightly higher popularity of Python and Java among students. It may also be worth remarking that several teachers introduce different programming languages and other design languages, such as *flow charts*, to analyze the control constructs.

Another general issue of relevance here concerns the extra-computing prerequisites. Large percentages of both teachers and students refer to the mathematical/logic background as well as to *text comprehension*[2] as critical—although often insufficiently developed—to the practice of programming. Interestingly, more than one third of the students mentions specifically De Morgan's formulas as poorly understood. Moreover, and quite surprisingly, about one fourth of them revealed to have faced problems with geometry, probably because of its connections with particularly motivating problem domains.

Introductory Programming in General. By looking again at Fig. 3, we can see the concepts that the students perceive (light-blue bars) and the teachers think of (orange bars) as serious learning obstacles. The chart should be self-explanatory. However, it can be observed that teachers are likely to underestimate the difficulties faced by some students with flow-control constructs; moreover, they do not seem to pay much attention on the understanding of recursion, perhaps because they presume it is hardly within the grips of most pupils. On the other hand, beside indicating a few of the key concepts taught, several interviewees emphasize the high-level thinking skills of abstraction and generalization (bottom bar).

Apart from recursion, according to the students the hardest concepts are arrays, data structures and subroutines, i.e. precisely the last topics introduced by their teachers, shortly before the end of a school year. Among the suggestions to the students, about half of the teachers give prominence to the use of "paper and pencil" to clarify ideas before starting to work with a computer. In the words of a teacher: *"read the text carefully, then analyze the problem and check a preliminary solution with paper and pencil"*. In addition, students are often encouraged to compare their programs with those of their peers. Most of the teachers assign also unfamiliar tasks, when their students have reached a sufficient degree of mastery of programming basics—tasks which more than 60% of the students feel nevertheless quite confident to achieve and which can provide further motivation to particularly brilliant learners.

As to the assessment, it emerged that the penalty for inefficient solutions can amount up to 20–25% of the marks, whereas the instructors tend to be less strict about programming style, so giving prominence to the fact that a program can work properly.

Focus on Iteration. Figure 4 reports the collected data about the major sources of difficulties with iteration. To some extent, teachers and students agree on indicating the complexity of loop conditions (in terms of use of logical connectives) and the treatment of the exit condition as problematic. However, they

[2] Text comprehension is an issue for 42% of the teachers and 27% of the students.

seem to have contrasting views as to the other aspects addressed. On the one hand, a number of teachers point out students' misuse of iteration constructs, in particular *while* vs. *do-while* and the overuse of *for* loops in situations where it is not an appropriate choice. On the other hand, students give far more prominence to dealing with nested iterations—42% of them report this being *the* major issue with iteration.

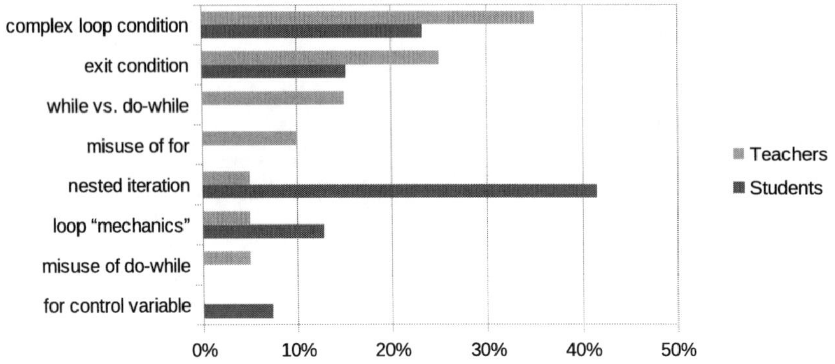

Fig. 4. Major difficulty with iteration in the teachers' and students' perception. Missing bars mean no available related option for students, 0% for teachers.

Now it is also interesting to compare students' (and teachers') perception of difficulty with their actual performance on the three questions that required an analysis of small programs based on iteration constructs. In a first task the students had to read carefully the statement of a very simple problem and identify the correct condition in a flow chart by simply choosing among four options, the only difference being the relational operator in the loop condition: "$<$", "$\leq$", "$=$" and "$>$". Less than 40% of the students provided the correct answer ($\leq$), whereas about as many chose one of the two seriously wrong options ($=$ or $>$).

The second task asked to determine the number of iterations of a short code fragment for a given input. The loop was characterized by a composite condition (using two *ands*) and a nested *if-else*. In this case, about 60% of the students identified the right answer (3 iterations). Finally, in the third task the students had to recognize functionally equivalent programs from a set of 5 items involving nested constructs (*if* and *while*) with simple conditions. Clearly, this task required a more comprehensive understanding of the effect of combining flow-control structures, and only less than 20% of the students were able to achieve it successfully. In particular, it appears that students' perception of difficulty with nested constructs is consistent with the actual state of affairs.

According to their teachers, students tend to avoid using Boolean operators to build efficient conditions. An interviewee argued that *"for loops are easier to students than while loops, since it is not necessary to figure out a suitable condition"*. To overcome these difficulties, several teachers insist on carrying out preliminary analysis steps based on flow-chart representations, so that students can clarify their ideas and understand the implied concepts in more depth. Also *"tracing the program execution with paper and pencil may be helpful to student, but similar tasks are only rarely done"*; indeed, the program code is *"less effective than a flow chart"* to visualize what is going on when a program is run. Incidentally, although loop conditions and the related border computations (first and last repetition) play a crucial role in the understanding of iteration, in general the teachers take into consideration a varied range of factors to assess students' programs (unless the focus of the assignment is precisely *on* the loop condition), depending also on the connections with the examples worked out in class.

When asked about the examples they commonly presented in class to explain iteration, the teachers mentioned the tasks listed below, the most popular ones being those related to elementary mathematics:

sum/average of a number sequence	power function
counting odd/even num. in a sequence	factorial function
min/max values of a sequence	Euclid's GCD algorithm
input data control (do-while)	math number sequence
first n multiples of a number	number base conversion
iteration over an array	pictures drawing with chars
nth element of a sequence	drawing a polygons

Unexpectedly, although all the interviewees said that they present the main forms of loop constructs—*for*, *while*, *do-while*—and treat their similarities and differences by showing appropriate examples, few teachers are also explicit about the mappings between such control structures, e.g. how to transform a *for* or a *do-while* loop into a *while* and conversely. One teacher, however, attempts to emphasize the role and power of iteration by discussing the universality of three basic control structures, as captured by Böhm-Jacopini's theorem.

General Educational Issues. From the interviews, it emerges that the teachers try to motivate their students by proposing interesting real world problems or the implementation of computer games and other graphics applications that are meaningful to them. Often, a driving factor to increase students' engagement with learning is their teacher's enthusiasm, e.g. while bringing to school the challenges faced in her/his professional experience. The educational objective is that students can make sense of the importance of mastering particular concepts and acquiring particular skills.

Other Thoughts. As seen from the outline in Fig. 1, each interviewee was asked for further possible ideas or suggestions she/he deems important to consider about the teaching and learning of programming. Here are the main points raised by the teachers, that go far beyond the scope of our present work:

- *Lack of alignment between informatics and mathematics topics.* A possible explanation of students' difficulties with the application of mathematical and logic concepts is that informatics and mathematics are not well integrated in the standard high-school curricula, recently subjected to reform. In other words, some of the mathematical topics may be covered either too early or too late to be effective when they are required to learn programming.
- *Robotics environments.* In order to enhance students' engagement, some schools have developed robotics laboratories. These usually successful experiences may also be proposed at earlier instruction levels, so that high-school students will be more familiar with informatics and programming concepts.
- *Object-first approach.* Some teachers are considering whether the learning of programming could be improved by starting from the beginning with the object-oriented paradigm.

5 Discussion

Once established that iteration is among the few most central concepts for novice programmers, a claim on which all the interviewed teachers appear to agree, the first question to ask is if students' difficulties with loop constructs are *really* a major issue in the learning of programming. By considering this concept only from a general point of view, based on the teachers' and students' perception it is so only to some extent, whereas other programming concepts are seen as more challenging—see Fig. 3. However, when we address the learning of specific features, such as the treatment of loop conditions or nested constructs, a different perspective emerges: students are not yet comfortable with these aspects.

As a matter of fact, students are aware of this, as the chart in Fig. 4 shows, but their difficulties are also confirmed by the performance in the three programming-related tasks included in the survey, briefly outlined in the previous section. This is perhaps not too surprising, in light of the fact that most of the program examples they usually see in connection with iteration are quite straightforward (see the list in Sect. 4) and tend to induce the use of stereotypical patterns. Thus, to help students work with nontrivial loop conditions and neat combinations of flow-control constructs, it can be desirable to develop a catalogue of significant examples presenting more varied and interesting structures. In a similar spirit, it may be helpful to investigate the role of iteration in the larger programming tasks in which the students engage (e.g. to solve "real world" problems, to implement computer games, etc.).

As recognized by several interviewees (see again Fig. 3), it is likely that the major issues depend on students' difficulties to take a more abstract, comprehensive perspective when dealing with programs. A possible way, identified by the teachers, to induce students to develop their abstraction skills is to contrast their tendency to approach a task by trial-and-error and require them to analyze the problem with paper and pencil. Another possibility is to demand that students organize their programs into several functions and procedures to introduce meaningful levels of abstraction. In addition, it could be interesting to envisage and to explore the effectiveness of methodological tools inspired by the notion of loop invariant, see e.g. the pedagogical work in [7,21], suitably adapted to fit less formal learning styles [1].

A final issue, emerged from the interviews, concerns the alignment between the learning of mathematical and logic prerequisites, which are part of the mathematics syllabus, and the learning of programming. Clearly, this issue should be addressed as part of the national education policies. However, at present what teachers can do is to strengthen the interdisciplinary work between colleagues teaching mathematics and informatics.

6 Conclusions

As part of a project aimed at identifying methodological tools to enhance a comprehensive understanding of iteration, in this paper we have discussed the outcome of the first two actions. More specifically, we have conducted face-to-face interviews with a pilot group of high school teachers to know their perspectives about the teaching and learning of introductory programming in general, as well as of iteration in particular. In addition, we have administered a survey to a sample of students to collect data both about their perception of these topics and about their performance on three tiny tasks concerning the iteration constructs.

In essence, data from teachers and students confirm that iteration is a central concept in the introductory courses and allow to identify the treatment of loop conditions and of nested constructs as major sources of students' difficulties with loop constructs.

Based on the results of these initial steps, we are now planning to design a survey to collect related information and good practices from a larger sample of teachers. Then, we will attempt to develop methodological tools and related material to enhance students' understanding of iteration.

References

1. Astrachan, O.: Pictures as invariants. In: Proceedings of the Twenty-second SIGCSE Technical Symposium on Computer Science Education, pp. 112–118. SIGCSE 1991, ACM, New York (1991). https://doi.org/10.1145/107004.107026
2. Barendsen, E., et al.: Concepts in k-9 computer science education. In: Proceedings of the 2015 ITiCSE on Working Group Reports, pp. 85–116. ITICSE-WGR 2015, ACM, New York (2015). https://doi.org/10.1145/2858796.2858800
3. Buchholz, M., Saeli, M., Schulte, C.: Pck and reflection in computer science teacher education. In: ACM International Conference Proceeding Series, 11 2013. https://doi.org/10.1145/2532748.2532752
4. Caceffo, R., Wolfman, S., Booth, K.S., Azevedo, R.: Developing a computer science concept inventory for introductory programming. In: Proceedings of the 47th ACM Technical Symposium on Computing Science Education, SIGCSE 2016, pp. 364–369. ACM, New York (2016). https://doi.org/10.1145/2839509.2844559

5. Cherenkova, Y., Zingaro, D., Petersen, A.: Identifying challenging cs1 concepts in a large problem dataset. In: Proceedings of the 45th ACM Technical Symposium on Computer Science Education, SIGCSE 2014, pp. 695–700. ACM, New York (2014). https://doi.org/10.1145/2538862.2538966
6. Fernández Alemán, J.L., Oufaska, Y.: Samtool, a tool for deducing and implementing loop patterns. In: Proceedings of the Fifteenth Annual Conference on Innovation and Technology in Computer Science Education, ITiCSE 2010, pp. 68–72. ACM, New York (2010). https://doi.org/10.1145/1822090.1822111
7. Ginat, D.: Seeking or skipping regularities? Novice tendencies and the role of invariants. Inf. Educ. **2**, 211–222 (2003)
8. Goldman, K., et al.: Setting the scope of concept inventories for introductory computing subjects. ACM Trans. Comput. Educ. **10**(2), 5 (2010)
9. Gomes, A., Mendes, A.: Learning to program - difficulties and solutions. In: International Conference on Engineering Education - ICEE, pp. 283–287, 01 2007
10. Jenkins, T.: On the difficulty of learning to program. In: Proceedings of the 3rd Annual LTSN ICS Conference (2002). http://www.ics.ltsn.ac.uk/pub/conf2002/tjenkins.pdf
11. Kaczmarczyk, L.C., Petrick, E.R., East, J.P., Herman, G.L.: Identifying student misconceptions of programming. In: Proceedings of the 41st ACM Technical Symposium on Computer Science Education, SIGCSE 2010, pp. 107–111. ACM, New York (2010). https://doi.org/10.1145/1734263.1734299
12. Lewandowski, G., Gutschow, A., Mccartney, R., Sanders, K., Shinners-Kennedy, D.: What novice programmers don't know. In: Proceedings of the First International Workshop on Computing Education Research, ICER 2005, pp. 1–12. ACM (2005)
13. Loughran, J., Mulhall, P., Berry, A.: Exploring pedagogical content knowledge in science teacher education. Int. J. Sci. Educ. - INT J SCI EDUC **30**, 1301–1320 (2008). https://doi.org/10.1080/09500690802187009
14. Luxton-Reilly, A., et al.: Developing assessments to determine mastery of programming fundamentals. In: Proceedings of the 2017 ITiCSE Conference on Working Group Reports, ITiCSE-WGR '17, pp. 47–69. ACM, New York (2017). https://doi.org/10.1145/3174781.3174784
15. Luxton-Reilly, A., et al.: Introductory programming: a systematic literature review. In: Proceedings Companion of the 23rd Annual ACM Conference on Innovation and Technology in Computer Science Education, ITiCSE 2018 Companion, pp. 55–106. ACM, New York (2018). https://doi.org/10.1145/3293881.3295779
16. Magnusson, S., Krajcik, J., Borko, H.: Nature, sources, and development of pedagogical content knowledge for science teaching. In: Gess-Newsome, J., Lederman, N. (eds.) Examining Pedagogical Content Knowledge, Science & Technology Education Library, vol. 6, pp. 95–132. Springer, Dordrecht (1999). https://doi.org/10.1007/0-306-47217-1_4
17. Mirolo, C.: Is iteration really easier to learn than recursion for cs1 students? In: Proceedings of the Ninth Annual International Conference on International Computing Education Research, ICER 2012, pp. 99–104. ACM, New York (2012). https://doi.org/10.1145/2361276.2361296
18. Saeli, M., Perrenet, J., Jochems, W., Zwaneveld, B.: Teaching programming in secondary school: a pedagogical content knowledge perspective. Inf. Educ. **10**, 73–88 (2011)
19. Schaffer, D.: An analysis of science concept inventories and diagnostic tests: commonalities and differences. In: Annual International Conference of the National Association for Research in Science Teaching (2012)

20. Shulman, L.S.: Those who understand: knowledge growth in teaching. Educ. Res. **15**(2), 4–14 (1986)
21. Tam, W.C.: Teaching loop invariants to beginners by examples. SIGCSE Bull. **24**(1), 92–96 (1992). https://doi.org/10.1145/135250.134530

What Are Computer Science Educators Interested In? The Case of SIGCSE Conferences

Ragonis Noa[1,2(✉)] and Orit Hazzan[2]

[1] Beit Berl College, Beit Berl, Kfar Saba, Israel
noarag@beitberl.ac.il
[2] Technion Israel Institute of Technology, Haifa, Israel
oritha@tx.technion.ac.il

Abstract. This paper explores the fields of interest of the computer science education (CSE) community during the 12 years between 2006–2018 as reflected in the professional content of SIGCSE conferences. For this purpose, we investigated four SIGCSE conferences—2006, 2010, 2014, and 2018—and identified main topics and themes addressed in the following three presentation formats: papers, panels, and special sessions. We defined five content categories derived from the different presentation content: teaching methods, curricula, CSE research, recruitment and retention, and educators. The paper compares the four conferences according to two main classifications (1) content categorization, according to the above content categories we defined; and (2) the most frequent keywords used by the authors to describe their work. These keywords were divided into three themes: CS curricula, CS topics, and pedagogy. Our analysis reveals that: (1) according to the content categorization, teaching methods received the most attention from the SIGCSE community, with curricula coming in second, at a substantial distance; (2) according to keywords categorization: (a) the most frequently used CS curricula keywords relate to CS1, followed by, at a significant gap, CS0 and K-12, following by computational thinking and interdisciplinary studies; (b) it is difficult to identify the most frequently used CS topics keywords (c) in relation to the pedagogy characteristic, the most frequently used keywords are: assessment, active learning, and team collaboration. In future work, we intend to check the consistency of the current findings with other journals and conferences in which the CSE community publishes its work.

Keywords: Computer science educators · SIGCSE conferences · Trends in computer science education · Teaching methods

1 Introduction

One of the challenges facing CS educators is coping with the rapid changes and developments taking place in the discipline of CS, in the students' interests and skills, and in teaching, learning and evaluating new methods. To prepare future computer scientists and software engineers for the largely unknown future work market, these

S. N. Pozdniakov and V. Dagienė (Eds.): ISSEP 2019, LNCS 11913, pp. 28–40, 2019.
https://doi.org/10.1007/978-3-030-33759-9_3

changes require CS educators, both in academia and in schools, to constantly adjust their course syllabi as well as their teaching methods. This need is reflected, for example, in the frequent requests posted to the SIGCSE mailing list, asking the community for course materials and advice on integrating new teaching methods into CS courses. Following are some random examples of such threads:

- Curriculum issues such as requests for learning materials for "preparing a basic concurrency course" (Sheldon, M., 10th June 2014), rethinking the first taught programming paradigm "functional programming in intro CS course" (Strout, S., 17th Feb 2018), and advice for "building a cybersecurity lab" (Weiss, S., 6th Nov 2017);
- Integrating up-to-date technological approaches to teaching CS such as "Smartphones' impact on student engagement and learning" (Hoffman. M.E., 10th Aug 2018), or about activating "MOOC on Software Engineering Essentials" (Bruegge, B., Krusche, S. and Seitz, A. (17th Oct, 2017);
- Exploration of teaching approaches such as a question on how to "correctly show dependence in UML with an abstract class" (Gates, E.A., 8th October 2017) and a discussion on the question: "Can multiple choice (or similar) questions be accurate and reliable as exam questions in CS1" (Vahid, F., 24th, July, 2018)[1].

The interest of the CSE community with respect to the contribution of SIGCSE papers over the years is expressed also in a special session held in 2010 conference titled: "Recognizing the most influential CS education papers". This special session was devoted to the recognition of the most influential CS education papers of the 20th century on the practice of CS education today. It served as a basis for the establishment of criteria for an award or other recognition for influential contributions to CSE [6].

Based on this recognition, we asked ourselves: What changes have taken place in CSE over the past 12 years, as reflected in the SIGCSE conferences? To exposure the changes, we chose four, not continuous, at the same interval of four years conferences and analyzed the topics of three presentation formats – papers, panels and special sessions. In the paper we present the research background, the research framework, the methods we used to analyze the data, and some of the main findings. We finalize with short discussion and future research we intend to conduct.

2 Research Background

The discipline of CS has undergone changes, which in turn have affected CSE. Chi [4], for instance, wrote: "The world has changed, and so should the computing science curriculum as well" and, after exploring the concepts included in the Internet Operating System [7], concluded: "How many universities can say that they have experts in all of these areas? These topics are often only covered in CS departments as either advanced topic courses, or, worse, not offered at all."

[1] The discussion is presented in ACM, SIGCSE-members: http://listserv.acm.org/scripts/wa-ACMLPX.exe?A0=SIGCSE-MEMBERS.

Such changes have caused CS departments to update their curricula. In Stanford, for example, "the previous core curriculum, which had become monolithic and inflexible, was pared in the re-design to just six core courses—three with a theoretical focus and three with an emphasis on programming and systems. [...] A number of relevant courses from other departments including, for example, biology, psychology, product design and studio art can be included as part of a student's program in CS."[2] This trend is reflected also in the new SIGCSE category added to the Curriculum Topics list: New Interdisciplinary Programs (CS + X). Furthermore, social media elements have been largely introduced into CS curricula and pedagogy in recent years (e.g., MOOCs, mobility, clouds, social networking, big data and more). These changes are reflected at SIGCSE conferences as well: the big data issue was first addressed at SIGCSE 2011 and MOOCs were first discussed a year later, at SIGCSE 2012.

Other ACM SIGs (Special Interest Groups) also refer to similar trends. For example, by mining the ACM Digital Library, Guha, Steinhardt, Ishtiaque and Lagoze [5] revealed evidence of transitions in the field of CS since the emergence of computer-human interaction as a distinct sub-discipline. Their results suggest shifts in the field due to broader social, economic, and political changes in computing research.

One way to explore changes in CS is by investigating the three versions of the CS Computing Curricula published by ACM and IEEE in 2001 [1], 2008 [2], and 2013 [3]. Even a superficial analysis of the top-level knowledge areas addressed in those curricula (KAs) reveals changes in the field (Table 1, N is the number of KAs).

As Table 1 reveals, the 2001 and 2008 curricula are almost identical. More profound differences are however exhibited between the first two curricula and the third curriculum, in which two main changes are evident in several categories (rows highlighted in grey). First, the Programming Fundamentals knowledge area has been split in 2013 into Software Development Fundamentals and System Fundamentals and, second, the knowledge area Net-Centric Computing, which appeared in both the 2001 and 2008 curricula, does not appear in the 2013 curriculum and, instead, four new KAs have been introduced: Information Assurance and Security, Networking and Communications, Platform-Based Development, and Parallel and Distributed Computing. No new CS curriculum has been published since 2013, but other related curricula have been updated and new curricula have been developed. For example, an updated curriculum for Computer Engineering was published in 2016 (the previous and first one was published in 2004), an updated curriculum for Software Engineering was published in 2014 (the previous and first one was published in 2004), and a new curriculum for Post-Secondary Degree Programs in Cybersecurity was published in 2017[3]. Similar updates were incorporated in the Information Technology and Information Systems

[2] Period of Transition: Stanford computer science rethink core curriculum, https://engineering.stanford.edu/press/period-transition-stanford-computer-science-rethinks-core-curriculum (June 14, 2012).

[3] ACM>Education>Curricula Recommendations: https://www.acm.org/education/curricula-recommendations.

Table 1. KAs in the 2001, 2008 and 2013 CS ACM and IEEE curricula

Year KA	2001 (N – 14)	2008 (N – 14)	2013 (N = 18)
Discrete Structures	+	+	+
Programming Fundamentals	+	+	
Software Development Fundamentals			+
System Fundamentals			+
Algorithms and Complexity	+	+	+
Architecture and Organization	+	+	+
Operating Systems	+	+	+
Net-Centric Computing	+	+	
Information Assurance and Security			+
Networking and Communications			+
Platform-based Development			+
Parallel and Distributed Computing			+
Programming Languages	+	+	+
Human-Computer Interaction	+	+	+
Graphics and Visual Computing	+	+	+
Intelligent Systems	+	+	+
Information Management	+	+	+
Social and Professional Issues	+	+	+ Practice
Software Engineering	+	+	+
Computational Science (CN) and Numerical Methods (NM)	+ CN + NM	+ CN	+ CN

curricula for bachelor and graduate degrees. The K-12 curricula standards[4] were developed in 2011 and updated in 2017.

3 Research Framework

3.1 Research Objective

Our research objective was to explore the changes that have taken place in CSE over the past decade, as they are reflected in conferences, discussion groups, and journals, in which CSE practitioners and researchers share their expertise and experience.

3.2 Research Questions

For the preliminary research stage, we posed the following question: What changes have taken place in CSE over the past decade, as reflected in SIGCSE conferences?

[4] CSTA K-12 Standards: https://www.csteachers.org/page/standards https://www.csteachers.org/page/standards.

3.3 Data Collected

We analyzed three presentation formats—papers, panels, and special sessions—included in the SIGCSE conference proceedings from four years: 2006, 2010, 2014 and 2018 (Table 2). Our assumption was that differences, if exist, will be more noticeable in non-consecutive years. Hence, we chose to examine conferences at 4-year intervals.

The three presentation formats are characterized on the conference website as follows:

- Papers describe an educational research project, classroom experience, teaching technique, curricular initiative, or pedagogical tool.
- Panels present multiple perspectives on a specific topic.
- Special sessions include a seminar on a new topic, a committee report, or a forum on curriculum issues.

For each item in each presentation category, we examined the following characteristics:

- Session head (in which the papers were presented)
- Presentation title
- Categories and subject descriptors (in 2006, 2010, 2014)
- General terms (in 2006, 2010, 2014)
- CCS concepts (in 2018)
- Keywords

As can be seen, the format requirements from authors was changed. In the first three conferences, authors were asked to include Categories subject descriptors, and General terms, and at 2018, authors were asked to specify the CCS concepts. Due to this inconsistency, we do not include these presentation characteristics in this paper.

The considerations for the data gathering and analysis are:

- *Session heads*: Session heads reflect the conference chairs' perspective on the conference topics and focal themes. Since the conference chairs give session titles to help the audience choose sessions that might be of interest, the session heads add information about the presentation content.
- *General terms*: We compared the General terms of the three first conferences but it did not lead to any valuable conclusion. Hence, it is not presented.
- *Categories and subject descriptors*: Till the 2019 conference, most presentations were classified as belonging to the K.3.2 - Computer and Information Science Education category, hence, this data was found to be less useful for our investigation of trends in CSE. In fact, the K.3.2 category was the category recommended by the conferences guidelines. For example, the SIGCSE 2014 website[5] specifically states, "most submissions are likely to use category K.3.2 Computer and Information Science Education". Indeed, some presenters were satisfied to use the high-level category, while others attributed several subcategories to their presentations. Despite the guidelines, several presenters used alternative categorizations, which are

[5] SIGCSE 2014 website: http://sigcse2014.sigcse.org/authors/format.php.

Table 2. Number of papers, panels, and special sessions presented at SIGCSE 2006, 2010, 2014 and 2018

Type of presentation	2006	2010	2014	2018
Papers	107	103	105	162
Panels	14	12	14	19
Special Sessions	10	12	12	16
Total = 576	121	127	131	197

also relevant for CSE (e.g., K.3.1 Computer Uses in Education: Collaborative learning; Computer-assisted instruction; Computer-managed instruction; Distance learning; or K.4 COMPUTERS AND SOCIETY: K.4.1 Public Policy Issues - Ethics; or K.4.2 Social Issues - Handicapped persons/special needs). In 2019, a new categorization system has been introduces - CCS CONCEPTS[6]. We guess it aimed at solving the above problem, and, at the same time, to integrate the two previous categories, General terms and Subject categories, into one classification.

- *CCS categories*: The new CCS categories tree of concepts is valuable and allows more accurate and up-to-date characterization of the presentations. Nevertheless, here as well, authors choose in different way. Some author mention only the concept that appears as a leaf of a categorization tree, other stop at inner nodes, and some describe complete paths. Therefore, comparative analysis may not be accurate.
- *Keywords*: Keywords express the presentations' themes, as defined freely by the authors. We initially assumed that this descriptor would best fit to compare and follow the CSE community interests. We found, however, a huge variety of keywords so that made it almost useless for statistically analyze, per-se. Further, not all authors included keywords.

Base on those insights, we set the analysis criteria presented next.

3.4 Data Analysis

Considering the data provided for each presentation, and the restrictions regarding each of the descriptors, we performed a two-way analysis of the data collected on each of the three types of presentations (papers, panels, special sessions): Content analysis (Sect. 3.4.1) and keyword analysis (Sect. 3.4.2).

The Content Analysis

Considering the session head in which the presentation was included, the presentation title, and if needed, its abstract, we defined five content categories, specified below, three of which have sub-categories. For each, we present examples of main original content that was associated with it. Each paper was allocated to one category according to its' identified leading content.

[6] See The 2012 ACM Computing Classification System: https://www.acm.org/publications/class-2012.

Teaching Methods

- Computerized tools: lab-related topics, animation, visualization, computerized tools that support learning processes, game programming.
- Active learning: all activities whose purpose is to promote student participation and engagement.
- Evaluation: evaluation methods - exercises and tests, project evaluation, peer evaluation, test design.
- Projects/peers: project development, project ideas, team formation, teamwork.
- Class organization: distance learning, working with teaching assistants, MOOCs.

Curricula

- K-12 curricula.
- Undergraduate curricula, including programming languages
- Interdisciplinary curricula.

CSE Research

- Including: conceptions, influence of teaching methods on student understanding, comparison between teaching methods, and *different* research methods.

Recruitment and Retention

- Including issues related to gender and disabilities.

CS Educators

- K-12 educators.
- Undergraduate educators.

We distinguish papers on 'Teaching Methods' from 'CSE Research' by the following criteria: CSE research papers describe a methodological research, including data collection tools and analysis; papers categorized as a Teaching Methods paper describe a teaching experience, highlighting some pedagogical method, and whose emphasis is not the research process.

The Keywords Analysis
After filtering keywords that add no relevant information for classification, such as CSE or Computing, we divided the keywords into three sub-categories: CS curricula, such as, CS1 and K-12; CS topics, such as, Cybersecurity and Logic Programming; and pedagogy, such as, Project-Based Learning, Automated Testing, and Gamification. When authors did not specify keywords, we retrieved keywords from the presentation title.

4 Findings: Trends in CSE

4.1 Content Categorization

The content categorization is presented for each of the presentations studied—papers, panels, and special sessions—with columns for each of the conferences (2006, 2010, 2014, 2018) and a Total column. The rows of Table 3, which presents the content categories for papers, are sorted in descending order of the Total column. To compare between the three types of presentations, this order is maintained also for the other two types of presentations, even if the Total column suggests otherwise.

Papers Content Categorization

Table 3 presents the frequency in percentages for papers according to the content categories (grey background) and sub-categories (white background) for each of the four conferences. The percentages of the categories represent their frequency in each conference, and as such, they express the degree of attention each category received in the said conference. In the Total column, percentages are calculated with respect to N = 477, which is the total number of papers presented in the four conferences.

Our main observations are that:

- *Teaching methods*: is the most frequently addressed issue in all conferences although interest is seen to decrease from 2014 (53%) to 2018 (37%)
- *Curricula*: Similar attention is given to the category of Curricula in the four conferences, but the focus shifted in 2018 and more attention was given to the K-12 and Interdisciplinary sub-categories.
- *CSE Research*: Interest in CSE research decreased from 2006 (21%) to 2014 (9%) and increased from 2014 (9%) to 2018 (15%).
- *Recruitment and Retention*: increased in 2014 and 2018;
- *CS Educators*: A noticeable change can be observed in 2018 (11%), after the category of Educators received only little attention at the previous three conferences. Specifically, in the K-* sub-category, in the 2006 and 2010 conferences, only K-12 educators were addressed, whereas in 2018, two new populations of educators were addressed K-8 and K-3.

Table 3. Relative frequency of the content categories of papers

Content categories/Sub-categories	2006 N = 107	2010 N = 103	2014 N = 105	2018 N = 162	Total N = 477
Teaching Methods	47%	47%	53%	37%	45%
Computerized tools	9%	20%	19%	9%	14%
Active learning	15%	12%	20%	7%	13%
Evaluation	8%	10%	6%	9%	8%
Projects/peers	8%	5%	5%	7%	6%
Class organization	6%	0%	4%	4%	4%
Curricula	22%	31%	27%	28%	27%
Undergraduate	8%	21%	21%	15%	16%
K-12	8%	7%	1%	5%	5%
Interdisciplinary	6%	3%	6%	9%	6%
CSE Research	21%	14%	9%	15%	15%
Recruitment and Retention	6%	6%	11%	9%	8%
CS Educators	4%	2%	0%	11%	5%
K-12	4%	1%	0%	6%	3%
Undergraduate	0%	1%	0%	5%	2%

Panels Content Categorization

Table 4 presents the relative frequency in percentages of panels according to the refined content categorization. Due to the relatively small number of panels presented at each conference, sub-categories are not specified.

Table 4. Relative frequency of the content categories of panels, in percentage

Content categories/Sub-categories	2006 N=14	2010 N=12	2014 N=14	2018 N=19	Total N=59
Teaching Methods	51%	42%	36%	32%	40%
Curricula	21%	33%	43%	42%	35%
CSE Research	21%	17%	0%	5%	10%
Recruitment and Retention	7%	8%	14%	11%	10%
CS Educators	0%	0%	7%	11%	5%

As Table 4 indicates, the frequency order of content categories associated with the panels is identical to that obtained for the papers (Table 3).

Special Sessions Content Categorization

Table 5 presents the relative frequency in percentages of special sessions according to the refined content categorization. Due to the relatively small number of special sessions presented at each conference, sub-categories are not specified.

Table 5. Relative frequency of the content categories of special sessions, in percentage

Content categories/Sub-categories	2006 N = 10	2010 N = 12	2014 N = 12	2018 N = 16	Total N = 50
Teaching Methods	30%	26%	50%	19%	30%
Curricula	30%	33%	25%	50%	36%
CSE Research	10%	33%	8%	19%	18%
Recruitment and Retention	30%	0%	17%	6%	12%
CS Educators	0%	8%	0%	6%	4%

As can be seen from Table 5, unlike papers and panels, Curricula received more attention in special session than did Teaching Methods, the category that received the highest attention in papers and panels.

4.2 Keyword Categorization

Keywords are defined freely by the authors and express their presentations' themes. As mentioned, we initially assumed that this descriptor would be found to be the best way to compare and follow changes in the interests of the CSE community. Since we found a huge variety of keywords[7], this descriptor was deemed unsuitable for statistical analysis; however, since keywords represent an important classification for authors, we nevertheless divided the keywords into three categories: (1) CS curriculum, (2) CS topics, and (3) pedagogy. This categorization appears to resonate the type of papers specified in the SIGCSE 2019 submission site[8]: (1) Curriculum Topics, Computing Topics and Education and Experience Topics.

Since the number of presentations in Panels and Special Sessions is relatively small, and as mentioned, the variety of keywords is great, we combine the keywords of all three presentation types together and present the number of appearances (and not percentages as presented in the content categorization).

Keywords that Address the Type of Curriculum

Table 6 displays the frequencies of keywords that address types of curriculum. The first line presents the frequency at which the global words curricula or curriculum was mentioned and the other lines indicate the particular curriculum topic mentioned.

The undergraduate curricula (CS0, CS1, CS2 and Software Engineering) are presented first, with the highest frequency for CS1 curriculum in all three conferences. In general, the frequencies of the undergraduate curricula are similar over the years, while CS1 leads high above, and the advanced curricula (CS2, SE) are addressed less. The STEM/ Interdisciplinary or Multidisciplinary curricula and the Computational Thinking curriculum come next and are discussed with respect to undergraduate programs and high school programs. Then, curricula for different school ages are presented. The increased interest in developing the young generation's computational skills is reflected clearly. This approach flourished followed Wing's [8] first call in 2006 to develop computational thinking skills within any discipline. CS in K-12 education is now an integral content of the SIGCSE conferences, with recently added attention to middle school and even to elementary school.

The bottom line of Table 6 presents the percentages of papers in each of the four conferences, which address the curriculum category. These percentages (in between 37% to 54%; on average of 45%) express a relatively high interest in this category.

Keywords that Address CS Topics

Table 7 displays the frequencies of keywords that address CS topics. In this category, the problem of multiple keywords without uniform representation is clearly expressed. The table presents CS topics that appeared at least in one conference and at least four times. These data do not allow retrieving any significant information and it warrants further investigation.

[7] This is correct also for the 2018 conference, in which more presentations were accepted.

[8] https://sigcse2019.sigcse.org/authors/papers.html.

Table 6. Frequency of keywords that address the type of curriculum

Keywords	2006 N = 131	2010 N = 127	2014 N = 131	2018 N = 197	Total N = 586
Curriculum/Curricula	16	18	14	16	64
CS0	8	8	5	3	24
CS1	13	15	16	17	61
CS2	4	3	3	5	15
Software Engineering	4	4	8	1	17
STEM/Interdisciplinary/Multidisciplinary	2	5	7	4	18
Computational Thinking		7	6	7	20
K-12	1	6	10	11	28
AP				3	3
K10			1		1
Middle School				2	2
Elementary/ Primary/K6			1	4	5
Percentage in the conference	**37%**	**52%**	**54%**	**37%**	**44%**

Table 7. Frequency of keywords that address CS topics

Keywords	2006 N = 131	2010 N = 127	2014 N = 131	2018 N = 197	Total N = 586
Algorithms	5	3	3	8	19
Networks	4	5	1	4	14
Cybersecurity	1		2	8	11
Parallel	1	5	3	2	11
Object Oriented	4	5	1		10
Compilers	5	3	1	1	10
Data Structures	1	1	4	4	10
Web	3	4	1	1	9
Graphics	5		1	1	7
Python	1	1	4	1	7
Distributed			4	2	6
Functional		1		4	5
Percentage in the conference	23%	22%	19%	18%	20%

The bottom line of Table 7 presents the percentages of papers in each of the four conferences, which address the CS topics category. These percentages (in between 18% to 23%; an average of 21%) reflect interest in this category which is only about half of the interest expressed in relation to the curriculum category.

Keywords that Address Pedagogical Aspects

Table 8 presents the frequency of the pedagogy-related keywords, sorted according to total appearance in the four conferences.

Table 8. Frequency of keywords that address pedagogical aspects

Keywords	2006 N = 131	2010 N = 127	2014 N = 131	2018 N = 197	Total N = 586
Assessment/Evaluation/Testing/Automated Testing	9	13	19	36	77
Teaching/Instruction	6	17	9	29	61
Collaboration/Peer/Pair	8	18	9	25	60
Gender/Diversity/Minorities/Culture	15	13	13	19	60
Active learning	11	6	8	16	41
Research	11	8	7	9	35
Visualization	6	10	6	7	29
Project	8	5	8	7	28
Games	6	8	4	9	27
Distance Learning/Flipped Class/MOOC	2	3	8	10	23
Percentage in the conference	63%	80%	69%	85%	75%

The bottom line of Table 8 presents the percentages of papers in each of the four conferences that address the pedagogical aspects category. These percentages (in between 63% to 85%; on average of 74%) express extensive and wide interest in this category. This remarkable interest is substantially higher than the interest expressed in the other categories and hints that the SIGCSE conferences fulfill their aims.

Here are several main insights with respect to pedagogical aspects:

- A significant increase is noted in aspects related directly to teaching practices, in particular, assessment, active learning, and collaborative learning. This resonates the categorization by content categories in which Teaching Methods received the highest attention.
- Focus is placed on collaborative learning, teamwork, and gender.
- A consistent increase is evident in aspects related to distance learning.

5 Discussion

The data analysis for the three types of presentations leads to several observations that enable to realize the potential of the SIGCSE conferences:

- Although the objectives of the three kinds of presentations differ, the different presentations address practically the same topics (and at, more or less, the same related frequencies).
- The dominance of the content category Teaching Methods is noticeable, especially compared with Curriculum.

- Although teaching methods receive a great deal of attention, only a small proportion of presentations address the CS educators themselves. Relevant topics that are neglected are, for example, barriers educators face while assimilating new teaching methods in different teaching settings (e.g., large university classes).

Following the exploration presented in this paper we intend to continue and analyze other venues that focus on CSE (journals and other CSE conferences) and to check how the topics addressed at the CSE conferences are related to trends in the discipline of CS itself.

References

1. ACM and IEEE: Computing Curricula 2001 - Computer Science (2001). https://www.acm.org/binaries/content/assets/education/curricula-recommendations/cc2001.pdf
2. ACM and IEEE: Computer Science Curriculum 2008: An Interim Revision of CS 2001 (2008). https://www.acm.org/binaries/content/assets/education/curricula-recommendations/computerscience2008.pdf
3. ACM and IEEE: Computer Science Curricula 2013 Curriculum Guidelines for Undergraduate Degree Programs in Computer Science (2013). https://www.acm.org/binaries/content/assets/education/cs2013_web_final.pdf
4. Chi, E.H.: Time to rethink CS education: The (social) web changes everything! BLOG@CACM (2010). http://cacm.acm.org/blogs/blog-cacm/82365-time-to-rethink-computer-science-education-the-social-web-changes-everything/fulltext
5. Guha, S., Steinhardt, S., Ishtiaque S.A., Lagoze, C.: Following bibliometric footprints: The ACM digital library and the evolution of CS. In: Proceedings of the 13th ACM/IEEE-CS Joint Conference on Digital Libraries (JCDL 2013), pp. 139–142. ACM, New York (2013). http://doi.acm.org/10.1145/2467696.2467
6. Kay, D.G., Bruce, K.B., Clancy, M., Dale, N., Guzdial, M., Roberts, E.: Recognizing the most influential CS education papers. In: Proceedings of the 41st ACM Technical Symposium on Computer Science Education (SIGCSE 2010), pp. 196–197. ACM, New York (2010). DOI: https://doi.org/10.1145/1734263.1734331
7. O'Reilly, T.: The State of the Internet Operating System. Radar, Insight, Analysis, and Research about Emerging Technologies. http://radar.oreilly.com/2010/03/state-of-internet-operating-system.html
8. Wing, J.M.: Computational thinking. Commun. ACM **49**(3), 33–35 (2006)

Holistic STEAM Education Through Computational Thinking: A Perspective on Training Future Teachers

Arnold Pears[1(✉)], Erik Barendsen[2], Valentina Dagienė[3], Vladimiras Dolgopolovas[3], and Eglė Jasutė[3]

[1] KTH Royal Institute of Technology, Stockholm, Sweden
pears@kth.se
[2] Radboud University and Open University, Nijmegen, The Netherlands
e.barendsen@cs.ru.nl
[3] University of Vilnius Institute of Educational Sciences, Vilnius, Lithuania
valentina.dagiene@mif.vu.lt
http://www.kth.se/larande, http://www.ru.nl/science/
http://www.vu.lt

Abstract. Computational thinking (CT) skills are argued to be vital to preparing future generations of learners to be productive citizens in our increasingly technologically sophisticated societies. However, teacher education lags behind policy in many countries, and there is a palpable need for enhanced support for teacher education in CT. This paper addresses this gap, establishing an intellectual framework with which to explore the manner in which CT can be inculcated in compulsory school students. Drawing on a deeper awareness of the broader societal and cultural context of the activities we introduce a new approach to designing teacher education. The novelty of our approach is that training computation thinking is framed as an integrative element rather than as a separate study subject. This approach provides better articulation between Engineering and Science oriented subjects and Arts, providing supporting methods to develop the professional skills of student-teachers.

Keywords: Computational thinking · Integration · Culture · STEAM · Compulsory schooling · Teacher training

1 Introduction

In order to educate future generations, new generations of teachers require the requisite skills and capability to scaffold learning in a societal context where technology, and in particular automation and computation threaten to eliminate many skilled professions [20]. By implication the tertiary education sector must respond in terms of teacher education, and their structure, conduct and outcomes to equip pupils with the new skill set required.

S. N. Pozdniakov and V. Dagienė (Eds.): ISSEP 2019, LNCS 11913, pp. 41–52, 2019.
https://doi.org/10.1007/978-3-030-33759-9_4

Responding to these challenges, the EU has announced new strategies and requirements for European Higher Education (HE). One of the declared priorities is "tackling future skills mismatches and promoting excellence in skills development" [1]. The motivation for this statement is clear, first, there is a decrease in interest and many "jobs are closely related to those areas that prepare students for jobs where shortages exist or are emerging" [2]. The areas of science, technology, engineering, (arts) and maths (STE(A)M), medical professions and teaching are focus areas.

The European Centre for the Development of Vocational Training (CEDEFOP) avers that the most highly demanded professionals are: "ICT professionals; medical doctors; science, technology, engineering and mathematics (STEM) professionals; nurses and midwives; and teachers" [1,2]. They also conclude that "all students in advanced learning, irrespective of discipline, need to acquire advanced transverse skills and key competences that will allow them to thrive" [1]. These skills, in addition to high- level digital competencies [1,8,10,21] include "numeracy, autonomy, critical thinking and a capacity for problem-solving" [1].

Computational models are central to a large fraction of modern scientific research, and therefore are also central to research-driven education. Computational models arise in collaboration with other disciplines outside computing. In these areas, in addition to the existing physical environment and specific content laboratories, computing can provide an opportunity for digital experiments and simulations. Then, in order to develop, implement, and study practical solutions based on computational models that include both technical and social aspects, students should have additional skills that allow them to develop or implement solutions in a highly digitised educational environment, such as decomposition and generalisation, and skills to design, create relevant algorithms, automate and calculate. Many argue that computational skills, in particular Computational Thinking (CT), are central to every discipline and profession.

Despite the importance attributed to STEM subjects by strategists and government documents [2], the need to motivate more people to study subjects related to STEM remains, including the problem of "tackling the under-representation of women, minorities and other under-represented groups in scientific and technical subjects in HE and subsequently in related professions" [1].

The role of school teachers is crucial to addressing this problem in a sustainable manner. School teachers are person who can motivate their pupils to take an interest in all subjects, including maths and sciences, and play an active role in helping to shape their future choices. During his or her teaching activities, the school teacher is a crucial agent, utilising knowledge, skills and competencies to enhance the intellectual development of students. Consequently, the role and responsibility of HE (especially in regard to the education of future teachers) is to ensure that study programs are provided which develop the required pedagogical models and competence.

This paper describes our recommendation for developing and contextualising future STEM education in the context of the European discourse on higher education and pre-service teacher education. Aligned with our previous discussion we suggest special attention be given to Computational Thinking and to the new demands placed on teachers. Our starting point is therefore to propose a framework of curriculum improvements with respect to computational skills in STEM teacher education in a manner that allows them to be contextualised into the complex European curriculum landscape.

Our target group for this project are teachers for: preschool institutions (kindergartens); primary school; middle and high school STEM and computer science subjects; foreign languages, arts and humanities. The concrete objectives are: (1) to improve the CT skills of prospective teachers, and (2) to foster the teachers' development of pedagogical content knowledge (PCK) related to the teaching and training of various aspects of Computational Thinking (CT). We recognise that it is impossible to provide a generic solution due to the different curricula for teacher education in different countries. However, the goal of the exercise is not to rewrite curricula, or propose new curricula, instead we focus on providing modules that provide practical assistance to teachers and teacher educators. The role of these resources, and how they influence curricula in countries beyond the scope of our initiative (our scope is primarily the Nordic and Baltic countries). We offer the model we have developed as a source of inspiration for others, and as an example of one approach to tackling this educational challenge.

2 Computational Thinking as an Integrating Skill

2.1 Research Perspective

Computational thinking and digital competence are closely related areas. The DigComp framework of the European Union [21] provides guidance in the process of identifying the necessary skills and competencies estimated to be required of future citizens. Jeanette Wing [22,23] widely popularised and promoted the central role of computational approaches. In this regard, a key aspect is the ability to understand the opportunities and limitations which the high speed computational capacity modern computers bring to the practice of all disciplines.

Here it is crucial to recognise that ideas of computation, and computability are not what is new. Computation and computing have been practiced since early times [18], and the ability to compute and automate has lead to large scale social re-organisation, for instance the impact of automation as a primary driver of the industrial revolution [7]. What is new is the rapidity with which calculations can be performed. The speed of calculation possible with modern computing machinery is unprecedented, and it is the application of this power, with the associated implications for what that makes possible that is crucial to the STEAM argument. But indeed, what is even more important, is what cannot be done despite this capability for rapid computation.

There are many ways to conceptualize Computational Thinking. Common aspects include Decomposition, abstraction, algorithms and automation, modelling and simulation, data collection, data representation, data analysis, and parallelisation. This skill set provides capabilities for designing content and context specific models and simulations with (or without) computers.

2.2 Scientific Literacy

The goal of science education is scientific literacy, therefore to teach scientific inquiry is one of the most important aspects for STEAM education. This includes (besides content specific skills) experimentation skills and argumentation skills.

Scientific thinking is understood as the ability to complete scientific inquiry within a specific scientific content. Knowledge of the basics and details of the content specific topics is important. In addition, students should acquire skills for experimentation and data processing, as well as logical thinking and generalisation skills. Creative thinking, as already mentioned, includes skills that allow students to incorporate aspects related to the environment and context into the model that they create and test during their project or problem based activities.

We treat Computational Thinking (CT) as an integrative skill within our holistic STEM model. This position is arrived at based on the following arguments. First, we wish to emphasise the primary role of computational models in modern scientific research and, therefore, in research-oriented education. Such computational models, in addition to the existing physical environment and specific content laboratories, provide an opportunity for digital experiments and simulations.

Subsequently it will be necessary to develop, implement, and study a series of practical modules imbued with the core competences in aspects related to the acquisition and development of CT skills. The process of such integration with the existing curricula will provide solutions based on computational models that include both technical and social aspects, [such that] students should have additional skills that allow them to develop or implement solutions in a highly digitised educational environment, such as decomposing and generalising skills and skills to automate, algorithmize, calculate, and design.

2.3 STEAM Integration

As for science, engineering and technology, focusing exclusively on specific technical knowledge in isolation no longer provides learning advantages. Contextualisation in terms of other disciplines emerges as important, and social contextualisation as a major factor in achieving broader representation of minorities. Revealing a "true" pragmatist approach, focused on the needs and expectations of the community, modelling of complex social aspects is a must for modern research and industry. Such requirements have a direct impact on modern STEM education.

There is a need for context-oriented STEM content and teaching resources, with a clear focus on the trans-disciplinary nature of emerging high level challenges. Indeed there are compelling calls to expand STEM to include aspects of design and the arts. In Sweden the national curriculum calls for CT content to be integrated into existing school subjects such as "art and craft" and Swedish language, as well as the more traditional targets, mathematics, physics and technology. To address this situation a point of departure in design, and a more holistic epistemology of STEM teaching embracing the Arts (STE(A)M) is proposed [19]. In the outline we present below, this integration is the central guiding principle.

To contextualise our effort further we consider the two main trends of development of post-industrial society related to education and research. Foremost digitisation, followed closely by the socialisation and contextualisation of knowledge and experience. There is a movement back to our "socio-cultural origin" - signified by a shift in popular perspective from industrial society with its clear focus on people as potential employees, to a post-industrial understanding of the complex interplay between the nature of people and society. These two directions are intertwined fostering nowadays post-industrial society to become even more complex to act, understand and model. Individuals are immersed in a kind of broth with human, inhuman agents and organisations. In the course of its daily activities, the industry must take into account the influence of the complexity of these social and contextual factors, and in practice this means even higher demands on employees related to skills and level of education [14].

Another argument for the integration is the failure of "automatic transfer" in the original Papert approach. One of the key ideas in Papert's (1980) classical work on the programming language LOGO [13] is that by learning to program, children would develop computational problem solving skills that they could apply to other contexts. Results of empirical studies on this expected transfer were mixed, however. Research suggests that sophisticated applications of computational thinking skills to other subject matter does not come by itself, but requires explicit instruction [16]. This is also confirmed by the work of Palumbo [12] which explores the evidence surrounding how problem solving can be supported by programming activities.

3 An Integrated CT Curriculum for Teacher Education

3.1 Content

There is a need to develop innovative educational approaches to practical STEAM education that are based on Computational Thinking (CT) as related to trans-disciplinary and holistic STEAM perspectives. We promote a pragmatic approach to CT as to a set of tools, techniques and approaches which enable a seamless transition from the early-aged child's unplug activities to a comprehensive modelling and computer simulation activities of K-12 and early years' university students. We put our research and implementation emphasis on educational programs and curriculum enhancement for education of prospective teachers focusing on CT and STEAM related aspects.

We propose an approach that promotes developing of skills related to the contextual environment, such as communication, research ethics, social modelling, politics and society, and include the development of emotional and creative thinking in addition to the skills of scientific thinking, mainly as related to project-based and enquiry driven education.

We propose a multidimensional model of curriculum development: the longitudinal dimension (personal childhood intellectual development), the skills dimension (scientific thinking skills, CT skills, and contextual thinking skills), the contextual dimension (community, society, communication, management, entrepreneurship, culture, diversity, ethics).

Within this three dimensional curriculum CT is positioned as an integrative skill set that links scientific and content- specific knowledge with contextual thinking skills, adding context-specific modelling skills (developing of models and simulations, including modelling of cyber-social systems).

The curricula philosophy emerges from the post scientific tendency to merge scientific and technical knowledge with social and humanitarian knowledge. Here we perceive contextual knowledge as the most valued, and adopt a pragmatist approach to education in terms of sharing community values and solving actual present-day problems. The adapted TPACK framework for CT and STEAM is applied to develop specific curriculum modules in the latter part of the paper.

Students are given the opportunity to evaluate their designs from an economic, environmental, political, and scientific point of view. In fact, the student teacher should also be able to develop and test the contextual model using assessment, evaluation, and communication.

3.2 Pedagogical Approaches

The evolution of school STEM pedagogy expands our scope beyond the traditional discipline specific STEM to tackle the complex challenge of embedding CT and other scientific thinking habits and practices into language and arts and craft subjects. Necessarily this integrated STEM must be seen as STE(A)M – that is include (integrate) arts and humanities subjects with traditional STEM. Our STEAM integration process is based on the development of models and/or simulations in curricula support modules (these could be computer/computational models or other forms of models and simulations) that will provide an appropriate grounding for students' cognitive processes. In doing so we place an emphasis on informatics (computer science) and/or CT.

Project based learning cycle (PBL) as related to STEAM includes practices and activities to (Young, 2018): (1) identify the problem; (2) identify criteria and constraints; (3) brainstorm possible solutions; (4) generate ideas; (5) explore possibilities; (6) select an approach; (7) build a model or prototype (computer model and/or simulation); (8) refine the design. Our approach leverages these stages as a way to scaffold module design.

What are the main aspects of school STEAM education? (1) We must provide students with the instruments to creatively solve the problems they face in their daily lives; (2) In the PBL cycle, students should be motivated to design the investigation to find the best appropriate solution from issues raised from the community; (3) the main principles for the curriculum: the situated problem, creative design, emotional grounding; (4) an integrative approach and focus on competences – scientific thinking, computational thinking, and contextual thinking; (5) systematic assessment.

The school (kindergarten) curriculum must comply with the earlier work of Armstrong [4]: (A) cycles of child's personal development; (B) a holistic longitudinal model of a child's personal development.

The holistic approach to design [3] involves increasing complexity – from simple tasks to complex projects; as we do so we eliminate compartmentalisation and sequencing of problem-solving tasks.

A context-based approach has been shown to be beneficial. In particular, context-based teaching provides meaning, coherence and relevance to conceptual subject matter. We develop a content based on real-world problems or tasks related to children's lives: the multidisciplinary nature of real-world problems places new demand on teaching, requiring collaboration between teachers with different content experiences and expertise.

4 Project: Developing Teacher Education on CT in STEAM

4.1 Objectives

We aim to contribute to the professional development of STEAM teachers by developing modules for teacher education in order to (1) improve CT skills of prospective teachers and (2) to improve pedagogical skills and competencies of prospective teachers based on the integrative multi-disciplinary model previously advanced by Seery et al. [19].

4.2 Design Principles

How should this be achieved? There are many approaches that have shown promise in engaging learners using an explorative/enquiry paradigm. We consider here some variants of problem based learning (PBL), as well as Design Based Learning (DBL) within the broader sphere of social-constructivist learning approaches.

The recommended assessment approach is based on a pragmatic methodology which includes theoretical study, and models practical design cycles including piloting and dissemination stages. As a final practical result, a number of curriculum modules result, providing the basis for training prospective teachers on various aspects of CT as related to STEAM project-based education for preschool and school levels.

The proposed modules adopt several crucial criteria: (1) they are self- sufficient, which allows them to be included in the existing university curriculum; (2) they form part of the coherent CT curriculum for STEAM and related subjects. Expected impact includes opportunities to improve current educational programs for prospective teachers, and in the longer term, to improve European STEM education by moving to interdisciplinary and pragmatic STE(A)M, thus increasing teacher and pupil involvement and increasing motivation of currently less represented groups in order to generate interest in professional careers in the field of science and engineering.

4.3 Methodology

The research and implementation process of the individual modules is structured in four phases: (1) Development and Design Phase: Literature review and/or research on existing practices, the development of a first draft of the intellectual output and its publishing on the web site; (2) Review and Pilot Phase: Refinement of the first draft based on peer review and feedback by experts as well as feedback from the piloting of the module in teacher education programmes responsible for the course of the training events. (3) Optimisation and Production Phase: Development of an improved version of the intellectual output and its publication on the research project web site. (4) Translation and Publishing Phase: translation of intellectual outputs into languages of the research project partner countries and national implementation of the outputs.

In the development of the modules we address the TPACK model, which offers: (C) knowledge of the content includes knowledge of CT and aspects related to STEAM and contextual modelling; (P) pedagogical knowledge includes knowledge related to: (a) pedagogy of CT as a whole, (b) STEAM pedagogy, including interdisciplinary, integrative and contextual aspects, (c) PBL pedagogy; (T) technological knowledge should provide support for PBL and related modelling; (CX) contextual knowledge, among others, includes knowledge of modern school reform and European educational policy. A partial evaluation of the efficacy of these modules and the integrated curriculum model can be conducted using the teacher self-efficacy instrument of Nordén et al. [11].

4.4 Module Structure

The conceptual core is the development of 10 modules for integrating of computational thinking (CT) into existing university trainee teachers' education. This implementation consists of learning resources which can be adapted, contextualised, and integrated into university teacher education covering science, technology, engineering, arts and mathematics (STEAM).

The structure of the pool of resources (see Fig. 1) is designed to cover all the main parts of the educational process. The output of the project is the 10 modules (O1–O10) described in Table 1. Output O1, along with outputs O2 and O9, provide the theoretical and methodological basis for all module development. Outputs O8 and O10 focus on specific CT and STEAM educational environments and aspects of instructional design. Other modules are subject and level specific and focused on CT for STEAM and related subjects. At the same time, each module is self-sufficient and includes supporting material in the form of descriptions and instructions for the user. Each module will ultimately be represented by its own web page on the research project website.

5 Implications

Fostering the application of CT in school subject areas suggests that the learning objectives in existing subjects should be examined for future alignment with

Table 1. Module overview

Module	Contents
O1	Framework for the development of the curriculum modules: CT & STEAM for education of prospective school and kindergarten teachers
O2	General Introduction of Computational Thinking: a basic module suitable for all teachers
O3	CT for pre-school (kindergarten) prospective teachers: specific features, approaches and practical solutions
O4	CT for primary education prospective teachers: specific features, approaches and practical solutions
O5	CT for STEM prospective teachers: specific features, approaches and practical solutions
O6	CT for languages, arts and humanities prospective teachers: specific features, approaches and practical solutions
O7	CT for languages, arts and humanities prospective teachers: specific features, approaches and practical solutions
O8	Educational environments for CT: design and aspects of integration
O9	Using Constructivism, and Project and Challenge Driven Pedagogy for learning Computational Thinking
O10	Technological, pedagogical and instructional design aspects of teaching CT for STEAM

CT competences. This requires developing suitable operationalisations of CT and investigating both generic linking principles and topic-specific connections to CT. Concrete CT 'hooks' have been developed for specific STEM subject matter, for example mathematics [9] and technology [5].

Most of the examples of embedding CT into an existing subject area involve some form of algorithmic problem solving in that subject area, often combined with the construction of digital artifacts such as computer programs or robot as a technological solution to the problem. In some cases, however, it would be preferable to use computational concepts to represent subject matter from another STEM discipline such as physics, chemistry, biology or mathematics, in order to better understand and explore fundamental principles.

An interesting example is the use of algorithms to model the concepts of natural selection and protein synthesis in biology [15]. In the case of such scientific phenomena algorithmic modelling can be utilised, and the phenomenon explored using simulations, stimulating analysis, evaluation and reflection skills. If the emergent properties differ from the expected, this "suggests the rules, and therefore the underlying understanding needs further refinement" [17].

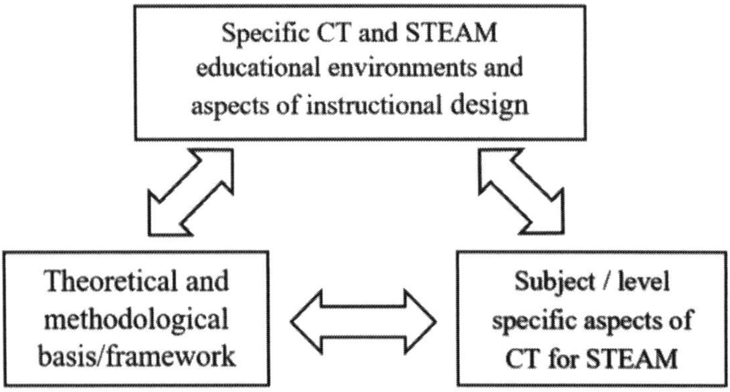

Fig. 1. Contextualised curriculum model

Teaching and assessing development in computational thinking has become one of the main issues in the field of modern education [3,6], and thus the discourse has moved beyond the boundaries of computer science. There is a tendency towards the integration of computational thinking skills into the skill set of today's learners regardless of their technical background. Therefore, to associate these skills with such courses as programming/computer literacy/digital competence might not be an effective or sustainable approach. However, as an alternative we suggest that a search for the possible ways to integrate computational thinking skills into the current educational settings provides a more constructive starting point.

Development of activities about computational thinking skills, and integration them into the curricula of various subject areas can be expected to help learners to meet the requirements of the information age paradigm of education. Teachers play a key role throughout this change because they are the ones who will embed the skills that contribute to the development of computational thinking skills in addition to practice the integrated activities. The computational thinking skills awareness of current teachers in the field of information technology (or computer science) is currently questionable. Moreover, the relationship between these skills and other subject areas are considerably weaker than is desirable. Our modularised approach strengthen that relationship, enhancing teacher education programs and providing support for curriculum revisions. It is expected that computational thinking skills will become obligatory fundamental skills, regardless of the subject areas of teachers. Moreover, the way teachers transfer these skills into their field of practice can be listed as one of the crucial teacher competencies in the near future. We believe that the approach we outline above addresses some central elements of this challenge.

6 Summary

In this paper we provide an educational science and resource design perspective on the challenge of integrating CT conceptual material into existing EU school teacher education programmes.

The aim of the curriculum modules for CT and STEAM education is two-fold: (1) to train pre-service teachers from various subject areas in order to develop their computational thinking skills, and (2) to model CT processes and thought structures to help integrate these skills into realistic educational scenarios. Our target group includes pre-service teachers in the one of the following fields: computer science, mathematics, science, foreign languages, craft, pre-school (kindergarten), and elementary education. Teacher education programs may naturally exhibit differences in terms of curriculum structure, and they can be shaped according to the local needs of countries. Any intervention designed for a single country might produce unexpected results for another one. That's why the context of the particular country should be well-defined by local researchers and thus the collaboration on a European scale developing the European dimension and character of education can become meaningful. In this way, countries can learn from each other's experience. It is consequently of the utmost importance that the pre-service teacher training interventions proposed here be tested and implemented in different countries.

Summing up the initiative and the manner in which it contributes to a new approach to STEAM teaching as an holistic pursuit we offer the following observations.

ELEMENTS OF INNOVATION include a pragmatic view on CT as on a set of tools and techniques which allow contextual integration of educational activities of school students of various levels of a STEM focused education. CT approaches in education, in addition to traditional approach to computer science and programming education, promote unplug activities, support project and design-based activities.

EXPECTED IMPACT (A) framework - is on (1) university teachers – provide a contextual description and module development paradigm; (2) curriculum developers – provide a framework for integration and adaptation of the developed. (B) research project web page – on all groups of interest and dissemination.

TRANSFER POTENTIAL is based on the universality of the structure, which ensures the consistency and self-sufficiency of the curriculum and other modules.

Acknowledgements. Some ideas in this paper are part of the outcomes of NordPlus Higher Education project NPHE-2019/10157. The main modules will be developed with the framework of the Erasmus+ project "Future Teachers Education: STEAM and Computational Thinking", 2019-1-LT01-KA203-060767.

References

1. EUR-Lex - 52017dc0247 - EN - EUR-Lex, https://eur-lex.europa.eu/legal-content/EN/TXT/?uri=CELEX:52017DC0247

2. Briefing note - The skills employers want!, April 2019
3. Angeli, C., et al.: A K-6 computational thinking curriculum framework: Implications for teacher knowledge. Educ. Technol. Soc. (2016)
4. Armstrong, T.: The Best Schools: How Human Development Research Should Inform Educational Practice. Association for Supervision and Curriculum Development, Alexandria (2006)
5. Atmatzidou, S., Demetriadis, S.: Advancing students' computational thinking skills through educational robotics: a study on age and gender relevant differences. Robot. Auton. Syst. **75**, 661–670 (2016)
6. Brennan, K., Resnick, M.: New frameworks for studying and assessing the development of computational thinking. In: Proceedings of the 2012 Annual Meeting of (2012)
7. Grier, D.A.: Human computers: the first pioneers of the information age. Endeavour **25**(1), 28–32 (2001). https://doi.org/10.1016/S0160-9327(00)01338-7
8. Kluzer, S., et al.: DigComp into action, get inspired make it happen a user guide to the European Digital Competence framework (2018)
9. Lu, J.J., Fletcher, G.H.: Thinking about computational thinking. ACM SIGCSE Bull. **41**(1), 260–264 (2009)
10. Mannila, L., Nordén, L., Pears, A.: Digital competence, teacher self-efficacy and training needs. In: Proceedings of the 2018 ACM Conference on International Computing Education Research, pp. 78–85. ACM (2018)
11. Nordén, L., Mannila, L., Pears, A.: Development of a self-efficacy scale for digital competences in schools. In: IEEE/ASEE Frontiers in Education Conference (2017)
12. Palumbo, D.: Programming language/problem-solving research: a review of relevant issues. Rev. Educ. Res. **60**(1), 65–89 (1990)
13. Papert, S.: Mindstorms: Children, Computers, and Powerful Ideas. Basic Books Inc., New York (1980)
14. Pears, A., Daniels, M.: Developing global teamwork skills: the runestone project. In: Castro, M., Tovar, E., Auer, M.E. (eds.) IEEE EDUCON 2010 The Future of Global Learning in Engineering Education (2010)
15. Peel, A., Friedrichsen, P.: Algorithms, abstractions, and iterations: teaching computational thinking using protein synthesis translation. Am. Biol. Teach. **80**(1), 21–28 (2018)
16. Perkins, D.N., Salomon, G.: Are cognitive skills context-bound? Educ. Res. **18**(1), 16–25 (1989)
17. Robins, A.V., Fincher, S.A.: The Cambridge Handbook of Computing Education Research. Cambridge Handbooks in Psychology. Cambridge University Press, Cambridge (2019)
18. Robson, E., Stedall, J.: The Oxford Handbook of the History of Mathematics. OUP Oxford, Oxford (2008). google-Books-ID: IieQDwAAQBAJ
19. Seery, N., Gumaelius, L., Pears, A.: Multidisciplinary teaching: the emergence of an holistic STEM teacher. In: 2018 IEEE Frontiers in Education Conference (FIE), pp. 1–6. IEEE (2018)
20. Tedre, M.: The Science of Computing: Shaping a Discipline. Taylor & Francis, Boca Raton (2014)
21. Vuorikari, R., Punie, Y., Gomez, S.C., Van Den Brande, G., et al.: DigComp 2.0: The Digital Competence Framework for Citizens, June 2016
22. Wing, J.M.: Computational thinking. Commun. ACM **49**(3), 33–35 (2006)
23. Wing Jeannette, M.: Computational thinking and thinking about computing. Philos. Trans. Roy. Soc. A: Math. Phys. Eng. Sci. **366**(1881), 3717–3725 (2008). https://doi.org/10.1098/rsta.2008.0118

Informatics Education in School: A Multi-Year Large-Scale Study on Female Participation and Teachers' Beliefs

Enrico Nardelli[1(✉)] and Isabella Corradini[2]

[1] Università di Roma "Tor Vergata", Rome, Italy
nardelli@mat.uniroma2.it
[2] Themis Research Centre, Rome, Italy
isabellacorradini@themiscrime.com

Abstract. This paper describes the outcomes of a multi-year large-scale study on Informatics education in school, involving an average of 3,600 teachers per school year of all school levels. The study has been conducted in Italy, where - generally speaking - there is no compulsory informatics education in school. Teachers have voluntarily enrolled in the "Programma il Futuro" project, running since 2014, and have taught short introductory courses in Informatics. Answering - anonymously - to monitoring questionnaires, they have indicated whether girls or boys were more interested in Informatics activities and whether girls or boys were more effective.

Answers show that the difference between the number of teachers thinking boys are more interested (or more effective) and the number of those judging girls more interested (or more effective) has constantly decreased over school years during the project. This variation in teachers' beliefs over school years - that we attribute to their involvement in project activities - is important, since teachers' beliefs are known to influence students' motivations, hence their future choices. Our opinion is reinforced by the results of a differential analysis, in each school year, between teachers repeating activities and those executing them for the first time.

Moreover, the analysis of disaggregated data shows that the difference between boys and girls relative to interest or effectiveness increases going up in school level. Our results provide an empirical support to the belief that it is important to start Informatics education early in school, before gender stereotypes consolidate.

Keywords: Informatics education in school · Broadening participation · Gender and diversity

S. N. Pozdniakov and V. Dagienė (Eds.): ISSEP 2019, LNCS 11913, pp. 53–67, 2019.
https://doi.org/10.1007/978-3-030-33759-9_5

1 Introduction

Many developed countries declare a shortage of workers well trained for computing related jobs [11,16]. This has become even more important in recent years, given that computing occupations are a larger and larger share of jobs [8].

Moreover, the existing information technology workforce does not adequately represent the diversity of society [10,21,38], largely due to the fact that too few girls and minorities enroll in computing related discipline [9,26,40].

The introduction of compulsory Informatics[1] education in schools and its extension to all school levels has been proposed as one possible measure to change this situation [6]. The rationale is that, by gaining since school a better comprehension of the real nature of the discipline, students - and girls in particular - can be more inclined to choose it for their university studies [28,39].

Related to this, it is also debated at which level of schools Informatics education should be introduced (see [15] and [42] for an in depth discussion), since some consider it an advanced discipline requiring students are mature enough to grasp it well. On the other side, there are some highly reputed learned societies who see it as fundamental as mathematics, hence advocate its introduction since the first years of school [1,37]. This is what happened, for example, in UK, where a computing curriculum became mandatory in 2014 for all levels of school.

In our study we investigated school teachers' beliefs in Italy regarding the interest and effectiveness of girls and boys towards Informatics. We think this is an important factor to increase female participation in the CS field, since teachers' beliefs are known to affect students' motivations, hence to influence their future choices of the university degree course to attend.

In this paper "kindergarten" indicates the pre-school level, for students up to 5 years old; "primary" indicates the 5 first years of school, attended by students aged between 6 and 10 (roughly, both endpoints included); "lower secondary" indicates the 3 years of intermediate studies, attended between 11 and 13; finally, "higher secondary" indicates the 5 last years of school, between 14 and 18. We always use these labels with the above described meaning, since this is their standard meaning in Italy.

2 Related Work

The introduction of Informatics education in school levels earlier than the higher secondary one is largely debated issue [3,15,42]. Even a country like, e.g. Poland, which has some form of compulsory Informatics education in higher secondary schools since the 80s, has not had compulsory Informatics education for primary school until a few years ago [35]. Duncan et al. [15] discuss that the best age for students to learn programming depends on many factors (cultural, environmental, social, personal, and instrumental) and should be considered in a multi-disciplinary context (e.g., psychology, pedagogy, mathematics, and language). In any case, they conclude "*it is clear from a variety of evidence that*

[1] We use interchangeably the terms Informatics and Computer Science (CS).

some exposure to programming before about 12 years old is both worthwhile and feasible". Also Armoni and Gal-Ezer [3] agree this issue is a complex one and "*cannot be addressed without deep and thorough research*".

It is also important to consider that the choice of the subject a student will study at the university and/or will do as a job is affected by many factors, beyond the actual age of her exposition to the subject during school years. Research has highlighted that students' motivation is affected by individual factors, situational ones, and how these interact [31,32]. Many studies support the conviction that teachers' beliefs affect student's motivation [5,20,22]. For a successful Informatics education uptake in K-12 it is therefore important to understand the actual teachers' viewpoint.

Moreover, social aspects cannot be neglected. In fact, negative stereotypes about girl's STEM abilities are transmitted to them by their teachers, shaping their attitudes and undermining their performance and interest [19,34].

In addition, it is known that well-designed educational programs can increase the participation of women to CS in college [17,23]. Research has highlighted the importance of acting at K-12 level, where girls risk to be discouraged and to lose interest in STEM careers [25], also under the influence of the stereotype seeing a CS student as a socially awkward and technology focused male [7, 26] and of social and cultural biases [10]. Moreover, role-model in K-12 is an important element [33], given its positive influence on girls' confidence when they are subject to negative stereotypes [27]. Finally, school performance in early STEM courses influences future students' choice of a major in the field [29].

By comparing female increasing participation efforts in computing to those in other disciplines, Zagami et al. [44] argue that the presence of a compulsory CS curriculum since early level of school might be the only measure able to sustain female participation over periods such as adolescence, a stage where students start making critical career choices [43]. The importance of acting since primary schools on the improvement of CS image so as to fight misconceptions and stereotypes and to increase female participation in computing has also been discussed in [18].

3 Methods

3.1 Context

Our analysis has been done in the context of Italian "*Programma il Futuro*" project[2] (PiF, from now on) for Informatics education in schools: it is a countrywide initiative which has been running since school year 2014–15 [12–14]. Italy does not generally have in place compulsory CS teaching in school, but for some types of upper secondary school. In the past, Informatics education has largely been focused on the operational aspects of using digital tools, like in many other developed ones [41]. Therefore, while it is under debate the possibility of introducing some form of compulsory Informatics education in schools, voluntary initiatives have flourished.

[2] https://programmailfuturo.it.

PiF's activities are grounded on both visual programming computer-based exercises *à la* Scratch (accompanied by video tutorials and automatically evaluated by the web platform supporting the project) and unplugged exercises on CS fundamental principles in the style of CS Unplugged (for which detailed lesson plans are made available). The teaching material is made available by Code.org and fully adapted to Italian by our team.

3.2 Questionnaires

Teachers involved in PiF are more than 33,000 at the beginning of school year 2018–19 (the fifth for the project). They voluntarily enroll, are generally not trained in CS, and usually teach a number of different subjects. A continuous communication action is deployed to keep them active and motivated.

Teachers are asked to fill out monitoring questionnaires with demographic and participation data. During each of the school years 2015–16 and 2016–17 they answered to two questionnaires (after three months and at the end) while in 2017–18 only one (the first one).

The goal of PiF is to spread information and awareness about the scientific nature of Informatics and not to investigate differences between boys and girls in attitude or performances related to Informatics. Nevertheless two questions in these surveys consider the possible imbalance between girls and boys in interest and effectiveness while carrying out the activities:

Q1 *In your classes, students* ***more interested*** *to project activities have been...*
Q2 *In your classes, students* ***more effective*** *in executing project activities have been...*

For both questions only one of the following answers can be chosen (they are presented to teachers in random order):

- equally students of both sexes
- female students more than male ones
- male students more than female ones

Note that activities carried out in classes are the same for both male students and female ones and are not elective, hence were attended by all female and male students. Note also that during the first year of PiF (2014–15) these two questions were not present in the pilot version of the monitoring questionnaire.

We are aware a better approach to the research question "At which school level is it better to introduce informatics education so as to reduce the gender gap?" would have been based on the measurement of the actual attitude or performance of students. However, considering the wide spectrum of school levels and the high number of project participants, it would have been a hugely complex task.

3.3 Population and Sample Demographics

We provide here some demographic data, during the analyzed school years, regarding both the *population* of teachers enrolled into PiF and the *sample* who

Table 1. Teachers' sex distribution

	2015–16		2016–17		2017–18	
	pop.	sam.	pop.	sam.	pop.	sam.
female	11,552	3,050	22,869	3,936	28,576	2,017
male	2,740	704	4,365	707	5,135	405

Table 2. Teachers' age distribution

	2015–16		2016–17		2017–18	
	pop.	sam.	pop.	sam.	pop.	sam.
to 30	89	*	191	31	214	13
31–40	1,617	*	2,853	487	3,154	204
41–50	5,547	*	10,217	1,924	12,033	906
51–60	5,782	*	11,140	1,930	14,096	1,112
61 up	1,257	*	2,833	271	4,214	187

* = this school year age was not asked

answered to the monitoring questionnaires. For those school years in which two monitoring questionnaires were issued, data from the second one reported here comes only from those teachers who did not answer the first one.

Table 1 shows how teachers are distributed according to their sex. In each school year the sample is a significant representation of the population with respect to sex, given that the average value[3] of the sum of the squared differences (ASSD) between values in the sample and their expected values[4] is less than 1.1% of the sample size in each school year. The percentage of women in the population (from 81% to 85%) is very close the actual percentage of female teachers in Italy (81%).

Table 2 shows how teachers are distributed according to their age. In each school year the sample is a significant representation of the population, with an ASSD value (computed as above) always less than 1.4%.

Table 3 shows how teachers are distributed according to the level of classes they teach in. In each school year the sample is a significant representation of the population also with respect to the school level, given the ASSD value (computed as above) is, again, always less than 1.4%.

A few teachers in each school year preferred not to declare the level of classes they teach in, hence the totals for the samples in Table 3 slightly differ from the corresponding ones in Tables 1 and 2, without prejudice for the analysis.

Monitoring questionnaires from school year 2016–17 onwards also investigated teachers' job seniority, a datum that is not collected when they enroll into PiF. Table 4 shows how they are distributed according to their teaching seniority in years. For both school years the sample is made for more than 84% by experienced teachers, which is a positive element in terms of the reliability of their answers.

3 Computed as $\frac{\sqrt{\Sigma_i (s_i - e_i)^2}}{N}$, where s_i is the actual value for the i-th class in the sample, e_i is the expected value (see next footnote) for the i-th class in the sample, and N is the number of classes.

4 Expectation is computed as $S \cdot p_i$, where S is the size of the sample and p_i is the percentage of the i-th class in the population.

Table 3. Teachers' school level distribution

	2015–16		2016–17		2017–18	
	popul.	sample	popul.	sample	popul.	sample
Kindergarten	433	55	1,391	183	1,992	73
Primary	7,799	1,969	14,822	2,606	18,262	1,431
Lower Secondary	3,911	1,149	7,155	1,252	8,586	626
Higher Secondary	2,248	555	3,866	590	4,511	287

Table 4. Teachers' seniority distribution

Years	2016–17	2017–18
up to 2	94	24
3 to 5	154	102
6 to 10	465	193
More than 10	3,930	2,103

Table 5. Classes and students involved

	2015–16	2016–17	2017–18
Classes	14,532	14,871	8,362
Students	272,529	297,272	153,697

We also asked teachers to report the overall number of classes they involved in Informatics education activities of PiF and how many students there were in their classes (see Table 5). We did not ask them the distribution per sex of their students but we consider that the study is based on a reliable sample of Italy's students also with respect to their sex, given (i) education is mandatory in Italy up to 16 years of age, (ii) teachers enrolled in PiF belong to all regions of Italy, and (iii) the very large number of students involved.

4 Results and Discussion

We do not discuss kindergarten data given these teachers are less than 4% of the sample size in each school year. Remember also that, for those school years in which two monitoring questionnaires were issued, data from the second one reported here comes only from those teachers who did not answer the first one. In the following subsections we first report results aggregated by school year (Subsect. 4.1.1), then results of the differential analysis (Subsect. 4.1.2) for each school year between teachers repeating activities and those executing them for the first time, and finally results aggregated by school level (Subsect. 4.1.3).

4.1 Aggregated Data

4.1.1 Results for School Years

Table 6 shows teachers answers to Q1 and Q2 in each school *year*. To make sense out of these data we computed for each year an indicator, the **interest gender gap**, that we defined as the difference, in that school *year*, between the number of teachers who rated male students more interested to project activities than female ones and the number of those who rated female more interested than boys (rows labeled respectively "M" and "F" in Table 6 and subsequent ones). We analogously computed the indicator **effectiveness gender gap**. To make these two indicators comparable across school years we normalized them, by computing their ratio to the total number of teachers who answered in each school *year*, and we present them in Fig. 1 as value per thousand teachers. As you can see both indicators are decreasing as the school years pass, roughly in the same constant way from a school year to the next.

Table 6. Answers to Q1 and Q2 for school years

	Q1 - Interest			Q2 - Effectiveness		
	2015–16	2016–17	2017–18	2015–16	2016–17	2017–18
Equally students of both sexes	3,223	3,987	2,133	2,885	3,639	1,976
Female students more	98	113	60	229	266	133
Male students more	352	348	151	559	543	235

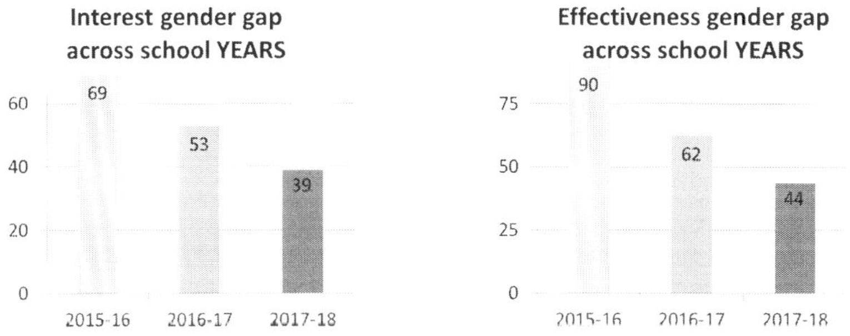

Fig. 1. Gap indicators across school YEARS (values per thousand teachers)

It is a widespread stereotype that female students' performances in science and maths are worse than their male companions' ones [7,10,25,27]. We do not know how much this stereotype was spread in our population before the beginning of PiF, but Fig. 1 shows the existence of a lower incidence of this stereotype with the progress of project activities over the years.

We hypothesize the involvement of teachers in project activities is the primary factor causing the observed variation of indicators. We think the observed phenomenon is relevant, since teachers answered anonymously to surveys, a condition that more likely can lead people to provide answers expressing a biased position [24,30]. We hence presume people answered honestly to our questionnaires. Moreover, if some remaining unconscious pressure not to express one's own gender bias had remained, its effect would only have reduced the size of the two gender gap indicators. Finally, even if in Table 6 the share[5] of teachers

[5] Computed as $\frac{F+M}{E+F+M}$.

having reported a difference between male and female students is just around 10% (for Q1-Interest) and 18% (for Q2-Effectiveness) of the total, we think that (i) given the overall number of answers this is a phenomenon which cannot be ignored, and (ii) given the above discussion of uneasiness in declaring a biased position the phenomenon's size might be even larger.

4.1.2 Novice and Repeating Teachers

To better understand the significance of the observed phenomenon we also investigated whether teachers executing PiF activities for the first time (*novice*) and those who were involved in previous years (*repeating*) had different beliefs. More specifically, we re-computed the two gender gap indicators shown in Fig. 1 separately for novice and repeating teachers for each of the school years 2015–16 (77% of novice), 2016–17 (52%) and 2017–18 (20%). Remember PiF started in 2014–15.

As you can see in Fig. 2, for each school years both indicators have a lower value for repeating teachers than for novice ones. In other words, in each school year, repeating teachers consistently show a lower presence of the stereotype that female students' performances in science and maths are worse than their male companions' ones. In our view, this result confirms and strengthens the observation made in Subsect. 4.1.1 of a lower incidence of the stereotype with the progress of project activities.

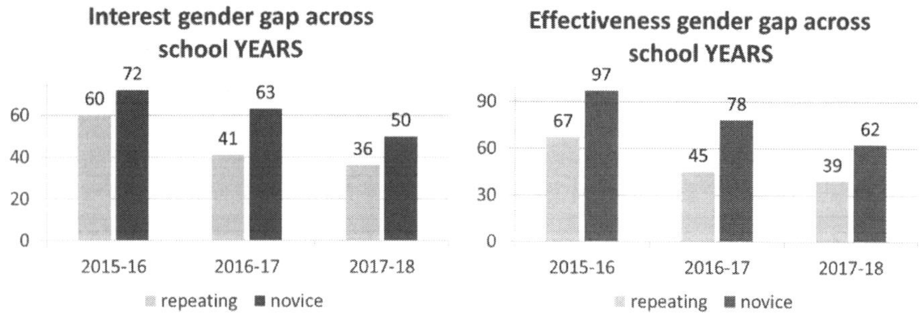

Fig. 2. Differential analysis of gap indicators across school YEARS

Note that the figure shows that the falling trends of the two indicators is present also for novice teachers who, by definition, cannot have been affected by the repetition of the activities. To understand this we have to consider that the increase in schools participation over the years is lower than the increase in teachers participation. The yearly increase in the number of participating teachers has been of 85% in 2016–17 and of 22% in 2017–18, while for schools it has been of 32% and 9% respectively.

This means that, roughly, for each new school entering PiF (clearly with a new teacher) there have been in the average almost two teachers entering the project in schools where their colleagues were already involved[6]. Therefore, a large part of novice is made up by teachers who have entered PiF because of their colleagues. Considering this element together with the concept of stereotypes as social and cognitive activity [4,36], a possible motivation is that beliefs of novice teachers have been affected by repeating teachers lowering their bias over the years.

4.1.3 Results for School Levels

Table 7 shows teachers' answers to Q1 and Q2 in each school *level*.

We computed again the two normalized indicators above described, this time on the basis of the difference, for each school *level*, between the number of teachers who rated male students more interested to project activities than female ones and the number of those who rated girls more effective than boys. Normalization was done with respect to the total number of teachers who answered in each school *level*. The indicators, shown in Fig. 3, are again presented as values for thousand teachers. As you can see both indicators are increasing going up with school level. This shows the existence of a higher presence, going up with school levels, of the stereotype considering girls worse than boys in science.

Table 7. Answers to Q1 and Q2 for school levels

	Q1 - Interest			Q2 - Effectiveness		
	Primary	Lower Secondary	Higher Secondary	Primary	Lower Secondary	Higher Secondary
E	5,606	2,596	1,137	5,603	2,353	1,084
F	99	93	79	296	232	100
M	301	338	212	647	442	248

Different approaches could be followed to fight this stereotype and possibly many of them need to be integrated to be effective. The starting point is to sensitize teachers in order to make them aware of the risks ensuing from the stereotype. In addition, given the social and cognitive nature of the stereotype, an early start of Informatics education in school would contribute to improve the attitude of teachers and students towards CS. Our result therefore provides an empirical support to those who advocate to start Informatics education in schools since the early years in order to fight this stereotype.

Moreover, note in Fig. 3 the big jump of the interest gender gap from Primary to Lower Secondary. While it is often said that middle school is the play-field where to win girls' interest to CS [2], we think this jump shows, instead, that Informatics education needs to start in Primary.

[6] The average number of teachers per school was 3.15 in school year 2015–16 and 4.95 in 2017–18.

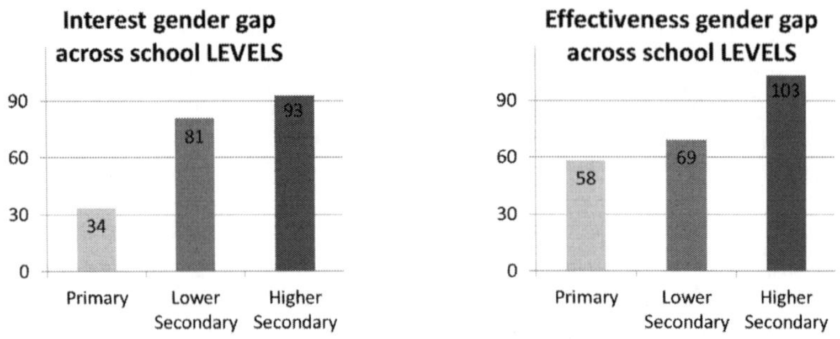

Fig. 3. Gap indicators across school LEVELS (values per thousand teachers)

Table 8. Answers to Q1 (*Interest*) for school years disaggregated by level of school

	2015–16			2016–17			2017–18		
	P	L	H	P	L	H	P	L	H
E	1,821	960	442	2,440	1,080	467	1,345	556	232
F	31	40	27	42	36	35	26	17	17
M	117	149	86	124	136	88	60	53	38

E = equally students of both sexes
F = female students more
M = male students more

Table 9. Answers to Q2 (*Effectiveness*) for school years disaggregated by level of school

	2015–16			2016–17			2017–18		
	P	L	H	P	L	H	P	L	H
E	1,606	865	414	2,214	983	442	1,243	505	228
F	100	90	39	127	96	43	69	46	18
M	263	194	102	265	173	105	119	75	41

On the other side, the larger jump of the effectiveness gender gap happens from Lower Secondary to Higher Secondary, which is consistent with the fact that the interest gap indicator tells girls have lost their interest in Lower Secondary.

An additional element contributing to the importance of the observed phenomenon (beyond the fact that teachers answered anonymously) is that the CS activities done in PiF were not elective for students but all students were exposed to them.

4.2 Disaggregated Data

We analyzed data disaggregated by level of school and by year of school to investigate the robustness of our results also within each school year and each school level (teachers provide their school level answering to the yearly questionnaires). Table 8 (for Q1) and Table 9 (for Q2) show data for school years from Table 6 disaggregated *by level* of school.

We show in Table 10 (for Q1) and Table 11 (for Q2) data for school levels from Table 7 disaggregated *by year* of school. Note that the sets of data in Tables 8 and 10 (resp. Tables 9 and 11) are the same sets of data, but presented with a different organization, for a better clarity.

Again, to make sense of these disaggregated data we considered the two normalized indicators previously described, but this time we computed them on

Table 10. Answers to Q1 (*Interest*) for school levels disaggregated by year of school

	Primary			Lower sec.			Higher sec.		
	Y1	Y2	Y3	Y1	Y2	Y3	Y1	Y2	Y3
E	1,821	2,440	1,345	960	1,080	556	442	467	232
F	31	42	26	40	36	17	27	35	17
M	117	124	60	149	136	53	86	88	38

Y1 = 2015–16 **Y2** = 2016–17 **Y3** = 2017–18

Table 11. Answers to Q2 (*Effectiveness*) for school levels disaggregated by year of school

	Primary			Lower sec.			Higher sec.		
	Y1	Y2	Y3	Y1	Y2	Y3	Y1	Y2	Y3
E	1,606	2,214	1,243	865	983	505	414	442	228
F	100	127	69	90	96	46	39	43	18
M	263	265	119	194	173	75	102	105	41

the basis of disaggregated data shown in Tables 8, 9, 10 and 11. We now discuss them separately for the two different presentations. In Subsect. 4.2.1 we discuss indicators for the data disaggregated by year of school reported in Tables 10 and 11, and in Subsect. 4.2.2 indicators for the data disaggregated by level of school reported in Tables 8 and 9.

4.2.1 Indicators Across School Years for Each School Level

In Fig. 4 we show the two indicators ordered by school year and grouped by level of school. You can see that within each level of school both indicators are decreasing as the school years pass, confirming the decrease seen in Fig. 1 for all levels of school together. Therefore, data disaggregated by school year support our interpretation at the aggregated level (Subsects. 4.1.1 and 4.1.2) that the involvement of teachers in project activities has caused this decrease.

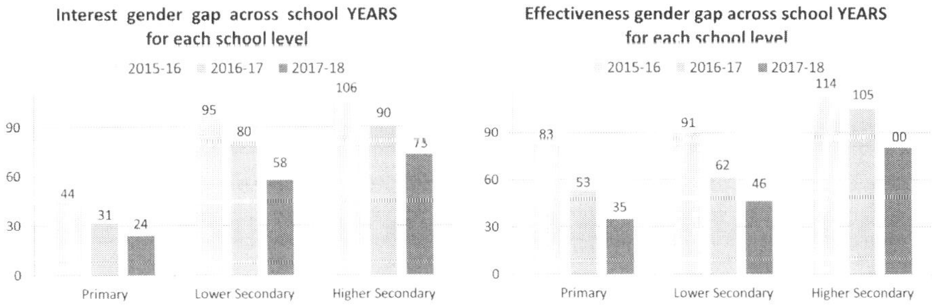

Fig. 4. Gap indicators disaggregated by school YEAR

4.2.2 Indicators Across School Levels for Each School Year

In Fig. 5 we show the two indicators ordered by school level and grouped by year of school. Again, both indicators increase, within each school year, going up with the level of school, confirming the increase shown in Fig. 3 for all years of school together. They also confirm the existence of a larger jump for interest

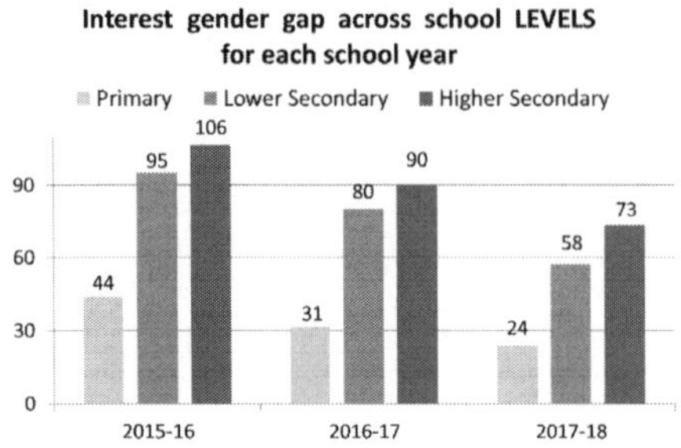

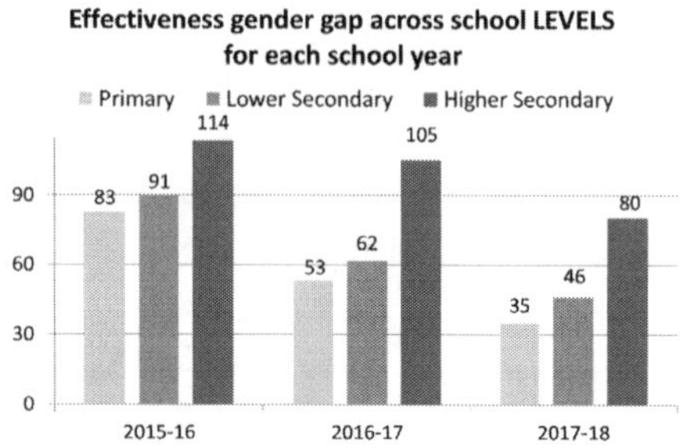

Fig. 5. Gap indicators disaggregated by school LEVEL

in the transition from Primary to Lower Secondary and for effectiveness in the one from Lower Secondary to Upper Secondary.

Therefore, also data disaggregated by school year support our judgment coming from the analysis at aggregate level in Subsect. 4.1.3 that Informatics education needs to be introduced in schools as early as possible in order to improve the attitude of teachers and students towards CS.

5 Conclusions

In this paper we describe the outcomes of a multi-year large-scale study conducted in Italy, where there is no general compulsory Informatics education in schools.

Teachers involved in this study (an average of 3,600 per year, belonging to all levels of school), have voluntarily enrolled in the "Programma il Futuro" project to teach introductory CS courses, grounded on both visual programming computer-based exercises and unplugged content, with dedicated support material.

Over the project years they have periodically filled monitoring questionnaires which examined, among others, whether they considered male students more interested or more effective than female students in carrying out project activities.

We introduced two indicators, called *interest gender gap* and *effectiveness gender gap*, to measure the difference between the number of teachers considering boys more interested (or more effective) than girls and the number of those rating girls more interested (or more effective) than boys.

These indicators therefore gauge what teachers believe about interest and effectiveness of female students relative to their male colleagues. This measure is important, since teachers' beliefs are known to influence students' motivations, hence their future choices. Answers were provided anonymously, a condition that more likely can lead people to honestly provide answers expressing a biased position.

Analysis by school year shows these gender gaps decrease as school years pass, primarily caused - in our opinion - by the nature of project activities and the continuous involvement of teachers. Moreover, analyzing separately in each school year the teachers involved for the first time and those repeating the activities, smaller values of the two indicators are found in the latter groups, reinforcing our interpretation.

When analyzed in the different levels of school (primary, lower secondary, higher secondary) both indicators instead increase in passing from a school level to the next higher up.

The two main outcomes are also supported by disaggregating data by both school level and school year. Within each school level, the behavior of indicators as school years pass confirms the trend measured for the aggregation of school levels. A similar confirmation happens for the analysis across school years.

Our study therefore provides an empirical support to the importance of fighting as early as possible the gender stereotype considering girls performing worse in science than boys. Hence, it also supports the introduction of compulsory CS school education as a way to increase the number of female graduates in computing-related disciplines and ultimately a more diverse IT workforce.

Acknowledgements. We greatly thank teachers and students involved in "Programma il Futuro" (coordinated by EN) and Code.org for their cooperation.

We acknowledge the financial support for school year 2018–19 of: Eni; Engineering; SeeWeb; TIM. Other companies have financially supported PiF in previous school years, see https://programmailfuturo.it/partner.

Rai Cultura, the culture department of Italian national public broadcasting company, is a media partner of the project since February 2017.

References

1. Académie des Sciences: L'enseignement de l'informatique en France: Il est urgent de ne plus attendre, May 2013. http://www.academie-sciences.fr/pdf/rapport/rads_0513.pdf
2. Accenture: Cracking the gender code (2016). https://www.accenture.com/us-en/cracking-the-gender-code
3. Armoni, M., Gal-Ezer, J.: Early computing education: Why? What? When? Who? ACM Inroads **5**(4), 54–59 (2014)
4. Augoustinos, M., Walker, I.: The construction of stereotypes within social psychology: from social cognition to ideology. Theory Psychol. **8**(5), 629–652 (1998)
5. Borg, M.: Key concepts in ELT: teachers' beliefs. ELT J. **55**(2), 186–188 (2001)
6. Caspersen, M.E., Gal-Ezer, J., McGettrick, A., Nardelli, E.: Informatics as a fundamental discipline for the 21st century. Commun. ACM **62**(4), 58 (2019)
7. Cheryan, S., Plaut, V.C., Handron, C., Hudson, L.: The stereotypical computer scientist: gendered media representations as a barrier to inclusion for women. Sex Roles **69**, 58–71 (2013)
8. Code.org: Computing occupations are now the #1 source of new wages in America (2016). https://blog.code.org/post/144206906013/computing-occupations-are-now-the-1-source-of-new
9. Code.org: Diversity in computer science (2018). https://code.org/diversity
10. Cohoon, J.M., Aspray, W.: Women and Information Technology: Research on Underrepresentation, vol. 1. The MIT Press, Cambridge (2006)

11. Computer Science Zone: The technology job gap (2015). https://www.computersciencezone.org/technology-job-gap/
12. Corradini, I., Lodi, M., Nardelli, E.: Computational thinking in Italian schools: quantitative data and teachers' sentiment analysis after two years of "Programma il Futuro" Project. In: ITiCSE 2017. ACM (2017)
13. Corradini, I., Lodi, M., Nardelli, E.: Conceptions and misconceptions about computational thinking among Italian primary school teachers. In: ICER 2017 (2017)
14. Corradini, I., Lodi, M., Nardelli, E.: An investigation of Italian primary school teachers' view on coding and programming. In: Pozdniakov, S.N., Dagienė, V. (eds.) ISSEP 2018. LNCS, vol. 11169, pp. 228–243. Springer, Cham (2018). https://doi.org/10.1007/978-3-030-02750-6_18
15. Duncan, C., Bell, T., Tanimoto, S.: Should your 8-year-old learn coding? In: Proceedings WiPSCE 2014, pp. 60–69. ACM (2014)
16. European Commission: The digital skills and job coalition (2014). https://ec.europa.eu/digital-single-market/en/digital-skills-jobs-coalition
17. Fisher, A., Margolis, J.: Unlocking the clubhouse: the Carnegie Mellon experience. SIGCSE Bull. **34**(2), 79–83 (2002)
18. Funke, A., Geldreich, K., Hubwieser, P.: Primary school teachers' opinions about early computer science education. In: 16th Koli Calling International Conference on Computing Education Research, pp. 135–139 (2016)
19. Gunderson, E.A., Ramirez, G., Levine, S.C., Beilock, S.L.: The role of parents and teachers in the development of gender related math attitudes. Sex Roles **66**, 153–166 (2011)
20. Hardre, P.L., Sullivan, D.W.: Motivating adolescents: teachers' beliefs, perceptions and classroom practices. Teach. Dev. **13**, 1–16 (2009)
21. Hill, C., Corbett, C., St. Rose, A. (eds.): Women and Information Technology: Research on Underrepresentation. AAUW (2010)
22. Hornstra, L., Mansfield, C., Van der Veen, I., Peetsma, T., Volman, M.: Motivational teacher strategies: the role of beliefs and contextual factors. Learn. Environ. Res. **18**, 363–392 (2015)
23. Klawe, M.: Increasing female participation in computing: the Harvey Mudd college story. Computer **46**(3), 56–58 (2013)
24. Lensvelt-Mulders, G.: Surveying sensitive topics. In: de Leeuw, E., Hox, J., Dillman, D. (eds.) International Handbook of Survey Methodology, pp. 461–478. Lawrence Erlbaum Associates, New York (2008)
25. Malcom-Piqueux, L.E., Malcom, S.M.: Engineering diversity: Fixing the educational system to promote equity. Bridge **43**, 24–34 (2013)
26. Margolis, J., Fisher, A.: Unlocking the Clubhouse: Women in Computing. MIT Press, Cambridge (2002)
27. Master, A., Cheryan, S., Meltzoff, A.N.: Reducing adolescent girls' concerns about stem stereotypes: when do female teachers matter? Revue internationale de psychologie sociale **27**(3–4), 79–102 (2014)
28. Medium: University computer science finally surpasses its 2003 peak! (2017). https://medium.com/anybody-can-learn/university-computer-science-finally-surpasses-its-2003-peak-ecefa4c8d77d
29. Miyake, A., Kost-Smith, L.E., Finkelstein, N.D., Pollock, S.J., Cohen, G.L., Ito, T.A.: Reducing the gender achievement gap in college science: a classroom study of values affirmation. Science **330**, 1234–1237 (2010)
30. Ong, A., Weiss, D.: The impact of anonymity on responses to sensitive questions. J. Appl. Soc. Psychol. **30**(8), 1691–1708 (2000)

31. Pintrich, P.: A motivational science perspective on the role of student motivation in learning and teaching context. J. Educ. Psychol. **95**(4), 667–686 (2003)
32. Ryan, R.M., Deci, E.L.: Intrinsic and extrinsic motivations: classic definitions and new directions. Contemp. Educ. Psychol. **25**(1), 54–67 (2000)
33. Sadik, O.: Encouraging women to become CS teachers. In: GenderIT, pp. 57–61 (2015)
34. Shapiro, J.R., Williams, A.M.: The role of stereotype threats in undermining girls' and women's performance and interest in STEM fields. Sex Roles **66**, 175–183 (2011)
35. Sysło, M.M., Kwiatkowska, A.B.: Introducing a new computer science curriculum for all school levels in Poland. In: Brodnik, A., Vahrenhold, J. (eds.) ISSEP 2015. LNCS, vol. 9378, pp. 141–154. Springer, Cham (2015). https://doi.org/10.1007/978-3-319-25396-1_13
36. Tajfel, G.: Human Groups and Social Categories. Studies in Social Psychology. Cambridge University Press, Cambridge (1981)
37. The Royal Society: Shut down or restart? The way forward for computing in UK schools, January 2012. https://royalsociety.org/~/media/education/computing-in-schools/2012-01-12-computing-in-schools.pdf
38. U.S. Equal Employment Opportunity Commission: Diversity in high tech (2016). https://www.eeoc.gov/eeoc/statistics/reports/hightech/
39. US News: Study: Middle school is key to girls' coding interest (2016). https://www.usnews.com/news/data-mine/articles/2016-10-20/study-computer-science-gender-gap-widens-despite-increase-in-jobs
40. Varma, R.: Why so few women enroll in computing? Gender and ethnic differences in students' perception. Comput. Sci. Educ. **20**(4), 301–316 (2010)
41. Vuorikari, R., Punie, Y., Gomez, S.C., Van den Brande, G.: DigComp 2.0: The Digital Competence Framework for Citizens. Luxembourg Publication Office of the European Union. EUR 27948 EN (2016)
42. Webb, M., et al.: Computer science in k-12 school curricula of the 2lst century: why, what and when? Educ. Inf. Technol. **22**(2), 445–468 (2017)
43. Weisgram, E.S., Bigler, R.S.: The role of attitudes and intervention in high school girls' interest in computer science. J. Women Minor. Sci. Eng. **12**, 325–336 (2006)
44. Zagami, J., Boden, M., Keane, T., Moreton, B., Schulz, K.: Girls and computing: female participation in computing in schools. Aust. Educ. Comput. **30**(2) (2015). https://journal.acce.edu.au/index.php/AEC/article/view/79

Inquiry-Based Learning in Computer Science Classroom

Zuzana Tkáčová[1,2(✉)], Ľubomír Šnajder[2], and Ján Guniš[2]

[1] Faculty of Science, Pavol Jozef Šafárik University in Košice, Košice, Slovakia
zuzana.tkacova@ukf.sk

[2] Faculty of Education, Constantine the Philosopher University in Nitra, Nitra, Slovakia
{zuzana.tkacova1,lubomir.snajder,jan.gunis}@upjs.sk,

Abstract. Inquiry-based learning in Slovak schools is still considered to be an innovative approach to teaching based on the active exploration of new knowledge by pupils themselves. It allows deeper involvement of pupils in the learning process, encourages motivation and differentiation with respect to individual learning preferences, creates space for pupils to develop cooperation and communication skills. Inquiry is a natural cognitive process for pupils, but its wider application is mostly in biology, chemistry or physics classrooms, while computer science in Slovak schools is still dominated by instructive teaching strategies. In the frame of the National project IT Academy we have focused on different fields of the computer science curriculum and we have implemented the 5E instructional model as an inquiry-based learning approach in 40 primary school lessons and 40 secondary school lessons. We provide teachers with complete lesson plans, including worksheets, supplementary work files and materials, or reference materials. These educational materials are being tested by teachers in Slovak schools. For both primary and secondary school teachers, we organize also professional development courses on innovative teaching strategies in the computer science classroom to make it easier for them to implement these new classroom learning practices. This paper presents the results of a survey on teachers' perception, attitudes, experiences, misconceptions and barriers to inquiry-based teaching strategies in computer science classrooms as the classroom teacher plays a key role in the successful implementation of these new learning strategies. Our research investigates how different factors affect teachers when considering the inquiry-based learning and its successful implementation in computer science classrooms highlights two major underlying factors, the teacher's personal contribution factor and a factor representing a collection of the teacher's readiness and teaching skills, which are further discussed.

Keywords: Inquiry-based learning · 5E Cycle · Active learning · Problem solving · Teaching methodology · Computer science teacher

S. N. Pozdniakov and V. Dagienė (Eds.): ISSEP 2019, LNCS 11913, pp. 68–79, 2019.
https://doi.org/10.1007/978-3-030-33759-9_6

1 Introduction

The unprecedented development of technical sciences over the past decades has brought the need to change the entire educational system so that its graduates are able to actively integrate into a dynamically changing society and become fully engaged in the labor market. We need to teach pupils to communicate, collaborate, make decisions, use information and formulate solutions to real world problems [1]. From the point of view of the educational process, a suitable educational model is sought, which, in addition to acquiring new knowledge, would also enable the fully-fledged development of the so-called soft skills. On the basis of an analysis of the results of international and national initiatives in the European Union for science education [2], experts agree on the important role of inquiry-based learning (IBL), which is based on a constructivist approach in which the pupil constructs knowledge himself based on experience gained during independent active activity [3]. The inquiry activities and the inquiry-based approach are gradually applied also in the didactics of computer science [4–6], although the lack of competence and readiness of teachers to implement IBL is a problem to the wider application in everyday computer classroom teaching.

One of the extended models of IBL is the 5E Cycle instructional model, which emphasizes constructivist principles and assessment of pupils' prior knowledge [3]. This model is far away from the traditional instructional approach that is still widely spread in computer science classrooms. The goal of the 5E Cycle instructional model is to enable pupils to understand the new concept (i.e. educational content) during a series of steps (Fig. 1) [7]. The first phase - **ENGAGE** - serves to motivate pupils to explore the presented topic, activate prior knowledge, identify misconceptions and create a link between past and present pupils' experiences with a suitable problem or experiment. The second phase - **EXPLORE** - is the main source of learning by pupils when they are actively discovering, collecting data, implementing practical activities and looking for connections. Pupils usually work in pairs or smaller groups, while the teacher acts as facilitator and observer. Phase three - **EXPLAIN** - helps pupils clarify the concepts they have examined. The teacher emphasizes the main findings by introducing new concepts that the pupils will explain based on the experience of the previous phase, and the teacher helps them formulate the results scientifically with the right language. Stage four - **ELABORATE** - provides pupils with the opportunity to expand, deepen and apply creative knowledge in new situations. By correctly setting up tasks and offering activities, differentiation is possible based on individual needs or pupil preferences. The fifth phase - **EVALUATE** - develops pupils' ability to assess, analyze and evaluate the results of their activities and creates opportunities for the formative and summative assessment for the teacher.

In the frame of the National project IT Academy [8] we have focused on different fields of the computer science curriculum and we have implemented the 5E Cycle instructional model as an inquiry-based learning approach in 40 primary school lessons and 40 secondary school lessons. These lessons cover programming (in Scratch, MIT AppInventor and Python), physical computing and

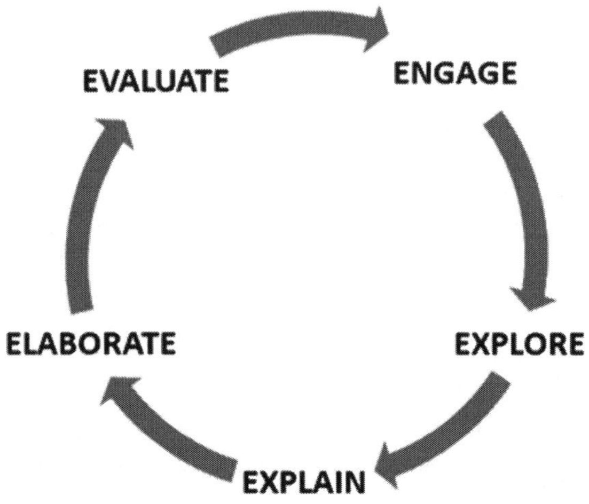

Fig. 1. The 5E Cycle instructional model

robotics (BBC Micro:bit, LEGO Mindstorms EV3, Raspberry Pi), artificial intelligence, 3D modeling and printing, as well as unplugged activities on information encoding and compression. We provide teachers with complete lesson plans, including worksheets, supplementary work files and materials, or reference materials. These educational materials are being tested by teachers in Slovak schools. For both primary and secondary school teachers, we organize also professional development courses on innovative teaching strategies in the computer science classroom to make it easier for them to implement these new classroom learning practices. As the classroom teacher plays a key role in the successful implementation of these new learning strategies, as part of our long-term research, we have decided to carry out a survey with teachers, participants in our training courses, on teachers' perception, attitudes, experiences, misconceptions and barriers to inquiry-based teaching strategies in computer science classrooms. In the following sections, we make a brief overview of the results of this survey.

2 Methodology

The primary objective of our research was to focus on the process of acceptance of IBL by computer science teachers and exploring the factors influencing their decision-making in the IBL implementation into their classrooms. We used a questionnaire as a quantitative method of data collection and statistical analysis. We added the following sections to our research question:

Q: How is IBL accepted by computer science teachers in terms of implementation into teaching practice?

- How do teachers perceive the benefits of IBL for computer science lessons?
- Which factors influence the process of implementation of IBL into computer science teaching?

Our total population consists of 45 teachers, participants of our professional development courses. As for the sample, we involved all these teachers who attended our courses (i.e. the convenience sampling was chosen), as the IBL approach is still new in Slovakia and these teachers have already become acquainted with it in our courses, we wanted to find out and analyze their opinions and experiences. The sample covers both experienced, fully qualified computer science teachers as participants of our specialized professional development courses (44%) and less experienced computer science teachers undergoing the initial training as a professional development course for teachers of other subjects to become qualified as computer science teachers (56%) - after completing the course activities. In our sample, 18% of teachers had less than 10 years teaching experience, 27% had 11–15 years of teaching experience and 55% have been teaching for more than 15 years. These teachers were mostly women (75%). Teachers were teaching at primary (55%) and secondary (45%) schools across our country.

Questionnaire consisted of single and multiple choice and open-ended questions mapping following areas of interest:

- theoretical background, sources of information on IBL,
- individual perception of advantages/disadvantages/benefits/barriers and personal identification of the teacher with IBL,
- individual interest and practical experience with teaching IBL and creating dedicated educational IBL materials,
- usability of IBL in computer science classrooms.

To further analyze the data, factor analysis [9–11] was used. This statistical data mining method serves as a useful tool for investigating variable relationships for complex concepts that are not easily measured directly by collapsing a large number of variables into a few interpretable underlying factors and thus factor analysis allows identification of the underlying factors that affect the results of our questionnaire.

3 Results

A basic statistical analysis of participants' responses for each of the areas of interest as well as factor analysis to determine latent factors was performed.

3.1 Theoretical Background, Sources of Information on IBL

In this part of the questionnaire, we investigated two questions:

How do you assess your theoretical knowledge of IBL?

As our respondents have already received information about IBL from our courses, 15% of them have said that so far they provide only the basic knowledge of the topic, while up to 85% of respondents said they have a comprehensive overview.

Where did you get the basic theoretical knowledge of IBL?

For this open-ended question, most teachers said that our courses were the main source of information for them. 18% of respondents reported self-study and only 9% of respondents reported other educational activities and seminars.

3.2 Individual Perception of Benefits/Barriers and Personal Identification of the Teacher with IBL

In this part of the questionnaire, we investigated five questions:

What are the most important benefits of IBL (from your point of view or experience)?

In this open-ended question, teachers most often mentioned:

- the activity of pupils,
- the persistence of information,
- the interest in pupils,
- the joy of discovering and experimenting,
- the higher motivation,
- teamwork,
- creativity,
- autonomy of pupils in the learning process.

What are the most important barriers of IBL (from your point of view or experience)?

In this open-ended question, teachers most often mentioned:

- the time-consuming activities during the lesson,
- the time required to prepare the teacher and to prepare teaching materials,
- problems with passive pupils,
- lack of pupils' self-activity,
- lack of pupils' responsibility,
- pupils' reluctance,
- managing individual differences among pupils,
- lack of teaching tools,
- lack of methodological support.

For whom do you consider IBL being beneficial?

In this one-choice question (for all pupils, only for skilful/weaker pupils), up to 67% of teachers perceive IBL as beneficial for all pupils, 33% perceive the appropriateness of this method only for skilful pupils.

Who do you consider IBL more appropriate for?

As many as 87% of respondents consider IBL to be suitable for both upper primary and secondary schools, 9% see the appropriateness of use only for upper primary school pupils, 2% only for secondary school pupils and 2% do not see this approach as suitable for upper primary or secondary schools.

How did you identify yourself with the 5E instructional cycle? On this issue, 53% of respondents said that they only partially identified themselves with the 5E Cycle, while 47% identified themselves completely. No respondent indicated that he did https://www.overleaf.com/project/5d19071be536f305643e2b35not

identify with this approach at all. On this issue, no significant difference was observed between the responses of primary or secondary school teachers. The link between the degree of personal identification of the teacher with the 5E Cycle and his perception of IBL being beneficial for all or only skilful pupils has not been statistically confirmed.

3.3 Individual Interest and Practical Experience with Teaching IBL and Creating Own Educational IBL Materials

In this part of the questionnaire, we investigated four single choice questions:

How do you assess your practical experience with using IBL teaching in your own computer science classroom?

On this issue, up to 78% of teachers answered that they had already started IBL teaching, while 22% said they had not yet taught IBL, but they are planning to test it.

How do you assess your practical experience in creating your own IBL teaching materials?

On this issue, 42% of teachers have confirmed that they have already created several IBL teaching materials. Up to 53% of teachers haven't created any IBL teaching materials yet, but they would like to try it. Only 5% of teachers report that they have not created any IBL teaching materials, nor are they planning.

What is your interest in teaching computer science using already developed IBL teaching materials?

We can observe a high interest in our IBL teaching materials – up to 73% of respondents are highly interested in teaching computer science using our already developed IBL teaching materials. The remaining teachers (27%) demonstrate only a moderate interest.

What is your interest in developing your own IBL teaching materials for computer science lessons?

It is possible to observe a large decrease in the interest of teachers in creating their own IBL teaching materials compared to using the already developed ones – only 20% of teachers demonstrate their high interest and 60% demonstrate moderate interest. There are 13% of teachers who have only a low interest in developing their own materials and 7% show now interest at all.

3.4 Usability of IBL in Computer Science Classrooms

In this part of the questionnaire, we investigated two questions:

Do you consider IBL for the computer science classroom being useful?

As many as 62% of teachers consider IBL teaching to be useful often for computer science classrooms, the remaining 38% find this approach only occasionally applicable. To specify the areas of computer science curriculum suitable for the use of the IBL approach from the perspective of teachers, we used the next question in our questionnaire.

For which areas of computer science curriculum do you consider the IBL teaching to be appropriate?

	F1	F2	F3	F4	F5
Theoretical background	0,386	0,576	**-0,642**	0,125	-0,239
Personal identification with 5E	**0,695**	0,086	0,066	0,629	0,333
Practical experience with IBL teaching	**0,238**	0,139	0,065	0,089	0,084
Practical experience with development of IBL materials	**0,590**	-0,390	-0,044	0,025	-0,068
Interest in using of developed IBL materials	**0,565**	-0,119	-0,106	-0,432	-0,057
Interest in development of own IBL materials	**0,626**	-0,469	0,014	-0,102	-0,186
IBL is useful for Computer Science	**0,622**	-0,069	0,106	-0,127	-0,020
IBL benefits for pupils	0,163	0,234	0,233	**-0,272**	0,251
Appropriate IBL usage	0,090	0,306	**0,423**	0,111	-0,246
Course type	0,195	**0,476**	0,137	0,002	-0,003
Teaching experience	0,191	**0,567**	0,061	-0,261	-0,122
Sex	-0,240	-0,211	**-0,384**	0,190	-0,136
School type	0,026	0,068	-0,373	-0,291	**0,492**

Fig. 2. Factor pattern before rotation

In this open-ended question, up to 82% of respondents mentioned programming as the main area for IBL use. 42% mentioned also the application software for data processing to be a suitable topic for IBL implementation. 22% of teachers consider the Internet and communication to be a suitable application area. 9% of respondents say it is an approach that applies in almost all areas of computer science curriculum.

3.5 Factor Analysis

For factor analysis, the results from questions focused on the following aspects have been taken:

- theoretical background,
- personal identification with 5E Cycle,
- practical experience with IBL teaching,
- practical experience with development of IBL materials,
- interest in using of developed IBL materials,
- interest in development of own IBL materials,
- assessment on how IBL is useful for Computer Science,
- assessment on IBL benefits for pupils,
- assessment on appropriate IBL usage in schools,
- assessment on course type,
- length of teaching experience,
- sex,
- school type.

First, the correlation matrix was calculated (Appendix A). As we can see from the correlation matrix, there is a partial correlation among the theoretical background of the respondent, his/her practical experience with development of IBL materials, assessment on how IBL is useful for Computer Science, personal identification with 5E Cycle, interest in using of developed IBL materials and interest in development of own IBL materials. Principal factor analysis was chosen as extraction method. Factor pattern show 5 latent factors (Fig. 2). Then, the Varimax rotation was used for the two most important factors (Fig. 3).

	D1	D2
Theoretical background	0,081	**0,689**
Personal identification with 5E	**0,579**	0,393
Practical experience with IBL teaching	0,149	**0,232**
Practical experience with development of IBL materials	**0,703**	-0,079
Interest in using of developed IBL materials	**0,557**	0,151
Interest in development of own IBL materials	**0,771**	-0,133
IBL is useful for Computer Science	**0,586**	0,222
IBL benefits for pupils	0,039	**0,283**
Appropriate IBL usage	-0,059	**0,313**
Course type	-0,043	**0,512**
Teaching experience	-0,088	**0,592**
Sex	-0,117	**-0,297**
School type	-0,008	**0,072**

Fig. 3. Factor pattern after Varimax rotation

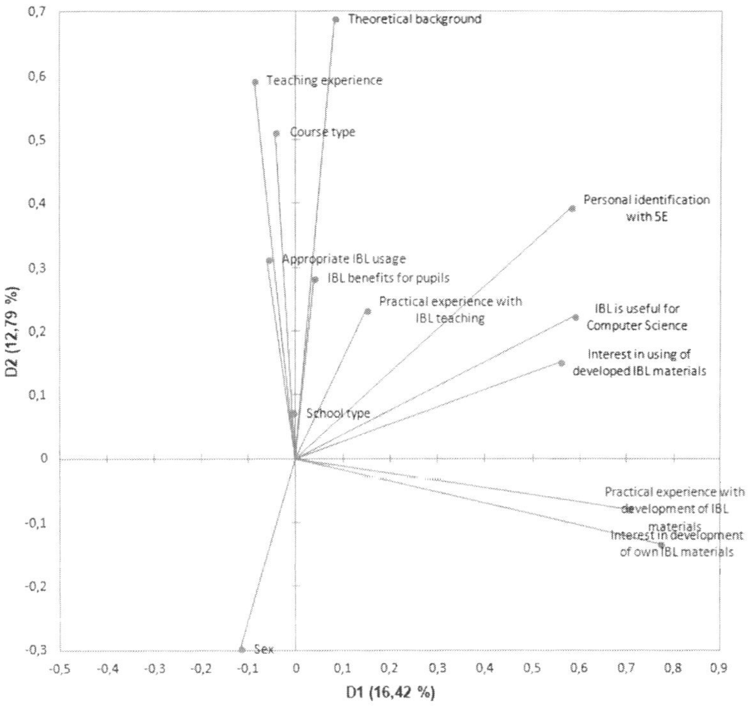

Fig. 4. Factor loadings (axes D1 and D2: 29,21%) after Varimax rotation

As demonstrated by the factor pattern after Varimax rotation (Fig. 3) and the diagram of factor loadings (Fig. 4), two latent factors can be identified. D1 represents the **personal contribution factor**, i.e. teacher's personal contribution to the IBL built on interest in development of their own IBL materials, practical experience with development of IBL materials, personal identification with the 5E Cycle, interest in using the developed IBL materials and assessment on how IBL is useful for Computer Science. D2 represents the **general**

background factor, i.e. teacher's readiness and teaching skills built mostly on theoretical background, length of teaching experience and IBL course type taken.

4 Discussion and Conclusions

In a number of papers, e.g. [12,13], it has already been confirmed that teachers have a positive attitude towards IBL - this work had been focused mainly on science teachers. Our research also points out that computer science teachers also see a promising tool in IBL to innovate their teaching. At the same time, IBL has proven to bring a great benefit in promoting autonomy of pupils in finding solutions before being shown them by the teacher. This aspect is also appreciated by the teachers in our study.

Based on our teacher training experience (and the results of our research have confirmed this) we can say that as teachers adopt the IBL approach, they go through several levels:

Level 1: Teacher goes through IBL lessons as a pupil (during our courses we start with IBL lessons where teachers learn as if they were pupils and then analyze this approach in the form of reflection)
Level 2: Teacher is acquainted with the didactic fundamentals of the IBL approach and then uses IBL materials (teacher is provided with methodological support, our developed materials and methodologies)
Level 3: Teacher modifies/adapts IBL materials for himself/herself (at this stage teacher has already accepted IBL as his/her own and begins to create his/her educational materials by modifying other materials)
Level 4: Teacher creates and validates his/her own IBL materials (teacher is already convinced of the importance of the IBL approach, has enough experience and is creative enough to start developing completely new educational materials that other teachers may also use)

It is clear that only a part of the teachers from the particular level will proceed to the next level due to the conservative nature of teachers and their fixed mindsets, as well as the typical mistake of taking the initiative instead of the pupils in the EXPLORE/EXPLAIN phase, remain a major problem, which disrupted the inquiry-based character of teaching during lessons and led to repeated unsatisfactory results and negative experiences for teachers and pupils.

In order to successfully implement IBL in the classroom, the teacher needs to have a theoretical background in the field of IBL and, above all, to identify internally with the ideas of the IBL approach. It turns out that the sequence of the four previous stages (resulting from our approach) is very helpful. The following considerations need to be considered [14]:

- the time-consuming nature of teaching (developing students' research skills requires more time, with the current broad requirements for computer science curriculum in Slovakia, usually only a few IBL lessons can be taught in a year, but elements of inquiry can be used in almost every lesson),

- a teacher with low knowledge of IBL and small experience with inquiry (a teacher who does not use inquiry himself would only hardly be a role model or a source of inspiration for the pupil to start the active inquiry),
- a teacher with unconvincing attitudes towards IBL approach in teaching (he/she will not be interested in developing pupils' inquiry skills, the priority still would be amount of knowledge),
- unusual, new topic (created IBL lessons can cover the curriculum at a different depth or at a different level structure as in a traditionally elaborated topic, which may discourage teachers accustomed to teaching their usual and proven topics),
- the reluctance of teachers to study methodological materials (computer science teacher is not accustomed to reading methodological materials because there is lack of these materials in our country, so teacher would appreciate rather completed worksheets, widgets, etc.),
- insufficient methodological support for the teacher (the teacher needs sufficient textbooks, worksheets, widgets, work files, methodological materials, training, discussion forums).

From the perspective of successful IBL implementation and its wider deployment in teaching, the teacher plays the crucial role. Therefore, in our National project IT Academy - Education for the 21st Century we are intensively working in teacher training. The results of our survey have shown that the impact of training on the attitudes and use of IBL in teaching is evident, especially with regard to promoting student autonomy, creativity and teamwork, while teachers need intensive methodological support and teaching materials for successful deployment. However, as it turns out, teachers are more interested in getting ready-made IBL materials than in developing their own IBL materials.

In our further research, we want to focus on both quantitative and qualitative analysis of the work of teachers - participants of our course activities, in order to assess their readiness and suitability for teaching as well as potentially problematic elements in their content.

Acknowledgements. This article was created in the framework of the National project IT Academy – Education for the 21st Century, ITMS: 312011F057, which is supported by the European Social Fund and the European Regional Development Fund in the framework of the Operational Programme Human Resources and in the frame of project KEGA 029UKF-4/2018 Innovative Methods in Programming Education in the University Education of Teachers and IT Professionals.

A Correlation matrix (Pearson(n))

Variables	Theoretical background	Personal identification with 5E	Practical experience with IBL teaching	Practical experience with development of IBL materials	Interest in using of developed IBL materials	Interest in development of own IBL materials	IBL is useful for Computer Science	IBL benefits for pupils	Appropriate IBL usage	Course type	Teaching experience	Sex	School type
Theoretical background	1	0,279	0,066	0,069	0,157	−0,037	0,171	−0,043	0,011	0,260	0,371	0,101	0,137
Personal identification with 5E	0,279	1	0,286	0,397	0,060	0,254	0,361	0,094	0,100	0,149	0,004	−0,117	−0,030
Practical experience with IBL teaching	0,066	0,286	1	−0,021	0,161	0,092	0,135	−0,038	0,100	0,263	0,054	−0,069	0,048
Practical experience with development of IBL materials	0,069	0,397	−0,021	1	0,400	0,614	0,276	−0,028	−0,080	−0,044	−0,123	−0,105	−0,044
Interest in using of developed IBL materials	0,157	0,060	0,161	0,400	1	0,404	0,463	0,107	−0,085	0,034	0,166	−0,125	0,135
Interest in development of own IBL materials	−0,037	0,254	0,092	0,614	0,404	1	0,467	−0,061	−0,032	−0,097	−0,032	−0,018	−0,039
IBL is useful for Computer Science	0,171	0,361	0,135	0,276	0,463	0,467	1	0,227	0,094	0,051	0,025	−0,197	−0,041
IBL benefits for pupils	−0,043	0,094	−0,038	−0,028	0,107	−0,061	0,227	1	0,132	0,063	0,286	−0,256	0,158
Appropriate IBL usage	0,011	0,100	0,100	−0,080	−0,085	−0,032	0,094	0,132	1	0,209	0,225	−0,150	−0,293
Course type	0,260	0,149	0,263	−0,044	0,034	−0,097	0,051	0,063	0,209	1	0,317	−0,301	0,010
Teaching experience	0,371	0,004	0,054	−0,123	0,166	−0,032	0,025	0,286	0,225	0,317	1	−0,212	0,026
Sex	0,101	−0,117	−0,069	−0,105	−0,125	−0,018	−0,197	−0,256	−0,150	−0,301	−0,212	1	0,012
School type	0,137	−0,030	0,048	−0,044	0,135	−0,039	−0,041	0,158	−0,293	0,010	0,026	0,012	1

References

1. Truesdell, P.: Engineering Essentials for STEM Instruction: How Do I Infuse Real-World Problem Solving into Science, Technology, and Math? ASCD, Alexandria (2014)
2. Rocard, M., Csermely, P., Jorde, D., Lenzen, D., Walberg-Henriksson, H., Hemmo, V.: Science Education NOW: A Renewed Pedagogy for the Future of Europe. Office for Official Publications of the European Communities, Luxembourg (2007). http://ec.europa.eu/research/science-society/document_library/pdf_06/report-rocard-on-science-education_en.pdf. ISBN 978-92-79-05659-8
3. Kireš, M., Ješková, Z., Ganajová, M., Kimáková, K.: Bádateľské aktivity v prírodovednom vzdelávaní, časť A. ŠPÚ, Bratislava, SVK (2016). ISBN 978-80-8118-155-9
4. Šnajder, Ľ., Guniš, J.: Inquiry based learning of selected computer sciences concepts and principles. ICTE J. **1**(1), 28–39 (2012). https://doi.org/10.1515/ijicte-2012-0003
5. Vaníček, J.: Programming in scratch using inquiry-based approach. In: Brodnik, A., Vahrenhold, J. (eds.) ISSEP 2015. LNCS, vol. 9378, pp. 82–93. Springer, Cham (2015). https://doi.org/10.1007/978-3-319-25396-1_8
6. Gordon, N., Brayshaw, M.: Inquiry based learning in computer science teaching in higher education. Innov. Teach. Learn. Inf. Comput. Sci. **7**(1), 22–33 (2008). https://doi.org/10.11120/ital.2008.07010022
7. Bybee, R.W., et al.: BSCS 5E instructional model: origins and effectiveness. BSCS, Colorfado Springs (2006). http://bscs.org/sites/default/files/_media/about/downloads/BSCS_5E_Full_Report.pdf
8. National project IT Academy - education for 21st century. http://itakademia.sk/
9. Han, J., Kamber, M., Pei, J.: Data Mining: Concepts and Techniques. Morgan Kaufmann Publishers Inc., San Francisco (2011)
10. Larose, D.T., Larose, C.D.: Data Mining and Predictive Analytics. Wiley, Hoboken (2015)
11. Chráska, M.: Metody pedagogického výzkumu. Grada, Praha (2007). ISBN 978-80-247-1369-4
12. Rammarain, U., Hlatswayo, M.: Teacher beliefs and attitudes about inquiry-based learning in a rural school district in South Africa. S. Afr. J. Educ. **38**(1), 1–10 (2018). https://doi.org/10.15700/saje.v38n1a1431. Art. # 1431
13. Dostál, J.: Inquiry-based instruction: concept, essence, importance and contribution. Univerzita Palackého, Olomouc (2015). https://doi.org/10.5507/pdf.15.24445076
14. Šnajder, Ľ., Guniš, J.: Bádateľsky orientované vyučovanie informatiky - priebežné výsledky pedagogického výskumu. In: Brodenec, I., et al. (eds.) Proceedings of conference DidInfo 2016, pp. 116–123. Matej Bel University, Faculty of Natural Sciences in Banská Bystrica, Slovakia (2016). ISBN 978-80-557-1082-2

Primary Education in Informatics

Introducing Informatics in Primary Education: Curriculum and Teachers' Perspectives

Valentina Dagienė, Tatjana Jevsikova(✉), and Gabrielė Stupurienė

Vilnius University Institute of Educational Sciences, Universiteto 9, 01513 Vilnius, Lithuania
{valentina.dagiene, tatjana.jevsikova, gabriele.stupuriene}@mif.vu.lt

Abstract. Informatics and especially its nowadays leading part, computational thinking, becomes an important and universal competence within the debate on 21st century skills and addresses the concepts and learning goals of Informatics (Computing or Computer Science). There are initiatives appearing worldwide that tend to include Informatics into early education. In this paper, we analyze implementation of Informatics as well as developing computational thinking competence on a primary school level. We survey the situation on Informatics in primary education in different countries (52 countries included), discuss the structure of draft curriculum for Informatics in primary education developed in Lithuania, and study primary teachers' readiness to integrate Informatics into primary education.

Keywords: Computational thinking in primary school · Computing in primary school · Informatics curriculum · Informatics in primary school · Primary education

1 Introduction

Computational thinking has been actively promoted through K-12 curriculum as a part of Informatics (Computing or Computer Science) subject or in an integrated way, as it addresses the concepts and learning goals of Informatics. Interest to teaching Informatics in primary school has increased during the last decade. Informatics education in Europe report, released in 2016, provides a recommendation: "All students must have access to ongoing education in Informatics in the school system. Informatics teaching should preferably start in primary school…" [1]. Basing on the findings of this report, an initiative of Informatics for all has been started and the strategy has been released [2] which states: "With its capacity to precisely describe how information can be automatically managed and processed, Informatics provides cognitive insights and a useful common language for all subjects and professions" [2].

Computational thinking encompasses a set of concepts and thought processes from Informatics that aid in formulating problems and their solutions in different fields. As Jeannette Wing defined, "computational thinking represents a universally applicable attitude and skill set everyone, not just computer scientists, would be eager to learn and

S. N. Pozdniakov and V. Dagienė (Eds.): ISSEP 2019, LNCS 11913, pp. 83–94, 2019.
https://doi.org/10.1007/978-3-030-33759-9_7

use" [3]. It is considered as a universal skill for all and one of the important 21st century skills. J. Wing later gave a more concrete definition, stating that computational thinking involves solving problems, designing systems, and understanding human behaviour, by drawing on the concepts of computational thinking [4]. It includes a range of mental tools that reflect the breadth of the field of Informatics.

Unless we can notice the separation of terms Informatics and Digital Literacy in e.g. [1, 2], some international initiatives, e.g. DigComp, include elements of Informatics (programming) into the digital competence area "Digital content creation" [5]. Terms of Informatics, Computing and Computer Science, used in this paper, refer to more or less the same thing, that is, the entire discipline.

"K-12 Computer Science framework", released in 2016, defines the main concepts that should be addressed in school Informatics education: computing systems, networks and the Internet, data and analysis, algorithms and programming, impacts of Computing [6]. Research on education in the early years has moved forward in the last few decades, informed by an understanding of the multimodality of young children's learning, as well as socio-political changes that emphasize the need to respect young children's views. As a result, it has been increasingly important to encourage children to reflect upon the world around them and to be engaged in real-world problems and solutions [7]. Visual gaming environments and tangible interfaces provide tools to learn Computing in early years [8], computer science unplugged activities [9] and Bebras international challenge task activities [10] for primary school provide possibilities to develop computational thinking without computer.

There are well known initiatives of Informatics implementation in primary education. For example, the Australian Curriculum: Digital Technologies is a new national subject within the Technologies learning area since 2016. The subject is mandatory from Foundation (Kindergarten in New South Wales) to year 8, with elective offerings following for year 9/10 students. The digital technologies curriculum includes fundamental ideas from the academic disciplines of Computer Science, information systems and informatics [11]. Media arts, online safety are integrated correspondingly into arts and health and physical education, while ICT is integrated across all subjects. The UK introduced new subject of Computing in 2014 that replaced IT, and guide for primary school teachers has been released [12]. The review of Informatics in K-12 education in Australia, England, Estonia, Finland, New Zealand, Norway, Sweden, South Korea, Poland and the USA provide information on initiatives, taking part in primary education as for year 2016 [13].

However, when introducing Informatics in primary education, we face many challenges. As Hubwieser et al. (2014) conclude in their research on Informatics education vision in primary and secondary education: (1) proper teacher education in substantial extent and depth seems to be one of the most critical factors for the success of rigorous Computer Science education on the one hand and also one of the hardest goals to achieve on the other; (2) there is a convergence towards computational thinking as a core idea of the K-12 curricula; (3) programming in one form or another, seems to be absolutely necessary for a future-oriented Computer Science education [14].

This paper aims to look at the tendencies of Informatics education in primary school, to analyze and share Lithuanian experience on introducing a primary school Informatics curriculum and teacher preparation.

Our main research questions we address in this paper are:

1. What is the up-to-date picture of introduction of Informatics in primary education in various countries?
2. What are the general differences in big topics (areas) of primary Informatics education curriculum?
3. How Lithuanian teachers are prepared for introduction of the new Informatics curriculum on the national level?

In order to answer Research Question 1, we survey the situation on Informatics in primary education in different countries (52 countries included) and present results of quantitative analysis (Sect. 2), discuss the structure of draft curriculum for Informatics in primary education developed in Lithuania (Sect. 3), and examinate primary teacher readiness to integrate Informatics into primary education (Sect. 4). Finally, we present a conclusion and discussion.

2 Informatics in Primary Education

2.1 Research Methodology and Respondents

In order to learn the most up-to-date information about the practice and situation of introduction of Informatics in primary education in different countries, a study of expert answers has been conducted during spring-summer period in 2019 instead of just literature review. In total, 52 experts representing different countries took part in this survey. It should be mentioned that requirements for the respondents (experts) of the study were very high: an expert was the one involved in the creation of national education system, curriculum and methodological material development in Informatics (Computer Science area), knowing the situation on primary education level. If expert could not answer all the questions by himself, the questions were redirected to another expert. In addition, we asked to self-evaluate the level of confidence of expert's answers on the scale from 1 (low) to 5 (high). General confidence level is evaluated as high (median: 5, mean: 4.6). List of countries, represented by experts, includes 34 countries of European region (Austria, Belarus, Belgium, Bosnia and Herzegovina, Bulgaria, Croatia, Czechia, Denmark, Estonia, Finland, France, Germany, Greece, Hungary, Iceland, Ireland, Italy, Latvia, Macedonia, Malta, Netherlands, Norway, Poland, Portugal, Romania, Russia, Serbia, Slovakia, Slovenia, Spain, Sweden, Switzerland, United Kingdom, Ukraine), and 18 non-European countries (Algeria, Australia, Cyprus, Cuba, India, Indonesia, Iran, Japan, Malaysia, Palestine, Philippines, Singapore, South Africa, South Korea, Thailand, Tunisia, Turkey, Uzbekistan).

The experts were asked the following questions:

- Students' age group, corresponding to primary education in your country.
- Is (Informatics, Computing or Computer Science) taught in primary school in your country? (Yes, as a separate subject; Yes, in an integrated way; No; Other).
- Is there a curriculum for the Informatics (Computing, Computer Science) in primary education? (Yes; No; It is being developed at the moment).

- If Informatics (Computing, Computer Science) is introduced in primary education, in which grade does it starts? (Please write grade number, e.g. 1st).
- Is Informatics included into primary teacher education programs? (Yes; Yes, mostly limited to common digital literacy; Yes, mostly limited to programming; No).
- If Informatics (Computing, Computer Science) is introduced in primary education, please mark areas of competence that are addressed: (Please mark one or more of the following answers that suite at least partly.) The six areas of primary Informatics education that were included into the Lithuanian curriculum were listed with general content explanation: Digital Content, Algorithms and Programming, Problem solving, Data and Information, Virtual communication, Safety and Copyright (see Sect. 3).

We posed the simplicity requirement for our questionnaire. However, experts could not only select suggested option of answer, but add their free-text comments as well. Most of respondents commented their answers due to the considerable differences within the country, no possibility to select between answer option, actuality of the problem, activities taking place in Informatics early education right now, etc. In this paper, we concentrate more on quantitative aspects of the study. But due to the active comments and information sharing by the experts, the study can be extended to qualitative research, what is positioned as future work. The study aims at answering Research Questions 1 and 2 of this paper (see Introduction).

2.2 Study Results and Discussion

It is important to know what students' age different primary education systems embrace. Age of students in primary education in surveyed countries ranges from 3 to 16. Most frequent lower and upper age boundaries are 6 and 11.

52% of surveyed countries (27 countries) have already introduced Informatics curriculum for primary education (Fig. 1). 56% of European region countries and 44% of surveyed non-European countries. There is no curriculum for Informatics in primary education in 27% of all surveyed countries, and the curriculum is being developed at the moment in 21% of all surveyed countries. Active development of new curriculum can be noticed in the surveyed countries of European region (91% of all respondents who stated that curriculum is under development).

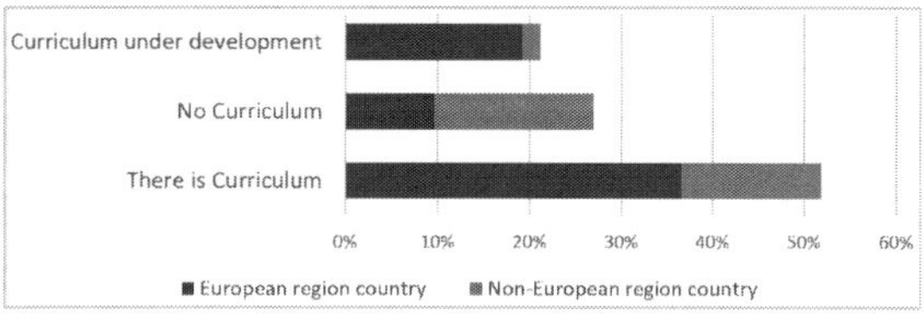

Fig. 1. Existence of Informatics curriculum for primary education in the surveyed countries, N = 52

The majority of surveyed countries introduces Informatics in the first year of primary school (44%), 22% of respondent countries introduces Informatics in grade 3, the same number (22%) in grade 5, and correspondingly 3% and 6% of countries introduce in grade 2 and grade 6 (Fig. 2).

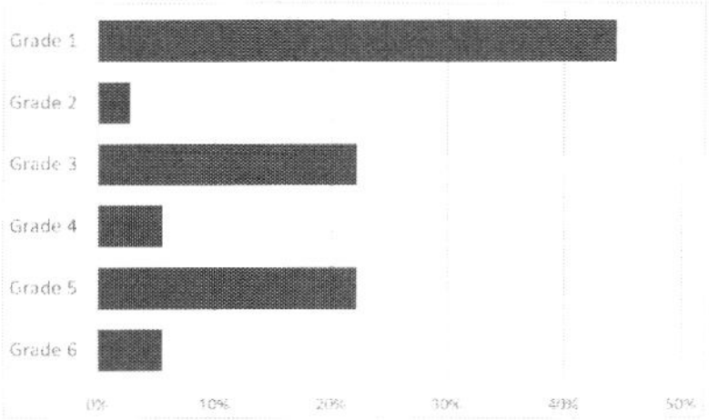

Fig. 2. Starting grade (school year) of Informatics introduction in primary education, N = 37

However, only 17 (33% out of all surveyed countries, or 46% out of countries with Informatics in primary education) introduce Informatics in grades 1 or 2 (Australia, Belarus, Bosnia and Herzegovina, Cuba, Denmark, Estonia, Greece, Indonesia, Norway, Poland, Romania, Russia, Sweden, Switzerland, Thailand, UK, Ukraine). All these countries (except for Thailand) reported to have/being developed Informatics curriculum for primary school at the moment of survey.

The vast majority of surveyed countries (83%) teach Informatics elements in primary education. However, there are a lot of differences in the level of Informatics implementation. Out of the countries who teach elements of Informatics, 26% have either non-compulsory (elective) Informatics subject in primary education, or the level of introduction of Informatics in primary education differs depending on the region, school type (e.g. private), choice done by school, etc.

Out of respondent countries who either have curriculum or undergo curriculum development process at the moment, 50% of countries introduce Informatics as a separate subject in primary education (Fig. 3), that is called differently across the countries, e.g. Computer modeling, ICT, Computing, Computer Science, Digital Technologies, Media education, etc. 21% of countries include basics of Informatics in primary education in an integrated way. Some countries introduce both as separate and as integrated either due to pilot study taking part at the moment (e.g. in Denmark), due to differences in school years (e.g. in Switzerland, for grade 1–2 the subject is integrated, for grade 3–4 the subject is separated), or due to possibility to select on a school level (e.g. Czechia).

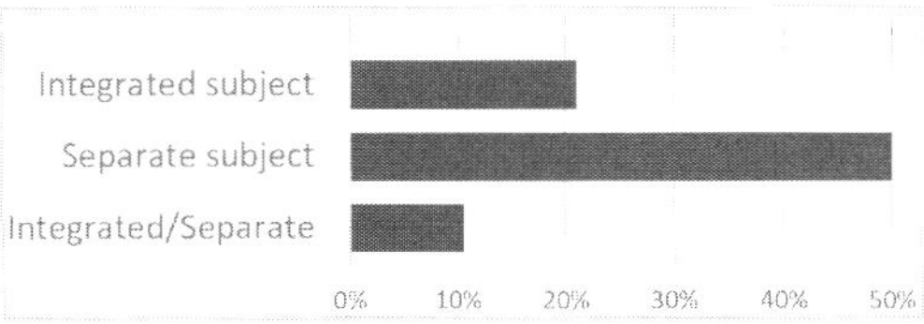

Fig. 3. Informatics elements introduction in primary education (integrated or separate subject) in the countries which have/develop Informatics curriculum, N = 38

A key question in quality of Informatics teaching in primary education is teacher training. In general (N = 52), 77% of surveyed countries have included elements of Informatics into primary teacher education programs (data for one non-European country is not available) (Fig. 4). 27% of countries include all main aspects of computational thinking in primary teacher training programs (answer "Yes"). However, almost in half of surveyed countries (46%) teacher training is mostly limited to digital literacy. In 2 countries (4%, Finland and Czechia) primary teacher training in Informatics mostly include programming.

It should be noticed that all countries who answered "Yes" to the question on teacher training, have Informatics curriculum in primary education.

Training in primary teacher education programs is limited mostly to digital literacy, dominates among all countries and even those who have introduced Informatics-related curriculum in primary education, or such curriculum is being developed.

Three experts, representing countries with Informatics-related curriculum in primary education but without teacher training included into primary teacher training programs, commented that it is planned to be introduced soon (Denmark), some programs do (Poland), or informatics teachers are teaching Informatics elements in primary education (Latvia).

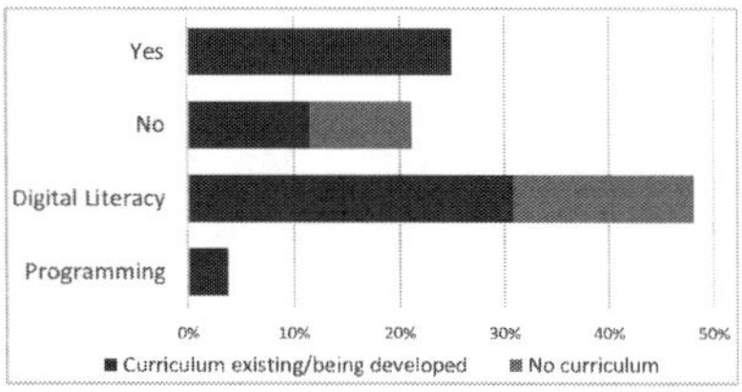

Fig. 4. Informatics inclusion in primary teacher education programs (N = 52)

Results on the main Informatics topics, being taught in primary education, are discussed and compared in the next section. Informatics content areas for primary education has been selected, corresponding to the curriculum main areas in the Lithuanian curriculum being developed, in order to compare implementation across countries.

3 Informatics Curriculum for Primary Education: Prospective Framework in Lithuania

Lithuania has experienced more than 30-year way of teaching Informatics in schools. Informatics in Lithuanian schools has been introduced as a compulsory subject since 1986. Since 1995, national exam in informatics has been introduced. The way of teaching informatics has been changing from theoretical aspects of Informatics in the first decade to more information technology-oriented subject in the second decade, and during the last decade we are moving to computational thinking oriented skills development. Since 2005, a compulsory subject, called Information Technology, has been introduced in schools since grade 5 (first year of basic education). It should be noticed that grade 5 in many countries at the moment of writing this paper is assigned to primary education level.

In 2016, working group of education experts, including Informatics teachers and primary school teachers, scientists, teacher trainers, educational policy-makers, business sector representatives, has developed a draft version of informatics curriculum framework for primary schools (grade 1–4). Lithuanian primary education typically embraces ages 7–11, i.e. 4 grades (now we are in a transformation phase to ages 6–11). As a result, six areas of Informatics have been identified [15] (Table 1).

Table 1. Lithuanian primary school informatics curriculum areas and basic skills

Area	Essential skills
1. Digital content	1. Familiarize with digital content diversity 2. Use digital content to learn in various subjects 3. Create digital content, using various technologies 4. Evaluate and improve digital content
2. Algorithms and programming	1. Understand an importance of algorithm and program for problem solving 2. Perform actions of algorithm/program 3. Identify sequencing, branching, loop actions and express them by commands, apply logical operations 4. Create and run programs using gamified programming tools and environments 5. Test, debug and enhance programs
3. Problem solving	1. Identify problems occurring when using digital technologies 2. Creatively use digital technologies learning various subjects 3. Select and apply appropriate digital technologies to solve tasks 4. Evaluate own digital skills
4. Data and information	1. Understand purpose and benefit of data and information management by digital technologies 2. Search information purposefully using digital technologies 3. Collect, store, manage data 4. Discuss and evaluate information relevance and reliability
5. Virtual communication	1. Understand purpose and importance of virtual communication 2. Communicate by the means of digital technologies 3. Collaborate by the means of digital technologies, share found/created digital resources 4. Discuss and evaluate possibilities and risks of virtual communication
6. Safety and copyright	1. Perceive the necessity to protect digital devices from malicious software 2. Protect personal data 3. Discuss copyright and piracy issues 4. Protect health while using digital technologies 5. Protect environment while using digital technologies

Correspondence of the designed curriculum areas and skills to the DigComp competence areas [5] can be found (Fig. 5). Probably the main difference is that Algorithms and programming which are most promoting computational thinking skills in Lithuanian curriculum is a separate area, while in "DigComp" it is included into Digital content creation competence area.

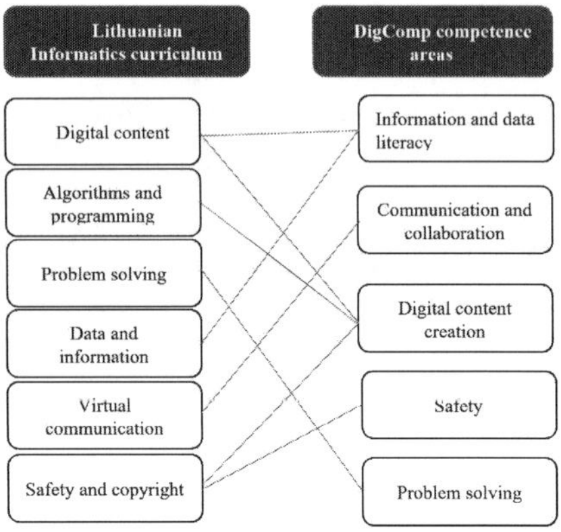

Fig. 5. Lithuanian prospective framework of Informatics curriculum area and DigComp competence area mapping

During the countries survey, discussed in Sect. 2 of this paper, we asked experts whether six areas of primary Informatics education are being developed in their primary education (each area had explanations on the content included into it). The reason of selecting such areas was to compare to the Lithuanian curriculum. The results are presented in Fig. 6.

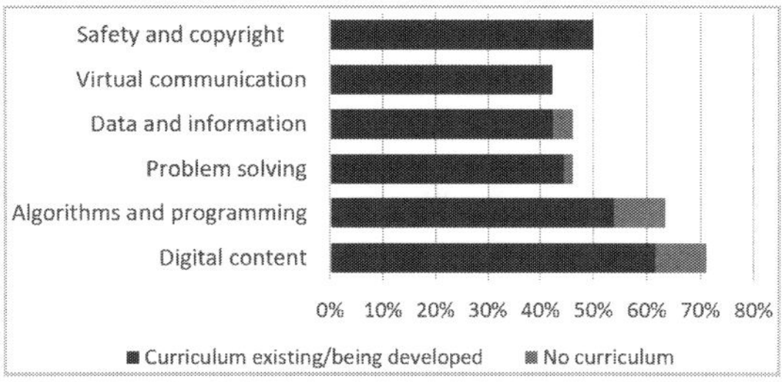

Fig. 6. Informatics content areas in primary education in surveyed countries (N = 52)

All of the areas are addressed in most surveyed countries in primary Informatics education. More often, Digital content (62%), Algorithms and programming (54%), Safety and copyright (50%) are taught. Digital content and Algorithms and programming are even taught in some countries that have not introduced Informatics curriculum.

However, only 33% of surveyed countries start Informatics from grade 1 or 2. In Lithuania, the Informatics is going to be introduced starting from grade 1 (before the reform to start primary education from age 6, Informatics is introduced starting from pre-school, i.e. one year before current grade 1). Out of these countries, 94% introduce Digital content skills, 71% introduce Algorithms and programming, Problem solving, Data and information Safety and copyright, 76% introduce Virtual communication topics.

4 Primary School Teachers Readiness for Informatics Curriculum Implementation

Introducing a new subject in primary education is a long process of discussions, pilot implementations, sharing best practices, teacher training, etc. Therefore, in 2017 Ministry of education, science and sport in Lithuania has launched project called "Informatics in primary schools". The goal of this project was to become ready for nation-wide Informatics implementation in primary schools. By competition means, 10 schools were selected, where primary teachers in school year 2017/2018 implemented practically draft Informatics curriculum, provided suggestions to curriculum correction, prepared various integrated activities to teach Informatics, closely collaborated with researchers who consulted them. A year later, 90 more schools have been selected for pilot implementation of Informatics curriculum. The finalized curriculum is planned to be implemented in all schools since 2020. But before activities with 100 schools have started, in the beginning of school year 2018/2019, a study [16] on teacher readiness to implement the new Informatics curriculum in primary schools has been run.

4.1 Research Methodology and Respondents

The participants of this study were 1342 primary school teachers (this makes up about 21% of all primary teachers in Lithuania) working in primary schools of different municipalities across all Lithuania (87% of all municipalities are covered).

The main research question of this study was "How Lithuanian teachers are prepared for introduction of the new Informatics curriculum on the national level?" (this is Research Question 3 of this paper).

The study has been run using internet-based questionnaire teachers had to fill in. We aimed to determine whether the skills, indicated in the draft Informatics curriculum, are already been addressed during regular primary school lessons (while Informatics is not compulsory subject yet) and how often. Another aspect of the study has been teachers' competence to teach Informatics in primary schools according to the new curriculum self-evaluation and comparison between those teachers who had digital competence training during the past 3 years and who had not.

4.2 Results and Discussion

The teachers, participating in the study, indicated for each Informatics curriculum area and its essential skill (see Table 1), how often do they include this skill into their regular lessons (almost every day, once or twice per week, one to three times per month, two to three times per half a year, very rarely or never).

The format of this paper does not allows us to present the detailed results for each curriculum area skills, therefore we generalize results by introducing numeric scale from 5 to 1: 5 – almost every day, 4 – once or twice per week, 3 – one to three times per month, 2 – two to three times per half a year, 1 – very rarely or never. Median values has been counted for each curriculum area and general result has been derived (Fig. 7).

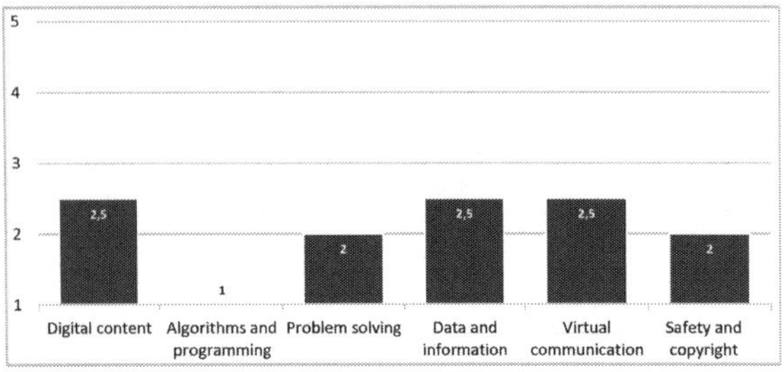

Fig. 7. Students' Informatics skills development during the lessons (generalized results), N = 1342

We see that for Digital content, Data and information and Virtual communication, appropriate skill training during the lessons is done almost one to three times per month. Approximately two or three times per half a year teachers include in their lessons Problem solving and Safety and copyright skills development. Unless, there are individual initiatives to develop Algorithms and programming skills, but generalized national results show that these area skills are almost not included into regular lessons.

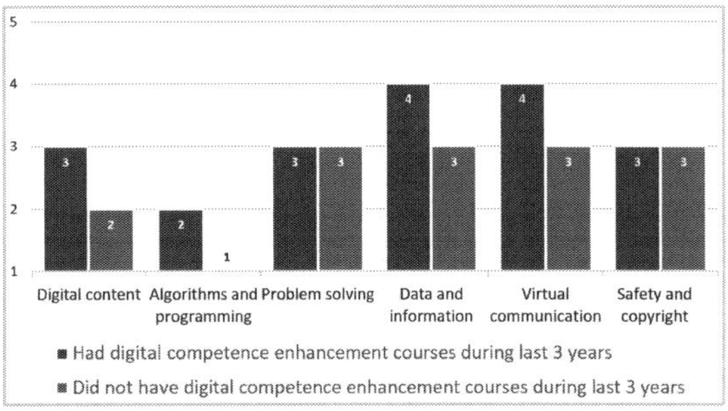

Fig. 8. Primary school teachers' competence self-evaluation to teach Informatics skills, N = 1342

In order to know how primary school teachers self-evaluate their competence to teach curriculum defined areas of Informatics, we asked them to use evaluation scale point from 5 to 1 corresponding to their preparation (5 – very good, 4 – good, 3 – moderate, 2 – weak, 1 – not prepared). The results (Fig. 8) show that teachers feel most prepared to teach Data and information as well as Virtual communication skills, has moderate preparation to teach Problem solving and Safety and Copyright skills. Less prepared teachers are to teach Digital content. And almost not prepared to teach Algorithms and programming.

We can also see the difference between self-evaluation of these teachers who had had digital competence training during the last 3 years and who had not. The difference per 1 scale point is seen in Digital content, Algorithms and programming, Data and information, and Virtual communication areas.

5 Discussion and Conclusion

We face three main challenges when introducing Informatics in primary school: (1) curriculum development; (2) teacher preparation; (3) research of implementation process and what should be taught [1]. In this paper, we addressed all of them and presented Lithuanian experience of Informatics introduction in primary school (grade 1–4).

Active participation of experts representing 52 countries in the study we run, indicates the importance of the problem. In 21% of surveyed countries (91% of these countries belong to the European region) Informatics for primary education curriculum is under active development at the moment.

Collected data has shown that Informatics in one or another way is taught in the majority of surveyed countries (83%) in primary education. However, there are a lot of differences in the level of Informatics implementation. It is quite a challenging task to compare implementation of Informatics in different countries due to the difference of education system. For instance, only 17 out of 52 surveyed countries (33%) introduce Informatics in grades 1 or 2. 19% of countries start teaching Informatics in grades 5 or 6 while in some countries (including Lithuania), grade 5 is a start of basic level of secondary school.

At the moment of research, countries pay priority to separate subject of Informatics in primary education rather than integrated. In Lithuania, we select integrated way of teaching Informatics. The results have shown that still more attention should be payed to primary teacher education. Training in primary teacher education programs, mostly limited to digital literacy, dominates among all countries and even those who have introduced an Informatics-related curriculum in primary education, or such a curriculum is being developed. Ongoing initiatives and experience in Lithuania (Informatics curriculum for primary school, pilot implementation in 10, then in 100 schools, collaboration with scientists, business representatives, teacher training activities and research) can serve as one of the possible models for countries who are going to implement Informatics in primary education.

Evaluation of teacher readiness to implement Informatics curriculum is an important element in the transformation phase. If there are initiatives of integration of Informatics elements into regular lessons nation-wide, even when there are no compulsory Informatics subject, this is a good indicator for launching Informatics as a new subject.

The future steps of the research include qualitative analysis of experience of difference countries.

Acknowledgement. We would like to express gratitude to the all international experts who took part in the survey on Informatics in primary education for active participation and collaboration. We also thank Education Development Center of Lithuania for the support of the research on primary teacher readiness to introduce Informatics in primary school.

References

1. Informatics Education in Europe: Are We All in the Same Boat. Report by The Committee on European Computing Education (CECE) Jointly established by Informatics Europe & ACM Europe (2016)
2. Informatics for All: The strategy. ACM Europe & Informatics Europe (2018). https://europe.acm.org/binaries/content/assets/public-policy/acm-europe-ie-i4all-strategy-2018.pdf
3. Wing, J.M.: Computational thinking. Commun. ACM **49**(3), 33–35 (2006)
4. Wing, J.M.: Computational Thinking: What and Why (2011). http://www.cs.cmu.edu/link/researchnotebook-computational-thinking-what-and-why
5. European Commission: DigComp into Action. Get inspired, make it happen. A user quide to the European digital competence framework. European Union (2018)
6. K–12 Computer Science Framework. ACM (2016). http://www.k12cs.org
7. Manches, A., Plowman, L.: Computing education in children's early years: a call for debate. Br. J. Educ. Technol. **48**(1), 191–201 (2017)
8. Garneli, V., Giannakos, M., Chorianopoulos, K.: Computing Education in K-12 schools: a review of the literature. In: IEEE Global Engineering Education Conference (EDUCON), pp. 543–551 (2015)
9. CS Unplugged: Computer Science without Computer (2019). https://csunplugged.org/en/
10. Dagiene, V., Stupuriene, G.: Bebras – a sustainable community building model for the concept based learning of informatics and computational thinking. Inform. Educ. **15**(1), 25–44 (2016)
11. Australian Computing Academy: Coding and Computational Thinking. What is the Evidence? https://education.nsw.gov.au
12. CAS: Computing in the National Curriculum. A Guide for Primary Teachers (2013)
13. Heintz, F., Mannila, L., Färnqvist, T.: A review of models for introducing computational thinking, computer science and computing in K-12 education. In: 2016 IEEE Frontiers in Education Conference (FIE) (2016)
14. Hubwieser, P., Armoni, M., Giannakos, M., Mittermeir, R.T.: Perspectives and visions of computer science education in primary and secondary (K-12) schools. ACM Trans. Comput. Educ. **14**(2), Article 7 (2014)
15. Education Development Center: Lithuanian Informatics Curriculum Outline. Preschool and Primary Education. Draft, 2019-06-30 (2019). https://informatika.ugdome.lt/lt/biblioteka/dokumentai/. [In Lithuanian]
16. Jevsikova, T.: School Potential and Readiness to Implement an Integrated Informatics Curriculum in Primary Education. Study Report. Education Development Center (2019). https://informatika.ugdome.lt/lt/tyrimas/ [In Lithuanian]

Observing Abstraction in Young Children Solving Algorithmic Tasks

Hylke H. Faber[1(✉)], Josina I. Koning[1(✉)], Menno D. M. Wierdsma[1], Henderien W. Steenbeek[1], and Erik Barendsen[2,3]

[1] Hanze University of Applied Sciences, Groningen, Netherlands
{h.h.faber,j.i.koning}@pl.hanze.nl
[2] Radboud University, Nijmegen, The Netherlands
[3] Open University, Heerlen, The Netherlands

Abstract. Abstraction is considered an essential aspect of computational thinking. Primary schools are starting to include computational thinking into the curriculum. However, in order to guide their support, teachers need to know how to recognize abstraction. In this paper, we present how we can observe abstraction in young children tasked with solving an algorithmic assignment. In order to operationalize abstraction, we have used the layers of abstraction (LOA) model by Perrenet, Groote and Kaasenbrood. This model was originally used in the field of computer science and describes programming behavior at the level of software development, but has since been extended for use in primary education. We have operationalized this model for use with 5 to 6 year old students tasked with programming an educational robot. Their behavior has been related to each of the four layers of abstraction.

Students were individually instructed with programming Cubetto, an educational robot, to reach a number of destinations, increasing in the level of algorithmic complexity. We analyzed audio and video recordings of the students interacting with Cubetto and a teacher. Verbal and non-verbal behavior were categorized by two researchers and resulted in an observation schema.

We conclude that our operationalization of the LOA model is promising for characterizing young students' abstraction. Future research is needed to operationalize abstraction for older primary school students.

Keywords: Computational thinking · Abstraction · Algorithmic thinking · Educational robots

1 Introduction

The term *computational thinking* (CT for short) has gathered a lot of interest in recent years. CT consists of a number of cognitive problem solving strategies where concepts of computer science are utilized, sometimes resulting in a solution

H. Faber and J. I. Koning—These authors contributed equally to this paper.

S. N. Pozdniakov and V. Dagienė (Eds.): ISSEP 2019, LNCS 11913, pp. 95–106, 2019.
https://doi.org/10.1007/978-3-030-33759-9_8

that can be interpreted by an information processing agent [17]. For instance, a computer might be able to solve certain aspects of a problem, assuming that the problem has been formulated in such a way that it can be interpreted by a computer. These cognitive strategies can be useful to solve problems outside the field of computer science.

In recent years, primary schools have started introducing CT classes for their students. However, as this is a relatively new field of study for primary education, without a clearly set curriculum, many schools feel unsure of what to do. After initially describing a possible learning trajectory in a series of lessons as a guiding example [2,3,6], we realized not enough research has been done on *how* young students develop CT. We believe that this is an essential first step in creating a research-based CT curriculum. So, our focus shifted towards tackling this problem.

As an institute for teacher education, we are interested in how teachers can better support their students. As CT is now slowly beginning to be included in the Dutch primary schools, we believe it is essential for teachers to foster CT development in students. Therefore, teachers need to able to recognize abstraction in young students' behavior. This paper presents our findings of developing an operationalization of abstraction. Furthermore, we discuss patterns in abstraction that emerge when young students are tasked with an algorithmic assignment. This represents a piece of the puzzle required for teachers to better support students' development of CT.

2 Background

While there exist many definitions of CT, abstraction is frequently mentioned as being an essential aspect of CT [1,13,17]. The core of abstraction is to view a situation at various levels of detail, all relating to the same situation and indirectly affecting details on other levels of abstraction.

As abstraction refers to a cognitive process, it is difficult to operationalize abstraction in terms of observable behavior. However, as it is an essential aspect of CT, teachers need to be able to guide their support to foster students' development of abstraction. For this to occur, teachers need to know how they can identify abstraction and how they can adapt their scaffolding process to guide their support. Furthermore, recent work by Rijke and colleagues [12] indicates that competence in abstraction, along with decomposition, increases with age among primary school students. To support this developmental process, teachers need to able to recognize how students use abstraction.

Recently, research has revealed interesting findings on the use of educational robots in primary school classrooms [9,14]. Work by Kalas and colleagues [5] explored computational task complexity in their formulation of a two-dimensional grid, consisting of two dimensions: control and representation. The dimension of control ranges from direct manipulation (directly moving a physical robot or dragging a character in a programming environment) to computational control (constructing a sequence of instructions that are executed at a later stage). The dimension of representation concerns the manner in which a constructed sequence of instructions is presented to the programmer (ranging from no representation, where the instructions are in no way represented, to external plan, where the sequence is reflected outside the direct context of the programmable entity). Within these two dimensions, various levels of abstraction can be identified. For instance, creating a sequence of instructions, instead of physically pushing a robot across a grid map, implies a higher level of abstraction. Furthermore, a programming device that presents the instructions that are being executed outside of the immediate context of the entity, allows students to operate on a higher level of abstraction that a device that offers no such representation.

While the aforementioned framework [5] can be used to characterize task complexity, the *layers of abstraction* model [10,11] (LOA) describes abstraction as a process of problem solving, in the field of computer science [4]. Each layer of abstraction encompasses a different level of detail and focuses on different aspects of the same situation. In order to gain insight in how student engage in abstraction, the layers have to be operationalized to include observable behavior.

2.1 Layers of Abstraction

The original model by Perrenet and colleagues [10,11] has been used to describe abstraction within the field of computer science. For this project, we aim to operationalize the LOA model in the context of primary education. Recently, both Statter and Armoni [13] and Waite and colleagues [16] have each presented their LOA model for use within a K-5 educational context, based on the model by Perrenet and colleagues (condensed from [16]):

- Problem: a verbal description of the problem, including requirements of the specific task or assignment.
- Design: a detailed depiction of the solution, without any reference to the specific programming language that is used to solve the problem.
- Code: a translation of the design; the code itself or a reference to the code, in a vocabulary that is specific for the chosen programming language.
- Running the code: the running code or any reference to the output of the code.

However, while this framework makes a distinction between the layers of abstraction on a conceptual level, they offer no concrete observable behavior that can be related to these layers of abstraction. In this study, we aim to operationalize abstraction, by formulating observable behavior that can be related to the layers of abstraction.

Furthermore, we are interested in how students switch between abstraction layers on a microgenetic timescale. Insight in this process can prove useful in shaping teacher support [15]. For this project, we would like to uncover insight in pattern of students' abstraction.

2.2 Research Question

Our research question for this study is as follows: *How can abstraction be operationalized to characterize behavior of 5 to 6 year old students tasked with programming an algorithmic task?* An answer to this question results in an observation schema for determining how students within this age group express abstraction in their behavior when solving an algorithmic task.

3 Method

The research group consisted of 17 students, For this research, a moderately sized primary school in a rural area was chosen, providing education to about 400 students. Here, CT currently is not part of the curriculum. We set out to get a clear image on how students react when confronted with a programmable robot for the first time. This will allow us to get a unbiased baseline view of their behavior, without any previous formally taught programming experience. Our research sample consisted of 17 students, 8 boys and 9 girls, at the 2nd grade of primary school. The mean age of the students was 5 years and 5 months. A licensed primary school teacher, different to the group's regular teacher, tasked the students with the different assignments and was present during the video and audio recordings.

3.1 Educational Design

The educational context for this study was designed using lesson materials by Koning and colleagues [6]. These materials are based on the picture book Hello Ruby [8], where a young girl named Ruby goes on an adventure to collect gems by solving computational problems. The original lesson materials by Koning and colleagues [6] prescribe the use of Beebot, a specific educational robot. However, considering Kalas' grid of task complexity [5], Beebot only allows for direct drive, without any relation to actual computational programming. Cubetto however, a different educational robot, does allow for computational control, as well as direct drive, and an external plan Therefore, for this research we chose to make use of Cubetto.

Cubetto (https://www.primotoys.com) is a physical programmable robot that can be used for early computing education. Cubetto can be programmed by placing plastic colored coding blocks in the correct order in a remote control board. Each coding block can be identified by its unique shape and color: 'move forward' (green), 'turn clockwise' (red), 'turn counterclockwise' (yellow) and 'execute function' (blue). By pressing the circular button on the right side of the remote control board, the constructed code is sent wirelessly to the robot, which starts executing the code immediately. Because the code is visible on the remote control board, students can more clearly relate the outcome of the code to their programming efforts. Furthermore, the constructed code is also clearly visible to the teacher, which allows a teacher to trace any errors made in the code.

Students were individually tasked with programming Cubetto to move on a map of Ruby's world, containing a gird of 15 cm x 15 cm squares. Depending on the specific task, Cubetto has to move from a fixed starting position to a destination. The complexity and required programming effort increases with every assignment. For instance, the first tasks consists of Cubetto having to move two squares in a straight line, which can be accomplished by only using two 'move forward' blocks. Subsequent tasks involve turning Cubetto, requiring the use of the 'turn clockwise' and 'turn counterclockwise' blocks. After a quick briefing by the teacher, students were given their first assignment. Students had a total of 30 min to complete all assignments, with most not finishing all assignments within that time period. The teacher was instructed to limit their support towards the students, as our aim was to capture the abstraction process of students.

3.2 Data Collection

Students' and teacher behavior was recorded using digital audio and video recordings. Cameras were placed in such a way that both the map and the remote control board were visible at all times.

3.3 Data Analysis

Constructing the Observation Schema. The two first authors jointly viewed the recorded videos and consulted on the behavior that should be categorized as indicative of abstraction. An initial observation schema containing definitions of each of the four layers was created, along with sample behavior indicative of each layer. Next, this schema was used by the first two authors to independently analyze the same video observation, categorizing all behavior on a 10 s interval to one of the four layers, with a fifth option being added, used to categorize behavior that was not related to one of the four layers. Afterwards, differences in categorization were discussed and the schema was refined, resulting in a definitive observation schema. This was used to categorize another set of videos, comparing results to calculate the inter-rater reliability by using Cohens kappa. Finally, the definitive observation schema was used to perform pattern analysis, using video data that was not analyzed previously. Table 1 presents an overview of how many videos were used during each step of the process.

Table 1. Developing the observation schema

Research activity	Number of videos analyzed
Initial analysis	11
Prototype observation schema	2
Definitive observation schema	2
Pattern analysis	4

A short description of *how* we constructed will be presented in the next chapter, as this concerns one of the results of this study.

Pattern Analysis. Next, after assigning behavior to one of the abstraction layers, using the observation schema we previously created, we analyzed the results to see in any emergent patterns could be identified. We expect that such an analysis can provide insight in the progression of abstraction during an algorithmic task performed by young students.

4 Results

Operationalization of the Model. After the introduction of the assignments by the teacher, the students were instructed on the first assignment. This gave us a chance to see how students explored the problem, at the *problem layer*. Students frequently pointed to the destination that Cubetto has to move to in order to complete the assignment. In some cases, students had vocalized the solution that they have planned to program, either by thinking aloud or telling the teacher about their intention. This led us to categorize their behavior at the *design layer*. Frequently, this was accompanied with the student drawing out a line, indicating the proposed route to reach the destination. Next, students were frequently observed to grab the colored coding blocks and placing them in the remote control board, allowing us to observe the code they constructed. This constructed algorithm was the result of efforts t hat took place on the *code layer*. After completing the algorithm, students pressed to button to send the code to Cubetto. Observation data revealed that students frequently observed Cubetto as it processed the code, at the *execution layer*. Moreover, students frequently predicted the outcome of either part of their code, or their code in full, which we also related to the *execution layer*.

The analysis of video recordings has resulted in the construction of an observation schema, containing definitions of the layers and samples of observable behavior (see Table 2). Using the definitive observation schema as explained above yielded a Cohens kappa of 0.74, indicating a substantial agreement.

Pattern Analysis. Graphing the layers of abstraction presents an overview of the process of abstraction (see Fig. 1). This gives an indication of how a student switches between the various layers, and how much time is spent on each layer before switching to another layer. The gaps in the graph represent instance where a student displayed behavior that was unrelated to the programming task. As shown in Table 1, more analyses have been made, but the two graphs presented here are indicative of the rest of the analyses, and give a good indication of how students operate on each of the layers when solving the task.

The pattern analysis revealed that students did not spend much time at all on the *problem* layer. After introducing a new assignment, students spend little time on the *problem* layer, and quickly moved to the *design* layer to start formulating

Table 2. Operationalization of the layers of abstraction model

Layer definition	Sample behavior
Problem layer: behavior related to understanding the task	– Pointing to the starting position of Cubetto is indicative that the child understands that Cubetto has to move from that position to the required destination – Pointing to the required destination is indicative that the child understands where Cubetto has to go – Searching for, finding and pointing to the bridge that Cubetto has to cross during the later assignments, indicated that the student understands that this symbolizes a new requirement for the design
Design layer: behavior related to designing a route for Cubetto, describing it in human language without using the coding blocks	– Pointing out the route Cubetto can take on the map by drawing a line with a finger indicates that the student has designed a solution for the problem – Counting the number of squares that have to be moved by Cubetto indicates that the child is more explicitly designing a route – Describing the route in terms of up, down and forwards
Code layer: behavior related to translating the designed route into a sequence of coding blocks	– Grabbing a coding block and placing the block in the remote control board – Removing a coding block from the remote control board – Making adjustments to the sequence of coding blocks after observing the outcome of the code
Execution layer: behavior related to the outcome of the translated code	– Pressing the button on the remote control board, executing the code – Carefully observing the behavior of Cubetto – Relating the outcome of the execution to the predicted outcome – Predicting the outcome of a section of code by reasoning on how Cubetto would interpret the code, without actually executing the code

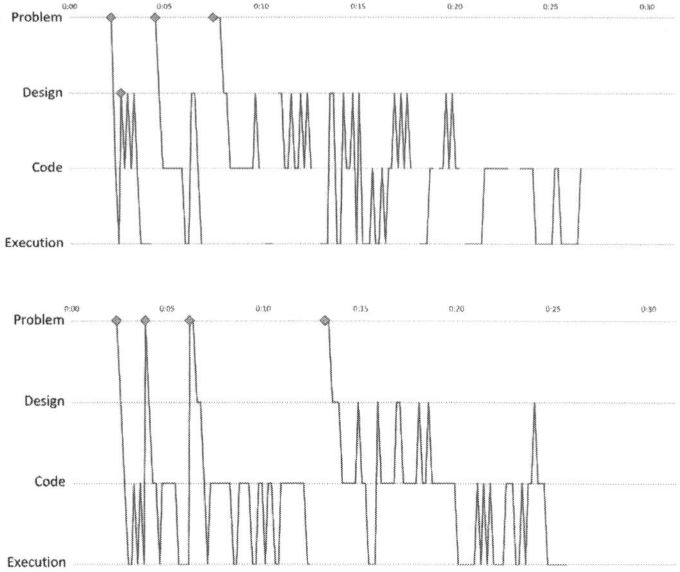

Fig. 1. Overview of the process of abstraction of two students, showing how students switch between layers over a timespan of 30 min. Green diamonds indicate when a new assignment was introduced. Behavior unrelated to solving the task is not shown, hence the gaps. (Color figure online)

a route (see Fig. 1). This could be related to the complexity of the understanding the assignments. However, all assignments we offered during this project were not difficult to understand: Cubetto has to move from a starting position to a destination. While a concrete solution might prove difficult, the assignment in itself was not very difficult to understand. Students therefore quickly moved on to subsequent layers.

Students were frequently observed to shift back to either the *code* or *design* layer, after observing the result of their code at the *execution* layer (see Fig. 1). In the event of an unexpected or undesired outcome, such as Cubetto stopping on a square adjacent to the destination, students switched back to the *code* layer to adjust the code and run the code again, indicating a process of *debugging*. In other cases, students decided that the route they chose had to be altered, switching back to the *design* layer, indicating a *redesign* of the solution. We believe both processes, debugging and redesign, can be explained using the LOA model:

- Debugging: We view the process of debugging as occurring between the *code* and *execution* layer. Students observe an outcome that is not expected. Debugging requires an adaptation at the code level, before running the program again to see whether the unwanted behavior persists. As such, debugging is related to switching back to the *code* layer, immediately after the execution process ends. Students were observed to switch numerous times between *code* and *execution*, most times adjusting only a single coding block.

– Redesign: In some cases, the outcome of the code infers that a redesign is required. Students were observed to choose, for instance, a new route for Cubetto, as the current design proved either too difficult or the student did not have enough faith to continue working on the design. In these cases, students switched back to the *design* layer and choose a different route for Cubetto. As such, the process of redesign is related to switching back to the *design* layer. Students were frequently unsure of the exact route that was taken. For instance, in many cases, students who were already constructing a sequence of coding blocks, switched back to the *design* layer to re-count the number of steps that were required to reach the destination. This was usually immediately followed by counting the number of coding block, indicating a switch back to the *code* layer.

5 Conclusion and Discussion

Coming back to our research question, we conclude that we succeeded to characterize abstraction in young students' behavior. We have demonstrated how we can use the layers of abstraction model to operationalize abstraction in observed behavior by students tasked with programming Cubetto (see Table 2).

Furthermore, our pattern analysis has yielded insight on *how* students engage in the process of abstraction over time, and what patterns emerge during that time. For instance, it is interesting to observe processes that one would expect in a more formal programming context, such as debugging and redesign, can also be observed in young students' programming behavior.

5.1 Cubetto

While Cubetto explicates the code that is being executed, the specific manner in which the coding blocks have to be entered into the programming board has, in some cases, led to a number of difficulties. The coding blocks have been designed in such a way that the remote control board only accepts the blocks when they are placed in their correct orientation. In some situations, this has led to frustration among students. This finding is in accordance with the study by Marinus and colleagues [9].

In some cases, students seemed to encounter difficulties, related to the shape and layout of the remote control board. The programming board allows for 12 blocks to be entered, among 3 rows. These rows are connected via a groove in the material of the board. At the end of the first row, where blocks have to be entered left-to-right, the groove makes a turn and continues on the right side of the second row. However, in some cases, observations led us to believe that a student believed that this turn would also cause Cubetto to turn. Another consequence of the second row of the remote control board being orientated right-to-left, is that the green "move forward" blocks are pointed to the left, instead of to the right, as they did when they were entered on the first row. The same effect has been observed with the directional blocks, as they point in different directions when they are placed in the first or second row of the programming board. These difficulties might have introduced a bias in the results, causing students to spend more time in the *code* layer than was expected.

5.2 Layers of Abstraction

In the original model by Perrenet and colleagues, the distinction between the *code* and *design* layer is based in part on the language that is used to describe the suggested solution. At the design layer, the solution is described using human readable language, without any reference to a programming language and the specific limitations of a specific programming language are not considered. At the code layer, the design is translated into a set of lines of code, specified to the programming language chosen to fit the solution.

While the distinction between human and programming language is in their case relatively clear, the same distinction is a lot harder to make in the context of this study. For instance, students were frequently observed to count the number of squares required to reach a certain destination. Initially, we related this behavior to the design layer, as we had previously decided that behavior on the code layer required interaction with the coding blocks, and this behavior did not concern the coding blocks. Counting the coding blocks, however, was related to the code layer, as that behavior did include interaction with the coding blocks. However, counting the squares could be considered a consequence of using Cubetto as a means of completing the task, as programming Cubetto requires knowledge of how many squares the robot has to move. Choosing a different educational robot, for instance, the Ozobot (https://ozobot.com/), would require a different approach. Ozobot is able to follow a black line on a surface. Therefore, the number of squares that needs to be crossed is irrelevant when choosing Ozobot to reach the destination. This finding aligns to the guidelines for teaching abstraction by Armoni [1] and observations Waite and colleagues [16], who both stress the importance of the *design* layer. Our method, prescribing the use of Cubetto beforehand, might have influenced students in their created designs, causing them to consider properties of Cubetto already at the *design* layer.

Subsequently, this finding initially led us to consider a split within the design layer. We considered an abstract design layer and a concrete design layer. An abstract design would be unrelated to the specific robot or programming language used to complete the solution. The concrete design, however, would describe the solution in human language, while also containing elements of the specific robot or programming language. The behavior of counting the squares on the map, as described above, would be considered an example of a concrete design, while a more global description of the route would be related to the abstract design. However, given the nature of the task, where Cubetto was pre-determined as the educational robot of choice, creating a design without considering the programming language of Cubetto would not make sense. For this reason, we chose to not further pursue a split at the design layer.

The aforementioned limitation of the assignment, where use of Cubetto was decided already at the start of the assignment, might have introduced a bias in deciding which behavior is related to the *design* and *code* layer. In a follow-up study, offering students a choice of robots or programming languages to complete the assignment could allow for a better distinction between the *design* and *code* layer.

Predicting the outcome of a section of code was considered a behavior related to the *execution* layer. However, this could also be considered a form of *tracing*, where a novice programmer determines the value of variables after execution [7]. According to Lister and colleagues, this operation does not imply abstraction, and could be considered a form of preoperational reasoning.

Due to the small number of (different) coding blocks needed to complete the tasks, it is difficult to determine whether a child is engaged in a process of debugging, or simply programming using a trail-and-error tactic, by looking solely at the constructed code. However, in these situations, verbal utterances by the child, in most cases, convinced us that trail-and-error was a seldom used tactic.

More research is required to further operationalize the LOA model for describing abstraction behavior for students in all age groups in K-6 education. Furthermore, we are interested to uncover how student behavior can be related to the LOA model when presented with various programming languages to choose from. As mentioned earlier, the two-dimensional grid by Kalas and colleagues [5] presents an interesting perspective on abstraction, that could be explored in further detail to relate task complexity to student abstraction. We aim to uncover how knowledge of these models can aid teachers in supporting the students. Furthermore, insight in emergent patterns of the sequence of abstraction layers, such as depicted in Fig. 1 might prove relevant for describing how other variables, such as teacher support or task structure, can have an influence on the development of abstraction. Finally, our ultimate goal is to uncover how teachers can use the LOA model to guide their support. This, in turn, can aid students in further developing their computational thinking abilities.

References

1. Armoni, M.: On teaching abstraction in computer science to novices. J. Comput. Math. Sci. Teach. **32**(3), 265–284 (2013)
2. Faber, H.H., van der Ven, J.S., Wierdsma, M.D.: Teaching computational thinking to 8-year-olds through ScratchJr. In: Proceedings of the 2017 ACM Conference on Innovation and Technology in Computer Science Education - ITiCSE 2017, p. 359. ACM Press, New York (2017). https://doi.org/10.1145/3059009.3072986
3. Faber, H.H., Wierdsma, M.D.M., Doornbos, R.P., van der Ven, J.S., de Vette, K.: Teaching computational thinking to primary school students via unplugged programming lessons. J. Eur. Teach. Educ. Netw. **12**, 13–24 (2017)

4. Hazzan, O.: How students attempt to reduce abstraction in the learning of mathematics and in the learning of computer science. Comput. Sci. Educ. **13**(2), 95–122 (2003). https://doi.org/10.1076/csed.13.2.95.14202
5. Kalas, I., Blaho, A., Moravcik, M.: Exploring control in early computing education. In: Pozdniakov, S.N., Dagienė, V. (eds.) ISSEP 2018. LNCS, vol. 11169, pp. 3–16. Springer, Cham (2018). https://doi.org/10.1007/978-3-030-02750-6_1
6. Koning, J.I., Faber, H.H., Wierdsma, M.D.M.: Introducing computational thinking to 5 and 6 year old students in dutch primary schools. In: Proceedings of the 17th Koli Calling Conference on Computing Education Research - Koli Calling 2017, pp. 189–190. ACM Press, New York (2017). https://doi.org/10.1145/3141880.3141908
7. Lister, R.: Concrete and other neo-Piagetian forms of reasoning in the novice programmer. In: Conferences in Research and Practice in Information Technology, p. 10 (2011)
8. Liukas, L.: Hello Ruby: Adventures in Coding. R. R. Donnelley & Sons Company, Crawfordsville (2015)
9. Marinus, E., Powell, Z., Thornton, R., McArthur, G., Crain, S.: Unravelling the Cognition of Coding in 3-to-6-year Olds: The development of an assessment tool and the relation between coding ability and cognitive compiling of syntax in natural language. In: Proceedings of the 2018 ACM Conference on International Computing Education Research - ICER 2018, Espoo, Finland, pp. 133–141. ACM Press (2018). https://doi.org/10.1145/3230977.3230984
10. Perrenet, J., Groote, J.F., Kaasenbrood, E.: Exploring students' understanding of the concept of algorithm. ACM SIGCSE Bull. **37**(3), 64 (2005). https://doi.org/10.1145/1151954.1067467
11. Perrenet, J., Kaasenbrood, E.: Levels of abstraction in students' understanding of the concept of algorithm: the qualitative perspective. In: Proceedings of the 11th Annual SIGCSE Conference on Innovation and Technology in Computer Science Education - ITICSE 2006, Bologna, Italy, p. 270. ACM Press (2006). https://doi.org/10.1145/1140124.1140196
12. Rijke, W.J., Bollen, L., Eysink, T.H.S., Tolboom, J.L.J.: Computational thinking in primary school: an examination of abstraction and decomposition in different age groups. Inform. Educ. **17**(1), 77–92 (2018). https://doi.org/10.15388/infedu.2018.05
13. Statter, D., Armoni, M.: Teaching abstract thinking in introduction to computer science for 7th graders. In: Proceedings of the 11th Workshop in Primary and Secondary Computing Education - WiPSCE 2016, pp. 80–83. ACM Press, New York (2016). https://doi.org/10.1145/2978249.2978261
14. Swidan, A., Hermans, F.: Programming education to preschoolers: reflections and observations from a field study. In: PPIG 2017 Proceedings, p. 10 (2017)
15. van der Steen, S., Steenbeek, H., den Hartigh, J., van Geert, P.: The link between micro-development and long-term learning trajectories in science learning. Human Development (in press)
16. Waite, J.L., Curzon, P., Marsh, W., Sentance, S., Hadwen-Bennett, A.: Abstraction in action: K-5 teachers' uses of levels of abstraction, particularly the design level, in teaching programming. Int. J. Comput. Sci. Educ. Sch. **2**(1) (2018). https://doi.org/10.21585/ijcses.v2i1.23
17. Wing, J.M.: Computational thinking and thinking about computing. Philos. Trans. Ser. A Math. Phys. Eng. Sci. **366**(1881), 3717–3725 (2008). https://doi.org/10.1098/rsta.2008.0118

Implementing a Reverse Debugger for Logo

Renato Menta[1], Serena Pedrocchi[1], Jacqueline Staub[1,2(✉)], and Dominic Weibel[1]

[1] Department of Computer Science, ETH Zürich, Universitätstrasse 6, 8092 Zürich, Switzerland
{rmenta,doweibel}@student.ethz.ch,
{serena.pedrocchi,jacqueline.staub}@inf.ethz.ch
[2] Pädagogische Hochschule Graubünden, Scalärastrasse 17, 7000 Chur, Switzerland

Abstract. Programming is a creative activity that teaches precision. In Logo, novices write simple programs that draw geometric shapes onto a screen. Logical flaws, however, cause unintended results and pose a major challenge for young programmers who yet need to learn how to search for errors in their code. We discuss the problems novices face when learning to program in Logo. Furthermore, we present a reverse debugger for Logo that enables programmers to step through their code in either direction. Using a stack, previous program states can be retrieved on demand. Our solution balances performance and memory consumption and hence can be used to debug even long and complex programs.

1 Introduction

Programming is a form of learning that is constructive, enriches creativity and teaches precision. Yet it is also strenuous and demanding at its very core: programmers are prone to committing numerous errors [13]. Learning how to cope with errors makes up a vital part of a programmers' competence [7]. In this work, we discuss the struggles novices face when learning how to program in Logo. Furthermore, we present a debugging tool that supports novices during the process of tracing semantic errors.

1.1 Making Mistakes: A Matter of Attitude

Humans cannot help but make mistakes. In the context of programming, computer science pioneer Ada Lovelace holds an exemplary attitude on this matter [15]: *"I used once to regret these sort of errors, & to speak of time lost over them. But I have materially altered my mind on this subject. I often gain more from the discovery of a mistake of this sort, than from 10 acquisitions made at once & without any kind of difficulty"*. Today, 180 years after this statement was made, much younger and less experienced pupils also learn programming and are still confronted with their own weaknesses. We can only hope they adopt a similar attitude to errors as Ada when they face issues in their programs.

S. N. Pozdniakov and V. Dagienė (Eds.): ISSEP 2019, LNCS 11913, pp. 107–119, 2019.
https://doi.org/10.1007/978-3-030-33759-9_9

1.2 The Rift Between Expectation and Outcome

By programming, pupils learn to express their ideas in a formal language. The resulting programs are written with clear expectations of what should happen when executed. Due to errors, however, a program may behave differently than expected. Seeing how a program has a different outcome than expected often has a shocking and somewhat alienating effect on novice programmers. In order to fix their program, they need to learn how to debug. Seymour Papert said [23]: *"When you learn to program a computer you almost never get it right the first time. Learning to be a master programmer is learning to become highly skilled at isolating and correcting 'bugs'. [...] The question to ask about the program is not whether it is right or wrong but if it is fixable"*. By learning how to fix incorrect programs, pupils become self-sufficient programmers: without external guidance, they write and refine programs with a specific purpose. Unfortunately, pupils' reality often looks different.

Without proper guidance, pupils are lost when facing semantic errors: they either start haphazardly tinkering with the code or they come to a full stop and wait for external support [21,24]. In order to cope with semantic errors autonomously, pupils need two fundamental skills: First, they need to be able to locate issues in their code. To find the needle in the haystack, they have to carefully trace the program logic one command at a time. Once an error has been isolated, a second skill comes into play: finding and implementing a solution. While the latter depends on the programmer's creativity, automatic tools can easily support the error-localization process. Special debugging mechanisms allow novices to trace their erroneous code more easily.

1.3 Semantic Errors vs. Syntactic Errors

Programming errors belong in one of two classes: syntactic or semantic errors. Syntactic errors (for example due to typos) cause the computer to fail during parsing and the program cannot be executed in the first place. These errors can be automatically detected and reported [12]. Semantic errors, on the other hand, are caused by flawed logic which computers cannot detect without knowing the programmer's intention. Programmers can write programs that parse correctly and run, but result in incorrect and unintended outcome. In this paper, we focus on the latter, semantic errors.

2 Background

Learning how to recover from semantic errors is an essential skill that is relevant to all programmers, independent of age and level of expertise. For a long time, various debugging tools and techniques have been developed for the professional community. Some languages for novices (e.g. Python) come with good examples of reverse debuggers. In the context of Logo, however, the potential of reverse debugging as not been explored so far.

2.1 Debugging: A Glimpse Back in History

The concept of debugging has been around since the early days of programming. Until Grace Hopper invented the first compiler in 1952, all instructions had to be given in a low-level machine language which was quite susceptible to errors. Code was hence usually first handwritten, line by line, on a standardized coding sheet [1]. Only then was it translated to punch cards and finally fed to the machine for execution. Along this way, various errors could have snuck in, causing unexpected output. Robert Campbell remembers [26]: *"We had to go through the operation step by step, until we found something which wasn't right"*. Using special "rollback" procedures, they tried to retrace the point at which the execution started to differ from what they expected [5].

With the invention of CRT monitors and command-line debuggers, error detection became significantly easier: programmers finally had the opportunity to inspect memory values directly on the computer rather than having to infer them on paper. In higher-level languages like COBOL and C, symbolic maps were used to link variable names and memory addresses [14]. The corresponding symbolic debuggers allowed programmers to dump and inspect memory by name. Breakpoints [19], conditional breakpoints [10] and the concept of single-stepping are used to inspect the program state at arbitrary points during execution. Originally, single-stepping was only possible in one direction (i.e., forward with regard of execution), but with the invention of reverse debugging [3], programmers could finally also step backwards through execution. Nowadays, debuggers are integral parts of most IDEs and allow professionals to conveniently program and debug in the same environment [9].

2.2 Debugging in Novice Programming Environments

Logical errors can occur in Logo just like in any other programming language. Thanks to turtle graphics, however, programmers can understand and trace their programs more easily: Incorrect implementations are characterized through visual defects in the resulting picture. In order to locate the root of such errors, programmers need to understand how their programs execute. The original Logo documentation [11] offered a command specifically for this purpose: `trace` prints all procedure invocations (input and output) that were called during execution. The command allows programmers to see what happened during execution and to perform error-analysis in a post-mortem fashion.

Since Logo was introduced, many new novice programming environments popped up and tackle the topic of debugging in their own way. Scratch [27] does not provide any notable debugging support any longer (the feature was discontinued when switching from version 1.4 to 2.0). In contrast, Smalltalk's Pharo [6] debugger allows programmers to change their code while debugging and the Python IDE Thonny [2] even offers reverse debugging. In the context of Logo, some environments (e.g., Turtle Blocks [4] and Robo Blocks [25]) provide debugging support through single-stepping, however, so far no Logo debugger allows programmers to also step backward in time. We address this problem and present a reverse debugger for XLogoOnline [18].

3 Typical Challenges When Learning to Program

To set the scope of this work, we present three fundamental programming concepts (i.e. sequential execution, repetition, and modularity) from our Logo curriculum [16,17] and discuss what challenges pupils face at the early stages of learning these concepts.

3.1 Sequences of Commands

Four basic movement and rotation commands (`fd`, `bk`, `rt`, `lt`) form the basis of what we know as the Logo programming language. Programmers steer a turtle on their screen, initially by executing single commands. This approach gives programmers immediate visual feedback, which is a great advantage concerning error handling. Novices often struggle with rotations since all Logo commands are interpreted relative to the turtle's perspective rather than the programmer's. When executing individual commands, mixed up rotations can be amended on-the-fly. They become a major hassle, however, once multiple commands are stringed together to form longer programs. From that moment on, novices need to learn how to sequentially trace their programs.

3.2 Repetition

Using repetition, pupils create shorter solutions that are less prone to copy-paste errors. New struggles arise from the more complicated execution order and being unaware of the program state:

1. **Execution order:** With repetition, execution order suddenly may be non-sequential. For instance, `repeat 4[fd 100 rt 90]` jumps back to previously executed instructions four times. The longer such a program and the more looping constructs it has, the more difficult it is to read and trace.
2. **Program state:** When learning about repetition, children encounter the concept of state. Knowing that the commands `fd 100 rt 90 fd 100` draw one step of a stair, we might expect `repeat 5[fd 100 rt 90 fd 100]` to draw five steps. This, however, is not the case since the turtle's orientation changes between the first and second iteration of the loop. Logo's state includes turtle attributes (such as orientation and location) and pen attributes (such as color and width).

3.3 Modular Program Design

Pupils learn to master complexity by extending the language with new custom commands. Drawing a house, for instance, can be done by first defining a square and a triangle method and using these as new building blocks. Tracing bugs in such nested programs, however, poses serious challenges for novice programmers: Errors can be hidden anywhere and so, children cannot help but meticulously skim through all the layers of abstraction searching for the root cause of an anomaly. The cognitive load involved is tremendous. We teach pupils to solve problems bottom-up and systematically test every module before using it. Rather than skimming through the whole stack and potentially counting hundreds or thousands of commands (just think about how many strokes an entire flower meadow might take), it suffices to trace the top-most layer of abstraction. With this approach, children learn to master arbitrary levels of abstraction.

Learning to program brings challenges that exceed simple syntactic issues. Every new concept makes tracing increasingly more difficult.

4 What Natural Coping Strategies Do Novices Use?

What approaches do children take when tackling algorithmic tasks? What typical errors occur? How do novices try to recover from semantic mistakes? To answer these questions, we observed pupils who tackled algorithmic tasks in Logo.

4.1 Setup

We conducted four Logo programming courses with primary school children aged 10 to 13. Each course took place at Swiss primary schools and lasted for twenty lessons. At different stages during the course (beginning, middle, and end), we handed out three algorithmic tasks, that the children were supposed to reproduce (see Fig. 1). We collected and manually evaluated the children's solutions and all their intermediate results.

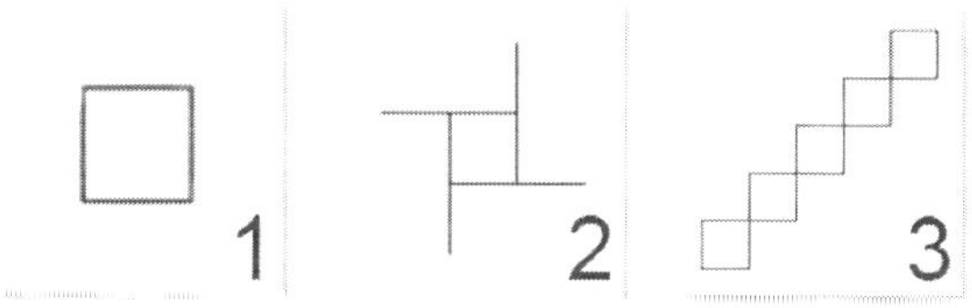

Fig. 1. The children's task was to reproduce these three pictures in Logo

4.2 Problem Decomposition: There Is No Single Correct Solution

Problem decomposition is the first step of the cognitive process a child goes through when solving a task. Different programmers find different solutions to the same problems. Even though all three tasks are rather small (it takes just a handful of lines to draw them), the participants found surprisingly many approaches that correctly solve the tasks. A square, for instance, is only composed of four simple lines and yet, depending on the starting point and the order of traversal, far more than just one or two solutions are possible. More complex shapes yield an even more diverse solution space. We distilled numerous different approaches from the children's solutions and illustrate eight of the approaches in Fig. 2.

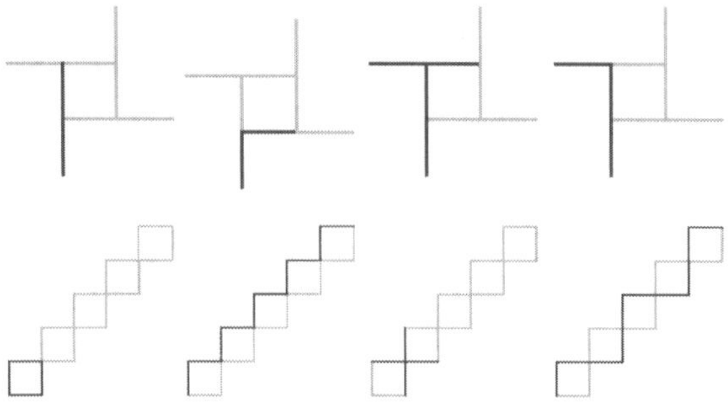

Fig. 2. Multiple ways exist to decompose a problem. In the above picture we show four approaches for each task. The highlighted lines show different fundamental patterns which all yield the same result when executed repeatedly.

4.3 Not Only Beginners Face Semantic Problems

Once pupils start programming, they inevitably face semantic errors. Three problems are typical among Logo programmers: (i) commands are used as black boxes without fully being understood yet, (ii) rotations are confused due to an inconvenient change of perspective, and (iii) novices neglect state invariants. The first two dominate in the beginning but over time, they reduce and give way to the third class of problems.

- **Semantic black boxes:** Most beginners use commands as black boxes and only gain an understanding for the underlying semantics and mathematical relations through experience. They learn that different programs can have the *same effect* (e.g. `rt 45 rt 45` and `rt 54 rt 36` and `rt 90` all have the same global effect). Using *inverse operations*, they learn to undo unwanted operations (e.g. `rt 100` can be undone with `lt 100`).
- **Clash of perspective:** Logo commands are interpreted from the turtle's perspective rather than the programmer's. Hence, novices need to put themselves into the turtle's position, which is cognitively challenging. Clashing perspectives have bewildering effects (e.g., `rt` and `lt` suddenly change their semantic meaning). Children learn to help themselves by aligning their perspective with the turtle – first physically, then mentally.
- **Managing complexity:** Logo is a stateful language and all of its commands have side effects on the turtle's state or the pen's state. Understanding Logo semantics means understanding what effect each command has on the overall program state. Managing local changes, however, is not enough: due to repeating programs, previously executed states may be revisited and pupils need to trace how the state evolves over time. Loop invariants are conditions that need to be upheld in every loop iteration (i.e. initial conditions that are restored in every iteration). They are important when reasoning about correctness and working towards modularity, however, novices often struggle with loop invariants.

Due to several reasons, pupils write semantically incorrect programs whose visual output does not fit their expectations. To recover from these semantic errors, programmers try to establish a connection between each command and its corresponding visual effect while retracing their code. The boy in Fig. 3, for instance, is trying to locate a semantic error in his code by simulating execution using pen and paper. He closely follows each instruction on the screen and draws the corresponding effect on paper. Several attempts on the paper indicate that he is facing difficulties while tracing.

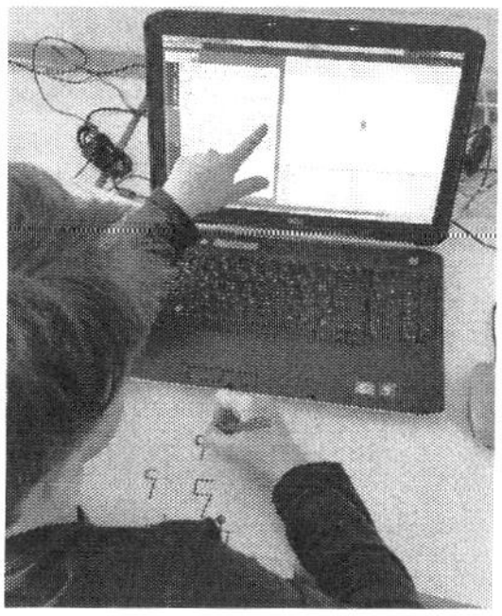

Fig. 3. Manual tracing

4.4 Discussion – Challenges in Tracing

While debugging, pupils need to iterate through their code and retrace each step. The main difficulty in tracing shifts from initially dealing with long and unstructured programs to later managing non-sequential information flow and complexity.

1. **Sequence of commands:** Programs formulated as sequences of commands are read and executed sequentially (Fig. 4a). The more complex a drawing, the longer its corresponding program. Long and unstructured programs, however, are difficult to trace since inexperienced programmers are likely to lose track.
2. **Repetition:** Repetition reduces the descriptive length of any program featuring recurring patterns (Fig. 4b). On the one hand, it takes fewer commands to describe repeating patterns, on the other hand the cognitive work involved in reading and tracing rises due to non-sequential information flow.
3. **Modularity:** By extending the language with new commands, pupils learn to hide complexity behind meaningful names (Fig. 4c). More and more complex programs can be written without increasing the cognitive complexity involved in tracing: Custom commands can be used as if they were built-ins as long as their functionality was tested beforehand.

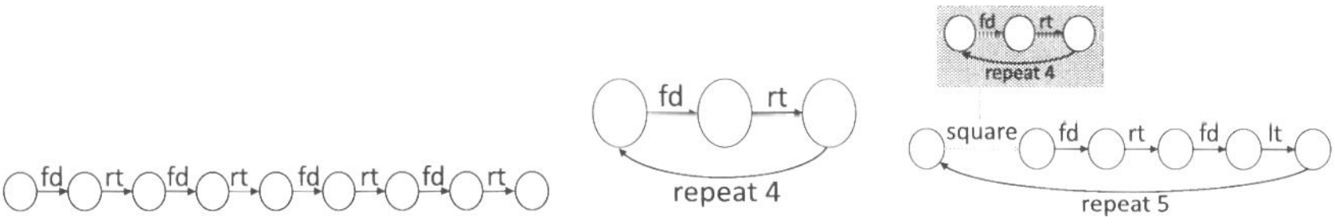

a: Sequences of commands b: Repetition c: Modularity

Fig. 4. Challenges involved in tracing change over time: First, pupils lose themselves in long and unstructured programs; later they struggle following non-sequential information flow; Finally, they learn to hide complexity in sub-modules.

5 Implementing a Reverse Debugger for Logo

In this section, we explain how we extended XLogoOnline with a reverse debugger that allows novices to trace their program during execution and step through their code forward and backward in time. We present our approach and explain how it balances performance against memory consumption.

5.1 Logo's Language Constructs

XLogoOnline is tailored for the Logo programming language and offers a number of programming constructs: commands and control structures.

1. **Commands** serve as functional building blocks with observable effects: Built-in commands (e.g. `fd, rt, setpc`) form the basic vocabulary which can be extended with user-defined commands (e.g. `square, triangle, house`).
2. **Control structures** steer execution: They manipulate the order in which commands are executed (e.g. `repeat, if`).

Programs can be written using only commands (e.g. `fd 100 rt 90 fd 100 rt 90`) or using a combination of commands and control structures (e.g. `repeat 2[fd 100 rt 90]`). Both programs yield the same result despite having different representations.

5.2 Execution: From Raw Text to Visual Output

Logo source code is provided in written form. As raw text, it cannot be interpreted by the computer directly and first needs to be transformed to a more structured intermediate representation. A syntax tree is a hierarchical representation that maps all syntactical elements (i.e. commands and control structures) to nodes that can be traversed in a pre-order fashion (see Fig. 5). When visited, each node triggers its characteristic effect.

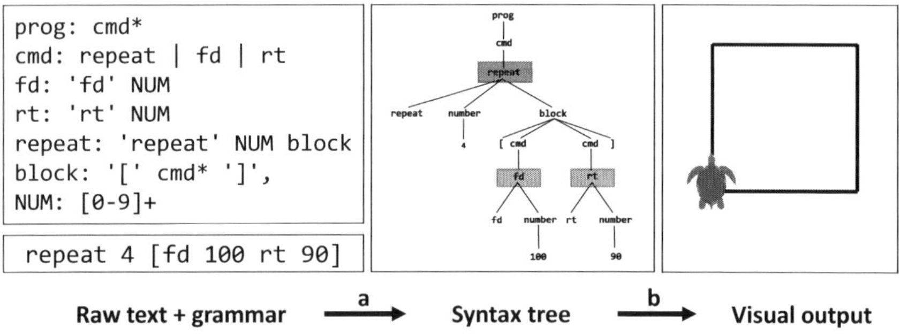

Fig. 5. A syntax tree is created from text and results in visual output once visited.

5.3 Single Stepping: Understanding Program Execution

In professional environments, execution of is often hidden from programmers: code magically produces some output while all intermediate steps remain a mystery. Understanding how solutions emerge, however, is a crucial part in debugging. *Single stepping* is a mechanism that visualizes all steps during execution (i.e., programmers see how the result incrementally develops) and hence gives programmers the opportunity to understand execution flow. We distinguish automatic from manual stepping depending on whether the programmer has manual control over execution or not.

- **Automatic stepping.** Execution can be visualized incrementally by immediately flushing all effects as the computer traverses the syntax tree. In Logo, any program execution can be visualized, yet different programs pose different demands on execution speed: Small programs with few commands (e.g. a square) execute within a fraction of a second. For execution to become observable, a massive slowdown in execution speed is needed. Other programs execute thousands of instructions (e.g. `repeat 360[repeat 360[fd 1 rt 1] rt 1]]`) and execution takes considerably longer. In those cases, a higher execution speed is more appropriate to not cause unwanted delay. In summary, finding a universal execution speed (i.e. flush rate) that works for any program is not easy. Hence, we allow programmers to pick a rate according to their needs and change it dynamically on demand.
- **Manual stepping.** Once execution speed reaches zero, the turtle's world freezes in its current state. Conceptually, this is the moment when automatic stepping turns into manual stepping, a mode that provides additional support in tracing. Programmers manually navigate from command to command and inspect how the program state evolves along the way. When debugging, programmers need to develop an understanding for how their program state evolved into an undesired situation. For this, manual stepping is useful since it assists programmers in tracing

5.4 Reverse Debugging: Can We Go Back in Time?

Even experienced programmers frequently step too far when debugging and run pass locations of interest. In reverse debugging, this problem is addressed by navigating through execution backward in time. We discuss how different approaches handle the trade-off between performance and memory consumption before presenting our approach that balances among both metrics.

Approach 1: Rerunning. One possibility to simulate the behavior of reverse debugging is to rerun the program from the start. With every step back, execution is re-initiated. All that needs to be stored is a single pointer to a node in the syntax tree that is currently being investigated. Instead of running through the entire program, we stop execution at whatever node the pointer currently points at.

Problem: One drawback of this solution is its poor scalability for long and complex programs that consist of many commands. For instance, `repeat 360[repeat 360[fd 1 rt 1] rt 1]` consists of several hundred thousand strokes. If taking one step back requires all of these instructions to be re-executed, the programmer would have to wait too long.

Approach 2: Inversion. An alternative to re-running relies on reverting the previously-executed instructions: we visit each node in the syntax tree in reverse order and undo each command along the way. This idea cannot be implemented for Logo in a purely mathematical way since some Logo instructions are inherently irreversible. In addition, state information can get lost due to being overwritten.

- **Insight 1: Not all commands are reversible.** Commands like `rt` and `fd` are reversible since they cause *relative change* (i.e. they perform additive changes to location and orientation). Other commands like `setxy`, `setpc`, and `cs` cause *absolute change* (i.e. they overwrite previous state) which makes them irreversible in a purely mathematical sense.
- **Insight 2: Reverse traversal is lossy.** Logo's irreversible commands overwrite information that cannot be retrieved later. For instance `setpc blue fd 100 setpc red bk 100` first draws a blue line which then is painted over in red. To correctly undo `bk 100`, we need to know what pen color was used before red, which is no longer known at that point. A stack allows us to solve this problem: state information can be stored to allow for lossless reversal of irreversible commands.

Approach 3: Snapshots. Using a stack, we can easily overcome the problem of lost state information. By taking snapshots of the program state, we capture how the program evolves over time. On demand, we can revert previously executed commands without even causing much computational overhead: the corresponding state can simply be retrieved from the stack. Each snapshot stores a copy of (1) the canvas and (2) the turtle's location and orientation.

Storing the entire bitmap of the canvas, however, consumes a significant amount of memory. Depending on the screen resolution, a considerable amount of information needs to be stored. For instance, during execution of the program `repeat 4[fd 100 rt 90]` eight commands are traversed and all eight states in between are stored on the stack (see Fig. 6). When executed on a screen with a resolution of 1920 × 1080 pixels, we end up with a gigantic amount of over 16 million pixels that need to be saved in memory.

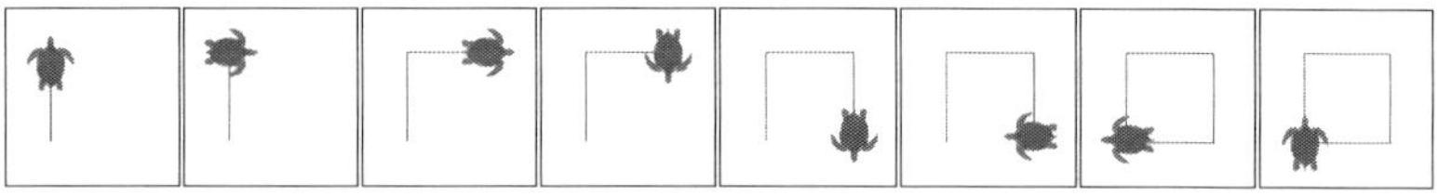

Fig. 6. All states that are traversed need to be stored on the stack

Memory consumption can be improved by changing the canvas' internal representation from bitmap to vector graphics. Rather than handling all pixels individually, we store a textual description of all lines visible on the screen (see Listing 1.1). Three attributes make up one line: a starting point (`x1`, `y1`), an end point (`x2`, `y2`), and the corresponding color (`stroke`).

Listing 1.1. The last of eight snapshots taken when drawing a square

```
<svg height="1080" width="1920">
<line x1="0" y1="100" x2="0" y2="0" stroke="rgb(0,0,0)"/>
<line x1="0" y1="0" x2="100" y2="0" stroke="rgb(0,0,0)"/>
<line x1="100" y1="0" x2="100" y2="100" stroke="rgb(0,0,0)"/>
<line x1="100" y1="100" x2="0" y2="100" stroke="rgb(0,0,0)"/>
</svg>
```

Vector graphics use significantly less space than bitmaps: before, a fixed large number of pixels had to be stored for each snapshot; now the size of each snapshot depends only on the number of lines visible on the screen. Most tasks in our curriculum (polygons, houses, etc.) use comparatively few lines and so the overall memory savings can be as large as three to four orders of magnitude. The overall reduction applies to each snapshot and so adds up to a memory consumption that allows arbitrary Logo programs to be debugged.

6 Conclusion

Young programmers need to learn debugging – it is an essential skill for any programmer since semantic errors can neither be prevented nor can a computer detect them automatically (unless the programmer's intention is known beforehand). Our debugger supports children in tracing through erroneous programs both forward and backward in time. By doing so, programmers get to observe how their code is executed and thereby acquire a better understanding for the notional machine underneath. Whether and how our debugger improves the pupils' understanding is subject to future research. Moreover, we will investigate whether there is a gender-related difference between boys' and girls' debugging behavior.

Our debugger has one limitation that is not critical for our target group but might be relevant for others: we decided to treat both built-in and user-defined commands as atomic operations. This decision fits our methodology which requires pupils to test new modules before using them. Since all program calls are considered atomic, we never step into them which, however, implies that recursive method calls cannot be debugged. This is a limitation that may be relevant for higher grades; on primary school level, it has only little impact since we do not teach recursion.

References

1. ABC. Berkeley to U.S. naval proving ground, ebp, 27 May 1946

2. Annamaa, A.: Introducing thonny, a python IDE for learning programming. In: Proceedings of the 15th Koli Calling Conference on Computing Education Research, Koli Calling 2015, pp. 117–121. ACM, New York (2015)
3. Balzer, R.M.: EXDAMS: extendable debugging and monitoring system. In: Proceedings of the May 14–16, 1969, Spring Joint Computer Conference, AFIPS 1969 (Spring), pp. 567–580. ACM, New York (1969)
4. Bender, W.: The sugar learning platform: affordances for computational thinking. Revista de Educación a Distancia (54) (2017)
5. Beyer, K.W.: Grace Hopper and the Invention of the Information Age (2015)
6. Black, A.P., Nierstrasz, O., Ducasse, S., Pollet, D.: Pharo by example. Lulu.com (2010)
7. Chmiel, R., Loui, M.C.: Debugging: from novice to expert. ACM SIGCSE Bull. **36**, 17–21 (2004)
8. Cuneo, D.O.: Young children and turtle graphics programming: Generating and debugging simple turtle programs. ERIC (1986)
9. Czyz, J.K., Jayaraman, B.: Declarative and visual debugging in eclipse. In: Proceedings of the 2007 OOPSLA Workshop on Eclipse Technology eXchange, pp. 31–35. ACM (2007)
10. Fairley, R.E.: Aladdin: assembly language assertion driven debugging interpreter. IEEE Trans. Softw. Eng. **4**, 426–428 (1979)
11. Feurzeig, W., et al.: Programming-languages as a conceptual framework for teaching mathematics. Final report on the first fifteen months of the logo project (1969)
12. Forster, M., Hauser, U., Serafini, G., Staub, J.: Autonomous recovery from programming errors made by primary school children. In: Pozdniakov, S.N., Dagienė, V. (eds.) ISSEP 2018. LNCS, vol. 11169, pp. 17–29. Springer, Cham (2018). https://doi.org/10.1007/978-3-030-02750-6_2
13. Gould, J.D.: Some psychological evidence on how people debug computer programs. Int. J. Man-Mach. Stud. **7**(2), 151–182 (1975)
14. Hennessy, J.L.: Symbolic debugging of optimized code (1979)
15. Hollings, C.: The lovelace byron papers. Transcript of folios, pp. 1–179 (2015)
16. Hromkovič, J.: Einführung in die Programmierung mit LOGO, vol. 1, 3rd edn. Springer, Wiesbaden (2014). https://doi.org/10.1007/978-3-658-04832-7
17. Hromkovič, J.: Einfach Informatik 5/6. Programmieren. Begleitband. Klett und Balmer AG Baar (2019)
18. Hromkovič, J., Serafini, G., Staub, J.: XLogoOnline: a single-page, browser-based programming environment for schools aiming at reducing cognitive load on pupils. In: Dagiene, V., Hellas, A. (eds.) ISSEP 2017. LNCS, vol. 10696, pp. 219–231. Springer, Cham (2017). https://doi.org/10.1007/978-3-319-71483-7_18
19. Johnson, M.S.: Some requirements for architectural support of software debugging. SIGPLAN Not. **17**(4), 140–148 (1982)
20. Klahr, D., Carver, S.M.: Cognitive objectives in a logo debugging curriculum: instruction, learning, and transfer. Cogn. Psychol. **20**(3), 362–404 (1988)
21. Lister, R., et al.: A multi-national study of reading and tracing skills in novice programmers. ACM SIGCSE Bull. **36**, 119–150 (2004)
22. Lyon, G.: COBOL Instrumentation and Debugging: A Case Study, vol. 13. US Department of Commerce, National Bureau of Standards (1978)
23. Papert, S.: Mindstorms: Children, Computers, and Powerful Ideas. Basic Books Inc., New York (1980)
24. Perkins, D.N., Hancock, C., Hobbs, R., Martin, F., Simmons, R.: Conditions of learning in novice programmers. J. Educ. Comput. Res. **2**(1), 37–55 (1986)

25. Sipitakiat, A., Nusen, N.: Robo-blocks: designing debugging abilities in a tangible programming system for early primary school children. In: Proceedings of the 11th International Conference on Interaction Design and Children, pp. 98–105. ACM (2012)
26. Tropp, H.: Campbell, interview, 11 April 1972 (1972)
27. Scratch wiki. Single stepping in scratch 3.0, Status as of August 30, 2019

Contemporary Computer Science Ideas in School Informatics

Unplugged Activities in the Context of AI

Annabel Lindner[1(✉)], Stefan Seegerer[1], and Ralf Romeike[2]

[1] Computing Education Research Group, Friedrich-Alexander-Universität Erlangen-Nürnberg, Erlangen, Germany
{annabel.lindner,stefan.seegerer}@fau.de
[2] Computing Education Research Group, Freie Universität, Berlin, Germany
ralf.romeike@fu-berlin.de

Abstract. Due to its great importance in the media, the start-up world and the political discussion, artificial intelligence (AI) is becoming increasingly relevant as a topic for schools. Until now, approaches to making AI tangible for students without actually programming an AI system have been rare. To address this circumstance, a teaching sequence of unplugged activities about AI has been developed and is presented. AI Unplugged provides CS Unplugged activities that present the ideas and concepts of computer science without using computers. The activities shed light on important concepts of AI and make it possible to convey the central ideas of artificial intelligence to the students. In addition, they offer starting points for discussing social issues around AI. This article describes the activities and their theoretical background, outlines a possible course of instruction, and describes practical experiences with *AI Unplugged*.

Keywords: Artificial intelligence · CS Unplugged · Machine learning · Teaching activities

1 Introduction

Probably no other computer science topic currently receives as much media attention as artificial intelligence (AI). AI is used in many areas: we speak with artificial intelligence systems like Siri, Cortana or Alexa, get "intelligent" product recommendations when shopping online or read computer-generated texts. More and more software products are advertised as AI-supported and governments are addressing the topic in strategy papers, e.g. [5]. This social significance also makes the topic relevant for schools, especially when taking into consideration that, e.g., according to a current survey, 65% of Britons have no or only limited knowledge of AI [12]. However, due to the complexity of the topic, a tool-based approach for mediating AI is, if at all, only suitable for older age groups. Unplugged Activities can make it easier for teachers and students to deal with the topic of AI and, therefore, can be used to introduce the topic even to younger learners.

S. N. Pozdniakov and V. Dagienė (Eds.): ISSEP 2019, LNCS 11913, pp. 123–135, 2019.
https://doi.org/10.1007/978-3-030-33759-9_10

2 Artificial Intelligence - Theoretical Background

Artificial intelligence has existed as a branch of computer science since 1956 [8], but its actual practical relevance has only come with the availability of corresponding computing capacities. The term *artificial intelligence* represents, above all, a comprehensive expression for different technologies and procedures, in which classic topics of AI and "newer" approaches can be distinguished. These two directions differ in the underlying paradigm. Especially in the field of machine learning, a change from symbolic knowledge representation, as it is applied in rule-based systems, to sub-symbolic knowledge representation has taken place. Sub-symbolic knowledge representation is, e.g., used in neural networks and does not permit an explicit representation of the aspects the system has learned [17].

The concept of machine learning is almost synonymous with these "newer" approaches. It describes the ability of AI systems to derive patterns and underlying rules from large amounts of data. The result of this learning process is a model that can be used for the successful processing of unknown data or problems. A technology that allows such learning processes is artificial neural networks. These networks consist of artificial neurons whose function is adapted from biological neurons in the human brain. Within the network, artificial neurons are connected to each other. They absorb information, process it and then pass it on within the network.

With regard to the learning process of artificial systems, three basic types of learning, which are used to train a model, can be distinguished. Supervised learning describes a process, where the expected result of an algorithm in response to a particular input is already known. The algorithm's actual output is compared to this expectation and conclusions are drawn as to how the model needs to be modified. Supervised learning mechanisms contrast with unsupervised learning, in which the model changes independently based on the similarity of inputs. This type of learning is especially used when no classified data for training the AI system is available. Reinforcement learning is the third basic type of learning. This method evaluates the reactions of a learning agent to certain input data. Based on the evaluation received, the system adapts its responses. In modern AI systems, these approaches often use a sub-symbolic representation of knowledge, i.e. the knowledge acquired by the system is only implicitly represented, e.g. by different edge weights in a neural network, and concrete solution patterns are not visible. The central principle of symbolic AI, on the other hand, is the explicit representation of knowledge and the application of logic. Typical topics of this classic AI are search procedures, planning, knowledge representation (e.g. with decision trees) and inference using logic [8].

3 Artificial Intelligence as a Topic in K-12

With the rising social relevance of artificial intelligence, which is primarily connected to great progress in the field of machine learning, AI is now increasingly discussed in educational contexts, for example in CS4All courses at universities [20]. Furthermore, the topic is gaining importance in the design of school curricula (e.g. [6] or [13]), and e.g. China has made AI a nationwide teaching content in general schools [25]. In order to achieve standarized curricular contents, suggestions for "Big Ideas" of artificial intelligence [22] have been made following the Big Ideas of K12 Computer Science Education [2]. A concept by Kandlhofer et al., which already starts teaching AI basics in kindergarten, also aims at the underlying ideas and principles of AI and the development of *AI Literacy* [15].

Especially for traditional AI topics, a number of learning materials can already be found. For example, computer science in context [16] offers a teaching series about chatbots, which works with Weizenbaum's ELIZA [24]. However, sub-symbolic approaches are also adapted for teaching: Kahn et al. present a concept that allows students to use different AI services in the programming environment Snap*!* [14], and Google provides a collection of AI experiments for learners[1]. Moreover, *Machine Learning for Kids* provides online demos in which students can train classification models and then use them in Scratch[2]. Additionally, there are approaches that use robots to teach AI topics[3].

However, such initiatives often do not cover the field of artificial intelligence extensively, but rather focus on smaller sub-areas (currently, a strong focus on machine learning can be seen). Thus, there are only a few approaches that try to convey the field of artificial intelligence in its breadth and with a comprehensive teaching concept until now. Moreover, in many projects, a purely application-oriented perspective is taken. Especially when complex technologies like neural networks are discussed, the aspect of exploring the ideas behind AI technologies is disregarded. However, the underlying concepts of artificial intelligence are difficult to grasp in pure application situations, so that AI systems remain a black box in such mediation concepts. Therefore, in order to foster sustainable education about AI, teaching materials should additionally take a structural and a socio-cultural perspective on AI as it is presented in the Dagstuhl triangle [4] into account and focus on the underlying ideas and concepts of AI.

For this reason, the unplugged activities developed aim to make the underlying concepts of artificial intelligence accessible without neglecting the breadth of the field. At the same time, a strongly formalized, mathematical representation, which would significantly complicate the access for students, is forgone.

4 AI Unplugged Activities

CS Unplugged provides a variety of activities that help learners of all ages understand the ideas and concepts of computer science enactively and without using computers. CS Unplugged activities have been employed in the context of computer science education for over 30 years [1]. For example, such activities are used to introduce students to programming in primary school [11], in extracurricular

[1] https://experiments.withgoogle.com/.
[2] https://machinelearningforkids.co.uk/.
[3] e.g. Cozmo (https://www.anki.com/de-de/cozmo) or PopBots [23].

learning laboratories [9] or in adult education [10]. In the field of AI, there is little Unplugged material available so far, although, due to the complexity and versatility of the field, Unplugged activities are well suited for the topic.

According to Nishida et al. [18], Unplugged activities show certain distinctive features that make them particularly suitable for learners. The following features are listed:

- There is *no direct use of computers* in the activity.
- A *game or challenge* is the central element of the activity so that CS is mediated playfully.
- The activity involves physical objects to foster *kinaesthetic engagement.*
- In the activity, *students are encouraged to interact* and discover big ideas of certain CS topics on their own.
- The activity is *easy to implement* and no expensive materials are needed.
- *Sharing* and remixing activities is important for the Unplugged concept.
- The activity offers a *sense of story* to engage (especially younger) learners.

In the following, the course and theoretical background of five AI Unplugged activities, which illustrate different elementary concepts behind AI systems and are based on the criteria of Nishida et al. [18], are outlined and discussed.

4.1 Activity 1: Classification with Decision Trees – the Good-Monkey-Bad-Monkey Game

Fig. 1. Activity 1: Finding classification strategies to distinguish biting and non-biting monkeys with picture cards.

How does a computer make decisions independently? How does it decide whether a person is athletic, should get a loan, etc.? Such classification processes are a common application of AI. In this activity, students create classification models to distinguish biting from non-biting monkeys by using decision trees. To achieve this, they examine how certain sample elements (picture cards with monkey faces) belong to a preset category (biting or non-biting monkey, see Fig. 1). In pairs, the students develop criteria for each category that can be used to classify new elements. The students' models are then tested with new examples and the accuracy of the prediction is evaluated to determine the best model. To show possible weaknesses of classification models, the students are furthermore confronted with elements that do not belong to any of the preset categories and encouraged to think about real-life examples where this could be problematic. The activity can, for example, be decontextualized with a learning task in which the abstraction process from the concrete game to general machine learning processes is made and where important terms like training and test data are introduced.

The activity is suitable to introduce basic aspects of machine learning and, at the same time, highlights problems that may arise from the use of AI systems for classification tasks. After working with this activity, students can explain how a computer learns to successfully classify elements using an already classified set of examples, describe the training process of a classification system, and emphasize the importance of training and test data. Furthermore, real situations in which decisions of artificial intelligence can be problematic can be described.

4.2 Activity 2: #deeplearning – Recognition of Images with Neural Networks

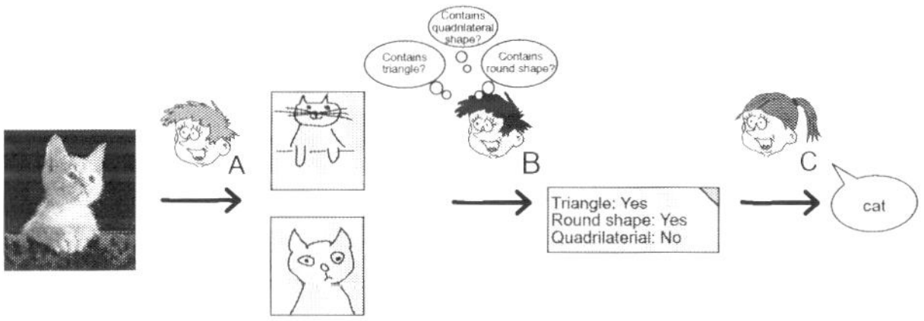

Fig. 2. Activity 2: students perform image classification.

How can a computer recognize objects? How does a computer decide whether a photo shows a dog, a cat, or a mouse? How can it tell buildings from people? It is very easy for people to recognize objects in their environment. However, for a computer, which, e.g., has to recognize objects to navigate securely in a self-propelled car, this is a complex task. In this activity, children and adolescents have the opportunity to understand how computers recognize the objects displayed in images. In addition, the term deep learning, which refers to the use of complex, multi-layered neural networks in AI systems, is taken up.

In this activity, students engage in teams of three or more and assume different roles (in the following called A, B, and C). A takes an image from a stack of photo cards (the cards show images of cats, houses and cars, A conceals the photo from B and C), quickly draws two different sketches of it and passes them on to student B. While making sure that C does not see the drafts, B checks whether quadrilateral shapes, triangular shapes or round shapes are included in the sketches. This information is collected by B and passed on to C. C then evaluates the information received using a preset table and announces whether the original picture was a house, a car or a cat. Finally, A confirms whether the solution is correct (see Fig. 2).

This activity, which centers around image recognition, invites the students to assume the roles of different layers within a neural network for image classification. In this process of extracting features from a photograph and classifying the image, the students recognize the limitations of the system (e.g. that only object categories which are already familiar to the network can be recognized and that more complex features are needed if they want to recognize new object categories) and consider what modifications to the network are necessary to achieve better results with their network. The activity introduces basic aspects of neural networks and their layered architecture and, at the same time, highlights challenges that may be faced when using AI systems for image recognition tasks. Afterwards, the students can explain how the number of layers in a neural network is connected to the identification of more complex features. They can furthermore describe on a basic level, how images are processed in image classification applications and which limitations these applications have.

4.3 Activity 3 and 4: Reinforcement Learning – Beat the Crocodile and Back to the Roots – Crocodile Chess and Classic AI

Computers that defeat humans in playing chess are not a new phenomenon. The Chinese board game Go, on the other hand, was considered so complex that only humans can master it – until Google proved professional human players wrong with AlphaGo. The AI system had developed a strategy which was far superior to the one of its human opponent. Activity 3 outlines how computers develop such strategies for playing games independently by using reinforcement learning, although they only know the rules and possible moves of the game. Activity 4 serves to show the differences between these learning AI systems and classic approaches to AI that aim to make knowledge accessible for machines by using logic and mathematically formalized knowledge. To achieve this, the reinforcement learning activity is implemented with an expert system instead. Although both activities can be used independently from each other, we recommend combining activity 3 and 4. In this way, students are able to compare "traditional" AI with machine learning techniques by basically playing the same game. They explore how machine learning algorithms can be implemented independently from the underlying game, while expert systems are difficult to initialize and require a lot of expert knowledge.

The game underlying both the activities "Beat the Crocodile" (activity 3) and "Back to the Roots" (activity 4) was initially created by Martin Gardner as *The Sweet Learning Computer* for Hexapawn [7]. Our version of the game contains a series of modifications compared to the original one: it uses the same storyline as activity 1 and is, therefore, realized as a monkey-crocodile mini-chess. Furthermore, awarding positive rewards, which is also an important part of reinforcement learning but not provided in the original game, has been integrated into crocodile chess. Additionally, the board position overview has been optimized by consequently subsuming symmetrical board positions. This increases the comprehensibility of the game and makes it easier for students to quickly find the matching positions on the game sheet.

In both activities, two students each play a game of mini-chess against each other (see Fig. 3). One pupil takes on the role of a "paper" computer. If the two activities are combined, the students should swap roles after the first game. In activity 3, the computer initially selects its moves randomly from a given list of all possible moves in any board position and gradually learns with a token system, which moves lead to victory and which ones end in defeat. By using this procedure, the computer develops a strategy and becomes better and better over time. In contrast, in activity 4, the computer does not learn its behavior, but works according to the rules of logic: this time, the computer's behavior is already preset and there is only one possible action for every board position. Consequently, the computer wins every game right from the start. After playing, the 3×3 chessboard is modified and the students are confronted with a 4×4 board. They have to consider now, how the computer can be adjusted to the new conditions when either machine learning or an expert system is used.

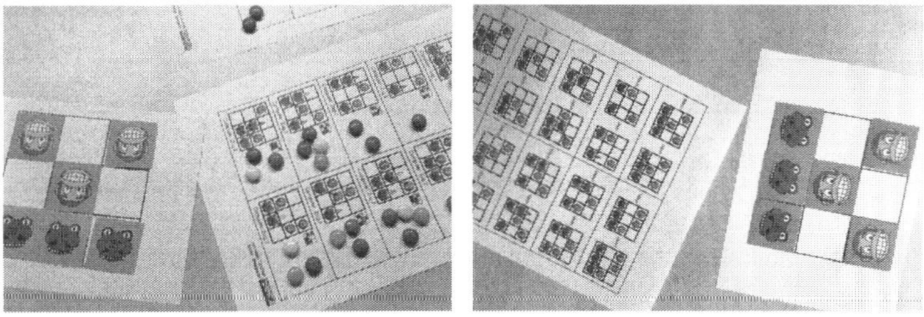

Fig. 3. Activity 3 and 4: students compare principles of machine learning (in this case reinforcement learning) and traditional approaches.

4.4 Activity 5: "And Oh! I Am Glad that Nobody Knew I'm a Computer!" - the Turing Test

What behavior does a machine have to show to be intelligent? What exactly does artificial intelligence mean? These questions have been on the minds of researchers since the beginnings of artificial intelligence. In 1950, Alan Turing developed the Turing Test, a method for determining whether a machine is intelligent. This activity, borrowed from the original unplugged materials [3], recreates the Turing Test with students and is intended to stimulate discussion as to whether computers can actually show something like intelligence. In addition, it becomes clear how easily one can be misled by a machine with carefully chosen examples of "intelligence". The activity suggests a series of questions that can be used to find out which student has taken the role of the computer and which student answers as themselves. However, teachers have the possibility to design further questions themselves or to let the students develop questions which can help to expose the computer. Afterwards, students can critically assess the intelligent behavior of AI systems and identify features that make the AI system appear intelligent when interacting with humans.

4.5 AI Unplugged and the CS Unplugged Criteria

The activities described align with the CS Unplugged criteria stated in [18]. Computers are not used in any of the activities. Furthermore, they all center around a game or challenge: activity 1 challenges students to compete against each other, activity 2 uses limited time frames to activate the students. In activity 3 and 4 students engage in a board game, while activity 5 asks learners to identify the computer. The activities involve physical objects such as picture cards, photographs, or board games which are interactively used by the students. To guarantee easy implementation, all the material needed is made available and can simply be printed. In order to be suitable for being used in class, all activities involve more than one student and foster interaction among the students. Moreover, the students have to explore the concepts that are mediated in the activities by themselves. The use of animals in activity 1, 3 and 4 (monkeys and crocodiles) is both appealing for younger learners and funny for adolescents or adults.

4.6 Unplugged Activities as Part of a Curriculum

Besides being used in individual lessons, the activities described in Sect. 4 can be conducted in a curriculum of six to eight lessons that serves to introduce artificial intelligence in K-12. The aim of the lessons is to discover and playfully explore the underlying concepts of artificial intelligence, a possible sequence of how this can be done is sketched in the following. The target group is in particular pupils at secondary school level 1 and 2, although some activities can also be used (possibly adapted) in other learning scenarios.

The sequence described addresses several of the content and process areas outlined in the educational standards for computer science in Germany [19] and, therefore, seizes on various competence areas. A particular focus lies on the content areas *computer science systems* and *computer science, man and society*, as well as the process areas *justification and evaluation* and *modelling and implementation*, but the other content and process areas are also partly applied. The sequence depicted in Table 1 wants to show that artificial intelligence can take many forms and that current AI systems are limited to highly specialized applications. In addition, the social effects of AI systems are discussed and it is illustrated that artificial intelligence is less "magical" than one might initially assume.

Table 1. Example course of lessons

Lesson	Topic	Description	AI Unplugged
1	Introduction to AI	Students explore the concept of machine learning and its effects on society	Activity 1
2–3	Neural Networks and Deep Learning	Using image classification with neural networks, the pupils explore another area of AI and analyze the functioning of neural networks. They also learn what is behind the term deep learning	Activity 2
4–5	Machine Learning and Classic AI	Using two strategies for the same game, the students compare "new" and traditional approaches to AI	Activity 3 and 4
6	What is artificial intelligence?	With the help of the Turing test, students explore the question of whether computers can really show intelligence and reflect on ethical aspects of AI	Activity 5

At the beginning of the sequence, the topic is introduced on the basis of object classification, which is, e.g., important for self-driving cars. Following this introduction, the image recognition activity serves as a context for machine learning with neural networks, before these machine learning approaches are compared to traditional AI. The game from activity 3 and 4 is used to highlight the difference between learning and rule-based systems so that the breadth of the subject area is illustrated. Finally, students reflect on AI and the question as to what extent computers can be intelligent is discussed. In a typical lesson structure, the Unplugged Activities open the lessons and are followed by a phase of decontextualization, where the concrete game or activity situations are abstracted and general principles are mediated by using learning tasks, group work, individual research, "re-plugged" activities etc.

This combination of Unplugged Activities with further approaches and activities is central to the success of the activities. As Thies and Vahrenhold [21] highlight, CS Unplugged Activities are most suitable for introductory and outreach purposes but should not be used as stand-alone units or instead of comprehensive teaching materials as their learning goals often do not provide the necessary depth and cover all cognitive processes. For this reason, the material presented should not be considered a fully extensive teaching unit but rather as introductory activities that need to be supported by further material adjusted to the setting and the group of learners.

5 Discussion

AI Unplugged was tested in a school experiment with a year nine and a year ten class of the German Realschule (ages 14 to 16). Even though most of the students already had a rudimentary idea of the term artificial intelligence, they did not have specific prior knowledge in the subject area. Prior to the intervention, many pupils associated the term with robots that acted independently and were capable of learning, they could not give any details about functional principles of AI.

Throughout the lessons, the students quickly and comprehensively grasped the principles of the activities, they were concentrated and had fun working in teams. For example, when it came to establishing rules for classifying monkeys (Activity 1), a competition developed to create the best classification model. This competition was followed by a lively discussion about how fair classification models could be. Thus, while exploring technical principles of AI, the students independently came across ethical and socio-cultural issues of AI and discovered limitations of AI applications. Furthermore, the students discussed questions and problems with their classmates and worked out solutions in teams without needing much assistance from the teacher. Even pupils who, in the beginning, were skeptical about the idea of doing computer science without computers were motivated by the activities and showed great interest in the topic afterwards.

During the subsequent decontextualization, a clear rise in knowledge was noticeable among the pupils: After the implementation of AI Unplugged activities, the pupils were able to explain the concept of machine learning and were able to discuss social implications of artificial intelligence on this basis. They quickly recognized the connections between individual activities and the underlying concepts of artificial intelligence and were able to draw parallels to phenomena they knew from everyday life (e.g. Captchas, Google image search, etc.). This created "aha" effects, even during the activities, and enabled the students to recognize the limits of corresponding AI systems.

Unplugged Activities are a popular way to teach CS concepts and successfully conveyed in teaching [21]. But are they applicable to complex fields such as AI as well? The use of Unplugged Activities in which the students take over the tasks of the AI and experience the functional principles of AI systems does not only support learning about AI but makes the students reflect about their own thinking and decision-making processes as well. Even though the starting point of these activities are questions like "How does a computer make decisions independently? How does the computer recognize objects?", they also stimulate reflections on one's own thinking by asking the students to fulfill the AI's tasks: "How do I make decisions? How can humans identify objects in their environment?" At this point, the strength of Unplugged approaches particularly comes into effect: the students can relate to previous knowledge about how their own thinking works when approaching the topic of artificial intelligence. They observe or compare how certain mechanisms of thinking are automated and how machine learning is realized so that the process of creating artificial intelligence can be retraced. Reflecting on their own thinking and ways of acting makes it easier for the students to fathom out the topic. Unplugged Activities foster this aspect and, therefore, make a detailed analysis even of complex topics possible. Nevertheless, certain principles of AI are hard to explain with human ways of thinking and are difficult (or nearly impossible) to understand for humans. Thus, it should be considered in future research if these concepts can be mediated with Unplugged Activities.

6 Conclusion

The AI Unplugged Activities are well suited to comprehensively present the complex topic of artificial intelligence. They allow action-oriented access to the topic of AI, without being dependent on a technical framework. The topic can thus be conveyed in a less complex way and, at the same time, can be expanded upon with various software tools. Additionally, for teachers wary of introducing the topic of AI due to its thematic complexity and the technical hurdles involved (setting up program libaries, etc.), the Unplugged Activities offer an opportunity to integrate the topic into the classroom.

Since AI Unplugged Activities incite the students to reflect upon their own ways of thinking and acting and to associate them with the computer's course of action, Unplugged Activities seem to be particularly suitable to introduce the topic of artificial intelligence. Furthermore, the conception of the activities makes it possible to use them as a coherent teaching sequence for AI, as well as to individually bring them in as an in-between activity or as a supplement to other approaches to AI. The material is available online under Creative Commons License.[4] The online offer also contains further material and links.

References

1. Bell, T., Rosamond, F., Casey, N.: Computer science unplugged and related projects in math and computer science popularization. In: Bodlaender, H.L., Downey, R., Fomin, F.V., Marx, D. (eds.) The Multivariate Algorithmic Revolution and Beyond. LNCS, vol. 7370, pp. 398–456. Springer, Heidelberg (2012). https://doi.org/10.1007/978-3-642-30891-8_18
2. Bell, T., Tymann, P., Yehudai, A.: The big ideas in computer science for K-12 curricula. Bull. EATCS **1**(124) (2018)
3. Bell, T., Witten, I., Fellows, M.: Computer Science Unplugged: Off-line Activities and Games for All Ages. Citeseer (1998)
4. Brinda, T., Diethelm, I.: Education in the digital networked world. In: Tatnall, A., Webb, M. (eds.) WCCE 2017. IAICT, vol. 515, pp. 653–657. Springer, Cham (2017). https://doi.org/10.1007/978-3-319-74310-3_66
5. Bundesregierung: Strategie Künstliche Intelligenz der Bundesregierung [German strategy for artificial intelligence] (2018). https://www.bmbf.de/files/Nationale_KI-Strategie.pdf. Accessed 18 June 2019
6. CSTA: About the CSTA K-12 computer science standards (2017). https://www.csteachers.org/page/standards. Accessed 15 June 2019

[4] https://ddi.cs.fau.de/schule/ai-unplugged/.

7. Demšar, I., Demšar, J.: CS unplugged: experiences and extensions. In: Brodnik, A., Vahrenhold, J. (eds.) ISSEP 2015. LNCS, vol. 9378, pp. 106–117. Springer, Cham (2015). https://doi.org/10.1007/978-3-319-25396-1_10
8. Ertel, W.: Introduction to Artificial Intelligence. Springer, Cham (2018). https://doi.org/10.1007/978-3-319-58487-4
9. Gallenbacher, J.: The adventure of computer science. In: Böckenhauer, H.-J., Komm, D., Unger, W. (eds.) Adventures Between Lower Bounds and Higher Altitudes. LNCS, vol. 11011, pp. 538–548. Springer, Cham (2018). https://doi.org/10.1007/978-3-319-98355-4_31
10. Garcia, D., Harvey, B., Segars, L.: CS principles pilot at University of California, Berkeley. ACM Inroads **3**(2), 58–60 (2012)
11. Geldreich, K., Funke, A., Hubwieser, P.: A programming circus for primary schools. In: Proceedings of the 9th International Conference on Informatics in Schools: Situation, Evolution, and Perspectives, pp. 49–50 (2016)
12. Holder, C., Khurana, V., Watts, M.: Artificial intelligence: public perception, attitude and trust (2018). https://www.bristows.com/assets/pdf/Artificial%20Intelligence_%20Public%20Perception%20Attitude%20and%20Trust%20(Bristows).pdf. Accessed 06 June 2019
13. International Society for Technology in Education (ISTE): Bold new program helps teachers and students explore the power of AI (2018). https://www.iste.org/explore/articleDetail?articleid=2229. Accessed 15 June 2019
14. Kahn, K., Megasari, R., Piantari, E., Junaeti, E.: AI programming by children using snap! block programming in a developing country. In: EC-TEL Practitioner Proceedings 2018: 13th European Conference On Technology Enhanced Learning, Leeds, UK, 3–6 September 2018 (2018). http://ceur-ws.org/Vol-2193/paper1.pdf
15. Kandlhofer, M., Steinbauer, G., Hirschmugl-Gaisch, S., Huber, P.: Artificial intelligence and computer science in education: from kindergarten to university. In: 2016 IEEE Frontiers in Education Conference (FIE), pp. 1–9. IEEE (2016)
16. Knobelsdorf, M., Schulte, C.: Computer science in context: pathways to computer science. In: Proceedings of the Seventh Baltic Sea Conference on Computing Education Research - Volume 88, Koli Calling 2007, pp. 65–76 (2007)
17. Langley, P.: The changing science of machine learning. Mach. Learn. **82**(3), 275–279 (2011). https://doi.org/10.1007/s10994-011-5242-y
18. Nishida, T., Kanemune, S., Idosaka, Y., Namiki, M., Bell, T., Kuno, Y.: A CS unplugged design pattern. ACM SIGCSE Bull. **41**(1), 231–235 (2009)
19. Puhlmann, H., et al.: Grundsätze und Standards für die Informatik in der Schule [Principles and standards for computer science education in schools]. Bildungsstandards Informatik für die Sekundarstufe I. Beilage zu LOG IN (150/151) (2008)
20. Seegerer, S., Romeike, R.: Was jeder über Informatik lernen sollte - Eine Analyse von Hochschulkursen für Studierende anderer Fachrichtungen [What everyone should know about computer science - an analysis of university courses for students from other fields]. In: HDI 2018, Potsdam, pp. 13–28 (2018). https://publishup.uni-potsdam.de/files/41354/cid12.pdf
21. Thies, R., Vahrenhold, J.: Reflections on outreach programs in CS classes: learning objectives for "unplugged" activities. In: Proceedings of the 43rd ACM Technical Symposium on Computer Science Education, SIGCSE 2012, pp. 487–492. ACM, New York (2012). https://doi.org/10.1145/2157136.2157281
22. Touretzky, D., Gardner-McCune, C., Martin, F., Seehorn, D.: Envisioning AI for K-12: what should every child know about AI? In: "Blue sky talk" at the Thirty-Third AAAI Conference on Artificial Intelligence (AAAI-19) (2019)

23. Williams, R., Park, H.W., Oh, L., Breazeal, C.: PopBots: designing an artificial intelligence curriculum for early childhood education (2019)
24. Witten, H., Hornung, M.: Chatbots Teil 1: Einführung in eine Unterrichtsreihe zu Informatik im Kontext (IniK). [Chatbots, part 1: Introduction to a teaching sequence about computer science in context]. LOG IN **28**(154/155), 51–60 (2008)
25. Yu, Y., Chen, Y.: Design and development of high school artificial intelligence textbook based on computational thinking. Open Access Libr. J. **5**(09), 1 (2018)

Machine Learning Unplugged - Development and Evaluation of a Workshop About Machine Learning

Elisaweta Ossovski(✉) and Michael Brinkmeier

Universität Osnabrück, Wachsbleiche 27, 49090 Osnabrück, Germany
{eossovski,mbrinkmeier}@uni-osnabrueck.de

Abstract. Machine learning, being an important part of artificial intelligence, is increasingly discussed and rated in the media without explaining its functionality. This can lead to misconceptions of its real impact and range of application, a problem especially concerning young people. This contribution focuses on the theory-driven development and practical experience with an unplugged workshop concept, which is about a simple technique of machine learning, as a basis for possible teaching units for high school students. For this purpose, the focus of the workshop is an action-oriented method to simulate the classification of screws with two different lengths. Workshop participants can reconstruct linear classification by moving a classifier represented by a wooden strip according to defined rules after each insertion of training data on a pinboard. The aim is to examine whether and how the topic can be made understandable at school. Pre- and posttests are used to evaluate the impact of the workshop on the participants' image of artificial intelligence and machine learning. The results of this research suggest that it is possible to reduce simple methods of machine learning for teaching this topic at school. Moreover, it seems that even a 90-min workshop can change the participants' conceptions of machine learning and artificial intelligence to a more realistic appreciation of their impact.

Keywords: Machine learning · Linear classification · Unplugged · K-12 education

1 Introduction

Being a part of artificial intelligence, machine learning is a current topic of discussion in the media, politics and economy. There is a constant stream of discussions that rate artificial intelligence either dramatically dangerous or as a miracle cure, when autonomously driving cars, diagnostic systems for disease risks or data processing by large corporations are debated.

Thus, there is a danger that an assessment of the topic will quickly develop, which, however, is strongly focused on the areas present in the media.

E. Ossovski—The author is an ELES research fellow.

S. N. Pozdniakov and V. Dagienė (Eds.): ISSEP 2019, LNCS 11913, pp. 136–146, 2019.
https://doi.org/10.1007/978-3-030-33759-9_11

This means that it is not necessarily based on knowledge of the actual functionality of machine learning and the diverse application possibilities. In the examined curricula for computer science teaching in Lower Saxony [10, 11], North Rhine-Westphalia [9] as well as Bavaria [13, 14] there are no topics covering any parts of artificial intelligence, only the effects of computer systems on society are discussed. This, however, tends to reinforce the possibly distorted media impression, since the pupils have to discuss the effects of systems whose technical functionality and significance they are not at all aware of. Additionally, the consideration of only the effects can lead to blaming machine learning methods for results generated by the given or collected data and not by the processing itself. It is seldom made clear by the media that methods of machine learning work in a non-deterministic way depending on the data sample as well as other factors and that the developer does not actively influence the result, but that statistical calculations often play a role. In the literature no overall concept could be found that didactically prepared the basics of machine learning, as well.

This paper describes an attempt how the topic of machine learning can be made understandable to pupils. In this context, it will be examined whether an unplugged concept, which is intended to make pupils understand the function of a linear classifier, can be implemented in practice. The main part is the development of a workshop in which machine learning is simulated in an action-oriented way without the use of real technical systems.

The evaluation gives a first impression of the impact the workshop can have on the participants. Special attention is paid to their assessment of the benefits and dangers of artificial intelligence and machine learning, and whether the topic can be adequately taught to pupils.

2 Action-Oriented Learning

Learning in school can take place in a variety of ways. A mostly positively evaluated kind [8, p. 402] is called *action-oriented learning*, which is however "used as a kind of collective name for quite different methodological practices" [5, p. 8, translated from German]. In contrast to frontal teaching, in action-oriented teaching it is not the teacher who is in the foreground, but the action that is guided by a teacher. The pupils themselves should be active during the learning process and work motorically in addition to pure reflection. Through their own efforts in developing the learning content, the learning can be more sustainable [8, p. 410]. In addition to the inclusion of different senses, the organizational form of group work is also associated with action-oriented learning [5, p. 86f.]. The curriculum for high schools in Bavaria emphasizes action-oriented teaching explicitly for the subject Computer Science [14, p. 32].

Other concepts that are closely linked to action-oriented learning include different levels of representation as a gradation for learning through concrete action. The *EIS principle* according to Bruner [6, p. 92f.] is a didactic classification of types of learning in three stages, whereby the materials used for learning play an important role. When an action-based experience is offered this learning is called *enactive*. An iconic form of representation is given by a visual experience and a symbolic form of representation consists of formal symbolic signs.

This concept of action-oriented learning was used for *CS Unplugged* [1], which offers a collection of materials for computer science teaching without using computers, focusing on middle school topics. For these materials some studies on motivation and benefit for computational thinking are already existing [12,15].

At the same time as this research Lindner and Seegerer [7] have developed some unplugged materials on artificial intelligence addressing decision trees and issues of general artificial intelligence topics among others mostly using decision trees and tables to represent the learning agent.

3 Concept and Workshop Design

Taking the didactic aspects mentioned above into consideration, a concept for a workshop was developed to examine whether the topic can be adequately taught to pupils in the high school.

3.1 Linear Classification

Linear classifiers have been chosen as the main machine learning method to be discussed in the workshop being a simple, but representative method. A linear classifier is a function that separates two linearly separable sets from each other as a hyperplane. It is formally defined as a perceptron function $P : \mathbb{R}^n \to \{0, 1\}$ with

$$P(x) = \begin{cases} 1 & \text{if } wx = \sum_{i=1}^{n} w_i x_i > 0, \\ 0 & \text{else} \end{cases} \tag{1}$$

for a weight vector $w = (w_1, ..., w_n) \in \mathbb{R}^n$ and an input vector $x \in \mathbb{R}^n$ [4, p. 170]. The training of such a classifier consist of gradually adapting an initially selected hyperplane to more and more training data. This is realized by changing the weight vector parameters in order to find a classifier that is as good as possible. Due to their equivalence to a two-layered, directed neural network and to the *Naive Bayes* method [4], linear classifiers also offer good starting points to more complex methods of machine learning. Linear classifiers can be used for various classification issues where the data is linear separable. If the data does not meet this requirements, a non-linear transformation with a support vector machine, which has a similar representation, can be applied [4, p. 253].

In a school setting, the representation of a linear classifier in 2-dimensional contexts is possible as a linear function or a straight line. The comparison to linear regression, which is already known to students as a method used with the calculator/CAS, offers a direct connection to other topics. While in regression a balancing line for a given amount of data is to be found, in learning an initial line for each data point is adapted in such a way that at the end of the learning process the separation is as good as possible.

Overall, linear classifiers represent an authentic introduction to machine learning and seem to be suitable in the school setting, since no competences beyond the mathematics teaching of an intermediate level are required for the understanding of 2-dimensional application scenarios.

3.2 Action-Oriented Unplugged Concept

The main focus of the workshop is on the action-oriented comprehension of the learning process of a linear classifier. At the core of the concept, there is the idea that learners handle data on their own as a computer could do with machine learning, but do not use a computer for this purpose. In an action-oriented unplugged scenario, all relevant details of the learning process are represented by objects and actions with which the process can be executed and tested. Each step of machine learning can be transferred to the unplugged concept and can be understood by the learner, who actively controls changes in the classifier function depending on the data.

Linear classifiers can be used in various situations. According to the requirements, an authentic but easily understandable example should be chosen for the workshop. After careful consideration of the advantages and disadvantages, screws have been chosen as the context for the workshop based on the resulting easy-to-handle data. A linear classifier should be used to distinguish between two screw types of different lengths.

The fictitious technical machine should work in such a way that the screws fall individually in a random position onto a slightly movable, centrally illuminated surface and are photographed from above. The mobility is intended to ensure that no screw is photographed in the head position. This avoids the situation where no difference can be detected between the short and the long screw. The aim is to be able to distinguish between short and long screws with the photo as data. On this photo the smallest possible rectangle with edges parallel to the edges of the picture in which the screw can be completely embedded is then determined (Fig. 1a). This rectangle is called the *Bounding Box*. The dimensions of the rectangle serve as the data, whereby the larger length determines the first vector component and the smaller one determines the second vector component. By the choice of such a two-dimensional example an action-oriented representation as well as the renouncement of formal representations are made possible and an overload of the learners is avoided.

These dimensions, shown on data cards (Fig. 1b), are inserted one after the other into a coordinate system represented by a pinboard using pins in a color according to the screw size. The current classifier is a thin wooden strip, which was previously fixed to the x-axis at one end after consideration by the participants. Figure 1c illustrates the result of a group of participants. This results in a representation that is both enactive and iconic. On the one hand, learners can actively insert data points and move the separation line. On the other hand, an iconic representation of the result similar to a function graph is achieved at

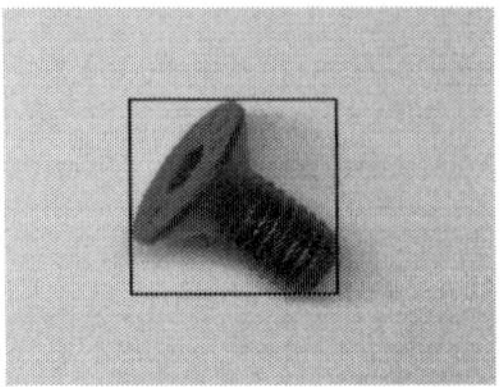

(a) Photo of a screw with its Bounding Box

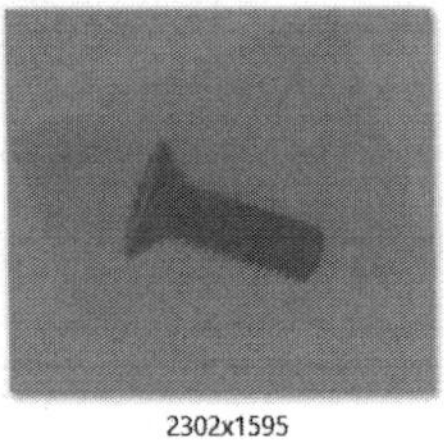

(b) Data card with pixel size of the measured Bounding Box

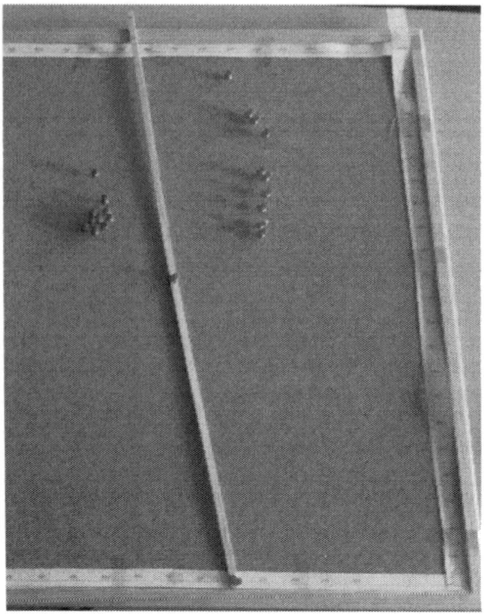

(c) Result of a group of participants

Fig. 1. Workshop material

the end. A formal mathematical level, where the straight line equation is determined at the end, could be discussed afterwards, but is not necessary for the understanding of the procedure and the training result. However, a basic knowledge of straight lines or linear functions is useful to see the possibility of algorithmically checking the final classification of data points. When selecting the screw lengths, an error tolerance must be ensured, since an absolutely exact placement of the pins cannot be guaranteed. Therefore, the data clusters must be far apart, which can be achieved by a sufficiently large difference in length.

A step of training is performed by taking a random data card from a face-down stack and entering the corresponding data point into the coordinate system with a pin. Afterwards, the separation line is adjusted according to the position of the newly inserted point by rotating the wooden strip at the non-fixed end by a fixed distance, which is reduced with increasing number of inserted data points according to a given scheme.

After a sufficient number of learning steps, the dimensions of the Bounding Box can be used to determine the type of screw by the help of the separating line. However, this requires a suitable selection of the initial straight line. A two-dimensional input vector and a straight line as a one-dimensional hyperplane are therefore sufficient for this context and are unlikely to overwhelm the learner.

The separating line is adjusted after each step of training, otherwise changes would occur only rarely if the line position was already well chosen at the beginning. The chosen procedure simplifies the usual procedure and makes it manageable.

3.3 Workshop Draft

The action-oriented part[1] of the workshop is accompanied by an introduction to the topic and a subsequent discussion. At the beginning an overview illustration (e.g. [4, p. 4]) is shown to clarify that the following application scenario is only an example of a method of machine learning and that the topic artificial intelligence covers a much larger area. An example of a classifier is given by explaining possible inputs and outputs of a face detection machine. It is explained that after a learning process such a machine is able to compute, for example, an estimation of age or even the emotional state of a person by some parameters taken from a video. As this example is too complex for the workshop the action-oriented comprehension is performed with a different issue with only a small number of involved parameters.

After this short theoretical impulse, the participants perform the described learning procedure in groups according to a previously explained instruction. 20 random data cards from the data set are individually marked on the pinboard and the wooden strip is moved in the direction of the inserted point. Then the participants briefly present their results to the other groups. Because the data and the classifier are represented on the pinboard, it is trivial to rate the success of the training process and to predict the classification of possible new data. During the presentation they should also explain their thoughts during the execution and answer some questions, e.g. which considerations led to the choice of the initial straight line and whether they consider a continuation of the procedure useful. The intention here is to realize the advantages of a computer in order to guarantee precision and to be able to carry out even small changes meaningfully. These characteristics cannot be fulfilled by the action-oriented representation, since a movement of the wooden strip by a few millimetres would not produce any significant results. The different results of the groups can be supplemented by further results documented on photos and taken as an opportunity to discuss the effects of different parameters such as the choice of the initial straight line as well as the selection and number of data cards. Then a more or less detailed theoretical analysis of the situation can be shown to the participants, depending on their mathematical interest.

The workshop concludes with a discussion of further cases such as very small or very high differences in screw sizes, non-linear separable data clusters and classification of more than two types of screws. This discussion makes it clear to the participants that the choice of a machine learning method should only be made after a thorough consideration of different factors. For example in the case of a very small difference it could happen that no well-classifiable datasets can be generated. In the opposite case other methods like simple weighting could be performed with significantly lower effort. Some participants may notice that the given data has a relatively high difference in screw sizes, but this is necessary to ensure a realistic success of the action-oriented learning method and can be considered for further discussion.

[1] The material used in the workshop is available at https://tinyurl.com/workshopuos.

4 Evaluation

In accordance with the evaluation concept described below, the workshop was already realized and evaluated with a group of eight computer science teacher trainees and eight Master of Education in computer science students and with three groups of eight to ten high school pupils each.

4.1 Evaluation Concept

A pretest-posttest design without a control group according to [3, p. 102] was chosen for evaluation. Participants are asked to complete a questionnaire with their assessments immediately before and after the workshop. An evaluation concept with a control group would be difficult to realize, as no alternative learning programs can be implemented without considerable effort and the interval between the two testing times is quite short. As possible other factors for changes to be considered besides the workshop regression effects can occur, which let extreme values tend to the middle during repeated measurement, as well as influences by the pretest [3, p. 202]. However, regression effects can be partially neglected, since the questionnaire is not a performance test. The evaluation takes place both quantitatively and qualitatively. We used the non-parametric *Wilcoxon-signed-rank-test* as well as the parametric *Student's t-test for matched pairs* for the quantitative evaluation of the items queried at both test times according to [2, p. 133] and [3, p. 738] because of the partly low numbers of participants in the different groups.

The pre- and posttest[2] largely contain the same questions that are regarded as statistical variables/items. In the posttest these were supplemented by three questions to evaluate the workshop with regard to understanding, coverage and relevance.

First, participants are asked about their personal definitions of artificial intelligence and machine learning. Since many participants have little previous knowledge of the topic before the workshop, the experiences and opinions on both terms are asked, as they are often used synonymously by the participants. Subsequently, the participants are asked to classify their personal impression into a five-level, verbalized Likert scale "positive (5) - rather positive (4) - neutral (3) - rather negative (2) - negative (1)".

Since a neutral impression is not unlikely, especially with little prior knowledge, a scale with a center was chosen here intentionally, while in the following more extensive statement part we omitted choosing such a scale. For various statements on benefit, danger and relevance for school teaching, the following levels can be selected: "agree (1) - rather agree (2) - rather not agree (3) - not agree (4)". The assessment of one's own knowledge of the topic is also asked. The questionnaire ends with a section for further comments.

[2] Available at https://tinyurl.com/workshopuos.

4.2 Discussion of the Results

First of all, we experienced that the workshop design was feasible as expected and no practical or organizational problems arose. The comparison of pre- and posttests of the eight computer science teacher trainees, eight Master of Education in computer science students and 28 pupils from grades 10 to 12 shows mainly small changes regarding the conception of artificial intelligence and machine learning. A significantly lower agreement (with significance level 0.05) to the statements *I think artificial intelligence is dangerous.*, *Artificial intelligence is a miracle cure.*, but also *I consider artificial intelligence to be an interesting topic.* could be determined. The lower agreement to the last statement can possibly be justified by an unrealistically high estimation in the pretest. Nevertheless the interest in the topic remains on a high level. Concerning machine learning the item about its usefulness shows a significantly stronger agreement in the posttest. Participants also rated their knowledge of artificial intelligence and machine learning significantly higher after the workshop. Although the impression of machine learning has not changed significantly among all participants, a significantly more positive impression can be observed if only the group of pupils is considered. When the groups were evaluated separately, fewer items changed significantly due to the low response numbers of some items.

Table 1. Significant ($p < 0.05$) results of evaluation (excepting first item with n = 39), partially rounded, n = number of paired answers given in pre- and posttest, 1 = agree to 4 = not agree/* 1 = negative to 5 = positive, gray: only pupils

item	n	mean pretest	mean posttest	tendency
My impression of machine learning is	39	3.5897*	3.75*	more positive
	21	3.5417*	3.8571*	more positive
I think artificial intelligence is dangerous.	43	2.5455	2.6744	lower agreement
Artificial intelligence is a miracle cure.	41	3.0238	3.1163	lower agreement
I consider artificial intelligence to be an interesting topic.	43	1.3953	1.6047	lower agreement
I know several things about artificial intelligence.	42	3.1	2.83	stronger agreement
I consider machine learning useful.	39	1.825	1.6429	stronger agreement
I know several things about machine learning.	41	3.2791	2.8049	stronger agreement

Overall, the pupils also tend to rate their knowledge as better than the trainee teachers and teacher training students. The results are listed in Tables 1 and 2. There have been no major differences in significance depending on the statistical test used. Since some participants in the pretest did not provide any information on specific items due to a lack of knowledge of the terms, only answers that were available in both the pretest and the posttest were included in the evaluation. This results in different numbers of answers included in the evaluation.

The items about the workshop, which were only occurring in the posttest, showed a slightly approving impression of the understanding, coverage and relevance of the workshop as an integral part of computer science teaching, with the group of trainee teachers and Master of Education students agreeing more strongly overall. The strongest agreement in both groups refers to the understanding, the weakest to the coverage. This may be related to the fact that the workshop only gives an insight into the topic and can therefore only be assessed as sufficient by a more detailed examination of the topic. The slight approval of the workshop as a fixed component of the computer science lesson can

Table 2. Significance results from Wilcoxon signed-rank-test (WSR) and paired Student's t-test (T), partially rounded, ($n = df + 1$), gray: only pupils

item	WSR: V-value	WSR: p-value	T: t-value	T: df	T: p-value
My impression of machine learning is	14.5	0.094	-1.843	38	0.0731
	0	**0,0147**	-2.892	23	**0.0082**
I think artificial intelligence is dangerous.	0	**0.0369**	-2.3508	42	**0.0235**
Artificial intelligence is a miracle cure.	4.5	**0.041**	-2.2207	40	**0.0321**
I consider artificial intelligence to be an interesting topic.	5	**0.0147**	-2.6678	42	**0.0108**
I know several things about artificial intelligence.	45	**0.0048**	3.1857	41	**0.0028**
I consider machine learning useful.	40.5	**0.0248**	2.4535	38	**0,0188**
I know several things about machine learning.	171	**<0.001**	5.595	40	**<0.001**

Table 3. Means of the workshop-related items, partially rounded, TT = Teaching trainees/M.Ed. students, $n = 16$; P = pupils, 1 = agree to 4 = not agree, $n = 28$

Item	Mean (TT)	Mean (P)
The workshop has contributed to my understanding of machine learning	1,75	2,2
The workshop gives a sufficient insight into the topic	2,0667	2,4231
The workshop should become an integral part of the computer science subject	1,9375	2,3478

possibly be understood as a basic approval of the workshop, but a weakening of the obligation in the statement. The exact results are shown in Table 3.

In the evaluation, we noticed a teaching trainee who demonstrated a strongly distorted view of artificial intelligence before the workshop and considered it to be very dangerous, but demonstrated a much more moderate attitude after the workshop. Among the students, it was noticeable that some who had not had computer science lessons before had no idea of the terms and therefore had difficulties filling them with content. Overall, many of the personal definitions referred specifically to workshop content and items related to machine learning and were answered more often and more detailed in the posttest.

5 Conclusions

The predominantly positive workshop feedback from pupils and teachers demonstrates that concepts of machine learning can be adequately taught even to pupils. Although the workshop is only content-oriented, we could ascertain an influence on the participants' perception, so that a reflection and analysis of the topic seems to take place. Even if the screw topic of the workshop is not the most interesting, it can help to focus the concentration on the learning procedure. In this way, participants can learn that machine learning can not only be used in areas of media interest. Continuing and extending the course into a teaching unit can therefore counteract a possibly distorted perception of artificial intelligence in schools.

References

1. CS Unplugged - Computer Science without a computer. https://classic.csunplugged.org/. Accessed 19 Aug 2019
2. Bortz, J., Schuster, C.: Statistik für Human- und Sozialwissenschaftler [Statistics for human and social scientists], vol. 7. Springer, Heidelberg (2010). https://doi.org/10.1007/978-3-642-12770-0

3. Döring, N., Bortz, J.: Forschungsmethoden und Evaluation in den Sozial- und Humanwissenschaften [Research methods and evaluation in the social sciences and humanities], vol. 5. Springer, Heidelberg (2016). https://doi.org/10.1007/978-3-642-41089-5
4. Ertel, W.: Introduction to Artificial Intelligence. Springer, London (2011). https://doi.org/10.1007/978-0-85729-299-5
5. Gudjons, H.: Handlungsorientiert lehren und lernen: Schüleraktivierung Selbsttätigkeit Projektarbeit [Action-oriented teaching and learning: student activation - self-activity - project work], vol. 8. Klinkhardt Bad Heilbrunn (2014)
6. Hefendehl-Hebeker, L., Schwank, I.: Arithmetik: Leitidee Zahl [Arithmetic: central idea number]. In: Bruder, R., Hefendehl-Hebeker, L., Schmidt-Thieme, B., Weigand, H.-G. (eds.) Handbuch der Mathematikdidaktik [Guide of mathematical didactics], pp. 77–115. Springer, Heidelberg (2015). https://doi.org/10.1007/978-3-642-35119-8_4. Chap. 4
7. Lindner, A., Seegerer, S.: AI Unplugged - Wir ziehen künstlicher Intelligenz den Stecker [AI Unplugged - we pull the plug on artificial intelligence]. https://ddi.cs.fau.de/schule/ai-unplugged/. Accessed 07 May 2019
8. Meyer, H.: Unterrichtsmethoden II: Praxisband [Teaching methods II: practical book], 14 edn. Cornelsen Scriptor Berlin (2011)
9. Ministerium für Schule und Weiterbildung des Landes Nordrhein-Westfalen: Kernlehrplan für die Sekundarstufe II Gymnasium/Gesamtschule in Nordrhein-Westfalen Informatik [Curriculum for secondary level II high school/comprehensive school in north rhine-westfalia computer science]. https://www.schulentwicklung.nrw.de/lehrplaene/upload/klp_SII/if/KLP_GOSt_Informatik.pdf (2014). Accessed 07 May 2019
10. Niedersächsisches Kultusministerium: Kerncurriculum für die Schulformen des Sekundarbereichs I Schuljahrgänge 5–10 [Curriculum for school types in lower secondary education years 5–10]. http://db2.nibis.de/1db/cuvo/datei/kc_informatik_sek_i.pdf (2014). Accessed 07 May 2019
11. Niedersächsisches Kultusministerium: Kerncurriculum für das Gymnasium - gymnasiale Oberstufe, die Gesamtschule -gymnasiale Oberstufe, das Kolleg Informatik [Curriculum for high school - upper school, comprehensive school - upper school, college in computer science]. http://www.db2.nibis.de/1db/cuvo/datei/inf_go_kc_druck_2017.pdf (2017). Accessed 27 Aug 2019
12. Rodriguez, B., Rader, C., Camp, T.: Using student performance to assess CS unplugged activities in a classroom environment. In: Proceedings of the 2016 ACM Conference on Innovation and Technology in Computer Science Education, ITiCSE 2016, pp. 95–100. ACM, New York (2016). https://doi.org/10.1145/2899415.2899465
13. Staatsinstitut für Schulqualität und Bildungsforschung München: Jahrgangsstufen-Lehrplan 11/12 Informatik [Computer science curriculum for years 11/12]. http://www.isb-gym8-lehrplan.de/contentserv/3.1.neu/g8.de/index.php?StoryID=26193 (2004). Accessed 07 May 2019
14. Staatsinstitut für Schulqualität und Bildungsforschung München: Der Lehrplan für das Gymnasium in Bayern im überblick [The curriculum for the high school in bavaria at a glance]. https://www.isb.bayern.de/download/1555/broschuere-der-lehrplan-im-ueberblick.pdf (2010). Accessed 07 May 2019
15. Thies, R., Vahrenhold, J.: On plugging "Unplugged" into CS classes. In: Proceeding of the 44th ACM Technical Symposium on Computer Science Education, SIGCSE 2013, pp. 365–370. ACM, New York (2013). https://doi.org/10.1145/2445196.2445303

About Classes and Trees: Introducing Secondary School Students to Aspects of Data Mining

Andreas Grillenberger(✉) and Ralf Romeike

Computing Education Research Group, Freie Universität Berlin,
Königin-Luise-Str. 24/26, 14195 Berlin, Germany
{andreas.grillenberger,ralf.romeike}@fu-berlin.de

Abstract. Today, data is no longer just important to computer science. Instead, basic competencies in managing, processing and using data are necessary in almost all other sciences and even in everyday life. Such competencies empower students to handle their own and others' data adequately and allow them to use data-related technologies and tools in a critically-reflected way. Although aspects of this topic are typically already part of computer science curricula for secondary schools, particularly fostering data-related competencies is often not the focus, so that large parts of this exciting topic have not arrived in the classroom yet. In this paper, we investigate the exemplary topic *data analysis and predictions* from a secondary education perspective. After summarizing the technical and didactic foundations, we describe a theoretically sound teaching concept which aims to foster the acquisition of basic competencies in this field and to contribute to a better understanding of these important aspects of the digital world. Besides presenting the teaching concept, the paper discusses the methodical structure as well as the software tool used. In addition, the mostly positive results and impressions of an evaluation with ninth-grade students are presented.

Keywords: Data · Data literacy · Data mining · Data analysis · Prediction · Teaching concept · Secondary education · Evaluation

1 Data in the Digital World

In today's world, data is an important basis of manifold developments which are often subsumed under the term *digitalization*. However, although everyone continuously generates and stores various data, when using those we typically take a rather passive role: Evaluating and processing all the data is mostly left to companies, whose products and services we use. Even more important is the limited or often lacking understanding of how such analyses work and hence also for their accompanying phenomena and impact: Despite an extensive discussion in the social discourse, it is difficult for large parts of the population to assess the power, possibilities and dangers of data analysis. Hence, they hardly have the

S. N. Pozdniakov and V. Dagienė (Eds.): ISSEP 2019, LNCS 11913, pp. 147–158, 2019.
https://doi.org/10.1007/978-3-030-33759-9_12

opportunity to position themselves accordingly. This is particularly important as today various decisions related to using data-driven services have to be made taking into account the personal cost-benefit ratio and the effects on society, for example when motor vehicle insurances desire to record driving behaviour. The ability to reflect such developments in a critically-reflective manner is particularly important when data-driven approaches are used in the background and/or without allowing people to decide for or against participating in this system: for example, rating persons based on data is not only carried out by well-known credit agencies, but increasingly also by government institutions. In China this development is already so far advanced that all inhabitants will soon be scored positively or negatively as part of a *social credit system*, with the aim to educate them to a desired behaviour [1]. The consequences associated with such developments can hardly be evaluated without a sound basic knowledge of how data are handled and used, otherwise the extent and possibilities remain hidden. In order to prepare for a self-determined and mature life in the digital society, school—and in this case particularly computer science teaching—has to provide insight into such developments and empower students to reflect them in a critically-reflected manner. Although different approaches for fostering basic competencies regarding handling and usage of data are already recognizable in computer science lessons, there is still a large gap [5] which indicates that computer science teaching in this area still has to develop further.

In this paper, we present a theoretically sound teaching concept focusing on *data analysis* and *prediction*. In the course of the lessons, students are not only given the chance to gain insight into the function of data analyses and predictions, but they are also empowered to carry out their own analyses based on real data sets and thus to fathom both the power and limits of automated data analyses. The teaching concept promotes a critical examination of everyday handling of data, but also enables students to deepen their experiences independently. In the following, we first summarize the state of research in this area and give an overview of CS teaching in this context. Then, before the teaching concept is presented in Sect. 3, the focus of the concept on aspects of data mining is discussed, relevant technical contents are outlined and the selection of the tool used is discussed. Finally, in Sect. 4 we describe the predominantly positive experiences gained during an evaluation of the teaching concept at school.

2 Current State of Teaching and Research

From a scientific perspective, the field *data* is particularly important: Not only is it an important basis for all developments summarized under terms such as *big data*, *data mining* and *data science*, but also for example in *machine learning*. But such developments are also triggering changes in other subjects, in particular related to research: For example, Hey et al. [10] emphasize the relevance of data-oriented research as a new research paradigm. In this context, also the need for fostering data competencies for everyone is stressed. The basic competencies everyone needs in this context are often summarized under the term *data literacy*.

Ridsdale et al. [14] describe it as "the ability to collect, manage, evaluate, and apply data, in a critical manner" and, in a summative research approach, also describe several key competencies related to this field. According to the common understanding, data literacy competencies have to be differentiated from such that are related to data science: Data science requires deeper competencies and focuses on professionally oriented aspects of the field *data*.

In computer science curricula, at the moment the extensive field *data* is mainly taken up with a focus on *databases* [5][1]. In this context, central basics are considered: in particular by introducing data models, the importance of defined data structures and of data types becomes evident, while at the same time key concepts are introduced, such as *redundancy*, *consistency* and *durability*. Beyond *databases*, however, data have rather little importance in current CS teaching: Although they play a certain role in programming and are also indispensable in topics such as *structure of the Internet*, the focus of these topics is usually different, so that data and related concepts are only considered marginally. Thus, the current role of this topic in the classroom hardly reflects its general importance. Accordingly, only few teaching concepts could be found which go a step further and take a broader look at the complete field. However, there are at least approaches that take up aspects of the topic which are typically less relevant in school teaching. For example, in a German simulation game [3], the idea of data protection is introduced. In another example, a teacher implemented a platform called InstaHub that allows students to build their own social network as well as a related teaching concept which allows students to get valuable insight into such platforms [4]. These and similar concepts deal with central topics of the field data. Yet, for several increasingly important areas such as data analysis and prediction, corresponding ideas are not yet to be found.

In computer science education research, however, progress has been made in recent years, particularly concerning the foundation of data-related aspects from an educational perspective: On the one hand, from a rather technical point-of-view, the entire subject area *data management* was investigated with the goal to identify key concepts and practices characterizing this field and to also consider recent developments [7]. Yet, as not only the technical aspects play an important role for teaching, also the perspectives of students, teachers and society as a whole have been investigated [8]. As part of this work, also a competency model of *data literacy* was developed, which, in contrast to the one by Ridsdale et al. takes the perspective of CS education and hence sets different foci [6], but in general both models are consistent. This competency model consists of four content and process areas each (cf. Fig. 1). Thus, it is not only focused on the concepts or technical content of this subject area, but also emphasizes the practical perspective on the topic. However, this project is not the only approach to consider rather modern data-oriented aspects in school: For example, in a joint project with mathematics education, currently Heimann et al. [9] develop a data science curriculum for secondary schools, which sets similar foci as the

[1] Although the study [5] is about five years old, there were only few changes in CS curricula in the last years.

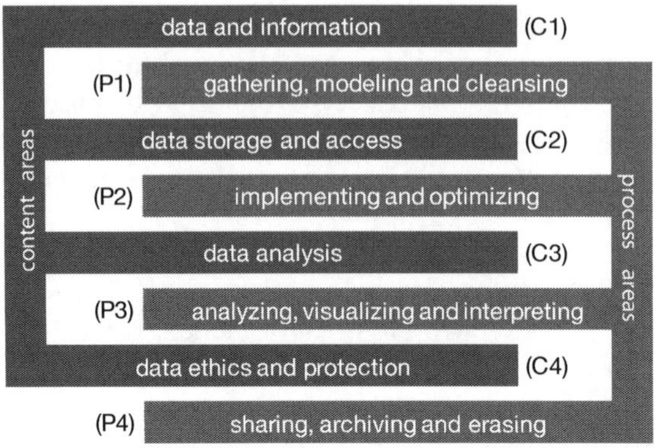

Fig. 1. The data literacy competency model used as basis for the lesson sequence [6].

competency model described before. Despite these different approaches to investigate the topic from a CS education perspective, the topic has so far remained a marginal topic in computer science education research and teaching.

3 Presentation of the Teaching Concept

In order to address the previously characterized gap in current computer science teaching, the lesson sequence presented aims to foster a basic understanding and the acquisition of competencies related to data analysis and predictions. The planned lesson sequence is designed for only four lessons of 90 min each, so that it can be flexibly included into teaching. However, of course it can be adapted individually if necessary, since a much more in-depth or somewhat more superficial examination is possible at various points. In general, we cannot expect students to have basic knowledge in how data analysis or predictions work, therefore the lesson sequence was designed in such a way that no previous knowledge needs to be built upon, which also makes it suitable for both lower and upper secondary level.

In order to decide which competencies are emphasized, we used the data literacy competency model mentioned before (cf. Fig. 1). This model is not only well-founded in CS education research but, by distinguishing content and process areas, it also helps to focus on both, content and practice, at the same time. In order to achieve the desired goals, from a content perspective the focus was set on *data analysis (C3)*, while also general aspects of *data and information (C1)* have to be taken into account, as we do not expect any prior knowledge. In addition, because of the relevance of this topic in society, also data *ethics and protection (C4)* cannot be left out, so that from a content perspective, we take up parts of all content areas except *data stores and data storage (C2)*. As we have designed this teaching concept so that it can be taught in only four lessons, we also could not include aspects from all process areas. Thus, we focus on the analysis and prediction itself, so that *P4 (analyzing, visualizing and interpreting)* is emphasized while the other process areas are at most considered marginally.

Hence, in the teaching sequence we particularly aimed at fostering the following data literacy competencies:

- explain why and how (possibly new) information can be obtained from stored data (C1/P3)
- characterize the difference between correlation- and causality-based relations in data as well as their respective meaningfulness (C1/P3, C4/P3)
- sketch the process of a (correlation-based) data analysis (C3/P3)
- characterize a typical analysis method and explain the underlying principle using a suitable example (C3/P3)
- perform a simple data analysis using a common method, manually as well as using a suitable software tool (C3/P3)
- predict missing attributes of a data set using a self-conducted data analysis (C3/P3)
- evaluate the outcome of the prediction and explain ideas for improvement (C3/P3)
- reflect the results taking into account ethical and social implications (C4/P3)

As we did not expect any prior knowledge, we decided to divide the course into two blocks: Initially, an introduction to the data analysis process is given in order to allow students to understand how the analysis process works. For this purpose, it is useful to focus on specific methods and on getting an overview of the analysis process. Afterwards, we introduce the students to some basics of data analysis and predictions without using digital analysis tools, as for this purpose we do not need to use larger amounts of data, so that analysis can be carried out manually in order to understand the important principles. Afterwards, in order to be able to estimate the potential and risks of automated data analysis and to get more valid and realistic analysis results, a software tool is used for analyzing data. At this step, we also switch to a larger data set that leads to more interesting results. While in the beginning we focus on a fictive data set (from the context of online shopping), the data set selected for the second block even more directly affects students, so that it leads to a critical discussion of the results and the analysis itself.

3.1 Basics: Data Mining, Classification and Prediction

Before we describe the lesson sequence in detail, we need to focus on the relevant basics of data mining and data analyses. While classical data analyses often pursue the goal to structure and summarize existing data, particularly by using aggregate functions in order to describe the data by minimum, maximum and average values, *data mining* follows a different approach: It focuses on discovering new information and often on predicting unknown attributes of a data set based on other data. The term *data mining* can be understood as an analogy to *gold mining*: It describes digging for valuable information in a large mountain of data. Different methods are used for this purpose, of which most can be traced back to the basic principles *classification*, *clustering* and *association*:

- *Classification* refers to dividing a data set into several classes. Often, the goal of a classification is to predict unknown attributes of one instance of the data set by looking at all the other instances of the same class. However, as using classification, the classes cannot be inferred from the data, the existing classes need to be known: For example, for classifying students by their performance in school, the classes may be derived from the grades, for classifying them by how far they live from school, it must be decided on which classes are introduced (such as less than 5 km, more than 5 km).
- *Clustering* addresses the limits of classification: It pursues the same goal as classification, but in this case the clusters are not predetermined but instead determined inductively from the data. Often, the rules for assigning instances of a data set to a certain cluster are an important result of clustering. So, for example, groups of people (i.e. clusters) knowing each other might be determined in social networks.
- *Association analysis* focuses on discover rules that describe a data set that either explain causal relationships or can be based on correlations. They are particularly useful for predicting unknown values. However, particularly in large data sets, finding associations is a complex task.

In the lesson sequence, the focus is on the methods *classification* and *association*, which are easy to understand, but also allow getting insight into how data analyses work. In this case, classification is used to find similarities in the data, to structure them accordingly and to derive findings from it, which are elaborated into rules as part of an association analysis. Thus, both methods go hand in hand and show how predictions work: By learning rules from an already classified data set, an automated classification of further data can take place, which allows for predicting unknown attributes of these data. In order to automate such analyses, a multitude of different classification algorithms exists, which often become very complex and are therefore not discussed in detail in the classroom. Instead, we focus on a basic method, the *classification tree*. These trees can be used as an intuitive approach to gaining an overview on association rules, as these rules are visualized as a decision tree, whose nodes represent decisions and whose leaves are used for class allocation. Hence, based on such a tree, predictions can easily be made, just by looking at a specific data set and following the tree's nodes from the root to a leave.

Besides the analysis methods, also the analysis process leading to a prediction is an important part of the teaching sequence: For making valid high-quality predictions, it is particularly important to consider the whole analysis process, as the quality is i.a. influenced by the selection of the sample on which the associations are determined. Hence, in the teaching sequence, we also give an overview on this process and relate the methods discussed in school to the overall process to give students an orientation during the analysis process (cf. Fig. 2).

3.2 Tool Selection: The Data Mining Tool *Orange*

While no software tool is necessary for the first part of the lesson series, in the second part the aim is to make the power and potential of data analysis

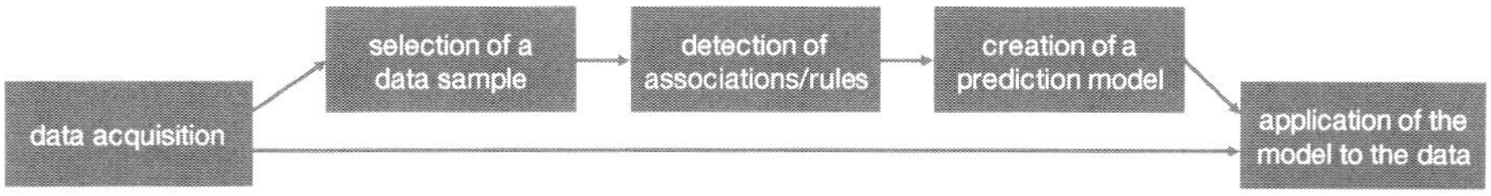

Fig. 2. Analysis process discussed during the lesson sequence.

visible for the students by enabling them to conduct their own analysis with real data. For this purpose, a suitable tool is needed. Again, the selection of the tool is particularly led by the criterion, that it should not require any prior knowledge and be intuitively usable. When selecting the tool, we also took the criteria into account that Resnick et al. established for tools that support creative thinking [13]: These tools should "*make it easy for novices to get started (low threshold)*"[2] [12,13], make it possible "*for experts to work on increasingly sophisticated projects (high ceiling)*" [12,13] and "*support and suggest a wide range of explorations*" [13] (*wide walls*). Accordingly, the use of a classical programming language such as Python, which is very common for professional data analyses, is hardly reasonable for this lesson series. Instead, graphically oriented analysis tools are particularly suitable, especially tools in which users describe the analysis as a data flow model, for example *rapidminer*[3] and *Orange*[4]: these tools allow students to directly transfer the knowledge on the analysis process to the automated data analysis. Both tools provide all the functionalities that we need for the specific lesson sequence, but they also offer many additional possibilities, so that they could be used also for more sophisticated analyses. We finally decided to use *Orange* in the classroom for two reasons: First, it was possible to further reduce the complexity of the tool since it was an open source program in which unneeded modules could be hidden. Furthermore, *Orange* can be used and distributed without any license to be required, while *rapidminer* requires both teachers and students to apply for an academic license, which is a barrier for using the tool. Some impressions of *Orange* are given later in Figs. 3 to 5.

3.3 Description of the Lesson Sequence

In the following, we give an overview of the course design. For a detailed description, refer to the overall concept published on the project website[5], which contains all the work materials and a detailed description for teachers.

In the first 90 min lesson, the central aspects of the analysis process are emphasized. For motivating the importance of the topic, at the beginning of the lesson sequence a newspaper article is presented, that describes the attempt of a US retailer to recognize whether its customers are pregnant in order to send

[2] Later, *low threshold* was also refered to as *low floor*.
[3] https://rapidminer.com/educational-program/.
[4] https://orange.biolab.si.
[5] https://dataliteracy.education.

them targeted advertisments [11]. This article encourages students to discuss how the retailer can determine that a customer is pregnant, which attributes about its customers it probably collects and how these attributes could lead to assuming a pregnancy. Thus, this discussion immediately draws students into the topic and also gives the teacher an impression of what students know about data analyses and how they think these work. Afterwards, based on other examples, the value and usefulness of data for different purposes, companies and business models is discussed and students can provide own examples they know from their daily lives. The teacher directs these discussions towards introducing the terms *causality*, *correlation* and *prediction*, which are relevant to be known for the complete lesson sequence. Starting with the students' ideas, afterwards a model of data analysis processes is being created.

Based on this introduction, in the next lesson, the process from a data set to a prediction is carried out manually, so that different principles of these analyses become recognizable, particularly the importance of a sufficient data sample, the selection of valid rules/associations and the creation of the data model. For this lesson, students work on a given simple and fictive data set (in the example from the context of online retail) and examine it for relations within the data, which are then formulated as rules (i.e. associations). In order to make these rules easier to grasp, to give a better overview of them and to simplify applying them to data, a (non-binary) decision tree is introduced as a form of representation. Afterwards, using this tree, the rules are applied to another data set with unknown attribute values. The given data set was designed in such a way that not all possible rules apply to all instances of the data set. Thus, students need to decide whether they consider an association as valid that is only valid for about 80% of the data. Hence, they also need to reflect about the targeted analysis quality and about problems resulting from unfavorably chosen rules. At the end of the lesson, the central task for the next lesson is introduced: to predict students' school grades based on a real data set.

In the third lesson, a freely accessible data set with (anonymised) data about Portuguese students [2] is analysed. This data set contains various personal data about more than 600 students (e. g. jobs of the parents, amount of spare time) as well as their grades in three exams. Using the tool *Orange*, which is not introduced in detail to the students, the aim is to generate a decision tree and hence a prediction model, which is then used for predicting the third grade from all the remaining data. As Orange not only allows viewing the actual results of the analysis, but also getting insight into the intermediate steps, students can for example have a look at the generated classification tree (Fig. 4), but also on the data sample that was selected randomly. By discussing the teacher's fictional goal of significantly reducing the correction effort by using analysis and predictions, students get into questioning and evaluating how good the analysis quality can get in comparison with the teacher's effort (size of the data sample). This is particularly interesting because of the high analysis quality, which students can for example observe by examining a confusion matrix (Fig. 5). Thus, the direct involvement of the students holds a high potential for critically discussing the possibilities and threats of data analyses and predictions.

The last lesson focuses on additional use cases and on a critical reflection of those: For this purpose, it is planned to transfer the competencies acquired so far to other contexts and thus, for example, to question the use of data in medicine, by insurance companies and banks and to discuss legal, ethical and moral aspects of these analyses within the framework of a jigsaw puzzle.

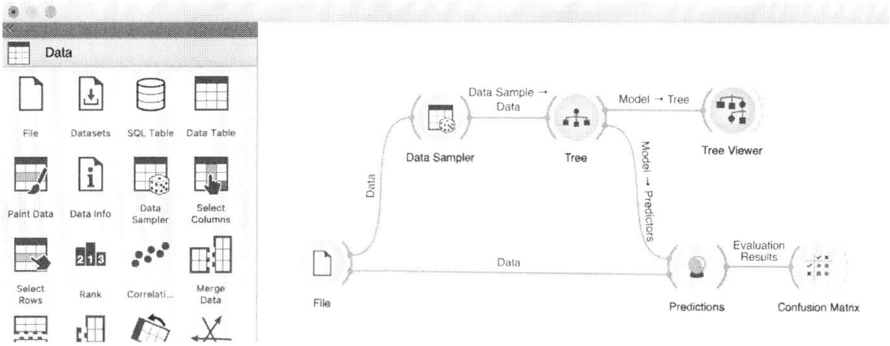

Fig. 3. Model of a data analysis in the analysis tool *Orange*. (Color figure online)

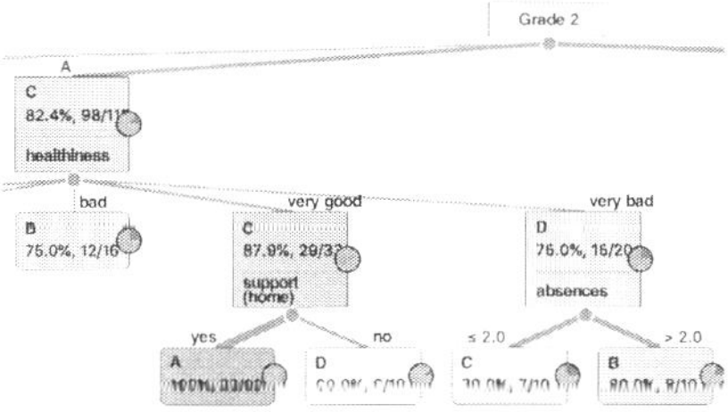

Fig. 4. Part of a classification tree in *Orange*. (Color figure online)

actual \ predicted	1.0	2.0	3.0	4.0	5.0	6.0
1.0	34	10	2	0	0	0
2.0	1	52	31	1	0	0
3.0	0	1	182	34	0	0
4.0	0	0	5	212	19	0
5.0	0	0	0	9	40	0
6.0	0	0	0	9	7	0

Fig. 5. Confusion matrix for examining the analysis quality.

4 Evaluation in School

The lesson sequence was evaluated in two ninth grade classes of a German secondary school with 15 (three female) and 12 (no female) students respectively. Both classes were taught by the same teacher and had no pre-knowledge from teaching regarding data in general, databases or even programming. For organisational reasons, only three lessons (90 min each) were available, hence we had to drop the fourth lesson and included some of the discussion aspects in the other lessons, so that those were very packed. The first author of this paper observed the lessons using observation sheets and conducted a guided interview with the teacher. Also, the students were interviewed with questionnaires at the end of the last lesson in order to cover different perspectives.

In general, the observations were rather positive: Although both courses were very different concerning students' interest in the topic and their motivation to participate in discussions, in general most students were taking part after a while, which was also surprising for the teacher, who did confirm this observation. Generally spoken, there was a large overlap between the researcher's and teacher's observations. In contrast, the students' perspective on the topic seemed a bit different in the questionnaires, but there was a high variation in their answers in almost all questions asked. As the questionnaire was handed to them as the last task of the lesson and hence also filled in by them very quickly, these results have to be considered carefully. Yet, taking together the three methods, there are some central results that can be deduced:

Interest and Motivation: Although the evaluation took place in two rather difficult, both inattentive and poorly motivated classes, both the classroom observation and the perception of the teacher showed a high interest and a motivated participation. According to the teacher, both the interest in the topic and the motivation seemed to be higher than for other topics. In addition, the frequent and intensive discussions were highly noticeable, which was unusual in particular for one of the classes. However, the student survey partly contradicted these observations, especially with regard to the perceived interest in the topic, which was rated as rather low.

Prior Knowledge and Experience: In the course of the lessons it became apparent several times that the examples used and the entire topic have strong references to the daily life of the students and to their experiences: In many cases, they additionally brought their own examples and were able to find intuitive explanations for questions that arose. Based on the students' ideas, even the data analysis process could be deduced well. Thus, it became clearly recognizable that data and data analysis play an important role in students' life and that they have some ideas on how these work.

Comprehensibility: In general, the topics considered in the lesson sequence seemed to be comprehensible and understandable for the students. This was particularly evident in the discussion phases, where they often included aspects in their argumentations that had been considered earlier. Only the distinction between correlation- and causality-based data analysis occasionally led to difficulties, so that more time should be devoted to this aspect. Also, the students stated in the questionnaire that the tasks were easy to solve for them and that they now feel to have an understanding of what can be done with data. So, in general, at least the basics of the subject area are comprehensible for the students.

Structure and Tool Selection: The structure of the lesson sequence was appropriate from both the teacher's and observer's point of view. However, the time should be distributed differently: The first block of manual data analysis was a bit too long, hence that it took considerable time before the students were allowed to conduct practical data analysis on the computer. This particularly seemed to lower their motivation as from previous teaching the students were used to working at the computer in every lesson, so this led to displeasure in the class. Therefore, a stronger integration of manual and automated data analysis has to be considered depending on what the students' are used to in class. Also, the lessons were a bit too packed, so that taking more time and adding at least a fourth lesson, as planned originally, seems necessary.

5 Summary

Summarizing, the developed lesson sequence could bring some important aspects of data analysis to school teaching. Particularly, it allows students to deal with this important topic and understand some of the underlying concepts. But it also helps them to develop some basic skills that are needed for conducting data analysis and for making predictions by themselves. It has turned out to be particularly important not to stop at the data analysis step, but instead to make predictions based on it, as this helped students to get into this topic, because they for example know that people are rated based on data in different contexts. Thus, the lesson sequence enabled students to understand aspects that are fascinating for them because of their "magical" effects, but can be explained with basic knowledge.

In general, the experiences of both, teacher and researcher, were very positive as this topic was not only important for the students, but as they also coped with the topic very well and developed a basic understanding. This particularly enabled them to discuss about this topic in a sound way and to conduct simple analyses by themselves. The active participation in the lessons confirmed the interest in the topic and the relevance for the learners. The choice of the software tool also seemed appropriate, as the students were not confronted with any challenges when using it and were able to master it intuitively.

However, the evaluation revealed aspects that should be taken into account in the future: In particular, the first phase with only manual data analyses was too long, as this contradicted the usual teaching. Accordingly, for motivational reasons, stronger intertwining the manual and automated data analyses will be sought in the future. In addition, it turned out that including further contexts, which was planned for the fourth lesson, was clearly lacking in the end, as the learners still found it difficult to relate the acquired competencies to new examples. Hence, shortening the topic to only three 90 min lessons seems not advisable.

Overall, the developed teaching concept and its implementation and evaluation reveal the potential of the topic for school and also confirms the assumption that this topic appears important for the students and is important for their everyday lifes. In particular, we were also able to show that this topic, which is often regarded as complex, can be reduced for and addressed in teaching even at lower secondary level, without having to abstract too much from the central aspects. Hence, the developed lesson sequence can be considered as a first step to bringing more data-oriented aspects to school teaching. However, when looking at the data literacy competency model used as a basis, there are many more aspects in this field that should clearly be addresses in teaching.

References

1. Botswan, R.: Big data meets Big Brother as China moves to rate its citizens (2018). https://www.wired.co.uk/article/chinese-government-social-credit-score-privacy-invasion. Accessed 09 June 2019
2. Cortez, P., Silva, A.: Using data mining to predict secondary school student performance. In: Proceedings of 5th Annual Future Business Technology Conference, Porto, 2008, pp. 5–12. EUROSIS-ETI (2008)
3. Dietz, A., Oppermann, F.: Planspiel "Datenschutz 2.0". LOG IN (2011)
4. Dorn, J.: InstaHub (2018). https://instahub.org. Accessed 09 June 2019
5. Grillenberger, A., Romeike, R.: A comparison of the field data management and its representation in secondary CS curricula. In: Proceedings of the 9th Workshop in Primary and Secondary Computing Education. ACM (2014)
6. Grillenberger, A., Romeike, R.: Developing a theoretically founded data literacy competency model. In: Proceedings of the 13th Workshop in Primary and Secondary Computing Education, WiPSCE 2018, pp. 9:1–9:10. ACM (2018)
7. Grillenberger, A., Romeike, R.: Key concepts of data management: an empirical approach. In: Proceedings of the 17th Koli Calling International Conference on Computing Education Research, Koli Calling 2017, pp. 30–39. ACM (2017)
8. Grillenberger, A., Romeike, R.: What teachers and students know about data management. In: Tatnall, A., Webb, M. (eds.) WCCE 2017. IAICT, vol. 515, pp. 557–566. Springer, Cham (2017). https://doi.org/10.1007/978-3-319-74310-3_56
9. Heinemann, B.: Drafting a data science curriculum for secondary schools. In: Proceedings of the 18th Koli Calling International Conference on Computing Education Research. ACM, New York (2018)
10. Hey, T., Tansley, S., Tolle, K.: The Fourth Paradigm: Data-Intensive Scientific Discovery. Microsoft Research, Redmond (2009)
11. Hill, K.: How target figured out a teen girl was pregnant before her father did (2012). https://www.forbes.com/sites/kashmirhill/2012/02/16/how-target-figured-out-a-teen-girl-was-pregnant-before-her-father-did. Accessed 09 June 2019
12. Myers, B.A., Hudson, S.E., Pausch, R.: Past, present and future of user interface software tools. ACM Trans. Comput. Hum. Interact. **7**(1), 3–28 (2000)
13. Resnick, M., et al.: Design principles for tools to support creative thinking. National Science Foundation workshop on Creativity Support Tools (2005)
14. Ridsdale, C., et al.: Strategies and best practices for data literacy education: knowledge synthesis report, Dalhousie University (2015)

Cybersecurity Within the Curricula of Informatics: The Estonian Perspective

Birgy Lorenz(✉), Kaido Kikkas, Tiia Sõmer, and Edmund Laugasson

Tallinn University of Technology, Ehitajate tee 5, 19086 Tallinn, Estonia
{birgy.lorenz,kaido.kikkas,tiia.somer,edmund.laugasson}@taltech.ee
https://taltech.ee/en/

Abstract. While the needs for generic IT staff have been generally addressed in many places, the lack of specialized workforce is a growing problem, especially in cybersecurity - falling behind in addressing cybercrime can lead to serious problems. Not only should the common cybersecurity awareness be raised, but more people should also be guided to specialize in cybersecurity. The cost of cybersecurity education and awareness campaigns is far less than the price of dealing with enormous consequences of cybercrime – in 2018, 600 Billion was reported in CSIS [17] by Internet Society, and it doubles annually.

In some countries, the problem has been recognized more than in others. The Estonian CyberSecurity Strategy (2019) points out the need to educate all citizens, improve education in schools and find new talents for the field [11]. The new curriculum of Informatics of which $\frac{1}{3}$ covers the cyber skills was developed in 2017, new materials will be available in 2019. In this paper we provide an overview of Estonian digital safety and cybersecurity curricula as well as discuss how to educate the masses and what to do with talents (how to detect talent and build up the talent pool). We will look at three years' work and studies (including the Cyber Olympics program) to offer ideas and perhaps inspiration to other countries. We also list a number of initiatives and tools that could help in updating the cybersecurity education and channeling resources in a more effective way.

Keywords: Curriculum development · Cybersecurity · Talents

1 Background

1.1 Digitalization and Goals for EU

Various strategies of the European Union have pointed out the need for a Digital Single Market [7] - everyone should have a possibility to conduct business or have access to the goods regardless of the location. The foundation of a Digital Single Market is formed by access, environment, economy, and society. This means that everyone should know how to use technology and the internet, as well as have access to it [4]. The downside is that cybercrime is also flourishing - not only are

S. N. Pozdniakov and V. Dagienė (Eds.): ISSEP 2019, LNCS 11913, pp. 159–171, 2019.
https://doi.org/10.1007/978-3-030-33759-9_13

companies developing services that are unstable and insecure, but many users having full access seem to lack any competencies other than click wherever you can, as fast as you can - unlike in city traffic, there is no driving license needed. Also, the interoperability of services cuts both ways, e.g. fewer attack vectors are needed for criminals [13]. Therefore the skill levels need to be raised for everyone, and getting more specialists to the field is inevitable [20]. According to ENISA [9], the focus has been on technical solutions - until the GDPR raised the issue of privacy to the wider public [8], yet overall awareness and behavioral aspects have but recently started to surface.

1.2 Developing Security-Aware Citizens for the Information Society

The latest DigComp 2.1 [2] points out that digital safety is among the five areas of digital skills that common people should obtain – essentially a part of lifelong learning. A lot of initiatives address coding and robotics (e.g. the Hour of Code and other similar events), while cybersecurity gets more attention during two months in a year - February being allocated for digital safety and behavior [22], and October as the "Cybersecurity month" is run by ENISA in the EU. As every country is free in their implementations, we studied various publications and reports to find out the current situation. For example, the overview provided by Informatics Europe [12] suggested that neither digital safety nor cybersecurity are not focused upon. While ethics and privacy get briefly mentioned this is not enough to successfully face the cybersecurity crisis that is coming our way.

Cybersecurity education in the EU and the US is mostly offered in the form of specialized courses at the university (BSc, MSc, PhD) level, while public awareness initiatives in the EU (e.g. Safer Internet) are commonly offered as extracurricular education and campaigns. There are some initiatives to work with technical talents within the framework of the European Cyber Security Challenge (led by military organizations, universities, NGOs and ENISA) where around 19 countries participate - 200 talents are tested annually on the EU level, 30–200 on the country level (average being around 100). This is not enough to meet the needs in cybersecurity. Likewise, we doubt that the related mass initiatives reach everyone. Even if countries participate in various other competitions like Cyber Patriot, Magic CTF or other Capture the Flag - style events, the amount of talents who have access to them is limited (usually, the same people attend all different events). Competitions for various skill levels are needed, widely distributed online training materials can also help - for instance, during the 2018–2019 season over 30 000 students participated in the CyberPatriot pre-competitions on many levels [6]. At the same time, a similar initiative in the UK (Cyber Security Challenge UK) is a more community-oriented NGO that provides programs for schools, educates parents and society. As for the Estonian approach, it is more akin to the wider, community-based UK model than the more vertical, competition oriented way of the US.

In Estonia there are also several initiatives that have been launched primarily by the Estonian Ministry of Defence through Cyber Olympic program (targeting young cybersecurity talents) and its many competitions: the easier, the test-like CyberCracker for 4–9th graders, the CyberCracker school round for beginner-level talents (7–12th graders and vocational schools) and the Cyber-Spike advanced-level talent competition for students aged 14–24 [5]. Estonia is also involved in the Safer Internet initiative [3]. For schools, there are several learning and teaching materials developed in 2018–2019. Until recently, the majority of teaching on cybersecurity depended on the initiative of teachers only as they invited guest speakers to talk about cybersecurity issues. Schools could also choose National Defence as one of their elective courses, this course included a part about cybersecurity.

The goal of this paper is to find out how to guide students in these directions. Starting from middle school (ages 12–14) we could see a more rapid change and improvement in the number of people entering the field, and discuss the *must have* and *nice to have* options and their impact to cybersecurity national strategy education subgoals. Creating this list is the theoretical part of the strategy building using the *top-down and bottom-up approach*. Feedback was also requested from 4 different ministries of Estonian government to suggest further adjustments that could be made without needing changes in curricula (a political decision).

2 Methods

We used a two-pronged approach in this study. In the top-down (from strategies to implementations) part, we analyzed related strategy and policy documents and their shortcomings in Estonia. In order to understand the current situation in teaching, we analyzed the different levels of curricula, as well as the best practices used, together with their shortcomings. In the reverse, bottom-up part, we used a list of shortcomings compiled with the help of experts as the starting point. The list was then sent to be evaluated by the ministry officials. The process and its analysis took place in 3 months from February to April 2019.

The list addressed

- Policy documents and reports that support the development of a national cyber strategy for schools in Estonia;
- Analysis of cybersecurity curricula development for all levels of education from basic school to graduate studies;
- Best practices that are supported by volunteers, supporting programs, competitions or other to update skills for both the masses and young talents (robotics and coding training, complementary IT education; cyber education through competition and awareness).

There were limitations for creating a list of initiatives - in the current situation, changing the current national curricula is not possible as there is no room for mandatory cybersecurity education for all the students. Also, all the initiatives should support community building to survive a decrease in funding in around 3–5 years. The effect of the initiatives would be measured by the number of people involved (mass education), but also by the quality (education for talents).

The expert group consisted of young cybersecurity talents (2 persons), industry experts (2 persons), representatives of gymnasium (1 person), vocational school teachers (1 person), and university researchers (2 persons). The list was compiled by reviewing the data (sent by email), open discussions, and online cooperation in a shared file. The list was later also evaluated by officials from 4 different ministries (Ministry of Education and Science, Ministry of Defence, Ministry of Economy and Communication, and Ministry of Internal Affairs).

3 Results

3.1 Policy Documents, Curricula, and Best Practices and Their Shortcomings in Estonia

E-safety and cybersecurity are taught at Estonian schools today within the elective courses of Informatics and National Defense. However, various aspects of cybersecurity are also integrated into other subjects (mathematics, societal studies). Most of the focus is on e-safety and cyber hygiene. To some extent, within the teaching of national defense, the questions of critical information infrastructure and cyberterrorism/cyberwarfare are also discussed. The national defense curriculum is coordinated by the Ministry of Defense; other subjects by the Ministry of Education and Science. The current national school curricula for all levels do not cover cybersecurity as a separate subject, but outline the main competencies the students should be able to possess upon graduation, also including cybersecurity-related competencies [25,26]. The first, second, and third level of school students (grades 1–9) should be able to – with the successive deepening of teaching – use computer programs for study and leisure and manage in the world of technology in a safe manner. By the end of the 9th grade, the student should be able to understand and analyze threats and opportunities arising from the use of technology. The PRÕK 2011 also states that theory should be amended with practical activities wherever possible. The objective for teaching Informatics, among others, is that the student recognizes and avoids threats to their security and personal information [26]. The Gymnasium level students should be able to use contemporary technology with responsibility and have an informed opinion on the trends of technology and questions related to its use [25]. The plan also prescribes compulsory crossover themes, one of them being Technology & Innovation. By the time of graduation, the gymnasium students should be prepared to use ICT in their everyday lives, studies and work. (ibid). Within the elective course of Informatics, the teachers mainly teach e-safety topics included in the national curricula. The elective course of national defense covers more specific areas, such as updates, firewalls, backups, encryption, VPN, and smart device security. The five main areas covered are computers, the Web, wireless networks, smart devices, and social networks.

With the introduction of the new National Cyber Security Strategy in 2019, there will be a renewed emphasis on cybersecurity awareness development at schools. The strategy also points out that we should strive to educate all citizens and hunt for technical talent. For the moment, a curriculum for an elective course on cybersecurity has been developed in 2017, and digital study materials for this course are being finalized. The course, together with materials, will be available to all schools in Estonia from September 2019 onwards.

3.2 The Curricula from a Cybersecurity Content Perspective

At the university level, there are programs for cybersecurity at Bachelor or Master level, and several open courses for anyone interested (see Table 1). The analysis of the quality and topics of the courses (showing that while some special branches give broad competencies and possibilities to specialize, the average IT student will face much less) is presented in the Digiturvis report ordered by the Ministry of Economic Affairs and Communications [18].

3.3 Nonformal Education

Today's children get their first IT experience very early. Outside the national school curricula, there are extracurricular activities offered by schools, different organizations or the private sector. Teachers will be the people who would follow the personality, development, interests, and skills of students throughout the years - this is important for attracting talent in positive rather than negative (i.e. criminal) ways. Prospective employers can have an early opportunity by providing either specific training courses, boot camps or other activities to young people in different age groups, but also by delivering information on options available to them in their future careers.

Several initiatives in Estonia have started to analyze the challenges and raise the interest of both students and schools to study IT [15], but the real impact still comes from extracurricular activities or competitions, where the primary focus is on development (programming). Most of these initiatives run solely due to a few motivated people in academia and industry. The number of extracurricular activities supported by the government is fairly low [19,28].

So far, the competitions have focused more on talents than numbers (see Fig. 1). Only the yearly tests for 4–9th grade and the activities of the Safer Internet (mentioned above) can be counted on to raise cybersecurity awareness on a wider basis. Below is an overview of competitions and initiatives involving cybersecurity and IT in Estonia. The comparison is made using DIGCOMP as a reference for explaining the level of IT skills taught. While it seems that there are many initiatives listed, the actual number of students that have access to them should be much higher in order to impact cyber-awareness.

The military sector has also been involved in the skills development - there is interest from the Estonian Defence League's Cyber Defence Unit to do voluntary work with youth [14]. An example of such work is assisting schools in introducing cybersecurity courses [21].

Table 1. Formal education and cyber security teaching

Level	Content from curricula
Basic	Digital safety is part of the new optional courses of Informatics. 1.–3. Graders (Digital Safety); 4.–6. Grades (Digital hygiene); 7.–9. Grades (Cyber Hygiene). The courses are influenced by DIGCOMP. Main content revolves around the use of technology (incl. Smart devices); information systems and online environments; identity, privacy; communication; health; problem-solving [10]
Secondary school	A 35-h beginner-level course focuses on an introduction to information society challenges (government services, terminology, and legislation); data protection; incidents and measures; improving one's skills from generic digital literacy to cybersecurity talent level [1]. Here, the talent means those taking part in nonformal education competitions for IT and cybersecurity (see the section for nonformal education below)
Vocational school	IT is taught at 12 schools, 11 of them training junior specialists of IT systems and 1 junior software developers), higher level skills are rarely seen. Cybersecurity is somewhat included in overall system security management training, but not in adequate levels and volume. 1–2 schools plan to start training IT security specialists from January 2020. An important factor is the chance to participate in various IT and cybersecurity competitions on both national and international level (see the *nonformal competitions* section below)
Bachelor studies	The IT College of Tallinn University of Technology offers a B.Sc. curriculum in CyberSecurity Engineering. Taught in English, it has the benefit of an international community and varying perspectives on cybersecurity [23]
Master studies	A joint MSc program between the two largest universities in Estonia (TalTech and UT). Courses include basic skills (e.g. Entrepreneurship and Business Planning or Organizational Theory and Psychology); basic IT (programming, data mining, system administration); crypto; cyber and forensics; special courses on attack and defense; human side (human, legal and management aspects, history of warfare) [24]
Doctoral studies	Thesis topics are chosen from technical perspectives to the gamification of cybersecurity to human aspects and management. There is no dedicated doctoral program for cybersecurity yet

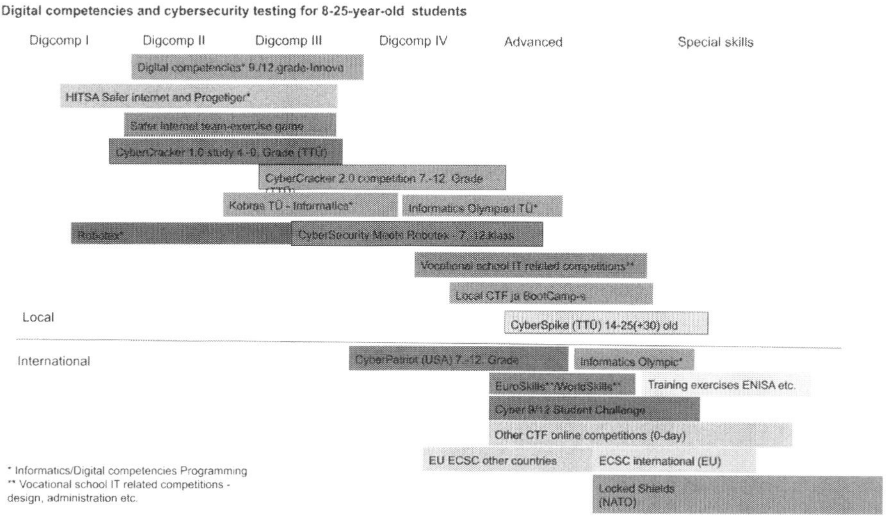

Fig. 1. IT and Cyber Security related Competitions in Estonia for the youth

The question is when to start – at the university level, during general education [16], or are there additional options and resources? One additional option that is being considered in order to attract young cyber talent could be military conscription, as it is mandatory for all male Estonian citizens aged 17–27 (and voluntary for females).

4 Recommendations

4.1 Formal Education

IT and cybersecurity are being taught within the traditional school curricula at all levels and within extracurricular activities [1,10] Table 2 shows the education, training, knowledge, and experiences of young people prior to joining the workforce compared to Table 1. There are also other education-related activities: international olympiads are held in various subjects and cybersecurity competitions are conducted. At gymnasium/high school levels there are national defense courses, which among other topics give an overview of cyberdefense measures in the military. There are also vocational schools where students get secondary education together with a vocation. When the first year is devoted to general studies and 2nd year to specialized studies (such as IT or cybersecurity-related topics), the 3rd year is generally meant for job-oriented, on-site vocational training together with more specialized training. Utilizing these students for the purposes of cyber conscription could prove useful.

For finding new talent, it will be important to not only have information about the academic background and abilities of young people but to also gain an insight into their other abilities. For example, a person without formal IT

Table 2. Education and training possibilities for youth

All levels of education	Extracurricular activities Olympiads Cyber competitions Youth organizations
Elementary school	Extracurricular activities Olympiads
Gymnasium/high school	Extracurricular activities Olympiads National defense studies
Vocational schools	Year 1: general studies Year 2: specialized studies Year 3: on-the-job-training
Universities	Academic studies

education might perform very well on some cybersecurity tasks. An important aspect of developing cyber talent will be on attracting those people to the field, who have not even thought about it for any reason. Studies have shown that interdisciplinarity is very important in cybersecurity, and attracting young people with other interests would widen the talent base, but also allow for more effective use of persons with specific skills.

4.2 Non-formal Education

The proposed list of activities and its impact were divided into a. talent hunt and competitions for masses regarding awareness (the focus group is students aged 8–24 years); b. International experiences and talent development c. Supporting training events for students and teachers; d. Development of the learning content; e. Support from research to evaluate the impact (see Table 3).

4.3 Based on the Findings, the Following Goals Were Delivered by the Experts

Goal 1: Every child in Estonia is cyber-aware and possesses measurable skills (CyberCracker) by 2022, 60% of the target group should participate;
Goal 2.1: in 2022, cybersecurity will be taught as an elective in at least 20 Estonian Gymnasiums;
Goal 2.2: Teachers of cybersecurity will be adequately educated and supported (community), more institutions will be involved in awareness campaigns to find and guide cyber talents;
Goal 2.3: Teachers are provided with modern study aids;
Goal 3.1: Continuity in discovering, supporting (community) and directing young talents (competitions, camps, community events);

Table 3. The proposed list of activities and its impact for cyber security

Initiative	Focus group	Goal
Talent hunt (a)	14–24 year old students, talents and potential talents	Local level competitions CyberSpike (online pre-competition, main competition) for 250 participants from basic to university level; CyberCracker School round for beginners once a year for up to 3000 students from 7–12th graders and vocational school. Local level Capture The Flag competitions at least 4 times a year; Vocational school CyberSecurity online competition once a year. Cyber Innovation hackathon once a year to develop new ideas, services, and products with the industry
Education for masses (a)	8–19 year old students, mass	CyberCracker study 1–2 times a year for 4–9th graders for 60% of the population, CyberCracker for Primary once a year for 1–3 graders (40% of the population)
International experience (b)	15–24 year old students, talents	Taking part of a different competition like European Cyber Security Challenge (EU), CyberPartiot (USA), Magic CTF (USA), 9/12 (USA); Nordic Security Competition (EU), Cyber Defenders Discovery Camp (Singapore) and more. Organizing international events in Estonia to attract foreign talents
Training for students (c)	10–24 year old students	CyberCamp 3 times a year for talents (a 25); local training events at least 4 times a year (a 25). Gymnasium level cyber security lessons (35 h) at 20 gymnasiums; Cybersecurity clubs (10 local clubs all over Estonia). CyberSecurity Roadshow (local events where experts come to visit - a 100 participants, 6 locations)
Training for teachers (c)	Teachers	Cyber seminars for teachers (3–4 times a year for 20–30 people), annual Cyber Conference for Education (150–200 participants). Expert teachers training for 10 teachers in a year
Development of learning content (d)	Teachers, Parents, Students	Beginner White-hat hacker exercise portal (12–20 new exercises annually); Learning videos (10 annually) with lesson plans; updating cybersecurity materials, lesson plans for basic school and gymnasium and make it publicly available (a 10 annually). Develop 3–4 learning games and scenarios in a year to teach theoretical models and terminology
Science (e)	Scientist, Ministries, Industry	Studies regarding monitoring initiatives and its success, modeling how one becomes a cyber talent and its shortcuts; curriculum development and testing results; improving discussion about cyber hygiene in society (academic seminars twice a year, summer schools once a year for 60 people)

Goal 3.2: Estonian cybersecurity talents will have opportunities to gain international experience at various European and world events (competitions, camps);
Goal 4.1: The CyberOlympics event series will be based on research and acquire international recognition;
Goal 4.2: Estonian research on cybersecurity is of good quality, results and best practices will be delivered both nationally and internationally.

5 Discussion

Nowadays, we see that Informatics taught within the third-level education is common, in the EU it is also being systematized for the first two levels. Nevertheless, cybersecurity has not found wider coverage, as seen from the "Are We in the Same Boat?" report by Informatic Europe [12]. Only privacy and security have been mentioned twice but in a rather passing manner. At the same time, our experience with commoners, managers and experts alike suggests that both securities of existing systems and awareness of the dark side of technology are of prime importance. Also, the DigComp recommendations for ubiquitous digital knowledge do include information security.

This raises the question: where should the sorely needed security experts come from? In the EU, the issue is discussed on the political level - but in practice, only volunteer enthusiasm is assumed through informal competitions and some enterprise initiative (mostly enterprise training programs - as only a few universities are capable of adequate training levels).

Moving to the first two levels of education, we see that there is a large gap between slogans and reality. Campaigns like "Come Study IT", "Hour of Code" or "Women to IT" are attractive but their practical results (people getting actually trained and employed) take years to achieve. We also see a bottleneck at teachers - the *fearful majority* frightened by technology is incapable of acquiring the necessary tech knowledge and thus also unable to pass it on to students.

From the results of the CyberCracker, we found that only $\frac{1}{3}$ of Estonian students saw themselves as prospective specialists and creators/developers of IT, the rest saw themselves as predominantly consumers. Thus, one of the key questions in getting more talent into IT and cybersecurity, in particular, is: how to direct the youth to accept responsibility and take initiative.

Another problem is that students do not get in touch with actual content creation at school, and the little they get would only be via social media. This has led to a skewed understanding of work in IT sector (or worse, no understanding at all) - when asked about the prospective paths in IT, *programmer* and *photographer* were the only ones named in several cases. The issue should be addressed by employers working together with each other (rather than competing) as well as other parties involved.

The current situation in Estonia is interesting - on the one hand, Informatics is not compulsory; on the other hand, new curricula have recently been developed to include various related topics (including cybersecurity). The government would rather see it become compulsory, but it hesitates - not fearing opposition to the very idea but rather the situation where there are no suitable people to teach the new topics. Thus, a prime issue here is to find ways to involve new teachers - whether by including enterprise, academy (even students), military, or just further promoting e-learning.

Looking specifically at cybersecurity, we compiled the following SWOT analysis:

- **Strengths:** small country - easy to change curricula, pilot and apply the changes. The government supports the idea and there is political readiness to back various initiatives to provide youth necessary knowledge and skills (competitions, camps, course development etc).
- **Weaknesses:** resources, especially funding and staff. Lack of teachers in cybersecurity and IT, in general, is a top concern (more so as cybersecurity has high pay levels).
- **Opportunities:** using existing young talent as teachers and course developers. Possibility to attract large international corporations by offering a uniquely positioned *testing ground* (Estonia is at the same time both a *post-Soviet* country and a thoroughly Western *startup dream* with ample possibilities and good infrastructure).
- **Threats:** the pace of development in the field will quicken further due to rapid implementation of AI solutions, making the country unable to cope with incidents, losing the image of an *e-country* and international reputation. As in many other countries, the next generation is a concern as talents leave towards wealthier countries. Another threat is the influence of services from countries whose values differ from European ones.

At the university level, we see the need for competence centers for IT teaching in various contexts. At Tallinn University of Technology, within its TalTechDigital initiative, an e-course called DigiTarkus (DigiWisdom) was piloted for all its staff in 2018 [27]. The aim of the course is to provide an all-covering basic set of digital skills (including basic cybersecurity) for both academics of various backgrounds and support staff alike. Building on the experience, we suggest a similar project - but this time, not for just mass education but rather a hub for developing and distributing a necessary skill set for teachers/trainers as well as future talent hunters.

6 Conclusion

Cybersecurity and -privacy, while having largely been a niche topic in education so far, move fast to become a central issue in digital education, and neglecting or downplaying it can seriously hamper the development of the whole field. Estonia is in a rather unique position to pilot an initiative for students to become digitally competent and show the results to the rest of the world. We feel that the orientation to generic awareness in today's Europe is a mistake as it will not direct enough young people towards proper IT careers - we may end up with either need to import the necessary workforce or just becoming passive consumers of external services.

Finding teachers and funding is a challenge in education both in Estonia and elsewhere, at the same time the number of cyber incidents is growing fast. Competitions are a good way to find interested young people - but if they remain isolated activities, the effect is not enough. The experiences of the UK and Estonia both suggest that while we need to start from the grassroots level, we also have to find ways to lead the talents to higher levels and specialist careers (among others, both parents and schools should be more involved). At the university level, cybersecurity should be offered on a wider basis - and again, both on the mass/common (to provide related knowledge and skills to academics with all backgrounds) and expert level (to train teachers who are capable of forwarding the knowledge and skills).

References

1. Estonian Atlantic Treaty Association: National curricula cybersecurity for secondary school in Estonia (2017). https://1drv.ms/w/s!AuRLzcD9FVl7ywlqPX-J4ewoLgIy
2. Carretero, S., Vuorikari, R., Punie, Y.: The digital competence framework for citizens with eight proficiency levels and examples of use. Joint Research Centre. European Commission. Luxembourg (2017). https://doi.org/10.2760/38842
3. Lastekaitse Liit. (Estonian) Union of Child Welfare: Targalt Internetis. About the project (Estonian) safer internet centre in Estonia (2019). https://www.targaltinternetis.ee/en/about-the-project/
4. Connectivity for a European gigabit society (2018). https://ec.europa.eu/digital-single-market/en/policies/improving-connectivity-and-access
5. CyberOlympic. About the project (2019). https://sites.google.com/view/kyberolympia/eng/about-the-project
6. CyberPatriot - the national youth cyber education program (2019). https://www.uscyberpatriot.org/
7. A digital single market strategy for Europe (2015). https://eur-lex.europa.eu/legal-content/EN/TXT/?uri=COM%3A2015%3A192%3AFIN
8. Drogkaris, P., Bourka, A.: Guidance and gaps analysis for European standardisation. ENISA (2018). https://doi.org/10.2824/698562
9. Drogkaris, P., Bourka, A.: Cybersecurity Culture Guidelines: Behavioural Aspects of Cybersecurity. ENISA (2019). https://doi.org/10.2824/324042
10. Information Technology Foundation for Education: National curricula informatics for basic school in Estonia (2016). https://drive.google.com/file/d/0B1-0pZFgjFnQX29Gb0ZYb1FMc0k/view?usp=sharing
11. Estonian cybersecurity strategy (2019). https://www.mkm.ee/en/objectives-activities/information-society/cyber-security
12. Informatics Europe & ACM Europe: Informatics education in Europe: Are we all in the same boat? Technical report, The Committee on European Computing Education (CECE), New York, NY, USA (2017). https://doi.org/10.1145/3106077
13. Interoperability & standardisation: connecting ehealth services (2018). https://ec.europa.eu/digital-single-market/en/interoperability-standardisation-connecting-ehealth-services

14. Kaska, K., Osula, A.M., Stinissen, J.: The cyber defence unit of the Estonian defence league: Legal, policy and organisational analysis. In: Estonia: NATO Cooperative Cyber Defence Centre of Excellence, p. 15. NATO Cooperative Cyber Defence Centre of Excellence (2013). http://ccdcoe.eu/uploads/2018/10/CDU_Analysis.pdf
15. Kooli, N.T.: Back to school programme (2019). https://tagasikooli.ee/?lang=en
16. Kori, K., Altin, H., Pedaste, M., Mäeots, M.: Why are students interested in studying ICT? (2017). https://sisu.ut.ee/sites/default/files/ict/files/kulli_kori_heilo_altin.pdf
17. Lewis, J.: Economic Impact of Cybercrime, No Slowing Down. McAfee (2018). https://csis-prod.s3.amazonaws.com/s3fs-public/publication/economic-impact-cybercrime.pdf
18. Lorenz, B., Laugasson, E., Püvi, S., Laanpere, M.: DigiTurvis - study report. Technical report, Tallinn University (2014). https://onedrive.live.com/view.aspx?resid=120A5B9B56F334F2!340&ithint=file%2cdocx&app=Word&authkey=!ALtyGq2CQwFt7Q4
19. Mektory tehnoloogiakool (2019). https://www.ttu.ee/kooliopilasele/tehnoloogiakool/
20. National coalitions (2018). https://ec.europa.eu/digital-single-market/en/national-local-coalitions
21. Põltsamaa gymnasium cyber security study programme elective subjects (2017). https://drive.google.com/drive/folders/0B431U6eEm9oVY081WEhMaENQSFk
22. Safer internet day (2019). https://xn-pev-qla.internet.ee/
23. TalTech: TalTech cyber security engineering (2019). https://www.ttu.ee/studying/tut_admission/programmes-in-taltech/bachelors/cyber-security-engineering/#specialty-4
24. TalTech: TalTech cyber security masters programme (2019). https://www.ttu.ee/studying/tut_admission/programmes-in-taltech/masters/cyber-security/#specialty-12
25. Teataja, R.: GrÕk. (Estonian) National Secondary School Curriculum (2011). https://www.riigiteataja.ee/akt/129082014021?leiaKehtiv
26. Teataja, R.: PrÕk. *Estonian* basic school national curriculum (2011). https://www.riigiteataja.ee/akt/129082014020?leiaKehtiv
27. Tallinn University of Technology: What is TalTechDigital? (2019). https://www.ttu.ee/projects/taltechdigital-2/
28. Tuisk, T.: Developments on science extracurricular activities 2013–2017 (2017). http://www.etag.ee/wp-content/uploads/2017/10/Terje_teadushuviharidus-2013-2017.pdf

Teaching Informatics: From High School to University Level

Person-Thing-Orientation and the Choice of Computer Science Courses in High School

Jascha Kemper and Michael Brinkmeier(✉)

Institute of Computer Science, Universität Osnabrück, Osnabrück, Germany
{jakemper,mbrinkmeier}@uni-osnabrueck.de

Abstract. Person-Thing-Orientation is a psychological trait that represents a persons interests in its social and physical environment. It often is measured by a standardised questionnaire, providing two scores for an individual, the Person- and the Thing-Score. In several studies they were shown to correlate to a persons tendency to select STEM-subjects at university and their persistence and success. In this paper the Person-Thing-Orientation of German high school students and its correlation to the choice of CS courses in the last two terms are examined. In addition to the standardised self-test the same questionnaire is used to obtain the Person- and Thing-Scores that the students ascribe to a typical computer scientist. Based on the collected data the correlations between gender, the choice of computer science courses and the self and foreign scores, as well as their distance, is analysed.

Keywords: Person-Thing-Orientation · High schools · Gender differences

1 Introduction

In Lower Saxony, and some other states of Germany, the students of the tenth grade are required to choose a series of courses for the last two years of high school. Usually these courses can be chosen as a *high profile course* with a large impact on their final exam grade, a *low profile course* with a lower impact a *regular course* with little or none impact at all. Some courses, like computer science (CS) can even be dropped completely.

One year before, they already have to choose some courses for the tenth grade. Regarding science, technology, engineering and math (STEM) the students have to select three out of physics, chemistry, biology and CS. While the first three are continuously taught, beginning in fifth or sixth grade, CS usually is a new subject, unknown to most of the students. Nonetheless, in many schools, which provide the possibility to choose CS[1], quite a large proportion of students select it, getting rid of one of the other three sciences. And, following oral reports of

[1] Not all high schools provide the opportunity to select CS.

S. N. Pozdniakov and V. Dagienė (Eds.): ISSEP 2019, LNCS 11913, pp. 175–188, 2019.
https://doi.org/10.1007/978-3-030-33759-9_14

teachers, the fraction of girls in CS courses during the tenth grade is quite high[2]. But at the brink to the 11th grade, many girls drop CS, reducing their fraction massively.

To validate this observations by numbers and to understand the reasons, a series of interviews with students and teachers of a high school were conducted. From these a questionnaire was developed, which was tested in the CS courses of a 10th grade in another high school. The survey took place several weeks after the students had selected their courses for the 11th and 12th grade. Therefore, they were aware of their reasons for dropping or selecting CS.

The survey was augmented by the standardised questionnaire for the Person- and Thing-Orientation, as introduced by Graziano et al. [3]. The resulting two scores are measures for the interest of the subjects in their social and physical environments. It was observed that these correlate with the likelihood that a person studies a STEM-subject and their persistence and success [4,6].

In addition to the individual Person-Thing-Orientation, the interest in a subject might be influenced by the stereotype of a person working in this field. If this image fits the own interests and personality, this might have a positive influence on the image of the subject itself. On the other hand, a large difference between the self image and the stereotype may lead to a principal rejection or disinterest in the subject. To measure this difference a second copy of the questionnaire with a slightly different setting was added. It was used to determine the Person-Thing-Orientation the students presume for a "typical" and fictitious computer scientist, subsequently called Foreign-Scores. The resulting difference between the Self- and the Foreign-Scores might correlate with the decision to select or drop CS-courses in the last two years of high school.

In this paper we describe the results of the questionnaire regarding the Person- and Thing-Scores and their difference between the Self- and the Foreign-Scores. In the next section we recollect results about the Person-Thing-Orientation and some observations documented in the literature about gender-based differences in interest in computer sciences. These results and some quotes from teachers, collected during the preparation of the questionnaire, are used to deduce some hypotheses regarding the correlation of Person-Thing-Orientation and the choice of CS courses, which we try to evaluate in the following.

2 Gender-Specific Differences of Interest in STEM Subjects

It is a well documented fact that women are under-represented in many STEM-disciplines and computer science in particular. This can already be observed in the last terms of high schools if the students have the opportunity to choose specific focus areas or to drop courses. One important factor causing this effect seems to be a specific psychological trait, the so called *Person-Thing-Orientation*

[2] Unfortunately we couldn't find a reference for this observation, apart from anecdotal reports of teachers.

Table 1. The questionnaire for Person-Thing-Orientation [4]

Item	Situation	Category
1	Redesign and install a stereo sound system yourself	TO
2	Take apart and try to reassemble a desktop computer	TO
3	Stop to watch a machine working on the street	TO
4	Listen in on a conversation between two people in a crowd	PO
5	Remove the back of a mechanical toy to see how it works	TO
6	Strike up a conversation with a homeless person on a street	PO
7	Try to fix your own watch, toaster, etc.	TO
8	Listen with caring interest to an old person who sits next to you on a bus	PO
9	Notice the habits and quirks of people around you	PO
10	Make the first attempt to meet a new neighbor	PO
11	Attend a speech given by a person you admire without knowing the topic on the speech	PO
12	Attempt to comfort a total stranger who has had a disaster happen	PO
13	Gain a reputation for giving good advice for personal problems	PO

[3–5]. One part of it, the *Person-Orientation*, describes the interest of a person in interpersonal relations, while the second, the *Thing-Orientation*, relates to the interest in technological concepts and things.

For each of the two traits a score can be computed from a standardised questionnaire (see Table 1, [4]). It was derived by factor analysis from a bigger version introduced by Little, containing 12 items per aspect [5]. The resulting questionnaire consists of a total of 13 items, 5 items measuring the TO and the remaining eight the PO. Each item describes an activity which has to be rated by the degree to which the subject would enjoy it. The ratings vary from 1 (strongly disagree) to 5 (strongly agree). The Person- and Thing-Scores are the averages of the answers to the PO and TO items.

Table 2. The relation between Person-Thing-Orientation and university subjects [4].

Category	Gender	Person-Score		Thing-Score		N
		Mean	SD	Mean	SD	
STEM	Female	2.58	0.83	1.81	1.21	30
	Male	2.24	0.75	2.76	0.97	137
Non-STEM	Female	2.59	0.60	0.87	0.89	109
	Male	2.39	0.72	2.06	0.96	126

Graziano et al. examined the influence of Person- and Thing-Orientation on the choice of STEM university courses [4] or as predictor for persistence and success in engineering [6]. They observed that women tended to have a higher Person-Orientation (PO) and men a higher Thing-Orientation (TO): "*men were higher in TO 1 ($M = 2.42$, $SD = 1.03$) than women ($M = 1.07$, $SD = 1.04$). Women, however, were higher in PO ($M = 2.58$, $SD = 0.65$) than men ($M = 2.31$, $SD = 0.74$)*" [4]. They and independently Tay et al. [8] disproved the hypotheses that the Person-

and Thing-Orientation contradict each other: *"TO need not be conceptualized as a bipolar opposite of PO, or even on a single common dimension with it."* [4, p. 474]. While a correlation between the Thing-Orientation and the choice of STEM-courses seems to be obvious, the Person-Orientation has an impact, too: *"On the other hand, students higher in PO may perceive more (or different) options for their personal and occupational lives"* [4, p. 475].

The fact that interest in CS seems to be gender specific was observed in other studies, too. For example in [7] Petrut et al. describe that in elementary schools boys seem to have a greater interest in technical devices, while girls seem to have a higher interest in solving difficult tasks. In addition the interest in Computer Science or computer related topics seems to be fixated at an early age. They further subsume, that the influence of specific interventions seems to be very limited. These observations are in accordance with the results about the Person-Thing-Orientation and their gender specific differences.

Some studies, like that of Romero and Dietrich [1] indicate that the observed early differences in the interest in computer science might stem from prejudices or stereotypes. They used the software *Sonic Pi* [2] to introduce students to programming. But instead of a STEM course, they did this in music lessons to prevent biases. They observed, that especially girls showed a long-term interest and remembered the key concepts after a longer period of time, indicating a higher interest in the topic. This might be caused by the fact that students connect music and musicians with another stereotype than CS and computer scientists. Therefore the girls may tend to develop a stronger interest in the application of computers and programming in this area.

2.1 Quotes from Teacher Interviews

During the preparation of the survey analysed in this paper, three teachers were interviewed. They were asked to explain the high fraction of girls in the 10th grade and the sudden drop in the 11th grade. Here we only recollect those statements, regarding the interest of girls in CS.

To begin with, none of the interviewed teachers denied the fact that the interest of boys in CS is generally much higher than that of girls. But this seems to contradict the fact that quite a large number of girls choose CS at the first possibility in 10th grade. Two teachers suggested explanations which would override the reduced interest, and thus explain this effect.

One teacher pointed out that girls often choose computer science in 10th grade to have more opportunities of dropping subjects or grades later on. Therefore it seems logical that they wouldn't continue CS in the last two terms. He stated that, provided they had the chance of dropping subjects or grades without starting CS, they certainly would have chosen that way instead. But he also states that nearly all girls who have chosen computer science show great effort in class.

Another teacher suggests that the main reason for girls dropping CS is not being disinterested in the subject, but their higher number of opportunities to select courses. His is due to their more constant performances over all subjects.

On the other hand, a special reason for many boys to elect CS would be their wish of dropping the second foreign language. He thinks that the specific topics in CS or other subjects would have no influence on boys or girls interests in the subject in general. He justifies this statement with the observation that the students' reactions on the topics were very different from class to class. In the end he is sure that the reason for girls selecting CS is not a gender specific difference of interest in the subject, but their higher number of alternatives because of their more constant performances in all of the other subjects.

These statements seem to indicate that a lot of girls chose CS in the 10th grade, even though they are disinterested in the subject. Regarding the Person-Thing-Orientation and the results of Graziano et al. [4] the girls in CS courses should not show a generally higher interest than the average. Therefore, the boys in CS courses still would have higher Thing-Orientation than the girls.

3 Hypotheses

In this section some hypotheses are stated, which will subsequently be evaluated using the concept of Person-Thing-Orientation.

- *Hypothesis 1.* The fraction of female students in CS courses drops significantly from 10th to 11th grade. This hypothesis stems from the anecdotal reports of teachers.
- *Hypothesis 2.* The Thing-Score of male students is significantly higher than that of female students. As the first hypothesis this is a direct consequence of published research on Person-Thing-Orientation. The Observations of Petrut et al. [7] point in the same direction.
- *Hypothesis 3.* The probability that a student chooses CS courses in high school correlates with his or her Thing-Score. This is a direct consequence of the observation of Graziano et al. [4,6].
- *Hypothesis 4.* The Person- and Thing-Orientation of female students in 10th grade CS courses do not differ significantly from the scores of all females. This hypothesis is a consequence of the teacher's statements. They claim that girls do not select CS courses in 10th grade due to a high interest in the topic. Instead they either choose it to drop another science or to obtain additional alternatives.

3.1 Self- and Foreign-Assessment of Person-Thing-Scores

As in [3,4,9] one copy of the questionnaire for Person-Thing-Orientation is used in a subjective perspective, i.e. the subject answers the questions from its own point of view. The resulting scores are the *Self-Assessment*. In addition to the studies mentioned above, and to our knowledge for the first time, a second copy of the questionnaire should be answered by the subject, taking the perspective of a fictitious computer scientist of roughly the same age. The resulting scores are called *Foreign-Assessment*. It is assumed to provide a measure for the presumed

Person- and Thing-Scores that the subject attributes to the fictitious and iconic character. In other words, we assume that the Foreign-Assessment describes the psychological traits connected with a stereotypical computer scientist.

Our interest in the Foreign-Assessment originates from the assumption that a student is more likely to select a course, if the covered topic is connected with a stereotype of persons similar to the own personality. We assume that this difference can be measured by the difference between the Self- and the Foreign-Assessment. Therefore, We will examine the correlation of this difference with the likelihood that a person chooses a course in computer science.

Hypothesis 5. We expected a high correlation between the difference of Person- and Thing-scores of the *Self-* and the *Foreign-Assessment* and their *Choice of CS courses.* Especially students dropping CS courses are expected to have a lower Thing-Self-Score as their Foreign-Score. On the other hand, we expect that persons with a higher Person-Self-Score than the Foreign-Score are likely to drop CS courses. The strength of this effect may vary between genders.

4 Method

The survey was conducted at a German high school allowing students to pick computer science as an examination course since 2006. It took place at the end of the term, a few weeks after the students selected their courses for the last two years. All students of the 10th grade attending one of the four computer science courses took part.

In total 74 students attend these courses, 37 of them female. 71 of them took part in the survey. The question for their gender was answered by 33 with "male", 34 with "female" and 4 with "other".

4.1 The Questionnaire

The questionnaire consisted of several sections, beginning with questions regarding the gender and the choice of CS courses in the last two terms. The second section consisted of questions regarding the motivation for the choice. These questions were constructed from the interviews conducted at a different high school. The third part consisted of the standardized questionnaire for the Person-Thing-Score, including the introductory text. The fourth section consisted of 46 theses to which the students had to agree or disagree on a 5-level Likert-scale. These were followed by a list of seven teaching methods which the students should rate. The last section consisted of the Person-Thing-questionnaire, but this time with the request to answer the questions from the perspective of a young computer scientist.

For the following analysis we only use the gender, the fact whether CS courses were selected or dropped and the scores obtained from the assessments.

4.2 Design

The survey is an empirical study with the independent variables *Gender*, *Choice of CS courses* and *Assessments*, the latter including the Self-Scores and the Foreign-Scores. The variable *Gender* is nominal with two values "male" and "female". The third option "other" was ignored due to the small sample size ($n = 4$). The nominal variable *Choice of CS courses* with the values "selected" and "not selected". The type of course is neglected, due to small number of cases in several categories.

The *Assessments* consists of the two factors *Self-Assessment* and *Foreign-Assessment*. The first are the Person-Thing-Scores resulting from the standard questionnaire, while the second are the Person-Thing-Scores resulting from the same questions with regard to a fictitious computer scientist. All four are ordinal variables with values between 1 (strongly disagree) and 5 (strongly agree).

5 Results

Due to space restrictions, this paper concentrates on the Self- and Foreign-Assessment of the Person- and Thing-Scores. The data collected from the 46 theses will be evaluated separately. The results regarding the *Choice of CS courses* are displayed in Table 3. Exactly two thirds of the male students picked CS as course in the last two terms, while only about one third of the female students did. From the raw data a series of values were computed for the analysis:

- Gender with "female" and "male" as possible values.
- SP/ST are the Person- and Thing-Scores of the Self-Assessment.
- FP/FT are the Person- and Thing-Scores of the Foreign-Assessment.
- PTDist is the euclidean distance between the 13-dimensional Self- and Foreign-Assessment-Vectors.
- PDist and TDist are the euclidean distances between the Person- and Object-Items of the Self- and Foreign-Assessment-Vectors.
- CSC with the value "dropped" if CS courses were dropped, and "selected" if a CS course was selected (neglecting the type of course).

Table 3. The Choice of CS courses

Type of CS exam	Male	Female	Sum
High profile exam	18	7	25
Low profile exam	2	0	2
Without exam	2	4	6
Dropped	11	23	34
Total	33	34	67

Table 4. Dependence of the Person- and Thing-Scores and the distances of Self- and Foreign-Scores on the factor gender.

Variable	$F(1,61)$	p	Effect sz. (η^2)
SP	2.464	0.122	–
ST	13.82	<0.001	0.185
FP	2.417	0.125	–
FT	7.174	<0.01	0.105
PTDist	16.51	<0.01	0.213
PDist	1.841	0.18	–
TDist	17.41	<0.001	0.219

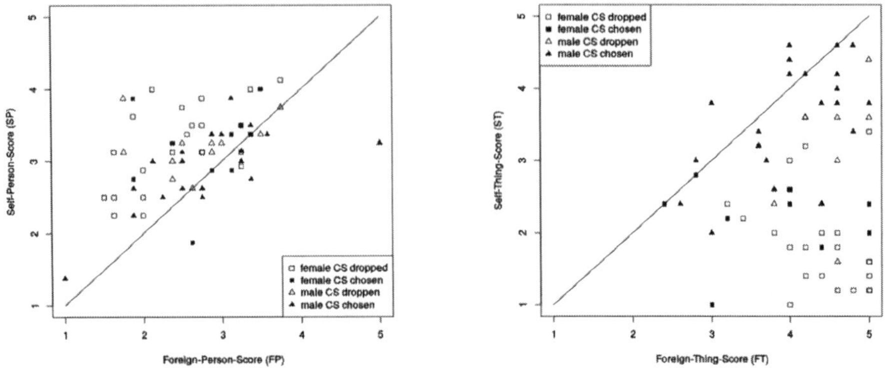

Fig. 1. Scatter plots of the Person- and Thing-Scores, marked by gender and CSC.

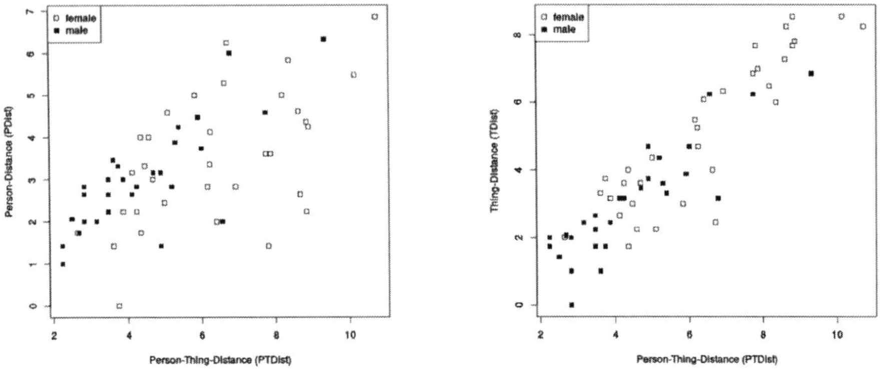

Fig. 2. Scatter plot of the Person- and Thing-Distances between Self- and Foreign-Scores plotted over the distance of all items and marked by gender.

5.1 Influence of Gender

Table 5. Means of Self- and Foreign-Scores

Gender	SP Mean (SD)	ST Mean (SD)	FP Mean (SD)	FT Mean (SD)	n
Female	2.21(0.50)	1.28(0.90)	2.54(0.64)	4.37(0.51)	33
Male	2.00(0.60)	2.16(0.93)	2.81(0.74)	3.93(0.78)	34
All	2.11(0.56)	1.72(1.01)	2.67(0.70)	4.16(0.68)	67

The Self- and Foreign-Assessments of the Person-Thing-Scores are plotted in Fig. 1, each dot representing one student, its shape showing the gender and its colour the value of CSC. Regarding the Thing-Score, it stands out that the Self Score (ST) and the Foreign-Score (FT) of male students seem to differ less than those of female students, which tend to a lower ST and a higher FT.

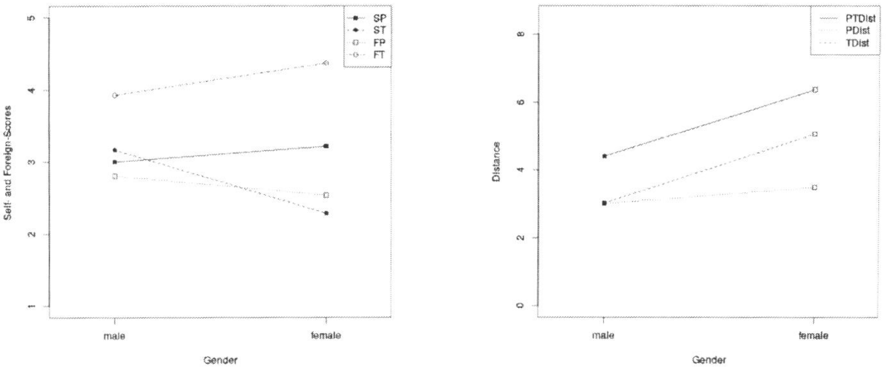

Fig. 3. Averages of Self- and Foreign-Scores and the distances of the vectors by gender.

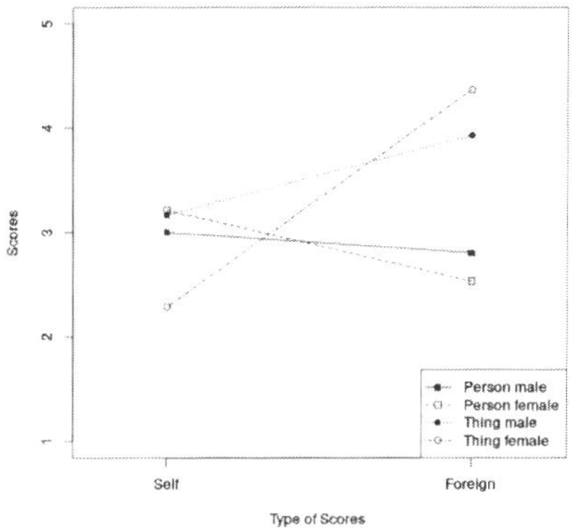

Fig. 4. The average Self- and Foreign-Scores by gender and type.

Since gender is a factor with two levels we use a between subject one way Analysis of Variance (ANOVA) for the analysis of its influence on the Self- and Foreign-Scores.[3] The resulting F-scores are given in Table 4. While the Person-Scores do not significantly depend on gender, the Thing-Scores do. This observation even holds for the Foreign-Scores, with males presuming higher values for FT. The effect size is given by the η^2-score. Values around 0.13 are usually deemed to indicate an effect of medium strength, while a vlaue of 0.26 is interpreted as a strong effect.

[3] All computations were performed using R.

5.2 Dependence of Foreign-Scores on Self-Scores

SP and ST are used as factors and FP and FT as dependent variables. We execute a two way ANOVA with the null hypotheses that the values of the Self-Scores have no influence on the means of FP and FT. The results are displayed in Table 6.

Table 6. The influence of the Self- on the Foreign-Scores tested by a two way ANOVA.

Variable	Factor	$F(1,59)$	p-value	Effect size (η^2)
FP	SP	15.2086	0.0002491	0.208
	ST	3.4984	0.0663896	–
	Interaction	1.0460	0.3106002	–
FT	SP	2.1226	0.1504	–
	ST	0.0010	0.9748	–
	Interaction	0.2021	0.6547	–

The null hypothesis is only rejected with high significance ($p < 0.001$) for the factor SP and the dependent variable FP. Thus the Self-Person-Score seems to influence the Foreign-Person-Score. The effect size is quite high. The left scatter plot in Fig. 1 indicates that a higher SP seems to be correlated to a higher mean of FP.

5.3 Influence of Scores on the CS Choice

Since CSC is a binomially distributed variable, the effects of the other variables cannot be measured using ANOVA. Instead we use Fisher's Exact Test to test the contingency table for homogeneity. I.e. in all cases CSC is the dependent variable and we test the null hypothesis that the distribution of CSC does not depend on the second variable. For the analysis the continuous variables were mapped to categories of given width. If the null hypothesis is rejected with high significance, Cramer's V is given as a measure for the effect size. In all cases its value is larger than 0.6, indicating a strong effect (Table 7).

Table 7. The influence of the different variables on CSC. In all cases CSC is the dependent variable and Fisher's exact Test is used.

Factor	p-Value	Interval	Level width	Cramer's V
SP	0.252	[0, 4]	0.5	–
ST	$8.424 \cdot 10^{-6}$	0.5	[0, 4]	0.699
FP	0.4711	[0, 4]	0.5	–
FT	0.5423	[0, 4]	0.5	–
PTDist	0.0001408	[2, 11]	1	0.632
PDist	0.3364	[0, 7]	1	–
TDist	0.0005121	[0, 9]	1	0.635

Due to the high significance, we reject the null hypothesis that ST has no effect on the mean value of Choice, being a measure for the probability. Hence we assume that ST has an influence on the decision to choose a CS course during the last terms. The same holds for the distance of Self- and Foreign-Assessment and especially for the distance between the scores of Thing-items. On the other hand, the ANOVA leads us to accept the hypotheses that SP has no effect on the mean of CSC, while PDist has a small influence on a low significance level.

Table 8. Influence of gender and CSC on Person-Thing-Scores tested with two way ANOVA.

Variable	Factor	(F1,59)	p-value	Effect size (η^2)
SP	CSC	0.7243	0.3982	–
	Gender	1.4195	0.2382	–
	Interaction	0.8394	0.3633	–
ST	CSC	42.1848	1.925e−8	0.480
	Gender	5.5425	0.02191	0.0466
	Interaction	0.0959	0.75793	–
FP	CSC	0.3507	0.5560	–
	Gender	1.5673	0.2155	–
	Interaction	0.2616	0.6110	–
FT	CSC	0.4447	0.507460	–
	Gender	7.4683	0.008273	0.111
	Interaction	0.8416	0.362664	–
PTDist	CSC	23.0809	1.105e−05	0.357
	Gender	8.0947	0.006095	0.0776
	Interaction	0.0022	0.962518	–
PDist	CSC	3.1215	0.08244	–
	Gender	0.5020	0.48140	–
	Interaction	0.5643	0.45551	–
TDist	CSC	30.1487	8.889e−07	0.409
	Gender	8.4006	0.005258	0.0733
	Interaction	0.2903	0.592084	–

5.4 Turning Things Around

Up to this point we interpreted CSC as the dependent variable and the Person- and Thing-Scores as independent. In the following this is turned around. We assume that gender and CSC are independent factors and that the Person- and Thing-Scores are dependent variables. In each case the test is conducted against the null hypotheses that the means of the corresponding scores do not differ between the groups defined by gender and CSC. If the hypothesis is rejected by at least a medium significance ($p < 0.01$), η^2 is used to measure the effect size (cmp Table 8).

In all cases in which the null hypothesis is rejected with high significance, the influencing factor is CSC. In contrast, the effect of gender seems to be less significant. This is confirmed by the effect size. For CSC the effect sizes are very high, with a maximum of $\eta^2 = 0.480$ for ST and a minimum of $\eta^2 = 0.357$ for PTDist. For the factor gender only a small effect can be observed.

6 Discussion and Conclusions

Before we discuss the results, we have to observe that the number of students is quite small and that the survey was only conducted at one high school. This may cause problems regarding the statistical significance of our analysis. Nonetheless many of the observed effects seem to be quite strong, which may be interpreted as support for the results.

To start up we can say that many result appeared exactly the way they were expected. *Hypothesis 1*, the anecdotal observation that the fraction of female students in 10th grade CS courses is quite high and drops drastically in the 11th grade, is confirmed by the numbers. In our sample the fraction of female students selecting CS courses is half as big as that of male students.

Hypothesis 2 is confirmed, too. Girls are slightly, but not significantly higher in SP while boys are much higher in ST (actually SP was quite homogeneous). As the analysis of the dependence of the scores on gender shows (cmp. Table 4), only the Thing-Scores – Self and Foreign – are influenced. Both genders have higher FT than ST and lower FP than SP on the other hand, although Foreign- and Self-Scores are independent. As girls are highest in FT we see that female subjects have a much higher foreign-self-distance than the males.

The data supports the third hypothesis that CSC correlates to ST. As the results of the statistical test show (cmp. Table 3) the hypothesis is confirmed with high significance and a high effect strength. On the other hand SP seems to have no significant influence. In fact, the effect of ST seems to be stronger than that of gender. This might imply that the differences observed due to gender may in fact be caused by the gender specific bias of ST.

Hypothesis 4 claimed that the SP and ST of girls in 10th grade CS courses do not significantly differ from the whole population. As a comparison of Tables 2 and 5 shows, the values of SP and ST between our sample and the values of [4] differ. In fact t-tests showed that in each case the means do significantly differ. This result is somewhat unexpected and may be caused by two factors. First of all, our sample is quite small, causing a deviation of the means. Secondly, the samples originate from different populations regarding age and cultural background.

Regarding hypothesis 5 that the CS choice correlates with the distance between Self- and Foreign-Assessment, we first have to observe that FP does not seem to depend on gender, while FT does with medium significance and medium effect strength. Female students tend to assign higher Thing-Scores to the stereotypical computer scientist as males. And their ST is lower than that of males. Therefore, the difference of FT and ST for females is much higher.

As the analysis of the interaction of the distance between Self- and Foreign-Assessment and CSC shows (cmp. Table 3), the influence of the distance between the person items is not significant. This is contrasted by the effect of PTDist and TDist, which are correlated to CSC with high significance and high effect strength.

Now we must ask if minimizing TDist can improve the number of students selecting informatics (especially females) or if TDist and CSC are just two factors resulting on a general disinterest in technology and CS. Interviews with 17 students, conducted during the preparation of the survey, showed that most of them have no idea what the job of a computer scientist looks like. Maybe this problem is the main reason for TDist being that high. We must ask how much effect more information about the professional profile and a weakening of the stereotype would have on TDist and maybe also on CSC.

On the other hand it is surprising that the triple interaction of gender, CSC and TDist was definitely not significant although the graphical representation strongly suggests this correlation. Maybe a higher number of subjects can improve this result. Nevertheless we can see that the group "girls dropping C" is both the group with highest TDist and with ST.

Subsuming the discussion, ST, PTDist and TDist seem to be predictors of comparable quality for the choice of CS courses in the last two terms of high school. Due to the small sample and the nature of the survey, we are not able to decide which one is better. In addition our claim that the Foreign-Assessment and the distances are a valid and reliable measure for the stereotype and its difference to the self image.

6.1 Possible Confounding Factors

To gain higher reliability the test should be improved at the sequence of the questions. As all subjects started with self-assessment before going over to foreign-assessment, it is possible that there was an influence on foreign-assessment, because subjects might have thought they must choose different answers that time. Maybe even a subconscious wish of a high or low distance to a computer scientist's character might have had an influence. Furthermore three subjects didn't answer the foreign-assessment questions maybe because they didn't see the sense of it after recognizing the questions as seen before. Therefore the difference must be pointed out even stronger. But this actually might lead to the subjects recognizing what the test is about to test, which in turn might worsen the influence of wishing results. Another question is, whether the person-thing items are suitable for all ages. E.g. a question is whether one would like to talk to a homeless. As students would associate a homeless with a person much older than themselves they might give a different answer. Nevertheless it is said that the person-thing questionnaire is constant for all ages (see [9]). Moreover there might have been an influence by all subjects visiting the same school which suggests many common live experiences. They could be strongly connected to a single item that thereby gets very high approval or rejection leading to a falsified average result on the scores.

6.2 Future Work

Even though the sample is quite small and restricted to the students of one school, the main effects seem to be quite strong. Therefore a larger survey and a more thorough analysis seems to be justified. Especially the correlation between the distances of Self- and Foreign-Assessments needs to be checked. This includes the examination of the claim that the Foreign-Scores measure the stereotype.

Furthermore, the claim that the Self-Scores of female students in CS courses do not differ from the whole population, can only be checked by a larger survey, including non-CS students of the same age.

The main job for further surveys is finding other factors on CSC and integrating them by an equal number of items. A much higher number of subjects is important in two ways: On the one hand it finally should lead to significant results and on the other hand it allows us to analyze the correlation between CSC and different profiles. This is not possible yet as e.g. less than 5% of the subjects chose the sport profile or none of the joining girls elected the social-science profile. Another important change in the selection of subjects should be also including those students of grade 10 (or grade 11 in future) who never elected CS and were missing in this poll because it was only to the CS courses of grade 10 asking who is going to continue. That way we can also get to know why not many girls of social-science profile choose CS. It will be especially interesting to see whether students dropping CS after one year have more in common with those continuing or with those who have never elected CS at all.

References

1. Alzate Romero, E., Dietrich, L.: Musikprogrammierung mit sonic pi. In: Informatische Bildung zum Verstehen und Gestalten der digitalen Welt, pp. 191–200 (2017)
2. University of Cambridge Computer Laboratory: Sonic Pi - The Live Coding Music Synth for Everyone (2018). http://sonic-pi.net/
3. Graziano, W., Habashi, M., Woodcock, A.: Exploring and measuring differences in person-thing orientation. Pers. Individ. Differ. **51**, 28–33 (2011)
4. Graziano, W.G., Habashi, M.M., Evangelou, D., Ngambeki, I.: Orientations and motivations: are you a "people person," a "thing person," or both? Motiv. Emot. **36**(4), 465–477 (2012). https://doi.org/10.1007/s11031-011-9273-2
5. Little, B.: Psychospecialization: functions of differential orientation toward spersons and things. Bull. Br. Psychol. Soc. **21**, 113 (1968)
6. Ngambeki, I., Evangelou, D., Graziano, W., Bairaktarova, D., Branch, S., Woodcock, A.: Person-thing orientation as a predictor of engineering persistence and success, January 2011
7. Petrut, S.J., Bergner, N., Schroeder, U.: Was grundschulkinder über informatik wissen und was sie wissen wollen. In: Informatische Bildung zum Verstehen und Gestalten der digitalen Welt, pp. 63–72. Gesellschaft für Informatik, Bonn (2017)
8. Tay, L., Su, R., Rounds, J.: People-things and data-ideas: bipolar dimensions? J. Couns. Psychol. **58**(3), 424–440 (2011). https://doi.org/10.1037/a0023488
9. Woodcock, A., Graziano, W.G., Branch, S.E., Habashi, M.M., Ngambeki, I., Evangelou, D.: Person and thing orientations: psychological correlates and predictive utility. Soc. Psychol. Pers. Sci. **4**(1), 116–123 (2013). https://doi.org/10.1177/1948550612444320

Wandering Micro:bits in the Public Education of Hungary

Andor Abonyi-Tóth and Zsuzsa Pluhár(✉)

Faculty of Informatics, Eötvös Loránd University, Budapest, Hungary
{abonyita, pluharzs}@inf.elte.hu

Abstract. Micro:bits have educational purposes, these Single Board Computers (SBC) were based on BBC's idea and developed by their supervision. The idea behind it was to give students an insight into programming and engineering science, encouraging them to choose their field connected to the STEM areas. These microcontrollers are ideal for supporting kids in learning the foundations of programming playfully. With the extensions, students experience the basics of robotics too.

The T@T Labor at Eötvös Loránd University has been working on experience-based education for decades. In the teacher training program and public education, the team is trying to use and introduce devices which can improve computational thinking skills. To achieve this, the University is coming up and organizes different projects.

The "Micro:bit botorkálás" ("Wandering micro:bits") was launched in October 2017. The aim of the program to send micro:bits as many schools as possible. Students can meet programming in a game-based way either inside the classroom or in after-school activities. Our 23 kits contain 10 micro:bits. The registered schools can use the kits free for a month, after that they must post the kit to the next. Till now (07/2019) over 15000 students in 160 schools met the kits.

We prepared a research survey to assess the effectiveness and success of our initiative, and to get to know the teacher's motivation and impressions.

In our article, we summarize and share our experiences on this device, based on those reports we got from the participating schools and the completed questionnaires (N = 78).

Keywords: Micro:bit · STEAM · Education · Learning-by-doing

1 Introduction

The increasing influence of ICT in everyday life and the currently used definition as a fundamental skill for everyone, not just for computer scientists – computational thinking [1] could change the views about skills, education and learning [2, 3]. However, the prevailing concepts about the term "user" have to be redefined, and it does not only cover user activities, such as browsing, chatting or interacting and using ICT tools, but more the ability to design and implement new ideas, and to be a "creative creator" [4].

S. N. Pozdniakov and V. Dagienė (Eds.): ISSEP 2019, LNCS 11913, pp. 189–199, 2019.
https://doi.org/10.1007/978-3-030-33759-9_15

The teacher's new role is to support both the formal and informal learning environment, and instead of only delivering factual knowledge and domain specific strategies to solve problems, rather enhancing the skills required by today's society [5].

In education teachers mostly work with well-structured problems – they have clearly defined initial states, goal states, and constraints. To solve them they must use procedural knowledge, step-by-step algorithms. In the real world they mostly found open or ill-structured problems, in which they do not know all elements of the problem, there can be multiple solutions or multiple solution paths and they can use multiple criteria to assess the solution [6].

A tool to support more dimensions of computational thinking and improve skills in ill-structured problem solving is to create a program [1]. It means not only coding, but phrasing ideas, expressing yourself, planning, developing, reflecting/reviewing, and creating a new product [7].

An other important ability that plays a significant role in future of students is how they can apply and reuse theirs knowledge and skills. The knowledge transfer, i.e. to adapt acquired knowledge and skills to other situations, other subjects, and use in real life and in multiple areas of science can be supported by STEAM (science, technology, engineering, art and math) in the education [2]. To focus STEAM education the discrete areas can be merged and consequently students can better understand their environment [8].

To combine programming with robotics and STEAM, the reason will be a "tool" where motivation and the concept of "learning-by-doing", "hands-on mind-on learning", project based learning can be improved and used and can be placed more and deeper emphasis on the learning process instead of the result only [7, 8].

2 T@T Lab

The Faculty of Informatics at Eötvös Loránd University, Budapest not only has to teach the theory of Computer Science, but also "has to use it in order to show its value in suitable applications that not only facilitate better learning processes, but also motivates learning and elevates its significance within the world of entertainment" [10, p 203].

In Department of Media and Educational Informatics we set up a special group: T@T Lab, the name whereof comes from the English initials TEL (Technology Enhanced Learning). The main goal of this lab is to create experience based learning activities and environments in education. We use the latest technological advances and tools in education, research and development to achieve this. Our aim is to improve and create innovative informal installations in education that can be used both in formal education or attract interest (e.g. in museums), increase motivation and facilitate the experience of discovery [9, 11].

The lab is physically in our IT Hut (T@T Kuckó) that functions as a technology playground for kids, students, parents, teachers and developers. In the IT Hut, we would like to more bring the developer (computer scientists) site closer to teacher training and public education. We organize our teacher training classes and innovative labs for programmers and computer scientists in our IT Hut to share methodology, new knowledge and cooperation, connection between the three key players in education: developer - teacher - student.

3 BBC Micro:bit

3.1 The Hardware

BBC micro:bit, a single board microcontroller allowing multiple educational applications. The screen with 25 red LED lights arranged in a 5 × 5 grid can display numbers, texts, icons, animations or sprites that allow various simple games to be programmed (Fig. 1).

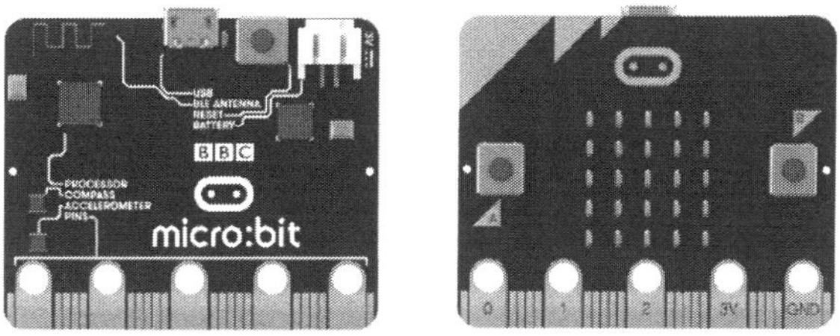

Fig. 1. The front and back view of micro:bit

There are several ways to interact with the device. The buttons (A and B) can be pushed or the built-in sensors such as the temperature and light sensor, motion detectors (accelerometer and compass) can be used to control the micro:bit using multiple gestures like shaking, flipping or sensing the changing of environment.

Not only the LEDs are available as output, but it can play sounds, or even music. The pins (edge connectors) enable the use of digital and analogue inputs and outputs - connect external sensors or motors. These increasedly accurate sensor and control solutions enable the application of micro:bits in robotic and STEAM education.

The devices support radio and Bluetooth communication, so users can develop applications where several micro:bits communicate with each other. Users can design and implement multi-user games or develop IoT-like systems where one micro:bit probes the environment and send the readings to the other device that acts in response by showing the changes which may represented as a diagram, or starting/stopping a motor.

Power to the micro:bits may be provided via USB connection, external circuits (two AAA batteries) or via the interface chip. So they can be used disconnected from the computer. Develop applications and games used in outdoor activities or worn as clothes as a step counter, jump counter, smart watch or remote controller to a mobile device. See [12–15].

3.2 Programming Micro:bits

The micro:bit is a microcontroller – it means you can upload the compiled program to it. Upload may be done via USB cable or Bluetooth connection supported by the micro: bit companion app on Android or iOS devices.

Programs can be developed in several programming environments [16, 17]: Microsoft Makecode Editor, Makecode for micro:bit, Scratch 3.0, Python editor, Swift and mBed OS 5. Some of them are block based languages, some are high level languages and some of them support switching between two views: block view and procedural language.

Several other programming environments developed by various companies or groups are available [18, 19].

3.3 Micro:bits in Education

Micro:bit can be used in several educational areas and subjects due to their versatility. The most important part of using this device in education is in information technology, because it could present motivating, enjoyable activities to most segments like algorithmic thinking, data modelling, programming, data visualization, problem solving, infocommunication, operating principles of IT devices and math in CS [19, 20].

However, it is also suitable for use in STEM or STEAM education – to connect multiple domains and subjects (from art to history, from maths to science), and solve problems where students have to use skills from several subjects, and through the activity they can learn (and gain experience) about multiple domains in an interdisciplinary, "out-of-silo" way.

The device can support project works, cooperation between students and individual work, as well [12, 13].

4 The "Wandering Micro:bits" Initiative

The T@T lab at Eötvös Loránd University in cooperation with the Public Education SIG of John von Neumann Computer Society started the "Wandering micro:bits" ("Micro:bit botorkálás") initiative in October 2017.

The main goal was to make BBC micro:bit – and its features in education – available in as many schools as possible even if just for a limited time. Students should try and come to know the potentials of the device, improve the computational-oriented thinking and their motivation for computer science through playful coding. We also would like to support teachers in deciding which device to buy if they have possibilities and/or would broaden their educational horizon. Testing and trying the device before buying it can help avoid buying devices they would not use later or having concerns about opening towards new things.

First, we bought two kits (10 devices in each kit) and sent them to the participating schools.

Teachers at schools could use the devices for 2–4 weeks free of charge. Initially the test period was two weeks in order to involve more schools in the program. Later this period was extended to four weeks as the number of available kits increased. We had only two requirements: send the kits to the next school by post and report their experiments. The report could be a posted on Facebook or sent as a document, the main goal was to help other schools with ideas on how to start using micro:bits. The initiative is running, we are looking forward to the registration of additional school.

In March 2018 the Hungarian distributor of micro:bits (Málna PC) donated a new kit to the programme, and in May 2018 the Hungarian office of the CPU producer, ARM extended the programme with 20 new kits. Consequently, we now use 23 kits, which requires extensive organization work, but now schools have the chance to use the kits for 4 weeks at a time.

The kits were available from the start in nearly 160 schools. Teachers could use the devices either during lessons or in after-school activities, project days or weeks.

To support the teacher's work in public education we published tutorials and materials in Hungarian. Among others, we prepared and published a free after-school activity curriculum [4]. This curriculum includes materials covering topics from animation through game programming to sensor uses and further utilization opportunities. The material comprises fully developed 14 sessions, 90 min each.

We realized during the preparation of the curriculum for after-school activity that the translation of the Makecode block environment was not well-prepared and was missing the underlying basic, standardized concept. We took a lot of effort into the translation and preparation of several materials.

5 Assessment of the Results and Impressions of Our Initiative

5.1 Scope of the Study, Methodology, Hypotheses

We prepared a research survey to review our original concept and the functioning the initiative.

In April 2019 a questionnaire was sent to the contact persons of the schools that participated in the programme, and finished the test period [N = 126]. We asked them about motivation, impressions, ideas and about how the kits were used.

The questionnaire had 21 questions. For attitudes and ways of use we used the five-point Likert scale, but for their impressions we preferred open answers.

Our hypotheses were as follows:

- H1. Mostly IT teachers will use the micro:bit kits in the initiative.
- H2. Most teachers (>75%) do not have any previous IT knowledge, and micro:bit will be the first device they use in education.
- H3. Mostly one teacher (the contact person) will use the kits in the applicant school.
- H4. The kits will be used in classes 5–8 (age 10–14) in most cases.
- H5. The most commonly used (>75%) programing environment will be block languages.

5.2 Participating Teachers and Schools

62% (N = 78) of the participating 126 schools completed our survey in April 2019.

Most teachers (99%) teach (at least) IT sciences that confirmed our hypothesis [H1] about it. Though the device could be used in several STEM (and STEAM) subjects, most teachers lack the required programming skills.

Our opinion is that teachers not specialized in IT could attend special teacher training courses to learn not only integrating micro:bits in education but the basics of programming.

We were interested in participants' prior knowledge of programming single board microcontrollers (e.g. Arduino, Raspberry pi, …) or robotics. We supposed that most teachers (>75%) do not have any previous knowledge, and micro:bit will be the first device they use in education. Our hypothesis [H2] was confirmed as most teachers (81%) did not have any knowledge or experience in this area. The teachers who already had some programming skills got the Bee Bot, Blue Bot or Mbot (6%), the LEGO robots (6%), Arduino (4%) and the ArTeC tools (4%).

5.3 Use of the Kits

As the number of travelling kits was increasing we could increase the duration micro: bits could spend at schools. More than half (59%) of the schools could use the kits for 3–4 weeks, 35% for less than 3 weeks and 6% for more 4 weeks.

We were curious how many teachers used the kits in each school. Our hypothesis [H3] was that mostly one (the contact person) because of teachers' extremely high workload and the difficulty to learn new technology, cooperate with others in unplanned activities and coordinate the sessions during the school year. We had to dismiss this hypothesis: based on the answers several teachers used the device in most schools (58%) (see Fig. 2).

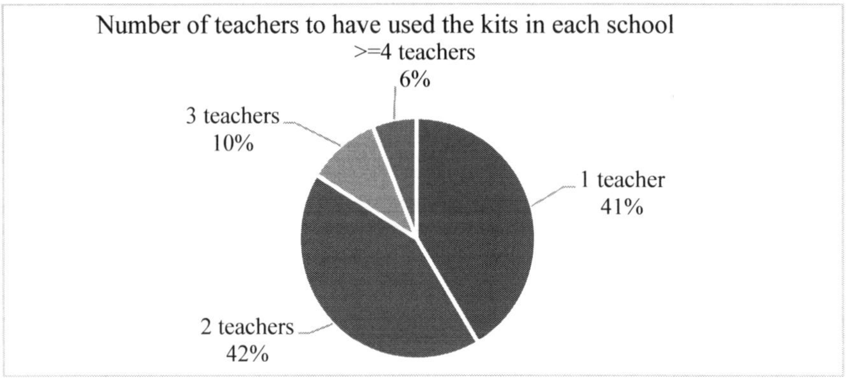

Fig. 2. Number of teachers to have used the kits in each school

Micro:bits can be used at various levels of education. We asked the teachers about students' ages to learn which age groups used the devices in the schools. Our hypothesis [H4] – mostly in classes 5–8 (age 10–14) – was confirmed. The highest number of students meet micro:bits in classes 5–8 (49%) (see Fig. 3).

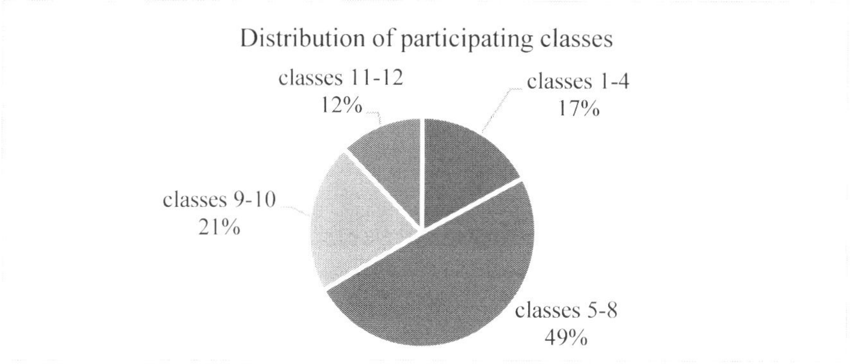

Fig. 3. Distribution of participating classes

Inside the Classroom

We asked the participants about using micro:bits in classrooms. Figure 4 and Table 1 shows the results.

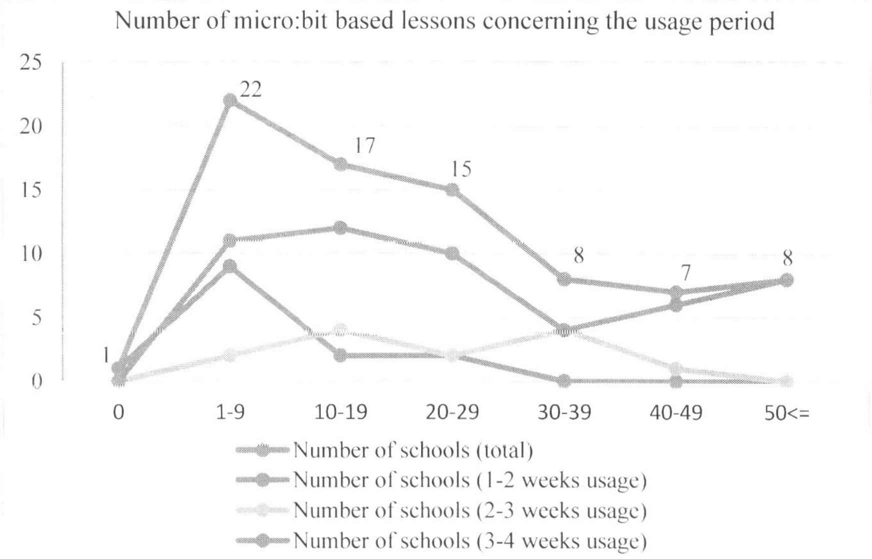

Fig. 4. Number of micro:bit based lessons according the usage period

There was only one school where the kit was not used in classroom activity, only in after-school activities. Teachers used the devices in 23 lessons on average in the given period. Most of them were IT lessons, however, some teachers also used them in geography, science, English, physics, math lessons and in e-library activities.

Table 1. Descriptive statistics of the number of micro:bit based lessons

	Total	1–2 weeks usage	2–3 weeks usage	3–4 weeks usage
Sum	1807	132	272	1403
Average	23,17	9,43	20,92	27,51
Median	16,5	8	20	20
Minimum	0	0	6	4
Maximum	88	25	40	88

We also surveyed the number of students. On average 114 students per school used micro:bits. The minimum value was 17 and the maximum was 500, while the median was 80. At least 4 teachers used the kit in the school with the maximum number of students.

After-School Activities

Approximately third (35%) of the schools did not use the kits in after-school activities. The others used them in extracurricular activities (73%), on project weeks, on Coding Week (33%), they organized career orientation (12%), project days (10%). Some schools used micro:bits at the Career Orientation Night[1] (2%) and/or demonstration class (2%).

On average 42 students per school used micro:bits in after-school activities. The median was 20, the minimum value was 2 and the maximum was 400.

Programming Environments and Advanced Application

As we presumed [H5], the favourite programing environments were block languages (87%) - Makecode (72%) and Scratch 3.0 (15%). Other than block based languages were mostly used with older students in secondary schools, but not exclusively (Table 2).

Table 2. Frequency of the programming environments

Programming environments	Count	Frequency (%)
Makecode environment (block programming)	67	72%
Makecode JavaScript programming environment	10	11%
Scratch 3.0	14	15%
Python	2	2%

We were interested if teachers could try the advanced opportunities despite the limited time, and if yes, which of them. Only 15 schools (19%) had time and external tools (like aluminum foil, crocodile clips, …) to try the following advanced activities:

- data transfer/communication between micro:bits
- wearable projects (like step counter)

[1] National event showcasing various professions.

- using external sensors
- robotics (control and line following projects)
- maths experiments in probability theory
- distance measuring by radio communication
- creation of a floor piano
- creating traffic lights
- reflex games, speed measuring
- smart house projects
- encryption, coding, decoding projects.

5.4 Teachers' Impressions

The results of numerous researches (UK, Western Balkans, Denmark) about experiences with using micro:bits in education are available on the micro:bit research website [21]. We can read positive feedback that the device helps to demonstrate that all kids can code, increases motivation, more girls will feel the power in CS (or STEAM) and teachers can feel more confident themselves.

We do not have any similar research in Hungary, and we were interested in both the positive and negative experiences with micro:bits.

The (free text) answers about positive experiences (N = 66) were diverse. We categorized the open-ended answers. The most frequent answers of the teachers included increased motivation (27%), user-friendliness (13%), spectacularness (9%), connection to the real world (9%), the potential in creativity (8%) and problem solving (8%), self-directed learning (6%), versatility (6%), the potential in differentiation (3%), low price (3%), novelty (3%), external scalability (1%), the potential in group work (1%), direct feedback (1%), on-line programming interface (1%), stand-alone operation without computer (1%).

Negative feedback (N = 23) included the lack of external sensors and motors (26%), difficult usage of the battery holder (17%), the smallness of the LED display (13%), relative slowness (9%), limitations of built-in sensors (9%), problems with USB connection (9%), vulnerability (4%), lack of user authentication on makecode portal (4%), problems with software uploading (4%), lack of operation indicator led (4%).

Future Plans

We asked about the participants' future plans with micro:bits: if the school would like to buy some devices or kits. Most schools (80%) found the device so useful and interesting that they plan buying, already ordered or they use their own (newly bought) devices.

We were interested whether participation in our initiative influenced the plans about buying micro:bits. The average of the answers on the five-point Likert scale was 4.7. So we think the initiative had a very strong influence factor.

Teachers' Feedback

We asked teachers about theirs opinion. 77 teachers answered this part of the questionnaire. Table 3 shows see the results with the most common answers set in bold.

Table 3. Distribution of opinions

5 strongly agree	4 agree	3 undecided	2 disagree	1 strongly disagree	5 and 4 together (mostly agree)
I. The device made the lessons and activities enjoyable for students					
87%	12%	1%	0%	0%	99%
II. I find the device perfect for improving algorithmic thinking					
82%	16%	1%	1%	0%	97%
III. I find the device perfect for improving problem solving skills (individual, in group work or in project work)					
81%	18%	0%	1%	0%	99%
IV. I feel more confident as a teacher in my subject by using micro:bits					
38%	**48%**	9%	4%	1%	86%
V. We can go beyond the built-in capabilities fast, so we need the advanced level and external extensions (external sensors, robotics, smart home, smart city applications)					
45%	35%	16%	3%	1%	81%
VI. This device is just like the others, i.e. after its novelty wears off, students' motivation will decrease					
4%	25%	**36%**	22%	13%	29%
VII. The device supports teaching facts and the curriculum					
31%	**44%**	18%	5%	1%	75%

5.5 Correlations

We could not find significant correlation between background variables (like previous knowledge in programming single board microcontrollers) and experience or opinions about the success of our initiative.

6 Conclusion and Future Works

Assessing the survey results, we obtained a bigger and in-depth picture about participants (schools and teachers), about the methodology and the experience of using new tools in Hungarian education.

Our results indicate that our initiative had a strong impact on the plans to buy devices and on future educational activities at schools, and accordingly, it fits the main idea to support teachers before knowing a tool and then decide about it. We will work on reaching out to new schools, promote the device among decision makers and prepare targeted tenders with industry partners to enable schools to have their own micro:bits and extension kits to use them in a variety education scenarios.

We intend to start teacher training courses in the coming years not only for IT, but other STEAM teachers focusing on micro:bits in education and robotics.

We believe that our initiative can also be successful outside Hungary, where the main goals are the same: support teachers to bring IT education to the next level – not only teaching how to use the devices, but focus more on logical thinking, creativity, cooperation, team and project works in IT and STEAM education.

Acknowledgments. We are grateful to our University (Faculty of Informatics at ELTE), the Hungarian office of ARM and Málna PC for their support and for funding this initiative.

References

1. Wing, J.: Computational thinking. Commun. ACM **49**(3), 33–35 (2006). https://doi.org/10.1145/1118178.1118215
2. Csapó, B.: A tudáskoncepció változása: nemzetközi tendenciák és a hazai helyzet. Új Pedagógia Szemle **2**, 38–45 (2002)
3. Molnár, Gy., Kárpáti, A.: Informatikai műveltség. In: Csapó (ed.) Mérlegen a magyar iskola. Nemzeti Tankönyvkiadó, Budapest, pp. 441–476 (2012)
4. Resnick, M.: Sowing the seeds for a more creative society. Learn. Lead. Technol. **35**, 18–22 (2007)
5. Greiff, S., et al.: Domain-general problem solving skills and education in the 21st century. Educ. Res. Rev. **13**, 74–83 (2014). https://doi.org/10.1016/j.edurev.2014.10.002
6. Jonassen, D.H.: Toward a design theory of problem solving. Educ. Technol. Res. Dev. **48**(4), 63–85 (2000). https://doi.org/10.1007/BF02300500
7. diSessa, A.: Changing Minds: Computers, Learning, and Literacy. MIT Press, Cambridge (2000)
8. Papert, S.: Mindstorms: Children, Computers, and Powerful Ideas. Basic Books, New York (1993)
9. Turcsányi-Szabó, M.: Aiming at sustainable innovation in teacher education – from theory to practice. Inform. Educ. Int. J. **11**(1), 115–130 (2012)
10. Turcsányi-Szabó, M.: Augmented Edutainment on campus, In: Gardner, M., Garnier, F., Delgado Kloos, C. (eds.) Proceedings of 2nd Immersive Education Summit, pp. 204–209. Universidad Carlos III de Madrid Departamento de Ingeniería Telemática, Paris, France (2012). ISBN 978-84-695-6427-1
11. Turcsányi-Szabó, M.: Online professional development for teachers. In: Knezek, G., Voogt, J. (eds.) International Handbook of Information Technology in Primary and Secondary Education, vol. 20, pp. 747–760. Springer, London (2008). https://doi.org/10.1007/978-0-387-73315-9_43
12. Sentance, S., Waite, J., Hodges, S., MacLeod, E., Yeomans, L.E.: "Creating Cool Stuff" Pupils'experience of the BBC micro:bit. In: Proceedings of the 48th ACM Technical Symposium on Computer Science Education, SIGCSE 2017 (2017). https://doi.org/10.1145/3017680.3017749
13. Ball, T., et al.: Microsoft touch develop and the BBC micro:bit. In: Proceedings of the 38th International Conference on Software Engineering Companion, ICSE 2016, pp. 637–640. ACM, New York (2016)
14. Micro:bit hardware guide. https://microbit.org/guide/hardware/. Accessed 05 May 2019
15. Micro:bit hardware description. https://microbit.org/hardware/. Accessed 05 May 2019
16. Micro:bit editors. https://microbit.org/code/. Accessed 05 May 2019
17. Micro:bit Third Party Editors. https://microbit.org/code-alternative-editors/. Accessed 05 May 2019
18. The micro:bit software ecosystem. https://tech.microbit.org/software/. Accessed 06 Apr 2019
19. Andor, A.-T.: Programozzunk micro:biteket! (2018). http://microbit.inf.elte.hu/szakkori-anyag/. ISBN 978-963-284-992-8. Accessed 05 May 2019
20. Péter, S., László, Z.: Informatika oktatása (2012). https://www.tankonyvtar.hu/hu/tartalom/tamop412A/2011-0052_34_informatika_oktatasa/index.scorml. Accessed 05 May 2019
21. Academic research into the BBC micro:bit | micro:bit, https://microbit.org/research/. Accessed 05 May 2019

Introduction to Computational Thinking for University Students

Zsuzsa Pluhár(✉) and Hajnalka Torma

Faculty of Informatics, Eötvös Loránd University, Budapest, Hungary
pluharzs@inf.elte.hu, hajnalka.torma@gmail.com

Abstract. Computer Science education has a long tradition at Eötvös Loránd University, Budapest. A lot of students apply for BSc studies that consists of 6 semesters, and it provides a general overview of the world of Informatics: the appropriate mathematical and theoretical background and practice in programming and software engineering. Our experiences show three basic problems of an computer science education at BSc level in English: an inadequate level of English language skills, the lack of the basics in mathematics, and inexperience in algorithmic thinking and problem solving. When applying to the university, students are tested for English language and mathematics skills, and based on the results they might be assigned to study in a preliminary year, where they have courses that improve their skills in English and mathematics. However, there was no course that aimed at improving algorithmic thinking and problem solving skills, and students' lack of these skills often resulted in problems and learning difficulties in the introductory programming course. This experience has inspired us to develop and start a new course (Introduction to Computational Thinking) that focuses on improving computational thinking skills, with emphasis on algorithmic thinking and problem solving skill development. The aim of our paper is to describe the structure of the course, to introduce what was done in the first semester, and present our first experiences with this course. We would like to follow our students as they progress to their first year in their university studies, look at their results in programming classes, and improve our course based on the results.

Keywords: Computational thinking · Algorithmic thinking · Programming

1 Introduction

In the higher education, the first years in programming are difficult. Having lower level skills in the basics of algorithmic thinking and problem solving strategies, and lack of understanding of abstract programming concepts might have a negative effect on students in their studies in the following semester [1]. Having worked with first year Computer Science BSc international students at Eötvös Loránd University, Budapest for several years, we experienced that they vary greatly in their knowledge and skills when they enter the university. They have more diverse backgrounds than the Hungarian students, thus many of them have shown having more gaps in theoretical background and knowledge than their Hungarian peers [1, 2]. To be more successful

S. N. Pozdniakov and V. Dagienė (Eds.): ISSEP 2019, LNCS 11913, pp. 200–209, 2019.
https://doi.org/10.1007/978-3-030-33759-9_16

with their studies, students' computational thinking, and, in particular, algorithmic thinking skills need to be improved.

1.1 Computational Thinking and Algorithmic Thinking

According to Jeanette Wing [3, 4] "Computational Thinking is the thought processes involved in formulating problems and their solutions so that the solutions are represented in a form that can be effectively carried out by an information-processing agent" [4, p 1]. Her definition has been discussed by many researchers, but the main ideas of logical thinking, problem solving, algorithmic thinking, analysis, systematic planning, generalization, and the skills of creating abstractions are common in most of the Computational Thinking (CT) definitions. These skills enable people to solve more complex problems [5–9]. According to Selby [11], CT consists of the ability of abstraction and generalization, algorithmic thinking, the skill of breaking problems into smaller sub-problems, and the skill of evaluation. Selby [11] stated that to be able to discuss whether students' CT skills have developed, the components of CT have to be clearly identified.

Among the components of CT, the algorithmic thinking skills get in focus during the learning of programming as algorithmic thinking is an essential skill in computer science. Algorithms are present in our everyday lives, and we use algorithms to solve computer science problems, as well. According to Zsakó and Szlávi [12], the levels of algorithmic thinking are the identification of an algorithm, the understanding of an algorithm, the execution of an algorithm, the analysis of an algorithm, the creation of an algorithm, and the implementation of an algorithm. This definition corresponds to the cognitive levels of Bloom's taxonomy [13, 14].

Improving Computational Thinking and Algorithmic Thinking. There have been several initiatives with the aim of improving computational thinking skills of students. These can be divided into 3 main categories. The first aims at integrating some specially chosen tasks into other fields of study, often during project work.

In the second method, computational thinking skills are analyzed and improved with the help of teaching programming skills and using simulations. Students might be required to develop new programming artifacts, including planning and implementation, or to integrate existing systems into their own projects [15–17]. The third approach does not involve programming, sometimes not even the use of a computer, but tries to develop students' skills with carefully designed activities [18–23].

Bebras and Unplugged Activities. Computer science unplugged activities can help to improve computational thinking skills without using a computer, without learning programming first. Focus can be given to hand made activities, and higher emphasis to learning by doing and learning-by-moving methodologies that support the efficiency of acquirement and motivation [24]. Moreover, several studies document the beneficial effects of Computer Science Unplugged towards recruitment and motivation [24–28].

Bebras, an international initiative to promote CS and CT among school students and teachers [10] is one activity where we can find unplugged possibilities. It can motivate students/kids to think about IT or CS and help them avoid negative attitudes. We can show students how important CS is in our world, and that they can find it everywhere around them [24]. The Bebras competition is present in Hungary since 2011, and last year more than 25,000 students participated in it [21]. One of the main aims of Bebras is that tasks should not require any previous, background knowledge to solve the problems, but students should "work" with typical CS problems and activities, and they unintentionally use strategies and algorithms from the area of IT.

Micro:bit, Robotics. The BBC micro:bit, a single board micro-controller can support several educational goals. The hardware allows us to use multiple inputs: not only pushing a button, but also sensing the environment in several ways. The output can be simple led lighting, or the activities could be extended with the help of pins (edge connectors). The tool supports communication via Bluetooth [30–32].

There exist several programming environments, both block and text based, and both procedural and object-oriented. Programming environment and language could be chosen based on the age, habits, attitudes or previous knowledge of students, or based on our goals in education [31–34].

As educational goals, micro:bit supports hands-on mind-on learning, learning-by-doing activities, STEAM (science, technology, engineering, art and math) ideas, cooperation and project work. It connects multiple domains and science areas [34, 35].

1.2 Programming Studies at ELTE University

The Eötvös Loránd University has a long tradition in programming education. Some parts of the curriculum require a high understanding of theory. In the first year of the BSc programming studies, there is a programming course - programming fundamentals, where students learn the theoretical background of basic algorithms and data structures in imperative programming paradigm. Later, other paradigms and languages, and more theories are built on these basics. The course consists of lectures about theory with some examples, and lab sessions where further tasks are presented to students, and students are required to work on their own, as well. The goal of the first year programming course is to provide the theoretical background of programming, and less emphasis is laid on syntax of a programming language.

Our previous findings and experiences have inspired us to develop a new course, Introduction to Computational Thinking, where the focus is on helping students to learn the basics of programming, improve algorithmic thinking and problem solving skills, and introduce some data concepts to students.

2 The Introduction to CT Course

The new course, Introduction to Computational Thinking, which was developed based on the discussed theoretical background, is aimed at students with little or no programming experience. The main aims of this course are

- to give an algorithmic thinking and problem solving basis for students;
- to provide students with an understanding of the role computation can play in solving problems;
- to help students write small programs that allow them to accomplish useful goals.

The course lasts for one semester ($\sim$12 weeks) with 4 contact hours per week. The course is accompanied by a course in the Canvas learning management system. All the course requirements, assignments and materials are uploaded to the Canvas course, and students have to submit their work to the online course, as well. The aim of having the online course is to make everything available for students wherever and whenever they would like to deal with the course material.

The main idea of the course is to facilitate students to explore fundamental computer science concepts through computer unplugged activities, code challenges and solving problems with the micro:bit. Four sections were planned that were build one upon other.

2.1 Bebras Tasks

The first section was planned as an introduction to the aims of the course. Our goals were

- to give a picture about computer science problems;
- support students to start thinking about problems on their own;
- give place and time to speak about problems, problem solving strategies, wording the questions and solutions in a problem;
- give the motivation for solving problems and thinking about strategies.

To achieve this, specially selected Bebras tasks were used in multiple formats.

First, Bebras cards [29], the Algorithms Unplugged version, were used. The students worked in groups, and each group had 10 cards – selected by the instructors. They had to solve the tasks, speak about them, try to find not only the solution but the connection to CS. Then students were asked to read the "why informatics" section on the card. Finally, they had to choose one task and speak about the problem for the whole group.

As the next step, we collected several Bebras activities from the UK Bebras challenge[1] for students to work with. The basic concept was the same: students worked in groups, and discussed problems, solutions and solution paths.

As closing this section we discussed the definition of problem solving, algorithm (as a step-by-step solving method), and the open or ill-structured problems. The discussion worked like a directed brainstorming.

Then we discussed the attributes of Bebras tasks (in wording, pictures, previous knowledge, etc.), and asked the students to write/prepare their own task.

2.2 Instructions in Unplugged Activities

In this section, we wanted to show the importance of precise and exact instructions that a computer can use.

We began with small games: The students worked in groups. One team member had to draw or move without to know the goal, and others had to give the instructions.

[1] https://challenge.bebras.uk/index.php?action=user_competitions.

With the "moving" version, the given instructions needed to be executed in reversed order, as well. As closing, after each game, we discussed the instructions, the success or failure of "output", how the instructor changed the instructions during the execution as he/she detected the different action, and the reasons.

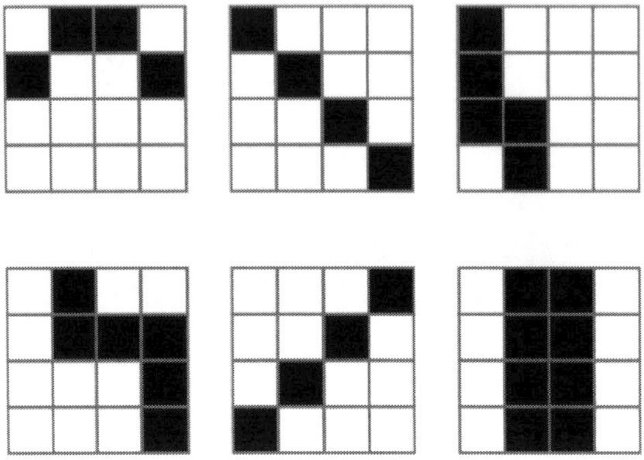

Fig. 1. One of the selected "instruction giving" tasks

After that, we restricted the possible given commands, and the students had to use only those instructions. (See Fig. 1).

The students often had to change their roles – each student acted as an "operator" (who gives the instructions) and was the guided (who follows the instructions).

2.3 Code Challenges

As the third part of the course, we collected several code challenges from code.org and from Bebras tasks. In this step, the students had to give instructions to the computer mostly like LOGO commands. First, we used the basics as "go forward" or "turn" with given attributes. Then we started to use loops and conditional branches.

A typical Bebras task was 2016-FR-04, where students had to solve several mazes. The students had to build the mazes from LEGO blocks, and then give the instructions so that 4 times repeated them the small robot can escape (see Fig. 2).

We used 3 levels for each tasks: an easy, a medium and a hard. The easy level was the trial, the students could understand the problem and the task, and it provided the motivation basis, as well.

Using these tasks, we had the opportunity to speak about the basics of programming languages - what could be the meaning of a "left" arrow (only turn left, or turn and step to the next place), and about that the differences in "codes" depend on the meaning. In this step we introduced the ill-structured problems: we spoke about different solution paths and different solutions in "code".

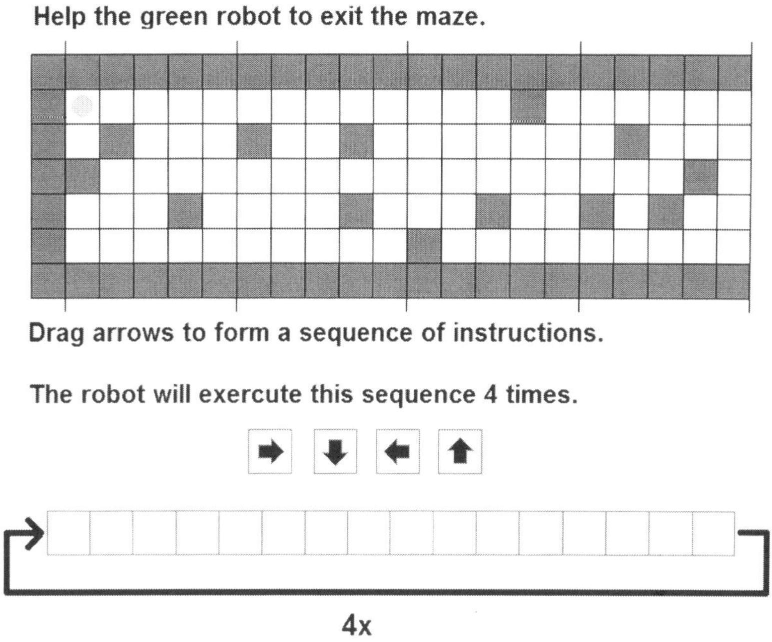

Fig. 2. 2016-FR-04 Bebras task – medium level

From code.org, we selected not only problems with control (such as the angry bird game[2]), but also other CS problems such as the text compression topic[3]. Students usually had to work in pairs or in small groups, however, students did the text compression tasks individually, comparing their results. All individual and group work was followed by class discussions.

2.4 Programming Micro:bits

After reaching an understanding in controlling, we started to use the computer, with the help of a block-based programming language, and sensing our environment.

In each class, first, we made a small introduction. From the second task on students had to prepare a small task where they needed to use the learned skills from the last occasions. When new things came up, we discussed the problems, talked about the algorithm and the solving process, and then coded it together. After this initial stage, students had to make some changes in the original projects, or prepare a variation to show that they are able to synthesize the old and new knowledge and skills. Students were told to work in groups, and discuss the processes, ideas, solutions.

The tools and the block-based environment was introduced with simpler projects such as animations, throwing the dice, rock-paper-scissors game and coin-flipping.

[2] https://studio.code.org/s/express-2018/stage/2/puzzle/2.

[3] https://studio.code.org/s/csp2-2018/stage/2/puzzle/1.

Then we started to use the inputs from the environment (like buttons and sensors), and experimented with events, measuring and game design. At the end, we prepared games with radio communication and voices from the planning phase to the programming and testing.

2.5 Extending Micro:bits

As the last part of the course, we showed the simplest extensions of micro:bit. We collected projects with simple circuits problems such as the frustration game[4], timing gates[5], and the Morse code transmitter[6]. The students worked in groups. They had to choose one of the projects, and follow the tutorial. When they understood the project, and it worked as it was expected, they had to change something in the project: add a new feature, increase the number of used micro:bits, or establish communication between micro:bits.

In this part, one of the main ideas was following tutorials and instructions of a document, and understanding a documentation about a project. We tested the understanding with the changes – if they could give simple modifications, new features, they understood the basic problems deeper and the problem solving action was not only a "following tutorial" method.

As the closing of the course, students had to present their projects in 10–15 min to the others. They were required to speak about the basic problem, about the solution path and the solution, and about their modification that was added as a new idea. We asked them to speak about their experiences that they had while they were working on the project - what had they found difficult or interesting, what was their motivation.

3 Impressions and Experiences from the Course

As the English language skills of many of the students in the preparatory year are lacking, at the beginning of the semester, it was only some students who were actively participating during the discussion of problems/tasks. However, all the students seemed to be open towards the course contents and aims, and were engaged in the given tasks. Their lack of language skills, later in the course, could be overcome by switching the language of the programming environment to their mother tongue, and by the provided step-by-step, easy to understand tutorials and other materials uploaded to the online course management system. We felt that many of the students were better at communicating, and more of them were taking part in discussions by the end of the semester.

As far as the assignments are concerned, the Bebras tasks submitted by students mainly required logical thinking skills which were more familiar to them, and it was difficult for them to distinguish between tasks that need just mathematical/logical skills

[4] https://learnlearn.uk/microbit/2016/07/05/steady-hand-game/.

[5] https://makecode.microbit.org/projects/timing-gates.

[6] https://tinkercademy.com/tutorials/microbit-morse-code-transmit-receive/.

or computational thinking skills. The micro:bit assignment which required them to take a micro:bit extension activity, create and then present it, was not successfully completed by all students. Some of them had not had any ideas about how to modify the original task to add something to it. Others had problems with STEM concepts, such as if they put their hands on the wire, it is them who the current flows through. However, they tried to overcome the difficulties, and their presentations were enjoyed by their peers.

The evaluation of the course was not just based on the submitted assignments, but also on the engagement and activity of students during the classes. This approach seemed to be unfamiliar to students, which was made more difficult for them by having to work together with two separate teachers at two different time slots. At the last class session, students got their grades for the whole course, and they were overall satisfied with their results. One student even asked for us to allow him to resubmit a task to get 100% instead of 96% (it's a grade "excellent" regardless). Our goal was to create a sense of self-achievement and motivation to study CS, and this last class was an indicator for us that this goal could be achieved.

4 Conclusion, Future Plans

Based on our experiences, in overall, the course was well-organized with a good theory background, which could be supported by the positive feedback from students. In classes, a hopeful progression in communication skills, in motivation and in thinking processes could be seen from the part of the students. Our plan is to make only some small changes to the course in the following semester.

To be able to see whether the course needs any serious modifications or the review of original goals, and to see whether the course adds to the success of students, the progress of students in their studies will be tracked. Their outcomes in other courses (such as the programming course in first year) will be analyzed to look for correlation between participation in this preparatory course (and in other pre-year courses) and the results of students in the next few semesters in their studies.

Currently, there is a selection process for international students before the beginning of the first year to decide whether they should go to the preparatory year. In the last few years, only language and math skills were tested. From the following term, this selection process will be extended with a computational thinking skills test. Bebras tasks or Bebras-like tasks will be used. There could be two outcomes: students could be advised to learn and improve some skills in CT, or they could start with their first year programming studies.

Such a test is planned to be used in the Hungarian computer science BSc program later. By defining several levels of CT skills in our students, a customized support and differentiation could be realized at our university.

References

1. Canedo, E.D., Santos, G.A., Leite, L.L.: An assessment of the teaching-learning methodologies used in the introductory programming courses at a Brazilian University. Inform. Educ. **17**(1), 45–59 (2018)
2. Pluhár, Zs., Torma, H., Törley, G.: Hallgatói teljesítményértékelés az algoritmikus gondolkodás tükrében. In: Szlávi, P., Zsakó, L. (eds.) InfoDidact 2018. Webdidactica Alapítvány (2019). https://people.inf.elte.hu/szlavi/InfoDidact18/Manuscripts/PzsTHTG.pdf. Accessed 10 May 2019
3. Wing, J.: Computational thinking. Commun. ACM **49**, 33–35 (2006)
4. Wing, J.: Research Notebook: Computational Thinking - What and Why? The Link. Carneige Mellon, Pittsburgh (2011). https://www.cs.cmu.edu/~CompThink/resources/TheLinkWing.pdf. Accessed 15 Oct 2018
5. Hu, C.: Computational thinking: what it might mean and what we might do about it. In: Proceedings of the 16th Annual Joint Conference on Innovation and Technology in Computer Science Education. ACM, Darmstadt (2011)
6. Casey, P.J.: Computer Programming: A Medium for Teaching Problem Solving. The Haworth Press, New York (1997). Computers in the Schools, vol. XIII, pp. 41–51
7. OECD (2010)
8. Csapó, B.: A tanulás dimenziói és a tudás szerveződése. Educatio **2008**(2), 107–217 (2008)
9. Adey, P., Csapó, B.: A tudományos gondolkodás fejlesztése és értékelése. In: Csapó, B., Szabó, G. (eds.) Tartalmi keretek a természettudomány diagnosztikus értékeléséhez, pp. 17–57. Budapest, Nemzeti Tankönyvkiadó (2012)
10. Chen-Chung, L., Yuan-Bang, C., Chia-Wen, H.: The effect of simulation games on the learning of computational problem solving. Comput. Educ. **57**, 1907–1918 (2011)
11. Selby C.C.: Computational Thinking: The Developing Definition. Submitted for ItiCSE Conference 2013 (2013). http://people.cs.vt.edu/~kafura/CS6604/Papers/CT-Developing-Definition.pdf. Accessed 15 Oct 2018
12. Zsakó, L., Szlávi P.: Informatikai kompetenciák: Algoritmikus gondolkodás. InfoDidact 2010 (2010). https://people.inf.elte.hu/szlavi/InfoDidact10/Manuscripts/ZsL_SzP.htm. Accessed 07 Nov 2018
13. Bloom, B.S., Krathwohl, D.R.: Taxonomy of Educational Objectives: The Classification of Educational Goals, by a committee of college and university examiners. Handbook I: Cognitive Domain. Longmans, Green, New York (1956)
14. Anderson, L.W., Krathwohl, D.R., et al. (eds.): A Taxonomy for Learning, Teaching, and Assessing: A Revision of Bloom's Taxonomy of Educational Objectives. Allyn & Bacon, Boston (2001)
15. Brennan, K, Resnick, M.: New frameworks for studying and assessing the development of computational thinking, AREA (2012)
16. Brennan, K.: Creative computing: A design-based introduction to computational thinking (2011). http://scratched.media.mit.edu/sites/default/files/CurriculumGuide-v20110923.pdf. Accessed 25 Oct 2016
17. Aiken, J.M., et al.: Understanding student computational thinking with computational modeling. In: PERC Proceedings (2011)
18. Bell, T., Witten, I.H., Fellows, M.: Computer Sciene Unplugged (2010). http://csunplugged.org/books. Accessed 25 Oct 2016
19. Dagiene, V.: Information technology contests – introduction to computer science in a attractive way. Inform. Educ. **5**(1), 37–46 (2006)

20. Cartelli, A., Dagiene, A., Futschek, G.: Bebras contest and digital competence assessment: analysis of frameworks. Int. J. Digit. Lit. Digit. Competence **1**, 24–39 (2010)
21. Pluhár, Z., Gellér, B.: International informatic challenge in Hungary. In: Auer, Michael E., Guralnick, D., Simonics, I. (eds.) ICL 2017. AISC, vol. 716, pp. 425–435. Springer, Cham (2018). https://doi.org/10.1007/978-3-319-73204-6_47
22. CS Unplugged website. http://csunplugged.org. Accessed 10 Nov 2018
23. Computer Science for Fun website. http://cs4fun.org. Accessed 10 Nov 2018
24. Bell, T., Curzon, P., Cutts, Q., Dagiene, V., Haberman, B.: Overcoming obstacles to CS education by using non-programming outreach programmes. In: Kalaš, I., Mittermeir, Roland T. (eds.) ISSEP 2011. LNCS, vol. 7013, pp. 71–81. Springer, Heidelberg (2011). https://doi.org/10.1007/978-3-642-24722-4_7
25. Bell, T., Witten, I.H., Fellows, M.: CS Unplugged (2015). www.csunplugged.org
26. Lambert, L., Guiffre, H.: Computer science outreach in an elementary school. J. Comput. Sci. Coll. **24**(3), 118–124 (2009)
27. Mano, C., Allan, V., Cooley, D.: Effective in-class activities for middle school outreach programs. In: Proceedings of 40th Annual Frontiers in Education Conference, FIE 2010, pp. F2E-1–F2E-6 (2010)
28. Taub, R., Ben-Ari, M., Armoni, M.: The effect of CS unplugged on middle-school students' views of CS. In: Proceedings of 14th Annual SIGCSE Conference on Innovation and Technology in Computer Science Education, ITiCSE 2009, pp. 99–103 (2009)
29. Dagiene, V., Futschek, G., Koivisto, J., Stupurienė, G.: The card game of Bebras-like tasks for introducing informatics concepts. In: ISSEP 2017 Online Proceedings. Helsinki, 13.11.2017–15.11.2017 (2017)
30. Sentance, S., Waite, J., Hodges, S., MacLeod, E., Yeomans, L.: "Creating Cool Stuff": Pupil's experience of the BBC micro:bit. In: Proceedings Of The 2017 ACM SIGCSE Technical Symposium on Computer Science Education, Seattle, Washington, USA, pp. 531–536 (2017). https://doi.org/10.1145/3017680.3017749
31. Ball, T., et al.: Microsoft touch develop and the BBC micro:bit. In: Proceedings of the 38th International Conference on Software Engineering Companion, pp. 637–640 (2016). https://doi.org/10.1145/2889160.2889179
32. micro:bit hardware description. https://tech.microbit.org/hardware/. Accessed 31 May 2019
33. Abonyi-Tóth, A.: Programozzunk micro:biteket! ELTE Informatikai Kar (2017)
34. Resnick, M.: Sowing the seeds for a more creative society. Learn. Lead. Technol. **35**, 18–22 (2007)
35. Jonassen, D.H.: Toward a design theory of problem solving. Educ. Technol. Res. Dev. **48**(4), 63–85 (2000)

Enhancing Student Engagement in Multidisciplinary Groups in Higher Education

Michael Opoku Agyeman(✉), Haiping Cui, and Shirley Bennett

University of Northampton, Northampton, UK
Michael.OpokuAgyeman@northampton.ac.uk

Abstract. Recently, there has been a rise in the integration of curriculum from different disciplines in higher education (HE) in response to the multidisciplinary nature of the skillset required by modern job market. In cases where the curriculum is delivered to students from the same discipline, it is intuitive for students to easily identify with the relevance the module. However, the aforementioned will not be as straightforward in situations where a curriculum/module from a particular discipline is taken by multidisciplinary groups of students. Consequently, there is a risk of disengagement of student groups from one or more of those disciplines. This report evaluates a strategy to enhance student engagement in modules taught to multidisciplinary groups in HE. For this purpose, a real-world case study of a module taken by Computer Science, Electrical and Electronics Engineering and Mechatronics Engineering Students at University of Northampton is used. Firstly, the report reviews the key problems in relation to student engagement. A review of recent literature is then presented to evaluate the state-of-the art approaches. An action plan/intervention is then proposed in response to the problem statement and findings from literature. Furthermore, an initial study based on an evaluation of the implemented action plan is then presented before a final conclusion remark.

Keywords: Computing education · Student engagement · Problem-Based learning · Learning in groups

1 Introduction

Computer Science and Engineering students often disengage from modules because of excessive, irrelevant or forced examples that do not relate to real-world applications [1]. While some students are interested in hands-on experience, others prefer theory [2]. This is exacerbated in cases where a curriculum/module from a particular discipline is taken by multidisciplinary groups of students. There is a higher risk of disengagement of student groups from one or more of the contributory disciplines. Studies have shown a positive correlation between student engagement and improved academic performance [3]. However, there are a range of different points of views reported in literature about effective student engagement techniques.

CSY2015 is a level 5 (second year) module taken by Computer Science, Electrical and Electronics Engineering and Mechatronics Engineering Students within the

S. N. Pozdniakov and V. Dagienė (Eds.): ISSEP 2019, LNCS 11913, pp. 210–221, 2019.
https://doi.org/10.1007/978-3-030-33759-9_17

Department of Computing. It has been observed over the years (at least 5 years under two module leaders) that the engagement of the students within the first teaching block is low. Particularly, a common trend is that some students believe that other students are more skilled in particular aspects of the module. For instance, engineering students expect computing students to be better at programming while computing students expect engineering students to be better at building circuits and mathematics. This belief, however, inhibits the learning experience of the students and also creates a disjoint in the engagement of aspects of the module. Moreover, most students feel they can at least disengage from the face-to-face sessions, read a book or engage with online resources with hope of passing the module. Student engagement is however, better in the second teaching block, possibly because they realize the significance of engagement with the face-to-face sessions after the first teaching block.

This case study evaluates how to enhance student engagement in this multidisciplinary module and the effectiveness of an implemented intervention. The aim of the intervention is to enhance the student learning experience through introducing specific engagement techniques right from the beginning of the first teaching block.

1.1 Possible Causes

1.1.1 Student Expectations

Some students may not believe that they have the required background for the module. Though students are aware that no prerequisite is assumed, they do not seem to identify with this. *Perhaps, providing reassurance throughout the teaching weeks will help.*

The belief that a student does not have the right background, creates a sense that students in other disciplines have been taught some modules that makes them better skilled for this module. **Hence, some students believe that other students are more skilled in some aspect.** Engineering students think computing students are better at programming, while computing students think engineering students are better at building circuits [3–5]. However, though the particular specialisms of the varied disciplines create some advantages, the module is designed and delivered to compensate possible issues that may be associated as both groups are exposed to the fundamentals during the initial weeks of the module. This assumption from the students seems interfere with of their learning.

Some students do not see the direct relevance to their programme of study and career because it is delivered by staff from a different discipline/department. Most Computing and Engineering dissertations in level 6 depend on Microcontrollers (the core of CSY2015). However, in level 5, students do not seem to see the relevance to their individual programme of study. Managing expectations by showing students relevant job advertisements and salary ranges from their respective disciplines seems to help.

Over the years, there has been an imbalance in the number of Computing and Engineering students enrolled onto the module. Though the total number of students vary each year, normally, the ratio of the number of Computing to Engineering students is about 4-to-1. This can create a sense of minority group among the Engineering students [6–8]. Furthermore, considering that the module is delivered within the

Computing Department, the Engineering students may not see the relevance of the module to their studies. This exacerbates the problem of students feeling that they do not have the right specialisms.

1.1.2 Computer-Based Multiple-Choice Questions (MCQ)

The module runs for 24 weeks with two summative assessment points: an interim computer-based MCQ (marking the end of first teaching block) and an end of module report, AS1, (marking the end of second teaching block). Most students feel they can at least disengage with the face-to-face sessions, read a book or online resources and/or try their luck with multiple-choice questions and at least pass [9]. Problem-based learning where students get to learn the theory through solving practical exercises may be a solution. This will not only ensure that they have transferable skills ready for the second teaching block but also help them identify how the theory links to practical solutions and their respective programme of study.

1.2 Challenge

In order to implement the right intervention to the aforementioned problem considering the possible causes and previous resolution attempts, there were 4 main challenges that needed to be addressed:

1. How does one redesign the delivery of the module to enhance the engagement of students from the different disciplines involved?
2. Are there any existing student engagement strategies that could be adopted or improved to resolve this issue?
3. What is the most feasible way to adopt the new strategies while keeping student-staff workload balance, without breaching the module specification and adhering to the learning outcomes?
4. What is the most effective mode of delivery to enhance student learning that could be incorporated in the module?

1.3 Possible Solutions Found in Literature

Many studies confirm that students' engagement is essential to their success [10, 11]. According to Willis [12], student engagement consists of academic engagement and institutional engagement. Similar to Renninger [13], academic engagement is defined by Ketele [14] as the ability to allocate metacognitive, cognitive and affective resources to a learning task. This case study focuses on how to enhance academic engagement of the students. Various literature has identified problem-based learning, active learning, collaborative learning and cooperative learning techniques as effective in engaging students academically [15–18].

Teaching via **problem-based** learning techniques normally involve putting students into small groups to work on tasks in an independent manner. Norman et al. [19], based on several meta-analysis, highlighted that the small groups help improve the academic achievements while the independent element of problem-based teaching has some negative effects on student learning. Some literature on the application of problem-based learning in teaching medicine [2, 20] claims that there is some level of improvement in the clinical performance at the expense of exams which had a negative correlation. A study by Bédard et al. [1], suggests that both medicine and engineering students find problem-based learning rigid and stressful [1, 2, 21]. In their study, students relate this rigidity to the requirement of having to work in groups and keep up with the group. The increase in stress levels were mostly related to the fear of failing a group work as an individual. In fact, among the four determinants of students' engagement identified by Bédard et al. [1] (self-efficacy, stress, new cognitive tasks, theories and beliefs about knowing), stress is the most predominant element of students' engagement. Vernon et al. [22] after investigating 35 studies between 1970 and 1992 concluded that problem-based learning improves students' attitudes. Moreover, work by Albanese et al. also confirm that both students and tutors have positive attitudes towards problem-based learning approaches, while Norman et al. [19] confirms that problem-based learning does not only challenge students but is also more exciting and motivating. In summary, problem-based learning has been extensively supported by literature to increase student engagement and attendance [2, 20, 23]. However, strategies must be put in place to reduce the level of stress and possible negative effects on assessment results.

Active learning techniques involve engaging students through meaningful learning activities. A common approach is to occasionally (twice or thrice in an hour) break the lecture for students to discuss their notes in pairs. A study by Hartley et al. [24] revealed that students' attention and retention reduce drastically with the length of the lecture. Interrupting lectures with relevant activities help refocus the minds of students and keep them engaged [2, 25]. Work done by Qin et al. [23], suggests that **cooperation** is more effective in producing high quality individual problem solving compared to competition. Their conclusion, however, is based on the findings that individuals in teams had better solutions to challenges compared to individuals working competitively. These findings do not necessarily conclude that students working in cooperative groups were more engaged or developed stronger transferrable skills or long-term problem-solving techniques. Problem-based learning helps resolve the issue of long lectures and students' disengagement. The activities give the students the opportunity to collaborate and cooperate in groups. Due to technology advancements, online learning and/or blended learning, where synchronous and/or asynchronous technology enhanced strategies are used as active learning techniques, have become increasingly popular. As highlighted by Reeves [21], depending on student's learning preference, synchronous and asynchronous sessions have their advantages and disadvantages in students' engagement. Some students feel safer to engage anonymously online while others engage more during face-to-face sessions. Reeves (2015) presented an interesting case of teaching hands-on laboratories online to multidisciplinary engineering students where the Virtual Learning Environment (VLE) was depended on extensively for student engagement. Their findings show that both asynchronous and synchronous sessions are useful in engaging students online. Kemp [26] however, revealed that students feel more engaged with face-to-face discussions with peers and instructors compared with online, though they prefer to do the activities online.

Though the findings above may help in improving the students' engagement of CSY2015, there are some associated challenges such as low grades and stress that need to be considered.

2 Preliminary Study

In order to gain a deeper understanding of the student engagement issues and associated challenges from the students' perspective, a study was conducted in-class, with the experimental group (CSY2015 2018/19), using an adopted empathy map adopted Ferreira et al. [27] (Table 1 and Fig. 1). It can be deduced from Table 1 that, while most students want to "gain" good programming skills and good grades in order to graduate and get good jobs, they fear the "pain" of not having enough prior programming skills and failing. As shown in Fig. 1, the study reveal that one student ("Student A") suffers from the fear of anxiety and depression, and feels overwhelmed by the impact of the study responsibility involved with taking several modules at the same time. This was taken into consideration in implementing the interventions discussed in this case-study (the details of the additional advice and support provided to "Student A" is beyond the scope of this report and hence not discussed). This study reveals that students see the relevance of the module to their future job opportunities. They want high grades; however, they do not have enough confidence in their own programming skills. Therefore, an intervention that gives students the opportunity to apply their theoretical knowledge to practical problems in order to help improve their programming skills while given them a feel of the work environment may be the right solution. Problem-based learning provides such an opportunity. Moreover, if given the opportunity to work with others, students do not only get to learn from each other but to also understand that they are not alone in some of the challenges encountered during the learning curve. A lesson the tutor gained from the study is to not overly complicate the problem-based learning activities, as this may rather demotivate the students or hinder their learning. Also, the use of interim but flexible deadlines will help ease the level of anxiety on students with regards to not being able to complete the tasks in time.

3 Intervention

3.1 Problem-Based Learning

The idea is to use problem-based learning with various hands-on laboratory activities to encourage experiential learning where students learn by doing [1, 18, 21]. CSY2015 involves physical computing where hardware (microcontroller) development tools are used. In order to help engage the students and to increase the relevance of the module to the individual disciplines, the most popular microcontroller programming hardware and software resources among both engineering and computing students for dissertations in Level 6 is selected for the activities of CSY2015. Problem-based learning theories suggest the use and effectiveness of small groups in improving academic achievements [19]. A similar approach is adapted (see Sect. 3.2) but with the aim of improving both student engagement and academic achievement.

Table 1. Results of student empathy study of CSY2015

What do they think and feel	What do they hear	What do they see	What do they say and do	Pain	Gain
Family	You cannot come this far to drop out of university	-Compete with Myself -See friends working	-Kind -Mind their own business -Motivated	Dropping out of University	-Being able to provide for the family -Plenty assets and stocks
-To run the program -The requirements in the table -Worry of the tasks not working	The advice given by others	-The program in the example -Classmates -Add more lines	-Curious -Ask for help from others -Check the program one by one	It is really hard for me because I have never learnt it before	-To learn how the program is running and what it means in partials -It seems that it always has errors
It is important to understand programming	It is useful and interesting, but it needs a lot of practice. It is good for the future job			Pressure, deadlines and working hard for all subjects at the same time	Good knowledge in programming to improve living once you achieve all your goals
Work Future Deadlines	Motivate	-Rainy days -Other groups Work	Friendly Work More Motivation	Feeling tired	Good grade Achievement
	They push me to continue writing harder and put extra effort	-The students around me -Most friends do easier courses which allows them more free time as compared to me	-Little to help when needed -Try to seem very in control -I try to behave as if each class is my last	Coping with financial struggle by maintaining a job while juggling university	Hoping to get a degree and make parents proud
Education and future The future and present	I try to surround myself with people who push me to	Weather and People Humans Characters	Friendly	Failing	Graduate with a good grade Whatever makes me and

3.2 Effective Large and Small Student Group Strategies

3.2.1 Rational

To make effective use of groups as an intervention to enhance student engagement, an adapted version of the 7 steps strategy proposed in [28] is used. The 7 steps strategy involves 1. Setting clear expectations for group work 2. Thinking carefully about the group size and composition 3. Helping to manage the logistics of the group work 4. Encouraging intercultural group work 5. Designing innovative group work activities 6. Monitoring the group's activities 7. Managing assessed group work.

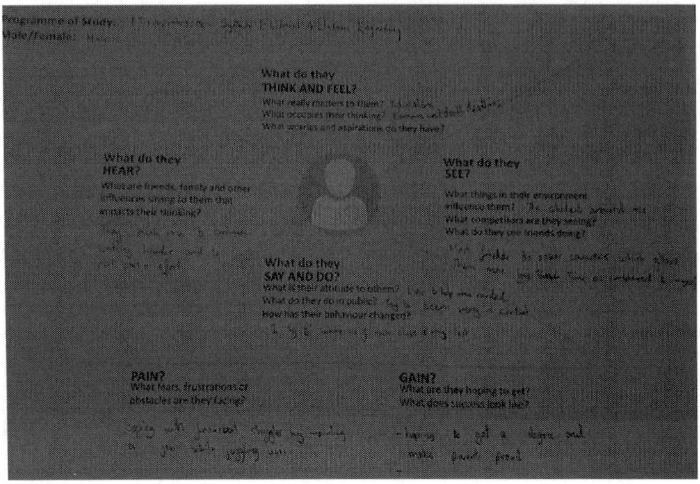

Fig. 1. Sample from student empathy study

3.2.2 Strategy

Set Clear Expectations for Group Work: Groups benefit from effective teamwork and planning (Livingstone, Lynch 2000) and hence students must be given enough time to evaluate practicalities of forming/joining a particular group [29]. Therefore, the new strategy is to help students familiarize themselves with each other in the early weeks of the module. The practical problems in the early weeks are formatively assessed in order to encourage students to get engaged in group activities without the fear of risking grades. Students are encouraged to either work in groups of 4 of their choice or individually (Gibbs, G. 1995b). They are given the flexibility to either stay in the same group throughout, or to form different groups for each session. Their progress is monitored during class and through group discussions (and through the project log/journal on the VLE).

Group Size and Composition: Existing research has shown that choosing the right group size can enhance student engagement [30]. It has been identified in the literature that the ideal group size is between four and six people [31–33]. Different strategies have been used to form working student groups (4 per group) in the second teaching block in the past which have had varied effects. For example, students have previously been allocated as follows:

1. A mixture of Engineering and Computing students. It was observed that, Engineering students either ended up dormant or relying too much on computing students for programming while computing students relied on engineering students for circuit building and report writing. There was not much interdisciplinary learning involved. Students from each discipline mostly concentrated on what they felt they were good at. This may not be an issue in the first teaching block which emphasizes individual learning. However, interdisciplinary learning is essential in the second

teaching block which emphasizes transferable skills and students' ability to work in a real-world industrial setting.
2. A mix of engaged (or promising) students and non-engaging (or at-risk) students. It was observed that non-engaging students depended too much on the "promising students" for the completion of the tasks and sometimes slowed down their learning curve.

In response to the above, the idea is to help students form teams rather than just groups to enhance engagement. The early weeks where students work individually or in larger groups are used to monitor engaging and non-engaging students. This helps to identify students at risk early enough to help put the right intervention in place. Afterwards (around weeks 5–6), smaller groups facilitated by the tutor are formed. Engaging students who have made significant progress can either work alone or with other engaging students or with students of their choice. Progress can easily be monitored by the quality of their contribution to the journal feature of VLE. Non-engaging students either get to work on their own or with other non-engaging students.

Though this intervention may seem like a bad idea, when implemented (in Week 7), the non-engaging students suddenly started showing some willingness to learn. They demonstrated a sense of responsibility to complete the tasks in their own creative way, knowing that they cannot hide behind the mask of other students. Moreover, after the implementation of this strategy, classroom attendance, student participation and interaction with the tutor (asking for clarification and feedback) has also improved greatly.

Encourage Intercultural/Interdisciplinary Group Work: Gibbs [34] emphasized that intercultural groups are more beneficial. In this context, the idea is to design the group activities in such a way that no particular discipline has familiar advantage over the other. Thus, to encourage interdisciplinary group work, each task requires building a circuit on a solderless breadboard and programming the circuit to work. This requires both Engineering and Computing skills without deviating from the learning outcomes of the module.

Innovative Group Work Activities: As emphasized by Gibbs [35] group activities should be of a complexity suitable for the collective effort and knowledge of all the group members. During the first few weeks where groups of 4 are used, students have to work collaboratively and creatively employ problem solving skills as well as subject knowledge to solve the problems. Groups are being introduced into the early teaching weeks as an intervention to encourage student engagement. Hence, the focus of the activities in this stage is to help students identify which group members they work best with, and whether they engage better with the module working alone or as a group. The goal here is not to use overly complex activities to ensure that each activity can be completed in within a week. This allows student to form new groups in different weeks in order to find the best group members for them.

Help Manage the Logistics of Group Work; Monitor the Group's Activities; and Manage Assessed Group Work: This involves the effective use of VLE's "group" resources. Using the group resource on VLE, students, can exchange files, create wikis, blogs, use journals and more importantly, these activities can easily be monitored and graded by the tutor. This has been implemented as an intervention in CSY2015. Students were advised to work within their groups and upload the findings of their completed task (by following a template) to their group page on the VLE site. Most students could not complete this during the class when it was first introduced as they had no prior experience with the group tool of the VLE. However, all the groups participated. Additional time was given to complete the task outside the face-to-face session. The statistics report from the VLE shows a high level of student engagement with the activities both during and outside the face-to-face session.

3.3 An Element of Game Theory

The fundamental of game theory is competition and reward. People are often motivated when there is a suitable reward which align with their goals [36]. The trick here is to assign a percentage (say 10%) of the assessment of the second teaching block (AS1) of the module to the problem-based activities [37].

AS1 accesses all the learning outcomes specified in the module specification of CSY2015. Hence, the problem-based activities are designed to map the learning outcomes of the module. It should be noted that one single submission point was used for AS1 for both the report on the project and the progress of the problem-based activities. Therefore, caution was taken in the allocation of the "reward" to ensure that the no rule is broken with regards to the module specification of CSY2015.

4 Quantitative Evaluation of Findings

In order to evaluate the impact of the intervention, effect sizes, a well trusted quantifying tool for evaluating the significance of an improvement, is used. The aim is to evaluate the effect of the intervention on the student engagement and academic achievement. The percentage difference between the number of students in 2018/19 (experimental group) and 2016/17 is 83.3% (see the table in Fig. 2) which is too significant to give a fair comparison of effect sizes. Therefore, grades of students from 2017/18 which has only 15.8% difference in student numbers with the experimental group was selected as the control group. Besides, the time overlap between the two academic years makes it more suitable to be selected for quantitative evaluation.

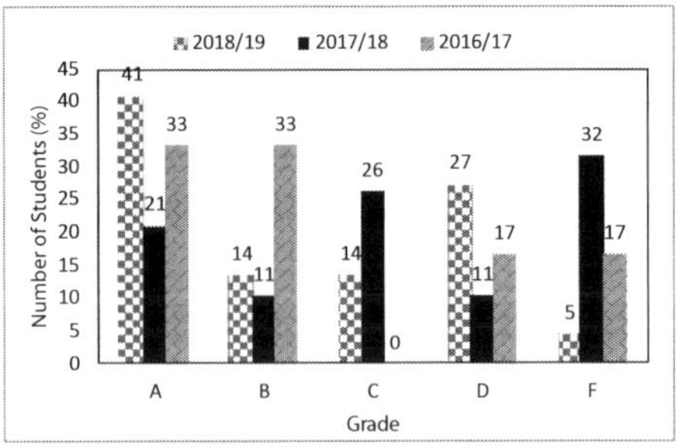

Academic Year	Number of Students	Percentage Difference with Number of Students in Experimental Group
2018/19	22	0%
2017/18	19	15.8%
2016/19	12	83.3%

Fig. 2. Assessment (MCQ) results of first teaching block of CSY2015

The average score was 64.4 in 2018/19, and 50 in 2017/18 with a standard deviation of 18.8. Hence the effect size is (64.4−50)/18.8 = 0.8. This implies that the grade of an average student in 2018/19 after the implementation of the intervention outperforms the grades of 79% of the students in the previous year. Effect sizes of 0.5 or higher (in this case 0.8) is much higher than most interventions reported in the literature [2]. Moreover, it has been confirmed in the literature that findings of effects sizes of 0.8 are rare as it demands significant gains [2, 20]. This therefore confirms that the intervention has a significant impact on the student's grades [3].

As shown in Fig. 2, students' grades in the MCQ test have greatly improved in 2018/19 compared to that of the previous two years. Though 2018/19 has the highest recorded number of students taking the test, 41% of the students had A while only 5% got F grade in contrast with the previous year which recorded 21% and 32% in A and F, respectively, with 19 students. An interesting observation, however, is that, the 5% of the students who got F is in fact a student who did not engage with the face-to-face sessions and only turned up on test date. The student's engagement with the online content and "possibly" his peers outside the classroom might have however, contributed to the F + instead of F or F-. Research conducted in [2] and [20] suggested a negative correlation between problem-based learning and test results. However, the results of the interventions prove that problem-based learning helps improves students' grades. The intervention in this case-study promoted competition through rewards, however, this did not have a negative effect on the quality of individual problem solving as implied by [23]. It rather had a positive effect on the quality of individual problem solving, student engagement and grades. The improved engagement and grades after implementing engagement strategies in the face-to-face session agrees with Kemp's work [26] which shows that students have a higher preference for engagement in face-to-face discussions.

5 Conclusion: Implications for Future Development and Teaching Practice

The use of larger but variable groups to work on formative assessment problems and eventually forming smaller groups to work on elements of the summative assessment is a particularly good technique for encouraging interdisciplinary learning, enhancing student engagement and given effective feedback. The problems-based approach to teaching theory is an effective technique for engaging students of varied abilities and disciplines. However, since the interim summative assessment is MCQ, it will be good to provide MCQ-based knowledge checks on the VLE site. It will also be beneficial to highlight the related learning outcomes within the activity briefs. The multiple-choice questions should be designed to draw on the experience and understanding gained through the problem-based learning without breaching the learning outcomes assessed in each item. It will be interesting to get external parties, such as employers, involved. For instance, the problems or activities could be linked to particular industrial projects and employers could be invited to give the briefing or help set the real-world scenarios. Alternatives such as giving labs and problems that cuts across the disciplines could be explored.

References

1. Bédard, D., et al.: Problem-based and project-based learning in engineering and medicine: determinants of students' engagement and persistance. Interdisc. J. Prob.-Based Learn. **6**(2), 8 (2012)
2. Prince, M.: Does active learning work? a review of the research. J. Eng. Educ. **93**(3), 223–231 (2004). https://doi.org/10.1002/j.2168-9830.2004.tb00809.x
3. Trowler, P., Trowler, V.: Student engagement evidence summary (2010)
4. Parnas, D.L.: Education for computing professionals. Computer **23**(1), 17–22 (1990)
5. McCracken, M., et al.: A multi-national, multi-institutional study of assessment of programming skills of first-year CS students. In: Working Group Reports from ITiCSE on Innovation and Technology in Computer Science Education (2001)
6. England, R.E., Meier, K.J., Fraga, L.R.: Barriers to equal opportunity: educational practices and minority students. Urban Aff. Q. **23**(4), 635–646 (1988)
7. Finn, J.D., Voelkl, K.E.: School characteristics related to student engagement. J. Negro Educ. **62**(3), 249–268 (1993)
8. Talbott, E., et al.: Making sense of minority student identification in special education: school context matters. Int. J. Special Educ. **26**(3), 150–170 (2011)
9. Dermo, J.: e-Assessment and the student learning experience: A survey of student perceptions of e-assessment. Br. J. Educ. Technol. **40**(2), 203–214 (2009)
10. Schmoker, M.: Focus: Elevating the Essentials to Radically Improve Student Learning (2018)
11. Eccles, J.S., Wigfield, A., Schiefele, U.: Motivation to succeed. (1998)
12. Willis, D.: Academic involvement at university. Higher Educ. **25**(2), 133–150 (1993)
13. Hidi, S., Renninger, K.A.: The four-phase model of interest development. Educ. Psychol. **41** (2), 111–127 (2006)
14. Pirot, L., Ketele, D.: L'engagement académique de l'étudiant comme facteur de réussite à l'université Étude exploratoire menée dans deux facultés contrastées. Revue Des Sci. De L'Éduc. **26**(2), 367–394 (2000)
15. Pirker, J., Riffnaller-Schiefer, M., Gütl, C.: Motivational active learning: engaging university students in computer science education. In: Proceedings of the 2014 Conference on Innovation & Technology in Computer Science Education (2014)
16. Attle, S., Baker, B.: Cooperative learning in a competitive environment: classroom applications. Int. J. Teach. Learn. Higher Educ. **19**(1), 77–83 (2007)
17. Burden, P.R., Byrd, D.M.: Methods for Effective Teaching. p. 160 (1994)
18. Freeman, S., et al.: Active learning increases student performance in science, engineering, and mathematics. Proc. Nat. Acad. Sci. **111**(23), 8410–8415 (2014)
19. Norman, G.R., Schmidt, H.G.: Revisiting 'effectiveness of problem-based learning curricula: theory, practice and paper darts'. Med. Educ. **50**(8), 793–797 (2016)
20. Albanese, M.A., Mitchell, S.: Problem-based learning: a review of literature on its outcomes and implementation issues. Acad. Med.-Philadelphia **68**, 52 (1993)
21. Reeves, J., Arnold, B.J.: Applying student engagement techniques to multidisciplinary online engineering laboratories. In: ASEE Annual Conference and Exposition
22. Vernon, D.T., Blake, R.L.: No title, Does problem-based learning work? a meta-analysis of evaluative research (1993)
23. Qin, Z., Johnson, D.W., Johnson, R.T.: Cooperative versus competitive efforts and problem solving. Rev. Educ. Res. **65**(2), 129–143 (1995)
24. Hartley, J., Davies, I.K.: Note-taking: a critical review. Program. Learn. Educ. Technol. **15** (3), 207–224 (1978)

25. Ruhl, K.L., Hughes, C.A., Schloss, P.J.: Using the pause procedure to enhance lecture recall. Teacher Educ. Special Educ. **10**(1), 14–18 (1987)
26. Kemp, N., Grieve, R.: Face-to-face or face-to-screen? Undergraduates' opinions and test performance in classroom vs. online learning. Front. Psychol. **5**, 1278 (2014)
27. Ferreira, B., et al.: Designing personas with empathy map. In: Seke (2015)
28. 7 Steps to: Using Group Work in Your Teaching. https://www.plymouth.ac.uk/uploads/production/document/path/2/2398/7_steps_to_using_group_work_in_your_teaching_March_2013__1_.pdf
29. Gibbs, G.: Learning in Groups: Tutor Guide. Oxford: Oxford Centre for Staff Development (1995)
30. Seethamraju, R., Borman, M.: Influence of group formation choices on academic performance. Assess. Eval. Higher Educ. **34**(1), 31–40 (2009)
31. Best, J.W., Kahn, J.V.: Research in Education (2016)
32. Keller, R.T.: Predictors of the performance of project groups in R & D organizations. Acad. Manag. J. **29**(4), 715–726 (1986)
33. Kitzinger, J.: Qualitative research: introducing focus groups. BMJ **311**(7000), 299–302 (1995)
34. Gibbs, G.: The assessment of group work: lessons from the literature. Assessment Standards Knowledge Exchange, 1–17 (2009)
35. Gibbs, G.: Learning in groups: tutor guide (1995)
36. Prensky, M.: The motivation of gameplay: The real twenty-first century learning revolution. Horizon **10**(1), 5–11 (2002)
37. Gibbs, G.: Using Assessment to Support Student Learning (2010)

Contests, Competitions and Games in Informatics

Situated Learning with Bebras Tasklets

Carlo Bellettini[1], Violetta Lonati[1(✉)], Mattia Monga[1], Anna Morpurgo[1], and Martina Palazzolo[2]

[1] Università degli Studi di Milano, Milan, Italy
violetta.lonati@unimi.it
http://aladdin.di.unimi.it
[2] Istituto Comprensivo 'Ilaria Alpi', Milan, Italy

Abstract. A Bebras short task, a *tasklet*, is designed to provide a source for exploring a computational thinking concept: at the end of the contest it could be used as a starting point to delve deeper into a computing topic. In this paper we report an experience which aims at taking full advantage of the potential of Bebras tasklets. A math teacher asked her pupils to act as Bebras "trainers" for younger mates. The pupils, in pairs, were assigned to design and prepare a tangible game inspired by a Bebras tasklet, devised for the younger pupils to practice. They also had to explain the game to the younger pupils, make them play and support them in solving it. In carrying out this assignment the pupils acting as trainers had to deeply explore the Bebras tasklet and face its computational thinking challenge, and also practiced soft skills as collaborating with peers towards a common goal, adapting language and communicative style to engage with younger mates, devising and designing a tangible object, and planning its creation. The experience proved that using Bebras tasklets as the social and cultural context for situated learning of computational thinking competencies is indeed quite productive.

Keywords: Computational thinking · Situated learning · Bebras

1 Introduction

Bebras, the "International Challenge on Informatics and Computational Thinking"[1] [7,9,13], is a popular initiative aimed at introducing to the fundamental concepts of informatics pupils from 1st grade to the end of secondary school, independently of their exposure to formal computer science studies. The challenge is organized on an annual basis in several (54 in 2018) countries since 2004, with almost three million participants in the last edition. The setting of the contest is slightly different in each country, but in general participants have to solve a set of about 10–15 tasks that are designed to be fun and attractive, adequate for the

[1] http://bebras.org/ 'Bebras' is the Lithuanian word for 'beaver': some countries translate it, and others use it as a brand name.

S. N. Pozdniakov and V. Dagienė (Eds.): ISSEP 2019, LNCS 11913, pp. 225–239, 2019.
https://doi.org/10.1007/978-3-030-33759-9_18

contestants' age, and solvable in an average time of three minutes, hence called *tasklets*. Moreover, since the contest is especially aimed at a non-vocational audience, tasklets should be independent of specific curricular activities and avoid the use of jargon. In fact, Bebras tasklets focus on that part of informatics that should become familiar to everyone, not just computing professionals. A number of tasklets are prepared every year by an international team of experts in computer science and computing education; then each national organization selects, adapts and translates a set of tasklets to be used in the local competition. After the contest, the translated tasklets used in the challenge are publicly released by most countries and can be used by teachers as teaching resources in their school practice [2,8]. In Italy, the challenge is proposed to teams of (up to) 4 pupils, divided into 5 categories according to contestant age (from 8 to 18 years), and administered by an online platform [3,4] that displays tasklets and collects the submitted answers. Once the contest is over, the same platform also allows pupils to access their answers and check the solutions. In particular, for each tasklet they can see the correct answer (or one of them, if applicable), compare their answer with the correct one, access the explanation on how the answer could be obtained, and read a short text ("It's informatics") about the informatics content of the tasklet. The system is available also beyond the contest, so that the challenge can be simulated and answers and explanation be accessed at any time. Usually, after the challenge pupils are eager to know whether the solutions they had submitted are right or wrong. However, when they have learnt they got an answer (partially) wrong, many are not too motivated to investigate further. During the last edition, we observed some pupils when the teacher disclosed the results, and they did not spend much time in examining the explanation or ascertaining they really understood the tasklet and the correct answer, even when the teacher urged them to. In order to encourage pupils' engagement, a math class teacher (author Martina Palazzolo) asked her 6th grade pupils to act as Bebras trainers for a primary school class (3rd grade); pupils were requested to design and prepare *tangible games*, inspired by Bebras tasklets, to be offered to younger pupils to practice in view of next year's Bebras Challenge. The trainers then had to explain the game to the younger pupils, make them play and support them in solving the tasklet. The last of these training sessions was observed by a computing education expert, member of the Italian Bebras Committee (author Violetta Lonati), whose observations were the basis for the assessment of the project. In this paper we report this experience and the related findings. In Sect. 2 we describe the activities that have been carried out and the project's learning goals and methodology. In Sect. 3 we present the tasklets chosen by the pupils and the derived games they built, and we report about the interaction of the pupils with their mates and their teacher during the preparation of games and the training sessions. In Sect. 4 we give some elements to evaluate the overall experience and we draw some conclusions.

2 Description of the Project

In this section we present the project, and in particular the context where it was proposed, the planned activities, the learning goals, and the methodology used to manage the activities and assess the results.

Context and Activities. The experience involved a 6th grade class of a publicly-funded school, composed by 22 pupils (age 10–11 years). This particular class of the school is involved in a three-year long experimentation on innovative teaching methods which involves all the class teachers. The class timetable schedules a two-hour weekly session of mildly structured activities devoted to the development of cross competencies, conducted by the math and science teacher (author Martina Palazzolo, from now on, *the Teacher*). This was the context where the project was conducted throughout the second term (January–May) of year 2019. All the pupils were familiar with Bebras tasklets since they had already played a simulation of the challenge in the first term. They had also spent a couple of hours working in groups to check their answers and study the explanations provided in the Italian Bebras Platform. At the beginning of the project pupils were informed by the Teacher that they were going to act as Bebras trainers for 3rd graders. From now on we will call these groups of pupils *trainers* and *trainees*, respectively. The project was thus organized in two phases: (1) *Preparation of the Games.* Working in pairs, trainers were asked to choose a Bebras tasklet, design a tangible game, and build it (with cardboard, etc.) so that it would be possible for the younger pupils to try it without accessing the original tasklet through the platform. This phase lasted around three months. The game had to be built in such a way that it would be clearly accessible and understandable by a peer. In particular, the requirements were that the title, the text, and question should be clearly readable, the game should be self-explanatory and have all the elements necessary to solve it, and it should be equipped with an envelope containing the correct answer. It was not requested though that the game were accessible by a 3rd grader without some help or further explanation by the trainers. (2) *Training Sessions.* Towards the end of the school year the trainers actually trained a 3rd grade class of 22 pupils by using their games. The trainees were invited to two training sessions, one held in April and one in May 2019, and played all the games. Between the two sessions, the Teacher conducted a discussion among the trainers: they were requested to report to their mates how the training sessions went and whether they thought their games needed some adjustments.

Soon after the project had started, a computing education expert and member of the national Bebras Committee (author Violetta Lonati, from now on *the Expert*) was asked by the Teacher to contribute to the project as a mentor and supervisor. The Expert's role was to support the Teacher in relation to the computational thinking aspects involved by the tasklets chosen by the pupils, and hence to help her understand how the project improved the learning of computational thinking skills. Teacher and Expert had already collaborated in other computing education projects in the past [5], after they had met several years ago in a refreshment course attended by the Teacher.

2.1 Learning Goals

The project aimed at several learning goals for the trainers. On the one hand, the trainers were expected to improve in the computational thinking skills (CT) implied by Bebras tasklets [2,8]. In particular the focus was on the following CT skills.

Represent—representing information through abstraction such as models, diagrams, symbolic encodings and understanding such representations;
Algo_think—automating tasks through algorithmic thinking (i.e., series of ordered steps);
Implement—implementing algorithmic solutions complying with some predefined syntax (*i.e., coding*);
Organize—logically organizing data;
Reason—analytically reasoning about data, objects, situations to check properties and draw logical conclusions.

In stating such goals, we adopt the framework discussed in [2], mostly based on the the operational definition of CT [1] developed by ISTE (International Society for Technology in Education) and CSTA (Computer Science Teachers Association). Only some of the skills described in the paper are mentioned here, namely those that are relevant with respect to the set of tasklets chosen by the pupils (see Sect. 3). In fact, since each pair of trainers chose a different tasklet, they actually practiced different skills among the above ones. We should also mention here that different (and only partially overlapping) definitions of CT exist; a good recent survey can be found in [6], which discusses also frequent misconceptions of CT by primary teachers. On the other hand, the project also aimed at promoting soft skills like: learning to learn; collaborating with peers towards a common goal; adapting language and communicative style to engage with younger mates; devising and designing a tangible object, and planning its creation; practically producing a tangible object identifying, getting and using the proper materials and techniques. In this paper we are mainly interested in reporting and discussing the findings concerning the CT skills, and we will consider the soft skills mentioned above as side learning goals only. For the trainees no learning goals were actually set, since they were involved in the activities only for two hours. However the training was useful to them as it gave them the opportunity to face the Bebras tasklets in a even more friendly setting than the online platform. A very recent work [10] describes a similar project conducted in Lithuania where game cards inspired by Bebras tasklets were proposed outside the challenge to foster CT. In this project too, tangible objects, mostly provided by the teacher, were used to support pupils in their solving process.

2.2 Methodology

During the whole project the Teacher acted more as a facilitator of the learning process than as an instructor, keeping in mind the constructivist view of learning: learners actively construct their knowledge and skills through reorganization of their previously acquired mental structure [15]. According to social-constructivism such construction of knowledge is also guided and influenced by the social context, and thus by the interactions with others and in particular by their use of language [16]. Hence the learning process is fostered by feedback, examples, and scaffolding by teachers, and interaction with peers rather than only by free exploration [14].

For this project, the Teacher designed the activities in a CSSC (Constructive, Self-Regulated, Situated, and Collaborative) learning environment [11]: the first phase required a mindful and effortful involvement by pupils in the exploration of the tasklets and allowed them to individually construct knowledge and meaning (*constructive*); pupils worked in pairs, exchanging ideas and mediating different points of view (*collaborative*); during the training sessions pupils acted in a social and cultural context, where learning was further enacted in the interaction with the younger pupils (*situated*); during the whole project the pupils were let free to decide how to use their time and how to plan their activities, while the Teacher monitored their work giving some feedback, avoiding to give direct instructions if not asked by the pupils themselves, and was available to support them upon request (*self-regulated*). The Teacher set some constraints in order to promote the expected learning outcomes in CT.

- Pupils were requested to design a game inspired by one among the tasklets they had not correctly solved in the first place. Hence, in order to design their game, they needed to examine the chosen task with care, understanding what it asked the solver to do, and how the correct answer could be found.
- In the transposition toward a tangible game, they were allowed to change some details and introduce variants to the original task, but the resulting game had to reflect the spirit of the original task and in particular be suitable to stimulate the same abilities.
- The rules and directions for the games had to be written in full on a poster to be made available to trainees.
- Pairs were broken up during the two training sessions so that each trainer was in charge of personally conducting the game in one of them.

At the beginning of the first phase, pupils were randomly split in pairs. As one could expect, several pairs were therefore composed by pupils with different levels of cognitive, linguistic, creative, and practical skills, and some of them were actually unhappy of the draw's outcome. This choice was discussed with the pupils and then motivated by the Teacher: they would be asked to collaborate with their mates as true professionals; moreover, identifying at least one positive trait in their mate was a target they had to achieve throughout the project.

During the training sessions (two hour long each), several table islands were arranged in the classroom where the games were displayed, and the trainees could move around the islands to play the games; each trainee was equipped with a card where trainers logged the participation to their games. During the games, the trainees could read the poster with the rules and directions for a game, however trainers were not forbidden to read aloud or explain in their own words the rules for the trainees, or more generally to interact with them.

To assess the project we took into consideration both the products of the pupils involved—namely the tangible games they built—and the overall learning process, focusing mainly on their interactions with peers, trainees, and their Teacher. In particular, the Expert attended the second (and last) training session as a non-participant observer. The observation goal was to detect whether and how the CT aspects underlying the Bebras tasklets had been grasped by the trainers. Both the Teacher during the first phase of the project, and the Expert during the last training session used the *anecdotal records* methodology [12], which consists of short descriptions of behavior as observed in specific situations. As typical in anecdotal records, the observed incidents have then been interpreted, and recommendations arising from the observations have been suggested and, in some cases, immediately implemented.

3 Process and Products

The 22 pupils in the 6th grade class were randomly split into 11 pairs. Three pairs chose tasklet "Birthday party" (`2018-RO-06`), two pairs chose tasklet "Drawing Game" (`2018-PK-01`), the other pairs chose one of the following tasklets: "Balls" (`2017-RS-02`), "Board jumps" (`2018-CA-06`), "Waiter" (`2018-IT-06`), "Room sharing" (`2018-DE-07`), "Finding the route" (`2018-CY-04`), "Dustmen robots" (`2018-SK-05`)[2]. Ten pairs succeeded in building their games. Most games were realized as posters (some of the posters are shown in Figs. 1, 2, 3, 4 and 5), and some of them also had mobile elements so that the interactivity of the original tasks could be simulated. One pair only (who chose "Birthday party") did not succeed in getting the game ready for the training sessions. Two pairs added some difficulties in their games that were not included in the original tasks (namely "Drawing Game" and "Birthday party"). Since such difficulties were deemed by the teacher too hard for 3rd graders, and other groups had chosen the same tasks, at the end only the latter games were used in the training sessions. During the training sessions most pairs were split, so that half of the 6th graders attended the first session and the other half attended the second session, and most trainers ran their game individually. Some exceptions occurred: some pairs were kept as such, mainly due to the presence of pupils with special needs; moreover, since "Drawing Game" was chosen by two pairs, but only one version of the game

[2] We report in bracket the international Bebras id code, although the tasklets were sometimes modified to exploit the interactivity potential of the Italian Bebras Platform and to take into account that the Italian contest is team based (whereas it is individual in most of the countries). The screenshots of the actual tasklets (translated to English for this paper) are given in Appendix A.

was suitable for the training session, the trainers did not work alone but were coupled with a member of the other pair.

In the following we give some details on the tasklets chosen and how they were used by the pupils. Due to space constraints we limit the description to five tasklets only, namely those which led to situations offering more elements for the discussion. We relate the tasklets to the CT skills we listed in Sect. 2.1 and we describe how the related games were realized and which differences pupils introduced with respect to the original tasklets. We also report and discuss the relevant incidents that occurred during the first phase and/or the training sessions. These facts shed lights on both the cases where pupils had understood the CT concepts, and the cases where critical issues came up.

3.1 Birthday Party

Tasklet. The tasklet, shown in Fig. 1, asks the solver to consider the friendship relationship among animals and place the animales around tables respecting some given constraints, thus it relates to the "Reason" skill. While reading the text one can start placing the animals, considering one constraint at a time, but there is some freedom in the choice of the tables, since some placements are fully determined only by forthcoming constraints. In particular, two critical situations might happen: i. if one places the Rabbit (the first mentioned animal) at the wrong table, she gets eventually stuck due to the different number of seats at the two tables; ii. all animals are placed before the text is over complying with all but the last constraint, but the placement might turn out not to satisfy the last constraint. In both cases, the solver needs to backtrack and reconsider the solution or start over.

Game. The trainers drew the two tables on the poster, and pieces of Velcro tape were stuck around each table as placeholders for the guests. The faces of the animals were drawn on cards, with Velcro on the back, so that they could be attached to the places around the tables. The cards were stored in an envelope attached to the poster. The task's text and the question were written on separate sheets and put in another envelope.

Anecdotal Record. At the beginning of the training session, trainers were very directive and basically guided the trainees step by step; when trainers read a sentence like "animal A is friends with animal B", they also added a comment like "then you have to put animal A at the same table as animal B", often pointing at the corresponding card. Moreover, when trainees got stuck because of the wrong choice of the table for the Rabbit (case i. above), they straightforwardly suggested to start over by placing it at the other table. Also, as soon as the trainees placed the last animal at a table, the trainers stopped the trainees (even though the text was not over yet) asked them to check the obtained situation against the solution in the envelope, and made them start over when they differed. In other terms, when something went wrong, the trainers did not wait for the trainees to discover the problem and try to fix it by themselves.

The Teacher advised the trainers to be more patient, but they appeared skeptical and indeed showed again the tendency of being too directive. After a second intervention, they succeeded in being more patient and realized that the trainees were actually able to eventually detect the inconsistencies by themselves without checking the solution, if allowed to conclude reading the text. Once, a trainee got stuck but refused to start over, asking instead try to fix the solution alone. He switched the tables and then re-checked that all constraints were satisfied. The trainers were really surprised that the trainee was actually able to fix the error by a different approach: "he did find the correct solution, but he found it without starting over!".

Discussion. Trainers were able to reason on the task's constraints, identifying the correct solution. They also showed to be aware of the two critical situations that might happen. However, the fact that they stopped trainees prematurely suggests that they probably did not identify the origin of the issue for case (ii). The last trainee described above showed good abstraction skills, being able to grasp that the relation "being at the same table with" is more important –in this tasklet– than the property "being seated at a certain table". Moreover, this interaction helped the trainers understand an important CT aspect: the same output or final result can be obtained with different strategies.

3.2 Drawing Game

Tasklet. The tasklet, shown in Fig. 2, is basically a programming question – the programs' goal being to draw shapes– and it relates to "Implement" and "Algo_think" skills. Due to the presence of multiple choices, the tasklet could be solved simply by executing the programs and checking if the obtained output is a square.

Game. The tasklet text was directly written on the poster, but the examples shown in the original were omitted. Moreover, the original tasklet presented a multiple choice question; the trainers opted instead for a constructive question, asking the solver to build a program with the provided commands. In an envelope attached to the poster, some white sheets were made available to write down the program, with lines numbered 1 to 6, to suggest that six commands were needed in the program.

Anecdotal Record. During the preparation of the game, the Teacher suggested that trainees would have benefited from manipulating some tangible objects when creating the program. Trainers were skeptical at first but then they used some cardboard to make four logs and a flag, so that the target drawing could actually be composed with objects. During the first training session, the trainers realized that writing the program on the sheets of paper was too time consuming. Hence, before the next training session, the trainers added some cards with the four available commands, that could be put in a sequence to form a program. During the next training session, however, they observed that multiple copies of each command were actually needed, since some commands had to be used more than once in the same program.

Discussion. The game resulted in a much more difficult task than the original one; according to the Bloom's taxonomy, the required cognitive skill moved from "apply" to "create". This fact suggests that the trainers mastered the CT content implied by the tasklet. During the training, they further realized the importance of re-using the same command more than once and in different positions. This is a peculiar aspect of programming, that does not often appear in other mathematical or logical tasks that require rearranging (e.g., sequencing) objects. Moreover, while supporting their trainees struggling in the program-writing process, the trainers came to understand better what is implied in such process: on the one hand one has to select and properly position the appropriate commands (write code), on the other hand one has to simultaneously simulate and trace the effect of the commands themselves (execute code).

3.3 Balls

Tasklet. The tasklet, presented in Fig. 3 focuses on LIFO stacks, and it relates to "Algo_think" and "Organize" skills.

Game. The ramps with holes and pins were drawn directly on the poster together with the tasklet's text and some new explanations on how the system was supposed to work. As in the original task, four possible alternative answers were given. An extra sheet with the ramp and the holes drawn on it was made available to track the rolling balls. The original number of balls was doubled from 10 to 20, the number of holes was increased from three to four with their capacity always of decreasing size.

Anecdotal Record. During the first phase, the Teacher suggested to prepare some tangible elements to simulate the process. The trainers did not accept the suggestion since "it will make the game too easy". Then the Teacher suggested that they could provide the trainees with some support to trace the process; they agreed but were not able to find a way. At the end, the Teacher suggested to draw the ramps with holes and pins on separate sheets, to be freely sketched by the trainees. During the first training session, the trainers did not use the sheets until after some iterations, when they saw trainees struggling with the task. At the end of the first training session, the trainer commented that the sheets were in fact useful. The trainer of the second session was very patient and intervened only when the trainees were stuck or made some errors in the executions of steps, by re-reading them the appropriate specification when needed, and advising them to trace the process step by step on the sheet.

Discussion. The fact that the trainer of the second session was so precise in reminding the relevant specifications at the exact moment they were needed is evidence that she had understood and remembered how the system worked and was perfectly able to follow the evolution of the system and apply the general specifications to its current state. The latter one is an important CT skill, especially useful when analyzing or debugging programs or systems. Moreover, her manner of supporting the trainees helped them in appreciating how the system evolved in a deterministic way, according to the specifications.

3.4 Waiter

Tasklet. The tasklet, presented in Fig. 4, asks pupils to choose among different representations (notes) of an order taken by a waiter. The tasklet aimed at promoting a reflection on how different ways of representing the same data can serve different purposes, hence it relates to "Organize" and "Represent" skills.

Game. The tasklet text was written on the poster, whereas the multiple choice answers were written on separate sheets and glued to the poster. Each answer had a piece of Velcro tape on top, and a Velcro cross should be used to select the right answer. The setting was changed with respect to the original tasklet: instead of a waiter, the main character was a shop assistant selling make-up products. The game presented only three multiple choice options instead of five. Moreover, the three options in the new setting did not present the same features as the original ones. In fact, each original option contained different pieces of information, whereas the new ones were actually equivalent with respect to the information they contained, differing only in the notation (numbers instead of letters, abbreviations, ...).

Anecdotal Record. During the training session, the game was easily solved by all trainees who simply had to pick the shortest option. When the Teacher asked the trainer to explain why they had changed the tasklet, the trainer only focused on the setting and not on the options and the differences in their information content (in fact, there were no differences). Only after recovering the original tasklet on the Bebras Platform and asking to check the correspondence between the options, the trainer realized that he was not able to match the modified ones with the original ones.

Discussion. Most likely, the trainers were able to identify the correct answer by simply recognizing the typical form of waiter's note, but they appeared to have missed the CT content in the explanation and comments to the tasklet. This interpretation is supported by the fact that the correct answer was faithfully transposed in the new setting, whereas the other options did not show the same features as the original ones. For instance, the explanation highlighted that the second option clustered the ordered items into two groups (Drinks and Foods) and could be useful if the service was prepared by two different people in charge respectively of drinks and foods only. This difference totally disappeared in the new setting.

3.5 Board Jumps

Tasklet. The tasklet, presented in Fig. 5, models a setting with pointers or jump instructions, and it relates to "Algo_think" skill.

Game. The game was built by using shoe boxes. Each of them was labeled, in order, with a capital letter from A to H, and a card with the instruction was glued inside each box. No poster was prepared and the tasklet text was written on a piece of paper. The correct solution was written on another sheet and put into an envelope. The text was changed; the basic instruction "2L means to open the box that is 2 positions to the Left" was rewritten as "move this box two positions to the left". Notice that this rule is not precise enough, since it is not clear what "move to another position" means, given that a box can be placed next to other boxes but cannot replace another box. Also, this new kind of rules does not fully determine the process, since it is not specified which box must be opened next. It was actually assumed that the boxes be opened in alphabetical order.

The question was changed too, in that solvers were asked to establish how the boxes are sorted at the end of the process. Notice that the new interpretation of the text changes completely the process and its outcome, since the solution of the original tasklet cannot be obtained following the text of the new game. However, the solution in the envelope reported exactly the correct solution of the original tasklet.

Anecdotal Record. During the training session, the trainer read aloud the tasklet's text, then waited for the trainees to start, by opening and moving the box labeled A. At this point the trainees were stuck and they asked what to do next, thus the trainer explained to follow the alphabetical order, *i.e.*, to open next the box labeled B. When the trainees concluded the game, their solutions inevitably differed from the expected one. The trainer then offhandedly explained the fact with vague remarks like "you did not move the boxes into the proper positions". The trainer never tried to repeat the process, showing or checking the proper actions to be carried out to reach the expected outcome. The trainees did not appear convinced but did not engage in any further discussion nor asked explanations.

Discussion. Manifestly, the trainer had not understood the tasklet and in particular the rules, their effect when applied, the overall process, nor the question. Surprisingly, even though the wrong interpretation of the rules and question was not compatible with the correct solution and its explanation (which reported step by step the complete process), the trainer remained comfortably in her interpretation. The trainer's imposing self-assurance on one hand, and the instructions' lack of rigor on the other hand, might have inhibited the critical thinking skills of the trainee. All in all, in this case neither the game preparation nor the training served as promoters of CT skills.

4 Conclusions and Further Work

The idea of asking 6th graders to train younger pupils with Bebras-inspired games they invented has proven to be a good opportunity for situated learning. All but one pair succeeded in finalizing the game they designed: the assignment and the time allocated seem to be well chosen for the age group. In most cases, we collected evidence that the pupils had understood the original tasklets, transposed correctly their core CT ideas, and were able to explain them to their younger mates. The interaction between trainers and trainees shows in more than one case (*e.g.,* "Balls" and "Drawing Game") that trainers were in fact able to follow the solving process of the trainees and support them appropriately. Not by chance, these are exactly the cases where the trainers intentionally made the tasklet's task more challenging, which is further evidence of their mastering of the implied CT skills. It is important for the teacher to monitor this aspect and make sure that the implied CT skills are preserved and the level of difficulty is kept adequate for the trainees' age.

With "Birthday party" and "Dustman robots" we also have evidence that the feedback from younger mates helped trainers in further improving their understanding of the task and the important elements therein. Finally, in many cases (*e.g.,* "Room sharing", "Drawing Game", "Dustmen robots"), pupils elaborated the original tasklet content, still preserving its sense and efficacy, showing in the process to be able to identify and abstract the important elements and properties of the entities involved in the tasklet, and the skills required to solve it. However, in two cases (namely "Board jumps" and "The waiter") the trainers clearly did not succeed in understanding the tasklet or the CT aspects, all the more so to convey them to the younger mates. For these pupils, most activities carried out during the project (and especially the whole training sessions) were not productive, as far as the CT aspects were concerned. At the end of the project, the Teacher reckoned that at first she was not familiar with those tasks and that she focused mainly in building a collaborative atmosphere within the class and in helping pupils with their design and creation of the game. These are probably the reasons why she did not notice at an early stage that the pupils were missing some meaningful points in the tasklets. Considering the results of the project, an important lesson learned by the Teacher is the need to spend some time to deeply examine the chosen tasklets (including the explanation and the commentary) in order to identify more clearly the important elements therein and the underlying CT content, so as to be able to monitor whether they are grasped during the activities or intervene in case they are not. As for the cross-cutting competencies, the pairs definitely practiced a number of them, *e.g.,* working towards a common goal, designing and building a tangible object, being patient in letting the younger work through the solution of the tasklet without stopping them beforehand, accepting and appreciating other ways of reasoning. We have to point out that initially the trainers displayed some resistance to building and providing trainees with tangible objects to work with, which instead proved to be helpful and appreciated by the younger pupils, as testified also in [10].

All in all, the experience proved that using Bebras tasklets as the social and cultural context for situated learning of CT competencies is indeed quite productive: pupils were generally captivated and showed signals of learning in all the phases. This approach provides many elements to the instructor to monitor the learning process and its effectiveness. Future work aims at measuring and evaluating more analytically the impact of such didactic interventions on improving computational thinking skills. Bebras can in fact be a valuable resource for learning activities, and the richness of the tasklets, sometimes overlooked during the short time available during the contest, is instead fully explored in the deep engaging series of activities such as the ones described here.

A Tasklets screenshots with games

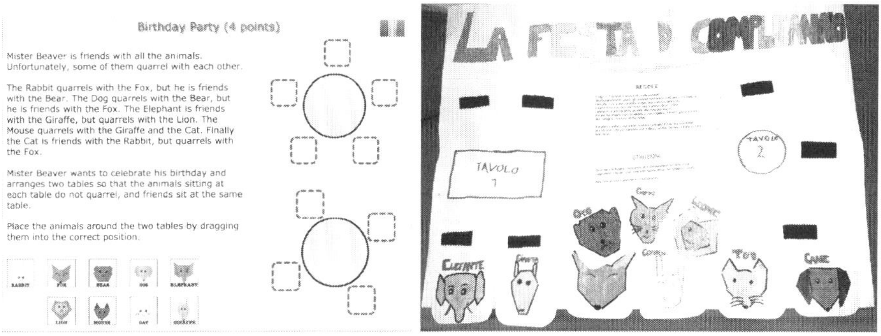

(a) Tasklet (b) Game

Fig. 1. Birthday party

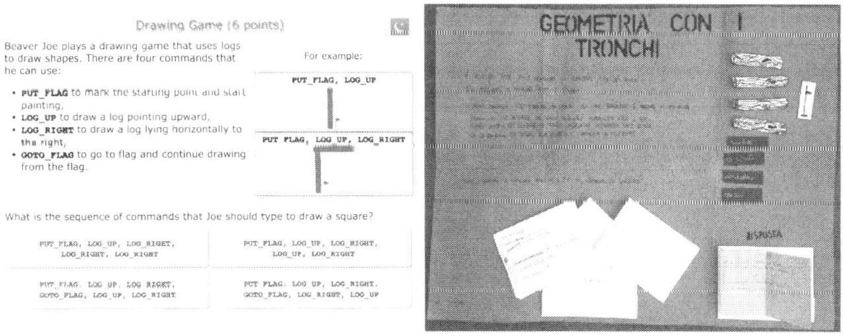

(a) Tasklet (b) Game

Fig. 2. Drawing game

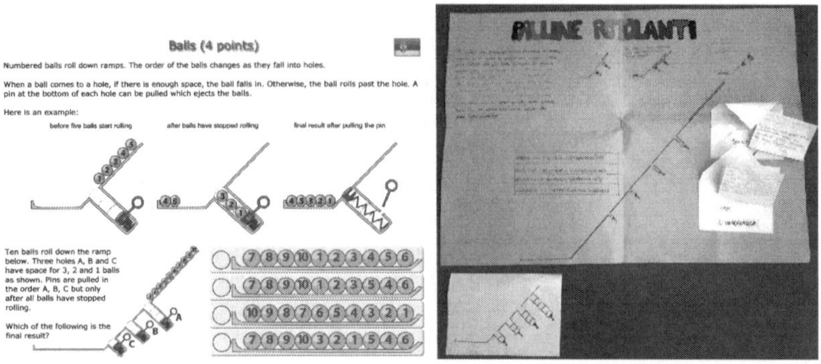

(a) Tasklet (b) Game

Fig. 3. Balls

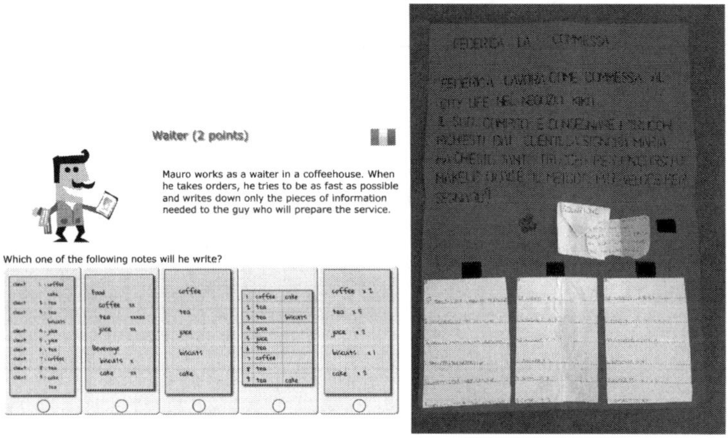

(a) Tasklet (b) Game

Fig. 4. Waiter

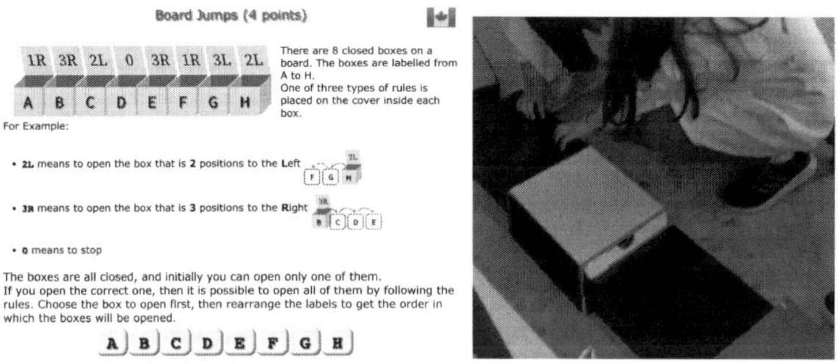

(a) Tasklet (b) Game

Fig. 5. Board jumps

References

1. International Society for Technology in Education & Computer Science Teachers Association: Operational definition of computational thinking for K-12 education. http://www.iste.org/docs/ct-documents/computational-thinking-operational-definition-flyer.pdf (2011)
2. Calcagni, A., Lonati, V., Malchiodi, D., Monga, M., Morpurgo, A.: Promoting computational thinking skills: would you use this bebras task? In: Dagiene, V., Hellas, A. (eds.) ISSEP 2017. LNCS, vol. 10696, pp. 102–113. Springer, Cham (2017). https://doi.org/10.1007/978-3-319-71483-7_9
3. Bellettini, C., et al.: A platform for the Italian Bebras. In: CSEDU 2018, vol. 1, pp. 350–357. SCITEPRESS (2018). https://doi.org/10.5220/0006775103500357
4. Bellettini, C., Lonati, V., Monga, M., Morpurgo, A.: How pupils solve online problems: an analytical view. In: CSEDU 2019 – vol. 2, pp. 132–139. SCITEPRESS (2019). https://doi.org/10.5220/0007765801320139
5. Lonati, V., Malchiodi, D., Monga, M., Morpurgo, A.: Is coding the way to go? In: Brodnik, A., Vahrenhold, J. (ed.) ISSEP 2015, pp. 165–174 (2015). https://doi.org/10.1007/978-3-319-25396-1_15
6. Corradini, I., Lodi, M., Nardelli, E.: Conceptions and misconceptions about computational thinking among Italian primary school teachers. In: Proceedings of the ICER 2017, pp. 136–144. ACM (2017)
7. Tatnall, A., Jones, A. (eds.) WCCE 2009. IAICT, vol. 302. Springer, Heidelberg (2009). https://doi.org/10.1007/978-3-642-03115-1
8. Dagienė, V., Sentance, S.: It's computational thinking! bebras tasks in the curriculum. In: Brodnik, A., Tort, F. (eds.) ISSEP 2016. LNCS, vol. 9973, pp. 28–39. Springer, Cham (2016). https://doi.org/10.1007/978-3-319-46747-4_3
9. Dagienė, V., Stupuriene, G.: Informatics education based on solving attractive tasks through a contest. KEYCIT **2014**, 97–115 (2015)
10. Dagienė, V., Futschek, G., Stupurienė, G.: Creativity in solving short tasks for learning computational thinking. Constructivist Found **14**(3), 382–396 (2019). https://cepa.info/6060
11. De Corte, E.: Constructive, self-regulated, situated, and collaborative learning: an approach for the acquisition of adaptive competence. J. Educ. **192**, 33–47 (2012). https://doi.org/10.1177/0022057412192002-307
12. Froehlich, C.P., Hoyt, K.B.: Guidance testing and other student appraisal procedures for teachers and counselors. Science Research Associates (1959)
13. Haberman, B., Cohen, A., Dagienė, V.: The beaver contest: attracting youngsters to study computing. In: Proceedings of ITiCSE 2011, pp. 378–378. ACM (2011)
14. Mayer, R.E.: Should there be a three-strike rule against pure discovery learning? Am. Psycol. **59**, 14–19 (2004)
15. Piaget, J.: The Child's Constructions of Reality. Routledge and Kegan Poul, Abingdon (2013)
16. Vygotsky, L.: Mind in Society: Development of Higher Psychological Processes. Harvard University Press, Cambridge (1978)

The Genesis of a Bebras Task

Christian Datzko(✉)

Wirtschaftsgymnasium und Wirtschaftsmittelschule Basel, Basel, Switzerland
christian@datzko.ch

Abstract. This paper reports the milestones a task proposal takes from its initial conception until its use in the Bebras International Challenge of Informatics and Computational Thinking and the experiences that Switzerland has with the procedures with the intent to share best-practices. This includes the Swiss Bebras Task Workshop, the International Bebras Task Workshop, the generation of the Swiss Task Set, the adaptation of a task proposal for the Swiss Bebras Challenge, the Contest System and the Brochure. Although the process is described from the point of view of the Swiss Bebras Challenge, the processes in some other participating countries are similar. The description of the process is accompanied by a task proposal of which the changes over time are documented. The basic findings are that during the year-long process a task proposal experiences several (re-)considerations, several stages of reworking and adaptation but that these reiterations serve towards quality improvement and ensure that each task proposal is up to standard to be offered to the more than 21,000 participants in Switzerland annually or even (up to and including the International Bebras Task Workshop 2019) 2.78 million students world-wide annually. This paper is targeted at the general audience interested in the process of developing high quality tasks, be it for contests or for general use. It may also be of interest to people working within the Bebras community to compare the Swiss process to their processes of preparing tasks.

Keywords: Bebras International Challenge of Informatics and Computational Thinking · Task preparation · Quality management

1 Background

The Bebras International Challenge of Informatics and Computational Thinking (short: Bebras) is an "international initiative aiming to promote Informatics (Computer Science, or Computing) and computational thinking among school students of all ages" [7]. Since its start in 2004 [4] it has grown to reach more than 54 countries and more than 2.78 million students annually by mid-2019 [5].

After a pilot run in 2009 using the German Challenge, Switzerland started to offer the challenge in 2010 in French, German and Italian. The annual participants in Switzerland have grown to more than 21,000 participants annually in 2018 [20].

S. N. Pozdniakov and V. Dagienė (Eds.): ISSEP 2019, LNCS 11913, pp. 240–255, 2019.
https://doi.org/10.1007/978-3-030-33759-9_19

The Challenge takes place online. Teachers enroll their students and let them participate in class [21]. The Challenge itself consists of 15 tasks for each age group except for 12 tasks for the age group 10–12, and 9 tasks for the age group 8–10 of which 1/3 are easy tasks, 1/3 are of medium difficulty and 1/3 are hard to solve, which are independent of each other and graded individually [16, p. 4].[1]

These task proposals (see Sect. 2) are conceived by individuals in the member countries of Bebras (see Sect. 3), aggregated nationally (see Sect. 4) and selected and reworked internationally (see Sect. 5) into a task pool. From there the member countries of Bebras select their own set of tasks for each age group (see Sect. 6), adapt them to their own language and national requirements (see Sect. 7) and implement them into their respective online system (see Sect. 8). Some countries including Switzerland publish them after the challenge (see Sect. 9). This process takes up most of the year: In Switzerland the task proposal generation starts in February and the brochure gets published after the challenge in mid-November.

Although generally the process described is similar for other countries participating in Bebras, the Swiss procedure especially before the International Bebras Task Workshop ensures that the submitted tasks have a quality regarded highly within the international community. This process has been improved gradually over the last 10 years and sharing it with a general audience hopefully helps other countries and other communities with similar processes to learn from the experience gained over time.

2 What Is a Bebras Task?

As in probably every active community of individuals from different backgrounds and with different experiences, the opinions on what a Bebras Task exactly defines differ in detail. However some basic categories for task proposals have been laid out early on already [11]. Since then there have been several approaches to refine these categories. One category of task proposals in particular, "Using computer systems", has been debated again and again. Many typical task proposals for this category require pre-knowledge that is not available to students of most participating countries, therefore it has been not used for task proposals in the recent years.

Lately there has been a proposal to focus the main informatics concept introduced in a task proposal [13]. This proposal is developed with aspects of computational thinking skills in mind. These categories are in use in the Bebras community since 2017.

Officially a task proposal has no requirements for the content [8, p. 6]. However there are suggestions about what a good task proposal is about.

[1] In this document the term "age groups" with a rough age range is given instead of the school years to enhance the international understanding of the target age of the students. Teachers in Switzerland however register the students based on the school year that they're in so it could be that some students are older and some students are even younger than the age group stated.

This document has been approved officially by the Bebras community and therefore sets the standards [8, pp. 6–7][2]:

- *"A good task proposal introduces or reinforces a topic in computer science.*
- *A good task proposal is quick and easy to understand...*
- *...but challenging to solve.*
- *A good task proposal is usable after the contest as a good example."*

The reason that these suggestions are not requirements is that the rules should not prohibit a task proposal to be made if it doesn't fall into one of the categories even though it touches an important or interesting topic of computer science. A task proposal can still be a good task proposal if it breaks the criteria cited.

Besides these internal definition there have some attempts to define or at least hint what a good task proposal is. Dagienė and Futschek [11, pp. 4–5], Dagienė [9], Vaníček [27] or even the project's own website [6][3] try to closer define it but most of these offer further refinements of the four criteria from above, some of them even deal with rather formal or practical aspects.

There are several formal requirements for a task proposal though. Besides some technical requirements like naming conventions and licensing information as well as a record of internal comments about the task proposal, a task proposal consists of [8, pp. 4–5]:

- a *title* which is displayed for the student and used as a name in brochures,
- a *body* which tells the story and explains the constraints,
- a *question or challenge* that the student has to answer or solve,
- either different *answer alternatives* for multiple-choice task proposals or an *interactive pane* in which the student can work on solving the task,
- an *answer explanation* which explains to the student which answers are correct and how they could be obtained,
- an *"It's Informatics"* section which explains to the student what the task proposal has to do with computer science,
- and optionally some *keywords* and *links to websites* for further reading on the computer science topics.

The last three categories of course are not presented to the student before or during the challenge but afterwards for example in the brochure (see Sect. 9). Although these formal requirements are like fields in a template to simply fill out [19], they are supposed to help the authors and editors of task proposals to make sure their task proposal is complete and adequate for students.

[2] This document has been prepared by Ivo Blöchliger, Christian Datzko, Mathias Hiron, Wolfgang Pohl, Eljakim Schrijvers, Alexandra Talon and Jiří Vaníček within the Bebras community.

[3] Some countries allow the use of pen and paper.

3 From the Initial Idea to a Task Proposal

To describe a creative process of getting an initial idea for a task proposal eludes the descriptions in many ways. However there are some aspects that can be perceived and improved like the aspects described by Paul and Elder [25]. What stands out is the fact that a single creative process must be accompanied by hard work to refine the initial idea [25, p. 45].

One way to get a first idea for a task proposal is to choose an informatics concept, develop a fitting cover story, add visual components and animation or interactivity and synthesize it into a task proposal [12, p. 258]. In some cases however it's the other way around: for the task proposal 2017-CH-08[a–b] ([15], [10, pp. 534–535]) for instance the cover story was first and then a fitting application of the story within computer science was found. Further approaches are mentioned by Vaníček [27, p. 24]. Switzerland even invites students from the age group 16–19 to submit task proposals (see also the experiences made by Manabe, Tani, Kanemune and Manabe [23]).

The task 2018-CH-11 [18][4] will serve as an example how an initial task proposal gets transformed into its final form. It was chosen because for it wasn't a "standard" task but offered some controversy, and also because for it all data for presenting it here was available. For obvious reasons task proposals that were discarded during the process were not taken into account.

This is how the task proposal was submitted originally[5]:

- Title: *Beaver-Modulo.*
- Body: *There are five little stones in the water arranged in a circle numbered from 0 to 4. Pfiffikus stands on stone number 0 and jumps from stone to stone clockwise. If he jumps 5 times, he will land on the number 0. If he jumps 8 times, he will land on number 3.*

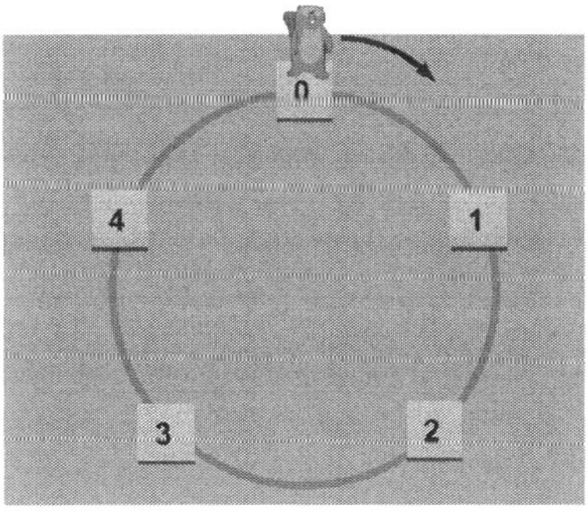

[4] Urs Hauser, Juraj Hromkovič, Regula Lacher, Jacqueline Staub, Christian Datzko, Susanne Datzko, Špela Cerar and Hanspeter Erni contributed to this task. Some of the comments about this task cited later were also done by Zsuzsa Pluhar, Emil Kelevedjiev and Wolfgang Pohl.

[5] The original graphics which were replaced later include work done by Vaidotas Kinčius.

- Question: *Pfiffikus is very athletic and jumps* 129 *times! On which number will he land?*
- Answer Alternatives: *Integer numbers from* [0, 4].
- Answer Explanation: *Number* 4 *because* 129 *mod* 5 *is* 4.
- It's Informatics: *The modulo operation is often used in computer science or number theory and finds the remainder after division of one number by another (sometimes called modulus). Given two positive numbers, a (the dividend) and n (the divisor), a modulo n is the remainder of the Euclidean division of a by n. For example is* 11 *mod* $5 = 1$ *because* $5 * 2 = 10$ *rest*[6] 1.
- Keywords: *modulo operation.*
- Websites: left empty.

From a formal point of view this task proposal is complete and the relation of the content to computer science is referred to in the "It's Informatics" section. It was originally aimed by the original author at students aged 10–12 with a medium difficulty (about the difficulty to assess the difficulty of a task see van der Vegt [28–30]).

4 The Swiss Bebras Task Workshop

Switzerland like other countries in Bebras holds a national workshop to collect the task proposals, to discuss them, to select those that will be submitted to the international community and to improve the selected task proposals based on the collected remarks. In some way that national workshop is similar to the international workshop (see Sect. 5). Because of its smaller scale[7] and the much lesser amount of work[8] it is less formalized.

The usual proceedings are:

1. Collecting comments on all task proposals.
2. Rating all task proposals based on their current state and their potential and calculating a weighted average (usually with twice the weight for the potential). All numbers are from 1 to 6 with 1 being the worst rating.
3. Discussing the task proposals from the top-scorer down and selecting which task proposals are to be improved and submitted to the international community.
4. Assign persons responsible for each selected task proposal and to double check the quality of the work.
5. If time permits starting the work on improving the task proposals to give new people in the team a chance to ask questions directly.

[6] This is a translation error from German to English: "Rest" in German should have been translated as "with a remainder of" in English.

[7] In the last years between 3 and 6 people participated in the Swiss Bebras task workshop.

[8] In the last years between 15 and 25 task proposals were collected, not counting variants of task proposals, from these between 9 and 13 were submitted to the international community.

After the national workshop the work is finished individually. Once the work is done, the task proposals are given a final check for formalities and submitted to the international workshop.

The task proposal 2018-CH-11 received a current state of 4.80 and a potential of 5.17 which gives a weighted average of 5.04. With this value it scored fourth out of the 19 task proposals (with their variants) of that year.

The following comments were made:

- *Mathematical task, modulo operations are used but not a "topic" for CS* [computer science].
- *Better to use "normal" names.*
- *However it is a very simple task and could be interesting for 5th6th graders* [age group 10–12]*?*
- *Try to get as much math out of it as possible.*
- *In the It's Informatics make sure this is more the interpretation of a dynamic process than applying modulo.*

The first comment already names one of the main discussions around this task: Is a task that has the modulo function in its core a task about computer science or is it a task about mathematics? Discussions like these happen again and again because computer science and mathematics are closely related and share methods and concepts. In this case at the end of the discussion it was decided that this task proposal was indeed about computer science, but that it should be noted in the internal documents:

> *"One could argue that this is a math task, because calculating the remainder of an integer division is a math competence students at target age might know. Also this concept is further explored in math applications like multiplicative groups of integers modulo n. However this task focuses on the dynamic process of jumping n rounds first and then (indirectly) asking how many jumps are left instead of asking what's 'left' after doing a regular mathematical operation. So in this sense the task is primarily about the analysis of a process and how to efficiently get the final result. It could even be gotten very quickly by an educated guess from the student: go 5 steps (124 to go), go 5 steps (119 to go), go 5 steps (*114 *to go) and see that the last digit is always either 9 or 4 so the answer must be 4 (since for 9 you could go another round and end up with 4 also)."*

The other issues were also addressed. In order to ease the difficulty of the task proposal which was considered harder than originally stated the short example of 8 jumps was elaborated. The graphics were redone to make them more appealing to students. The answer explanation has been extended to make it easier to understand by students, especially the term "lap" was introduced in order to make the concept of the integer quotient more understandable (it is commented: *"when doing endurance sports, often events are done in laps (like how many times a race track has to be completed or how many times one has to swim back and forth in a swimming pool); this association with sports is very near to students at target age and closely associated with the story of the task")*. The "It's Informatics" was completely rewritten in order to make the connection between what the students might know from math class and the modulo operation and to show applications of the method.

The task proposal was submitted into the international community like this:

- Title: *Beaver-Modulo*
- Body: *In order to train for the annual beaver challenge some beavers train a lot. Today the task is to jump from rock to rock in clockwise direction as indicated by the arrow starting from rock number* 0. *So if he jumps* 8 *times, he'll end up on rock number* 3:

$$0 \to 1 \to 2 \to 3 \to 4 \to 0 \to 1 \to 2 \to 3.$$

- Question: *One of the beavers shows off and jumps an astonishing* 129 *times. On which rock did he end up?*
- Answer Alternatives: *Integer numbers from* $[0, 4]$
- Answer Explanation: *If a beavers jumps* 5 *times, he ends up where he is, let's call it a "lap". To find out where he ends up after* 129 *jumps we have to find out how many "laps" he jumps and how many jumps he still has to do after that. In this case it's* $129 = 25 \times 5 + 4$. *So jumping* 129 *times will have him end up at the same place as if he just had jumped* 4 *times, he ends up on stone number* 4.
- It's Informatics: *You may have seen this operation in math class before. It's part of what you might know as the* Long Division *or the* Euclidean division *which calculates an integer quotient and a remainder.*
  In this case you're asked to calculate the remainder of $129 \div 5$. *Since this operation is used very commonly in computers, it has a name:* modulo operation. *Usually "%" or "mod" is used as an operator. So for our equation we could write:* $129\%5 = 4$.
  Typical applications of this operator are in loops of programs (just like our beaver jumping in loops), when variables overflow or even for the widespread cryptosystem RSA.
- Keywords: *modulo operation.*
- Websites: https://en.wikipedia.org/wiki/Modulo_operation
  https://en.wikipedia.org/wiki/Long_division

https://en.wikipedia.org/wiki/Euclidean_division
https://en.wikipedia.org/wiki/RSA_(cryptosystem)

During the improvement of the task proposal the following alternative has been considered and discarded but viewed as relevant to note in the internal comments: *"I have considered to further explain that for* $129 = 25 \times 5 + 4$ *that the number* 25 *is irrelevant, especially since for a divisor* 5 *or* 10 *it's very simple to find the remainder. However this would make the answer explanation longer. Further I have decided to not go further into applications of the modulo operation, especially considering the target age group. This could be elaborated."* This kind of consideration is typical for tasks: on one hand most tasks open up a topic of computer science where many interesting things could be written, but on the other hand a task including the information only used for after the challenge should be as short as possible to avoid information overload.

5 The International Bebras Task Workshop

Each year the Bebras community meets for a week at the International Bebras task workshop. One of the main goals of that event is *"to discuss and prepare tasks"* [2]. The participants are mostly computer scientists, computer science teachers and computer science teacher educators, but also some representatives from companies working in the area of computer science challenges or representatives from ministries of science or education. However, virtually every participant works in one of the pre-assigned working groups.

Since the recommendations of the pre-workshop review process [8] were begun to be implemented before the workshop, the community is asked to comment and rate task proposals. Although the review system is improved every year the basic idea is the same: every task proposal gets rated based on its current state and on its potential (using the same 1 to 6 scale) and further comments are collected. Unlike in the corresponding process at the Swiss Bebras task workshop a task proposal receives only a few ratings since in the last years there has been a surge of task proposals (between 194 and 250 task proposals annually) which lead to 1 to 3 reviews per task proposal. Consequently the ratings are only moderately comparable to each other, but in most cases at least hint the general direction. The comments serve a much higher value because they allow the task proposers before the workshop to improve their task proposals based on the comments. The comments and ratings are also available to the working groups during the workshop.

During the workshops the task proposals are assigned to working groups consisting of about 8 members which work on roughly 20 task proposals (depending on the number of task proposals and the number of participants of course). The method of working is up to the working group leader, but most working groups do their own rating (current state and potential again like in the review) to have a better base to decide on which task proposals to work on with higher priority. Especially those task proposals with a big difference between their current state and their potential are improved and worked on significantly. This is usually done in pairs with a second pair responsible for double checking. Some work is outsourced: graphics are created by experts brought to the workshop by some countries and the programming of interactive tasks which depends on the contest system being used (see Sect. 8) is skipped and left to the countries to develop after the workshop. Instead a description on how the interactive parts should work is given.

Towards the end of the workshop all groups give a final rating of the new current state and select those that they deem as suitable for the national challenges. These form the "task pool" from which the national task set is chosen (see Sect. 6).

The task 2018-CH-11 received two reviews in the pre-workshop review process. The current state was rated 3.50 and the potential 4.00. The review comments were: *"Can a beaver jump? It is more counting (math) for me. But because of the inf.part* ['It's Informatics'] *and the comments could be used."* as well as *"The task is more suitable for a mathematical competition"*. This on one hand shows the question originally raised in the Swiss Bebras task workshop whether the task proposal is sufficiently about computer science, but the first comment also mentions that the approach to make the computer science aspects in this task proposal more visible in the "It's Informatics" section was successful. The other issue is: beavers usually don't jump but rather swim or walk. However using the beaver as a fairy tale character instead of the animal it would be can be viewed as acceptable [27, pp. 24–25].

Later during the workshop the working group commented: *"good presentation, math background, make water lighter"* and gave it a rating of 4.67 (current state) and 4.88 (potential). The task proposal was ranked second out of the 20 task proposals in that particular working group.

The working group changed some details of the text and changed the color of the lake. The changed parts now looked like this:

- Body: *Some beavers took part in the annual beaver challenge. Their first task was to jump from rock to rock in a clockwise direction, as shown by the arrow, starting from rock number 0. So, if a beaver jumped 8 times, he will end up on rock number 3:*

  $$0 \to 1 \to 2 \to 3 \to 4 \to 0 \to 1 \to 2 \to 3.$$

  The color of the water was brightened.
- Question: *One of the beavers showed off and jumped an astonishing 129 times. On which rock did he end up?*

The task was given a final rating of 4 (ranking 15th out of the 21 tasks worked on with in that working group[9]). These ratings of course cannot be compared to the previous ratings because many tasks have changed and the demands for a task to receive a good grade were raised during this process. It is still interesting

[9] One of the tasks got split up into two variants.

to note that the rank dropped so clearly for no obvious reason. The task was assigned by the working group to age group 12–14 with a medium difficulty. It was assigned to the task pool and thus classified as suitable.

6 Selecting Tasks for the Swiss Task Set

From the task pool every country selects those tasks that they deem suitable for their national challenges [2]. In order to do that, for every age group that they offer they have to select tasks. Switzerland offers the age groups 8–10, 10–12, 12–14, 14–16 and 16–19. With overlaps this resulted in 37 to 45 tasks in total in the last few years.

Traditionally Switzerland cooperates with Austria, Germany and Hungary for the selection of a task set. As a result from that the vast majority of the tasks used in these countries were the same although some details differed to make up for regional needs.

The task selection is done in a meeting of representatives of these countries. Before the meeting members from these countries rate all tasks in the task pool and comment on them. This gives a uniform rating (see Sect. 4) and ensures that the rather similar opinions on what a good task is are the base for the selection of the tasks. Of course during the meeting still sometimes controversial discussions about some tasks were held. For a task set not only the quality and suitability of individual tasks are important, but also the construction and balance of the whole task set has to be taken into account. The students have to be presented with a number of tasks that to some extent show the breadth of computer science. Tasks about similar aspects of computer science in the same age category should be avoided. Although for the countries mentioned above no mandatory national curriculum exists, selecting topics that would be adequate for a certain age category is also taken into account. In the end each age category should offer an attractive insight in computer science.

The task 2018-CH-11 received diverse feedback. The 7 ratings resulted in an average of 3.86 with a quite high standard deviation of 1.86 (again on a scale from 1 to 6). The only comment reiterated the two criticisms of the task: *"Beavers do not jump! This is a maths task, we should not present it as CS, in spite of modulo being used in many computing applications"*. The same person even stated later: "[for my country]*: maybe not*" and indeed that country did not select the task. The rating was fixed as "medium" for the age group 12–14 and "easy" for the age group 14–16.[10]

7 Adapting a Task for the Swiss Bebras Challenge

After the selection of the tasks they are first adapted to the German language. In some cases this includes major changes in the wording, especially of the answer

[10] The complete Swiss task set can be derived from the brochure [16].

explanation and the "It's Informatics". This is because not every country publishes brochures and in some cases doesn't need these texts. For Switzerland the brochure is valued quite highly because it will be available for students and teachers for the years to come for instance to be used in class (see Sect. 9). Also in many cases the graphics are reworked. This is not true for the translation into French and Italian afterwards where a rather close translation is strived for to offer the same experience to the whole country.

The adaption work is done by members of the team, usually in cooperation with Austria and Germany. After the adaption an experienced team member double checks it and if the task had been adapted by Austria or Germany adapts it to the local language specialties so that in the end two or three persons have approved it.

Offering the same challenge in three languages (French, German and Italian in the case of Switzerland) is a huge effort. Subtle differences may already make a huge difference in how easy it is to solve a task (there is an interesting study about this done by Tomcsányi and Vaníček [26]). This is especially true if language is involved in the task, for instance as a text that has to be decrypted. For that reason Switzerland also assigns two people to each task for the translation into French and two people for the translation into Italian. One is doing the translation and the other one is doing the double checking.

The time to create the translations is limited and most of the work is done in the spare by volunteers. Switzerland tries to reserve four weeks for the translation of the tasks from German to French and Italian. Besides the actual translation work the texts would have to be available in a proper format for reuse for the contest system and the brochure. Also the text for some graphics and some interactive systems needs to be adapted. It is however typical for Switzerland to care for their local languages and so this effort is regarded as worth it.

For the task 2018-CH-11 not many changes were made for the adaptation into German. The title was changed to *"Biber-Wettbewerb"* ("beaver challenge") to avoid the likely unknown word "modulo" for the students and as a pun on the German name of the challenge: "Informatik-Biber Wettbewerb". The story was refined a little bit (it now was about a training instead of the challenge itself). The equation $129 = 25 \times 5 + 4$ was explained as "25 *Runden plus* 4 *Sprünge"* ("25 laps and 4 jumps"). Otherwise it was more or less a literal translation of the final English version of the international workshop. For the graphics it was decided to go with the original darker blue color of the lake instead of the newly introduced light blue color. The task in the challenge was identical to the version in the brochure [18]. The difficulty of the task was kept at "medium" for the age group 12–14. The task 2018-CH-11 was then translated into French by Elsa Pellet [24] and into Italian by Andrea Adamoli [1].

8 The Task in the Contest System

Many countries use their own online system for letting students participate in their contest ([14, pp. 233–238], [3]). However the effort to develop and maintain an online system which is used once a year for two weeks and must be compatible with many different clients is quite an effort [22, pp. 78–80]. Therefore Switzerland like roughly 1/3 of all countries participating in Bebras has been using an external contest system from the beginning [17]. It provides all the means for running the challenge in three languages, has the necessary IT knowledge and hardware and is offering appropriate third level support.

The tasks have to be implemented in the contest system. In the case of the contest system used by Switzerland that means that the task has to be recreated in HTML and that all graphics have to be available as SVG (or PNG for the few pixel graphics used). To ensure a unified look of all tasks, the HTML used is handcrafted and done as simple as possible. The HTML for all tasks is first created in one language and then the source code is copied and the text replaced again to ensure the uniformity.

The tasks are then tested in different browsers on different operating systems based on what typical and wide-spread setups are. This is necessary because some bugs in the graphics or in the interactive tasks only show in special combinations. Especially if different versions of the same browser are wide-spread (like Microsoft Edge and Internet Explorer) testing is quite an effort.

The implementation of 2018-CH-11 was pretty straight forward. By using only the `<p>`, `<img>` and `<em>` (to highlight the question) tags and some basic CSS like "`text-align: center;`" the whole task was implemented.

The task gave the results presented in Table 1:

Table 1. Results of 2018-CH-11.

	12–14				14–16			
	Students	Correct	Percentage	Rank	Students	Correct	Percentage	Rank
French	1014	467	46.1%	6	1125	754	67.0%	4
German	4838	3071	63.5%	5	4540	3422	75.4%	3
Italian	140	64	45.7%	6	52	31	59.6%	4
Total	5992	3602	60.1%	5	5717	4207	73.6%	3

The numbers for Italian should be read with care, because the absolute numbers are so low. The percentages between the different languages should not be compared directly because the students that take part are not chosen in a representative way: it depends on which teacher chooses to let his students take part and if the teacher chooses to let every student take part or just some students he selects (perhaps to promote gifted students or as part of an elective subject). It also depends on the region which teachers are reached: in Switzerland for those age groups classes are often separated depending on their performance in earlier years and the Swiss Bebras cannot reach out to every school in the country.

All in all however one can say that the tasks rating as "medium" for the age group 12–14 is rather correct (the rank should have been between 6 and 10; two tasks that were rated "easy" actually were perceived as "hard" by the students) and for the age group 14–16 correct (the rank should be between 1 and 5). Judging from the ranks of some other task proposals in the same age group, however, the process of assigning a task difficulty based on the average opinion of the persons who decide on the task set is to be questioned. Van der Vegt [29] aggregates some more systematic methods that could raise the quality of these assessments.

9 The Task in the Brochure

Many countries offer the tasks in form of a brochure after the challenge. The idea is not only to document the tasks but also to offer them as a resource for students and teachers to use in class and at home. Since 2013 the Swiss Bebras offers the brochure with all questions and solutions right on the Monday after the challenge. That way the teachers can address the tasks in class directly after the challenge when the memories are still fresh. Since 2015 the Swiss Bebras offers not only one brochure for each language with all questions and answers, but a total of 36 brochures: one for each of the five age groups as well as one with the tasks of all age groups and this with and without solutions and for each of the three languages.

In order to reduce the amount of work and because of the high redundancy of these 36 brochures an automated system is used to generate these brochures. Unlike the contest system the brochure system is developed and maintained within the Swiss Bebras. Based on the experiences of the first brochure system used in 2014 and 2015 it was rebuilt from scratch in 2016 by using LaTeX only with as much modularization as possible. A task for instance is a single LaTeX file for each of the three languages and only contains the information for that task.

In the case of 2018-CH-11 the implementation of the task in LaTeX was nearly as simple as the implementation in the contest system. Besides the definition of the meta information of the task only the commands `\emph{}` and `\begin{center}\end{center}` were used besides some math commands. In order to automatically generate the list of involved authors [16, p. 100] LaTeX variables are used as tags for which later the authors get aggregated automatically.

In the last years in Switzerland the brochure was actually prepared before the implementation of the tasks in the contest system. This ensured that the answer explanation was ready and checked before the implementation of the task in the contest system. In a few cases this also gave a last chance to correct aspects of the task itself, for instance unclear wordings or missing detail information in the task itself.

10 Conclusion and Further Considerations

The development of a Bebras Task is a year-long process (see Sect. 1) which involves many spiral-like iterations [12, p. 258] of improving a task. Therefore many people are involved in the process which leads to a quality control on several levels.

Almost all work for the Swiss Bebras is done voluntarily by teachers and people from Universities in Switzerland. The work is rewarded by a rising number of participants and some nice feedback mostly from teachers whose students participate. Without the dedication of these people to deliver reliably high quality work the Swiss Bebras wouldn't be possible.

The extra amount of work put into a task proposal before submitting it internationally leads to the fact that Swiss task proposals tend to require less work during or after the international Bebras task workshop, which eases the workload in preparation of the national challenge and of course makes the work available to everyone in the Bebras community. The work for the adaptation of some other tasks selected after the international Bebras task workshop is necessary for those tasks which have a rather high potential but have not yet been polished enough yet.

The Swiss Bebras still holds a treasure chest of research opportunities. Especially the setup with offering the same task in three languages with translations being as close as possible (as opposed to what Tomcsányi and Vaníček found in their research [26, p. 219]) raises interesting questions. Also the self-developed brochure system might be worth some more analytical attention. A comparison of slightly different versions of the same task in different countries of the same language (Austria, Germany and Switzerland) could give interesting results.

Acknowledgments. The author would like to thank Juraj Hromkovič for the encouragement to start this paper. He would also like to thank his wife Susanne for proof reading this paper in its various stages. This paper would not have been possible without the experience earned within the Swiss Bebras team lead by Hanspeter Erni and by the support we get from Eljakim Schrijvers and his team. A special thanks is owed to Willem van der Vegt who reviewed this paper from the point of view of the Bebras community and gave some valuable feedback. Thanks is also owed to Frances Rosamond and Michael Fellows who reviewed the paper and gave some good advice. The author would also finally like to thank the reviewers for their constructive feedback.

References

1. Adamoli, A., Datzko, C., Datzko, S., Erni, H. (eds.): Quesiti e soluzioni 2018 – Tutte le Categorie. SVIA-SSIE-SSII Società Svizzera per l'Informatica nell'Insegnamento, Zürich (2018). https://www.informatik-biber.ch/documents/2018/Castoro-informatico-2018-TutteLeCategorie-conSoluzioni.pdf
2. Bebras International Challenge of Informatics and Computational Thinking: Bebras task workshops (2019). https://www.bebras.org/?q=workshops
3. Bebras International Challenge of Informatics and Computational Thinking: Contest management systems (2019). https://www.bebras.org/?q=technology
4. Bebras International Challenge of Informatics and Computational Thinking: History (2019). https://www.bebras.org/?q=history
5. Bebras International Challenge of Informatics and Computational Thinking: Statistics (2019). https://www.bebras.org/?q=statistics

6. Bebras International Challenge of Informatics and Computational Thinking: What is a Bebras task (2019). https://www.bebras.org/?q=goodtask
7. Bebras International Challenge of Informatics and Computational Thinking: What is Bebras (2019). https://www.bebras.org/?q=about
8. Blöchliger, I., et al.: Pre-workshop review process (2014). Unpublished
9. Dagienė, V.: What kinds of tasks are good for contests? In: 6th International conference on Creativity in Mathematics Education and the Education of Gifted Students, Riga, pp. 62–65 (2011). https://www.bebras.org/sites/default/files/documents/publications/DagieneV-2011.pdf
10. Dagienė, V.: Resurgence of informatics education in schools. In: Böckenhauer, H.-J., Komm, D., Unger, W. (eds.) Adventures Between Lower Bounds and Higher Altitudes. LNCS, vol. 11011, pp. 522–537. Springer, Cham (2018). https://doi.org/10.1007/978-3-319-98355-4_30
11. Dagienė, V., Futschek, G.: Bebras international contest on informatics and computer literacy: criteria for good tasks. In: Mittermeir, R.T., Sysło, M.M. (eds.) ISSEP 2008. LNCS, vol. 5090, pp. 19–30. Springer, Heidelberg (2008). https://doi.org/10.1007/978-3-540-69924-8_2
12. Dagienė, V., Futschek, G., Stupurienė, G.: Teachers' constructionist and deconstructionist learning by creating Bebras tasks. In: Sipitakiat, A., Tutiyaphuengprasert, N. (eds.) Constructionism in Action 2016, pp. 257–264. Suksapattana Foundation, Bangkok (2016). http://e-school.kmutt.ac.th/constructionism2016/Constructionism
13. Dagienė, V., Sentance, S.: It's computational thinking! bebras tasks in the curriculum. In: Brodnik, A., Tort, F. (eds.) ISSEP 2016. LNCS, vol. 9973, pp. 28–39. Springer, Cham (2016). https://doi.org/10.1007/978-3-319-46747-4_3
14. Dagiene, V., Stupuriene, G., Vinikiene, L., Zakauskas, R.: Introduction to bebras challenge management: overview and analyses of developed systems. In: Dagiene, V., Hellas, A. (eds.) ISSEP 2017. LNCS, vol. 10696, pp. 232–243. Springer, Cham (2017). https://doi.org/10.1007/978-3-319-71483-7_19
15. Datzko, C., Datzko, S., Erni, H.: Der einarmige Biber. In: Datzko, C., Erni, H. (eds.) Aufgaben und Lösungen 2017 – Alle Stufen, pp. 15–17. SVIA-SSIE-SSII Schweizerischer Verein für Informatik in der Ausbildung, Zürich (2017). https://www.informatik-biber.ch/documents/2017/Informatik-Biber-2017-Alle-Stufen-mitLoesungen.pdf
16. Datzko, C., Datzko, S., Erni, H. (eds.): Aufgaben und Lösungen 2018 – Alle Stufen. SVIA-SSIE-SSII Schweizerischer Verein für Informatik in der Ausbildung, Zürich (2018). https://www.informatik-biber.ch/documents/2018/Informatik-Biber-2018-Alle-Stufen-mitLoesungen.pdf
17. Eljakim Information Technology bv: Bebras (2019). https://www.eljakim.nl/project/beverwedstrijd/
18. Hauser, U., et al.: Biber-Wettbewerb. In: Datzko, C., Datzko, S., Erni, H. (eds.) Aufgaben und Lösungen 2018 – Alle Stufen, pp. 43–44. SVIA-SSIE-SSII Schweizerischer Verein für Informatik in der Ausbildung, Zürich (2018). https://www.informatik-biber.ch/documents/2018/Informatik-Biber-2018-Alle-Stufen-mitLoesungen.pdf
19. Informatik-Biber Schweiz: 20XX-YZ-01a-eng (2018). https://informatik-biber.ch/wordpress/wp-content/uploads/2014/01/20XX-YZ-01a-eng.odt
20. Informatik-Biber Schweiz: Chronik (2019). http://www.informatik-biber.ch/de/geschichte/
21. Informatik-Biber Schweiz: Teilnehmen (2019). http://www.informatik-biber.ch/de/teilnehmen/

22. Kristan, N., Gostiša, D., Fele-Žorž, G., Brodnik, A.: A high-availability bebras competition system. In: Gülbahar, Y., Karataş, E. (eds.) ISSEP 2014. LNCS, vol. 8730, pp. 78–87. Springer, Cham (2014). https://doi.org/10.1007/978-3-319-09958-3_8
23. Manabe, H., Tani, S., Kanemune, S., Manabe, Y.: Creating the original Bebras tasks by high school students. In: Olympiads in Informatics, vol. 12, pp. 99–110 (2018). https://ioinformatics.org/journal/v12_2018_99_110.pdf
24. Parriaux, G., et al. (eds.): Exercices et solutions 2018 – Tout âge. SVIA-SSIE-SSII Société de l'Informatique dans l'Enseignement, Zürich (2018). https://www.informatik-biber.ch/documents/2018/Castor-informatique-2018-ToutAge-avecSolutions.pdf
25. Paul, R., Elder, L.: The Thinker's Guide to The Nature and Functions of Critical & Creative Thinking. The Foundation for Critical Thinking, Dillon Beach (2008)
26. Tomcsányi, P., Vaníček, J.: International comparison of problems from an informatics contest. In: Mechlova, E. (ed.) ICTE 2009: Information and Communication Technology in Education 2009, Ostrava, pp. 219–223. Ostrava University Editorial Centre (2009). https://ioinformatics.org/journal/INFOL127.pdf
27. Vaníček, J.: Bebras informatics contest: criteria for good tasks revised. In: Gülbahar, Y., Karataş, E. (eds.) ISSEP 2014. LNCS, vol. 8730, pp. 17–28. Springer, Cham (2014). https://doi.org/10.1007/978-3-319-09958-3_3
28. van der Vegt, W.: Predicting the difficulty level of a Bebras task. In: Olympiads in Informatics, vol. 7, pp. 132–139 (2013). https://ioinformatics.org/journal/INFOL127.pdf
29. van der Vegt, W.: How hard will this task be? Developments in analyzing and predicting question difficulty in the Bebras challenge. In: Olympiads in Informatics, vol. 12, pp. 119–132 (2018). https://ioinformatics.org/journal/v12_2018_119_132.pdf
30. van der Vegt, W., Schrijvers, E.: Analyzing task difficulty in a Bebras contest using Cuttle. Olympiads Inform. **13**, 145–156 (2019). https://ioinformatics.org/journal/v132019145156.pdf

From Bebras Tasks to Lesson Plans – Graph Data Structures

Lucia Budinská(✉) and Karolína Mayerová

Department of Didactics in Mathematics, Physics and Informatics, Comenius University, Bratislava, Slovakia
{lucia.budinska,mayerova}@fmph.uniba.sk

Abstract. In this paper we focused on graph tasks from Slovak Bebras Challenge with the intent to use them as a teaching and learning material. Based on qualitative categorisation of tasks together with quantitative analysis of contestants results we chose three tasks that were the most suitable for lower secondary schools Informatics in Slovakia. We used qualitative research methods to better understand what had caused the most significant problems. Based on these results we have prepared lesson plans with objective to teach pupils to understand, read, edit and to create specific graph structures. Taking Bloom taxonomy into account, worksheets were created and for each learning objective, there is at least one subtask in a worksheet. The main parts of this paper are pre-research and preliminary results of testing worksheets with pupils in the 5th and 6th year. We describe differences between groups based on gender and age. These results help us understand the reasons of contestants' mistakes in the original tasks and of gender- and grade-specific performance in these tasks. We plan to further develop the lesson plans as we found them valuable not only as a method of research but also as proof that tasks from Bebras Challenge could be used for learning and for teaching.

Keywords: Graph data structure · Graph task · Bebras challenge · Lesson plans · Worksheets · Qualitative research

1 Introduction

The Bebras Challenge is a great opportunity for every pupil and student to get in touch with computer science and computational thinking. The Slovak version of Bebras, called iBobor (as in "informatics beaver") is widely known throughout the country as in the school year 2018/19, 77,928 pupils and students from almost 1,000 schools (both primary and secondary) took part in the challenge. The iBobor's aim is not only to bring some of computer science concepts to schools, but also to inspire teachers and to give them a chance to teach parts of the informatics curriculum that are not contained in the textbooks. This is also the aim of our research presented in this paper, where we were looking for a way how Bebras tasks could be used in Slovak schools to help pupils learn graph structure topic more in depth and more precisely.

S. N. Pozdniakov and V. Dagienė (Eds.): ISSEP 2019, LNCS 11913, pp. 256–267, 2019.
https://doi.org/10.1007/978-3-030-33759-9_20

1.1 Context

To better understand why we chose Bebras task as a way to teach some topics, it is important to state that while Informatics is mandatory subject from third grade (8–9 years old pupils) to eighth grade (13–14 years old pupils) with one lesson per week in Slovakia, more than 40% of informatics lessons in lower secondary education (fifth to ninth grade) are taught by teachers with different specialisation (based on data from Slovak School Inspection). These teachers therefore, in many cases teach more digital skills and are not willing to try to teach programming or more specialised areas of computing. This problem is interconnected with another one – there are no official up-to-date textbooks. The old ones were created in 2005 and the National Educational Programme (NEP) [1] has been changed since the books' publication. Therefore there are some areas which these textbooks do not cover. This leaves a lot of work to teachers – they need to adjust old materials, create their own or search for materials from different teachers or even countries and adapt or translate them for their students. From teachers' feedback to Bebras we know that many of them use Bebras archive throughout the school year to teach some informatics areas or just to make it easier for them and more fun for their students. Based on this we assumed that Bebras seems like a good starting point to create new learning and teaching materials, as many pupils and teachers are familiar with the challenge which creates a higher chance of them using it.

Which topic to cover stemmed from experience of one co-author who is a teacher in lower secondary school. While we had many materials for each area from NEP, the biggest issue was with the part *Structures – Graphs*. We were not able to find a good materials which were suitable for pupils of age 10 to 12. What were we looking for? In NEP, there is stated that pupils at the end of the sixth grade (12 years old) should know: "to orientate in a simple structure (searching and obtaining information from structure based on some criteria); to organise information to structures (creating and manipulating with structures with data and simple relations, e. g. tables, graphs, sequences of pictures or numbers); and to interpret information from structures (deducting existing relations from data in structure, retelling information in structure using own words)" [1].

Another reason for using task from Bebras was categorisation of graph task created in Slovakia [2] based on tasks which were used in Slovak contest. One of the main objectives in this categorisation are methods and strategies used in solving process, which are (1) trying all possibilities, (2) the "look-see" method, (3) graph search with constraints, (4) uncovering a strategy, (5) creating a strategy. Connecting this categorisation with NEP, we focused on the first three categories, as the rest of them are more suitable to algorithmic thinking and their main goal is not to work with structures.

1.2 Literature Overview

While looking through the literature concerning the use of Bebras tasks in schools we found many interesting ways – for example adapting Bebras-like tasks into a computational thinking test or tests to evaluate their knowledge and skills from the computing [3]. There were many articles where authors were describing what can Bebras teach, using categorisation of the tasks, e.g. [4,5]

Valentina Dagiene and Gabriele Stupuriene's [6] way of bringing Bebras to school unplugged and not as a part of evaluation or assessment was adapting Bebras tasks to playing cards, which can be used in many ways in lessons. One of them is letting pupils solve the task individually and later grouping them and encouraging them to talk about their ideas. These cards were used in primary school level and increased motivation of both pupils and their teachers. On one hand they helped pupils to think about concepts, but on the other hand, there were some misconceptions which partially came from some teachers' lower qualification in informatics.

This all led us to question whether pupils of this age can gain a deep understanding of some concepts through a small task which can be usually solved in 3 min. Do they learn what we think they do? Can they find similarities in different contexts? A teacher is a crucial part in this constructionist process and while we also deal with teachers who are not qualified in informatics, we need to create some materials which can guide pupils through them, making smaller steps and then trying to generalise what they learnt. To better distinguish between steps, we find Bloom taxonomy of learning objectives [10] to be the best alternative, as slovak teachers are (more-or-less) familiar with it and it is used in many textbooks or teachers' materials.

An inspiration how to use task from competition in school was found in paper about a Slovak contest for talented students in lower secondary education PRASK [7]. The author, Michal Anderle showed how these tasks can be adapted to high school lessons and why it is important to divide them into subtasks. He mixed individual, pair and group work in one lessons and we believe this is a good approach.

2 Research Methods

Our research is a part of long going mixed methods research [8]. The main goal of this paper was to find out how can be Bebras tasks transformed and implemented into school informatics with emphasis on enhancing pupils' skills in orientating, interpreting and organising graph structures. Which can also enhance their computational thinking skills, as abstraction and generalisation. Our research is divided into several phases which have different ways of collecting data, and also their analysis (qualitative and quantitative). In this paper we discuss mainly three phases (see below) and one pre-phase which was an important part of creating the whole research idea.

2.1 Zeroth Phase

In this phase we analysed the National Educational Programme in Informatics (NEP) [1], as one of the main documents used in creating curriculums and lesson plans, and we were looking for suitable tasks from Slovak Bebras contest which could satisfy its requirements. We identified tasks which could be used in schools as a learning material, as they contain all processes needed. Theoretical analysis of documents was used in this phase. We also used graph task categorisation from Budinska and Mayerova [2], which was the result of open coding of tasks. And this results in finding graph tasks suitable to use in schools.

2.2 First Phase

In previous phase a group of tasks was chosen, and in this phase we analysed contestants' results from these tasks to better understand if tasks were easy or difficult and if there are any problems in tasks' text, pictures or proposed answers. For analysing data, the quantitative methods were used. We used statistical methods – both basic descriptive statistics (percentage of correct answers for each year) and statistical hypothesis test (chi-square test, Pearson standardised residuals [9] in which we tested differences between gender and school grade groups.

2.3 Second Phase

Based on results from previous phase, we knew only global results of these tasks but we wanted to see how pupils solve them and if our hypothesis about what was causing the errors were true. Therefore, the second qualitative phase was conducted in October 2018 in the fifth (7 pupils, 3 boys) and the sixth grade (10 pupils, 4 boys) of one lower secondary school. We chose three tasks from Bebras, all of them were easier with higher success rate but still with a good potential to learn basics of graph theory. They were proposed in a form of a worksheet.

Pupils solved worksheet individually and for each task they were asked to describe how they found the answer. After individual solving, each class was grouped into two groups – boys and girls as one of our aims was to better understand what could have caused the gender-specific differences in solving these tasks. Each group had time to discuss their answers and to find one that all of them think is correct. This is an example of focus group [8], where there is no moderator but instructions in worksheets take his role. All pupils have a chance to say something, and their goal is to find an answer they all agree on.

Discussions were recorded (each group had their own recorder) and later rewritten and analysed using axial coding [8]. To make sure all pupils in the group understand how to solve these tasks, another worksheet was made with only slight changes for each task. Teacher motivated pupils that if (and only if) pupils from the whole group would have correct answers for all three tasks in it they all would get bonus points in Informatics as a reward. Both worksheets were analysed using codes and interjoining it with information from the recordings. To ensure the triangulation of the data the researcher (teacher) took field notes which provided us with more insight to what was happening (e.g. when pupils were showing each other something in worksheets).

2.4 Third Phase

In the third phase, which was taking place in May 2019, we created worksheets for each of the originally tested tasks. We were taking into account the results of previous phase and trying to create tasks in each stage of Bloom taxonomy of learning objectives [10]. To address some problems with original tasks, we proposed some introduction to worksheets, which should be done together with the whole group. We showed worksheets to two groups of primary and lower secondary school teachers and they gave us a lot of ideas about methods that could be used in lesson plans.

First test of first worksheet was made in May 2019 in the same classes as research from previous phase. While most of them saw these tasks before, we saw from their reactions that many of them had no deeper insight into graph tasks, but it is possible, that some pupils created good mental models of family trees. The worksheets adapt only a concept of original task and not the task itself, so they could be suitable for pupils who are new to the topic and others could challange their mental models. From this research we have field notes from the teacher and student products – filled worksheets. All of them were analysed, coded, and evaluated using a point system. Due to problems with time at the end of the school year we were able to test only one of three worksheets, as one testing takes approximately one lesson and these classes have only one informatics school lesson per week.

3 Results

In this article, we focused on three tasks which were analysed, tested with pupils and based on the results, worksheet for each task was created. In this part we present whole analysis, observations and worksheets, separately for each task to make it easier to understand.

3.1 Family Relationships Tree

The first task we chose for this research was the task called *Family Relationship Tree* that was used in the competition in the school year 2013/14 in the category Benjamin (in that time 5th to 7th grade). This task had been proposed as easy and its real success rate was 48.8%. As can be seen in Fig. 1, there is a graph showing family relationships, that the lower secondary school pupils should be familiar with. For finding the right solution, the direction of the arrows is important, indicating who has a family relationship with whom.

The right answer was an arrow pointing from Maria to Tomas. 46.4% of boys and 51.8% of girls answered this task correctly, which is a statistically significant deviation (Pearson's coefficient was 7.08 for girls). The difference between boys and girls success rate was significant for all age groups of competitors, but from the results it was also visible that with increasing age the error rate of competitors has decreased.

Based on the graph task categorisation, we thought that pupils mostly use "look-see" method, therefore they obtain information from graph structure and then they interpret them.

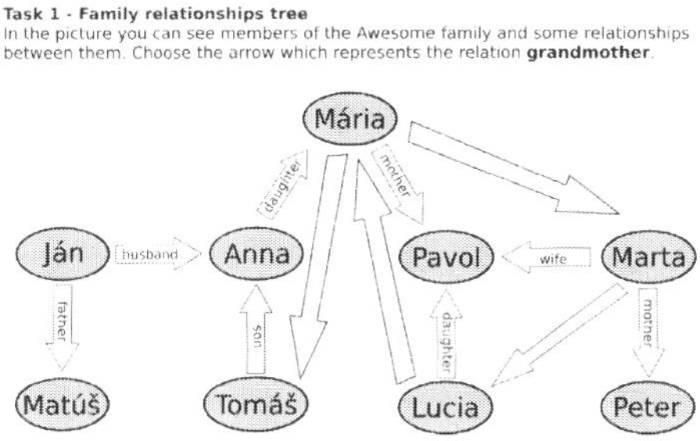

Fig. 1. The task Family relationships tree from second phase worksheet

3.2 Results of the Second Phase

When working alone, pupils spent either very long time on the task Family Relationship Tree, or not enough time and they did not check their answers. In all four groups, pupils came to the conclusion that Maria was the grandmother. The boys in the sixth grade, even originally just circled the name Maria, so the teacher had to coordinate their solutions, pointing out that they should select an arrow. In the end, both boys' groups chose an (wrong) answer, an arrow pointing from Lucia to Maria. It has been said several times that "Lucia is the grandmother of Maria" together with "Maria is the grandmother". It is clear from both debates that some pupils understand what the direction of arrows means, but it seems as if they did not combine these two contradictory pieces of information. In both boys' groups they spent more time discussing family relationships ("Lucia is Mary's granddaughter because...") and they were less focused on the direction of the arrows. Girls' groups have been more focused on the direction of arrows than family relationships. In both girls' groups, they correctly read from the graph that Mary has (at least) two grandchildren – Lucia and Thomas. Both groups discussed a lot whether the arrow direction indicates "the relationship of whom or relationship from to", while trying to base their opinions on the rest of the relationships shown in the graph. Both girls' groups found the right answers.

The validation task for the Family Relationship Tree was named The Clever Family and it consisted of graph constructed with the same rules as in the previous task. Pupils were asked to name one relationship in the blank arrow. Interestingly, three out of four groups named it correctly – both girls' groups and the fifth grade boys' group. In the sixth grade boys' group only one pupil had correct answer, three other boys in this group all had incorrect answer "daughter", that means they again changed the meaning of the arrows' direction.

Based on this observation we identified the main problems in this task – (1) the meaning of arrows direction is ambiguous, (2) boys in this groups had problems with naming the family relationship names, (3) the pupils intuitively understands who is in which relationship with whom but they did not pay attention to direction of this relationship. We addressed these problems in our proposed worksheet.

3.3 Results of the Third Phase

The worksheet consists of 9 tasks, each one focusing on one Bloom cognitive development stage. Before working on the worksheet there is a time for talking about relations name in the family. The names of relations in the family should be written down on a blackboard, as it helps pupils to focus on the task and not to find the right relation (therefore, it deals with the problem (2)). Our solution of problems (1) and (3) was gradation of the tasks. First three tasks used one graph and in the text we explicitly named two relationships from it (e.g. Adam is Simon's son). In the first task pupils should write down the relationships which are directly visible (and one is also written in the text). In the second task, they need to complete the relationships which are not directly mentioned (the opposite or missing relations). In the third task pupils were asked to draw two specific relationships to the graph and create one on their own. In the fourth task we tell them three relationships and they need to choose one of four graphs which represents them. In the fifth task pupils draw graph based on written relationships. The sixth and the seventh task are very similar – we used the same graph and were asking for the same relationships, but in the sixth task we drew the graph and in the seventh task we wrote down the relationships. We wanted to find out if there is a difference between these two ways of solving the problem and we also asked pupils which one is their preferred one and why (the eighth task). The last, ninth, task was to create own relationships graph, it could be based on their family tree or they could imagine one.

On average, after scoring each answer, fifth grade pupils got 79% of points, while sixth grade pupils got 85%. The lowest success rate was in the third, fifth and ninth task. In the third and the fifth task pupils were drawing arrows and most of their mistakes were based on wording – while *Hana is Simon's wife* was incorrect in 5 times, *Lenka has a brother named Albert* was incorrect 10 times. We chose the wording on purpose because both ways are used in the real life but it changes the direction of the arrows in our graph and we wanted pupils to understand it. Because this was one of the biggest issues in our worksheet, in the next version we would like to add one task were we explicitly ask pupils to write down what the direction of the arrow means. This could help them to think about it and to validate their intuitive grasp of the concept.

In the sixth and the seventh task there were no significant differences between pupils' results, but we saw that they needed more time to answer the task without the graph and a lot of them draw their own graph while solving it. Based on pupils' answers in the last task where they were drawing their own family graph we can see that they only had a little problem with it, but they were losing points for forgetting to write two relationships in sentences (e.g. My mother is Eve.). Some of them changed a direction of a few arrows, and another group was using only lines (not arrows) and naming relations such as "siblings", "couple", etc. This could arouse the discussion with the whole group and the teacher about representation of the structure, the logic behind it and even about how computers store some data. All of this will be added to the lesson plans.

4 Tram Lines

The second task analysed in this research was the task from the Benjamin category (fifth to seventh grade) in the school year 2015/16 called Tram Lines. The picture shows a map of tram lines and the contestants were supposed to find out what tram a boy used, see Fig. 2. The description of his route (turning and final stop) has been described in the text. 51.9% of the girls and 49.6% of the boys solved this task correctly. This difference is moderately significant (Pearson coefficient 3.38 in favor of girls). From the results it was visible that while in the fifth grade the differences between boys and girls were negligible, in the seventh grade they were markant. Also, the success rate increased significantly with age. Pupils had to use a textual description of the route, which contained several conditions. Therefore, we consider searching a graph with constraints as a suitable method for solving this task. From the NEP point of view it is connected with obtaining information according to specified criteria.

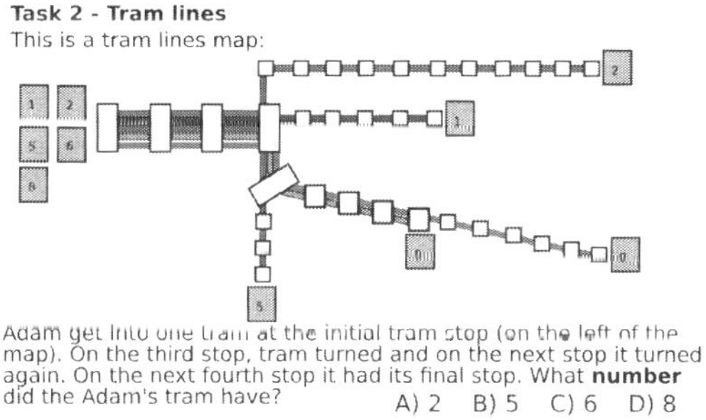

Fig. 2. The task Tram Lines from second phase worksheet

4.1 Results of the Second Phase

When solving the Tram Lines task, many pupils initially did not understand the picture. After explaining that white rectangles are stops, they understood what to do. They also gave hints to each other with examples from the real environment familiar to them. Some pupils guessed the answer, the rest got it right. In this task pupils could not easily explain why their answer was correct. When they explained it to each other, they traced the route with their fingers or pencils. Therefore, they were following steps written in the text on the graph representation. The sixth grade boys had the biggest problem with explanation to this task, they all guessed the answer and were not able to tell why. It turned out they used method of exclusion to find the correct answer when they were working together. The problem in this task proved to be that the starting stop is not counted and therefore many pupils got stuck at the first statement. Finally, all the groups agreed on the correct answer.

The variation in the second worksheet was the task named Trams in Beartown, in which the pupils were supposed to determine which trams the boy was allowed to go by. There were no differences between boys and girls, and both groups solved the task correctly. The difference was only between the fifth and sixth grade – in the fifth grade only one girl found two possible lines, but in the sixth grade there were six (out of ten) answers with the two lines. Wrong answers did not occur in this task. The main problems we found were that (1) pupils were not able to understand a graph structure quickly, (2) some wording could be ambiguous (e.g. "initial stop", "turn") and (3) younger pupils were not looking for more than one correct answer.

4.2 Proposed Worksheet

In the worksheet, tasks were created using Bloom taxonomy. Each subtask is trying to reach one objective. As we were not able to test this worksheet with pupils, we describe only tasks and not their results. To deal with problems with Tram Lines task, we slightly changed the structure and made it more similar to real-life line maps – that means we added places and names into it. In the first task pupils need to find basic concepts ("stop", "initial stop") in the graph structure. This could help with problems (1) and (2). In the next task they count stops of some of the trams – so they need to find which line in graph represents which tram, in the third task they need to decide which tram to take based on some criteria. There is implicitly stated that sometimes there are more options available and then there is more space for pupils to fill in their answers. In the next task they need to choose the better line. The synthesis is represented by the task where pupils design their own tram lines in the "city", and the last task is to discuss why their map is better than the proposed one and what they think is important when creating such a map.

In the lesson pupils could talk with their teacher about why is it sometimes better to use this kind of diagram instead of the real map. They could also find some maps of public transport from the different cities and towns, and talk about how they think the Internet search tool for transportation could work and how computers know where you should transfer.

5 Bracelet Machine

The task, originally called Mother's Day, but in our worksheet changed to Bracelet Machine, was the third and final task in the research described in this paper. It was used in 2013/14 in the Cadets category (eighth and ninth grade), with 82.0% boys' success rate and 85.6% girls' success rate. The gender difference was statistically significant with a Pearson coefficient of 5.6 in favor of girls. Gender differences are equally significant in both age groups. Although the task was designed for a higher age category, its very good results and a small error rate convinced us that this task could be suitable for younger pupils too.

The task uses a finite state machine model (considerably simplified) and the contestants need to comprehend the rules of making bracelets, which are shown in the graph, see Fig. 3. An example was used to describe how bracelets were made. Since the task contained four possible answers, it was advisable to resolve it by eliminating each option, or in other words, by trying all the options. In this task, the pupils manipulated with the data (pictures) in the graph and, based on the rules, constructed the results (bracelets).

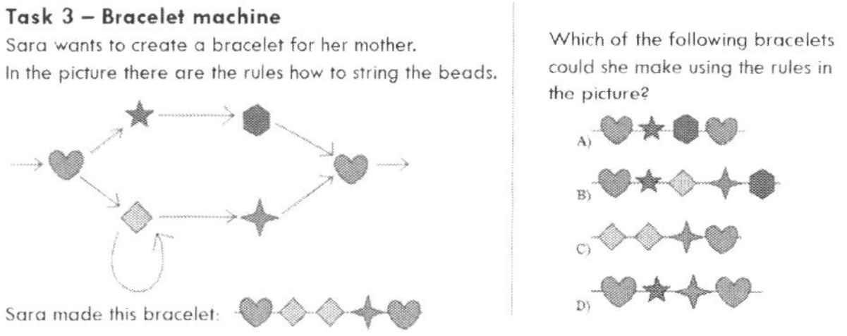

Fig. 3. The task Bracelet machine from second phase worksheet

5.1 Results of the Second Phase

The Bracelet Machine task was the most problematic for many pupils in our testing groups – many of them did not know what the rules in the picture meant and how to interpret them. The most common explanation for choosing the answer A was: "She went through the bottom path, now she'll go through the upper." Some pupils chose answer B with the argument that it contains all the shapes which were in the picture. The argument for C was that shapes were in the right order. The boys' groups chose a strategy of exclusion, in discussion in the sixth grade one boy clearly defined the rules for bracelets. In each group it was said that the loop under the pink diamond meant "that it could go twice this way," none of the groups thought about going more than twice.

It was clear from the discussions that the pupils understood the graph only intuitively and could not fully explain why their answer was correct. This has proven to be a problem in the solution of a similar task in the next worksheet called Bracelets. Only slight changes were made to the original graph – we let them write down (or more accurately draw) their own bracelets made with "machine" from the graph. We were interested if they understood the rules in the graph and how they would work in looking for two different answers.

Pupils who did not engage in the groups discussion of previous task or it was clear from their words they did not understand it, had problems with solving the Bracelets task. There was a pupil in each group except the fifth grade girls, who just redrawn the diagram – they considered it a bracelet, as all of them later explained, "the bracelet is circular". All fifth grade girls wrote more than two options, in every case at least two of them were correct. The common mistake was to miss the shape from the beginning or end of the bracelet, or to repeat the shape that did not have a loop above it. The remaining pupils had the right answers – they all chose both possible ways and if there was a loop on the way they used it. The problems we identified were (1) more difficult comprehension of rules from graph for this age group and (2) not clear understanding what the loop means.

5.2 Proposed Worksheet

In proposed worksheet we addressed these problems with small steps which pupils need to take in order to understand the structure. Firstly they see some bracelets which were made by the machine and they need to draw the "way" how machine was creating them – to address the second problem we used loop zero, one and three times. In the next task they are asked to fill missing piece into bracelets. Then they decide which bracelets were made by machine in the picture, and in the next task they are shown three machines and six bracelets and they connect each bracelet to related graph. In synthesis we let them write their own bracelets for the graph and then they are supposed to write down what are the rules for the bracelets (with what shape it starts, with what shape it ends...). To make it more interesting for more motivated pupis an additional task is at the end of the worksheet – to create their own machine (it could create bracelets, funny words or whatever they want).

The discussion following the worksheet could be about simplifying the rules to follow by drawing them into diagram like this one. With pupils, who did not have problems with the worksheet, the teacher could have a discussion about determinism and nondeterminism (e.g. what would the machine do if there are two possible ways each starting with the same shape).

6 Conclusion

In this paper we presented the results of using Bebras graph task in lower secondary school as a part of the learning process. We chose three tasks which seemed to meet the criteria from the National Educational Programme, analysed their results from the competition and let two groups of pupils from fifth and sixth year solve them. While analysing methods they used, errors they made and misconceptions they gained, we were able to identify the most significant problems and we tried to overcome them with creating worksheet for each task. Subtasks in worksheets are created with Bloom taxonomy in mind, so for each cognitive objective there is at least one subtask.

Even though we could not test all three worksheets, based on the results of the first one, it appears to be a good approach to teach graph data structures. We are aware of the small group of participants, and we are planning to test them with different setting groups. To find them, we presented the worksheets to the two groups of primary and lower secondary school teachers and they gave us more ideas and insight to what they need. They liked the idea and they agreed that it is not so easy for them to use Bebras tasks in lessons if they do not have a good understanding of the informatics concept behind it. Also, some ideas about post-worksheet discussion arose from the results and teachers opinions, as well as many different uses of worksheets – it can be done individually, in pairs, in groups or even with a different approach for each task. Some of the teachers are willing to participate in later rounds of the research starting in the new school year, which could bring a new perspective to all of it.

Acknowledgment. This research was supported by the Comenius University in Bratislava Grant UK/373/2019.

References

1. Slovak innovated National Educational Programme in Informatics for lower secondary eduaction http://www.statpedu.sk/files/articles/dokumenty/inovovany-statny-vzdelavaci-program/informatika_nsv_2014.pdf. Last accessed 25 May 2019
2. Budinská, L., Mayerová, K.: Graph tasks in bebras contest: what does it have to do with gender? In: Proceedings of the 6th Computer Science Education Research Conference, pp. 83–90. ACM (2017)
3. Román-González, M., Moreno-León, J., Robles, G.: Combining assessment tools for a comprehensive evaluation of computational thinking interventions. In: Kong, S.C., Abelson, H. (eds.) Comput. Think. Educ., pp. 79–98. Springer, Singapore (2019). https://doi.org/10.1007/978-981-13-6528-7_6
4. Dagienė, V., Sentance, S.: It's computational thinking! bebras tasks in the curriculum. In: Brodnik, A., Tort, F. (eds.) ISSEP 2016. LNCS, vol. 9973, pp. 28–39. Springer, Cham (2016). https://doi.org/10.1007/978-3-319-46747-4_3
5. Calcagni, A., Lonati, V., Malchiodi, D., Monga, M., Morpurgo, A.: Promoting computational thinking skills: would you use this bebras task? In: Dagiene, V., Hellas, A. (eds.) ISSEP 2017. LNCS, vol. 10696, pp. 102–113. Springer, Cham (2017). https://doi.org/10.1007/978-3-319-71483-7_9
6. Dagiene, V., Stupuriene, G.: Short Tasks - Big Ideas: Constructive Approach for Learning and Teaching of Informatics Concepts in Primary Education. In: Dagiene, V., Jasute, E. (eds.) Constructionism 2018. Vilius (2018)
7. Anderle, M.: Transformation of tasks from competition to high school lessons - Binary search trees. In: ICERI2018 Proceedings, pp. 6549–6557 (2018)
8. Creswell, J.W.: Educational Research: Planning, Conducting, and Evaluating Quantitative and Qualitative Research. Pearson Education Inc., London (2015)
9. Agresti, A.: Categorical Data Analysis. John Wiley & Sons Inc., Hoboken (2002)
10. Bloom, B.: Taxonomy of Educational Objectives: The Classification of Educational Goals. Handbook 1 Cognitive Domain McKay. New York (1956)

CITY: A Game to Raise Girls' Awareness About Information Technology

Evelyn Saxegaard and Monica Divitini(✉)

Department of Computer Science, Norwegian University of Science and Technology, Trondheim, Norway
divitini@ntnu.no

Abstract. Worldwide there is a significant under-representation of females considering Information Technology (IT), and more in general STEM, as a career option. The missing women in IT have long been a topic of concern and several factors are known to contribute to this gender gap. Among the factors identified in the literature, there is a misconception of the role of IT and its role in everyday life. In turn, this might result in a decrease in interest. The aim of this research is to explore the possibility to increase girls′ awareness about IT in an accessible and engaging way. With this objective, the paper presents the design of CITY, a game concept aiming at explaining the role that technology plays in everyday life. The paper also presents the evaluation of the game.

Keywords: Gender gap · Serious games · IT education · Awareness

1 Introduction

The reduced number of women in Science, Technology, Engineering, and Mathematics (STEM) has long been a topic of concern [4]. Different factors influence the gender gap in STEM, including stereotypes, missing awareness, lack of role models, and the view on girls' abilities. In particular, lack of information leads to misunderstandings and misconceptions about the field that might negatively influence girls [2, 7].

In this research we investigate how to address the lack of information with an informative serious game. Several studies described such games as effective both for motivation and learning [10, 18]. This research will therefore focus on the use of serious games to present information about IT with the aim to raise awareness among girls about IT as an interesting subject of study and a possible meaningful career option.

The research presented in this paper follows the Design Science paradigm [11], aiming at developing an artifact in form of a game prototype that is grounded in current understanding of the problem domain as well as in the body of knowledge in serious games.

Next section elaborates on related work. We then present the game in Sect. 3 and its evaluation in Sect. 4. Section 5 concludes the paper and points out directions for future work. The game is available online at https://techinthecity.firebaseapp.com (in Norwegian).

S. N. Pozdniakov and V. Dagienė (Eds.): ISSEP 2019, LNCS 11913, pp. 268–280, 2019.
https://doi.org/10.1007/978-3-030-33759-9_21

2 Serious Games for Providing Information

Most research on building awareness and behavior change has been carried out in the field of healthcare [14, 17]. For example, the games PROCEE [8], NutritionRush [3], and RebEarth [1] all utilize information as an important tool throughout the game play to increase players' knowledge about the topic at hand. The evaluation of these three games, as presented in the referenced papers, reports good results suggesting that the use of information can be an effective tool to make players more aware of a topic.

When exploring the use of informative serious games to raise awareness about IT, both learning elements and game elements are important to take into account, as the player's educational experience must be supported by fun and engaging activities. The construction of an engaging, informative learning environment ensures that the player does not passively receive information, but that new knowledge is obtained through active tasks. However, balancing learning and fun is challenging, as informative serious games might struggle to present information without being tedious.

Different game elements are identified in the literature to help keeping the player engaged. For example, Boller described Conflict, Cooperation and Competition, Strategy and Chance, Aesthetics, Theme, Story, Resources, Rewards, Levels, and Scoring as the fundamental game elements [5]. Many elements are also identified as essential to promote learning. Quizzes and active game tasks, such as collecting items or controlling the character, are wide-spread learning elements. For example, the game in Cosma et al. [8], and many of the games mentioned in the literature review by Mortara et al. [15] use question and answer-based exercises to make the player more aware of the consequences of a decision or to improve their knowledge about a topic. Storytelling and choice-driven elements are also frequently used to compel the player to feel an affiliation to the plot and the game. Stories grounded in the subject of the serious game are often used to combine the serious content with the game's entertaining side [13]. This ensures that the player sees the game as a meaningful activity.

When designing games targeting girls it is important to be aware of possible gender issues that might dis engage girls. For example, a study by Kafai [12] shows that girls tend to prefer realistic game environments with little violence or negative feedback for taking wrong decisions. Similar studies revealed the value of having meaningful content presented through dialogue and character interaction [6, 16]. The role of the game's narrative was also found to be central to females' enjoyment of games. This gave them the opportunity to explore and engage with characters facilitating social interaction [6].

Table 1 provides an overview of elements from the literature that are identified as relevant in the design of CITY. The first column (a) lists game elements that can be used to promote learning, while the second column (b) lists game elements that can be used to promote engagement.

Table 1. Overview of learning and engaging game elements

(a)

Learning Elements
Provide information
Quiz
Consequential play
Repetition
Emotions
Points
Real scenarios
Sophisticated graphics and sound design

(b)

Engaging Game Elements
Rich narrative
Reward
Meaningful dialog
Engaging characters
Consequential play
Appropriate level of challenge
Cooperative
Vicarious adventure

3 CITY Game Design

CITY is an online game targeted toward female teenagers in secondary schools with the aim of increasing their awareness of IT. The storyline is summarized in Table 2. The game does not aim at providing a comprehensive coverage of the topic. IT is an umbrella term that makes it almost impossible to include all aspects. A few topics have therefore been selected based on girls' interests and the likelihood of them finding the chosen scenarios engaging and attractive. The chosen narrative makes it easy to add additional areas in a later phase. The story and the information are presented in Norwegian, but the game could be easily made available in any other language.

Table 2. CITY storyline

You are in "CITY", a peaceful town with a lot of technological resources. However, the mayor has decided to ban all Information Technology because it steals jobs from hard-working people, huge corporations misuse the citizens' personal data, and people are more occupied with checking their phones than talking to others *(i.e. common concerns about technology)*. He wants to create an inclusive and caring society where people interact with each other the way they used to before technology changed everything. Although the intentions of the mayor seem good, ignorance concerning technology can be dangerous. You need to get enough information to convince the mayor that banning technology is not the right decision. Although his claims have some truth to it, understanding the underlying causes is imperative in any situation. You will move around the city to learn about IT. Inside each location you can talk to employees and visitors, and play minigames, to gain insight into what technology is and how it affects us. At the end of the game, you will use your new awareness about IT to convince the mayor to change his mind.

The game is built around four interrelated information pillars: (i) What is technology; (ii) What is technology used for; (iii) How is technology created; and (iv) who uses and creates technology. An important part is to emphasize women's position in the technology industry and other industries where IT is used, challenging the existing stereotypes many girls have about people working with technology.

The game is divided into 8 scenes: (1) Introduction; (2) Walking in town; (3) Hospital; (4) Walking to the next location; (5) IT-business; (6) Travel to the mayor′s office; (7) City hall; (8) End of debate.

SCENE 1 and 2. Introduction

The player gets a brief introduction to the story and the mission. The player meets a woman that urges her to visit various locations in the city (Fig. 1). This will provide the knowledge needed to change the mayor′s mind about banning technology from the city. The player is also given tips on how to interact with the game.

Learning Goal. The aim of Scenes 1 and 2 is to set the scene for the player and give a preliminary introduction to technology. The general concept of what technology is and what it can be used for is presented, setting the context for the rest of the game.

Game Elements. The woman that the player meets provides basic information. Presentation of information in a conversation is more engaging than reading it in a non-contextual manner. The scene is driven by the narrative and curiosity. The narrative provides the player with a story and a mission to fulfill, creating an atmosphere that allows the player to immerse herself in the experience. Curiosity is tightly coupled with this as the game seeks to increase the player's spirit of inquiry to learn more about how to reach the goal. In addition, following the idea of flow [9], it is important that the first phase is simple to carry out. This gives the player a chance to get to know the game before the difficulty is increased. Short hints about how to play the game are provided to ensure a smooth start.

Fig. 1. CITY - Starting scene

SCENE 3. Hospital
The first location the player encounters is the hospital. Here the player is presented with a hospital building (Fig. 2), with objects and characters that are clickable. By selecting these elements, the player is taken to new scenes where information related to the clicked object will be presented or interaction with the characters is started. There are four interactive scenarios in the hospital: (1) a female doctor discussing technology in the health sector; (2) a male doctor explaining the use of artificial intelligence in medicine; (3) a patient with a pace-maker describing how technology keeps him alive, and lastly, (4) a person in the waiting room wearing an activity tracker.

Fig. 2. Representation of the hospital as the player sees it

Learning Goal. The learning goal of this scene is to make the player aware of the use and impact of IT in the health sector, an area that many girls find interesting. The themes for this location are (i) general information about technology in hospitals, (ii) the type of technology used, (iii) how artificial intelligence is used to improve diagnostics, (iv) patients' view on technology, and (v) wearables that track activity.

Game Elements. The provision of information is central throughout all the gameplay. In this scene, the player is presented with general knowledge about technology in hospitals. Central game elements in this phase are the player's opportunity to select what she wants to know more about; choose to participate in a minigame; gather light bulbs; and be intrigued by a vague hint in the smartwatch scene.

SCENE 4. Travel Between the Hospital and the IT business
Upon leaving the hospital, the player returns outside. It has begun to darken, and the mayor's meeting is starting in only a few hours. As she hurries to the next location, the player is able to pick up a newspaper laying on the street, with an article describing how the mayor has already started turning off technology. When putting down the paper, the player receives a notification on her phone informing that the Internet has been switched off. She then hurries to the next location, i.e. the IT business.

Learning Goal. In this part of the game, the learning goal is to make the player reflect on a scenario where technology is not available, possibly seeing the benefits of using technology and understanding its importance.

Game Elements. The main learning elements in this scene are providing information and to benefit from the user's emotions. The newspaper is a way of presenting information that the player has not seen before. This breaks with previously used approaches to form a more diverse and interesting game. Additionally, the scene is aimed at generating emotions in the player by having them experience the time rush and the disappearing of the Internet. The player is motivated to continue the quest when she is driven forward by elements such as the dark skies, her encounter with the consequences of removing technology, and the desire to get to the next location.

SCENE 5. IT Business

Similar to the hospital, the IT business is depicted as a building with transparency of the various office rooms (Fig. 3) and the player can interact with the characters in different rooms. There are five different scenarios at this location: (1) A female developer asking the player her thoughts on programming, (2) a male developer explaining the value programming holds, (3) a female programmer talking about her experience with code, (4) a room where two people are testing virtual reality equipment, and (5) a computer that demonstrates examples of what you can do with coding.

Learning Goal. In contrast to the hospital location where the goal was to show the player the practical use of technology and its benefits, the IT business is designed to demonstrate how technology is created and who is behind it. The location aspires to generate positive associations to IT and convince the player that programming is less frightening than many might think. The female developers work as a role model.

Game Elements. The information is presented either as a speech, an image, or as text. The image is a new medium not previously experienced in the game and is meant as a tool to make the presentation of the information more engaging. As in the hospital, the use of real-world examples is an important aspect. Using realistic examples allow the player to identify with the characters and the information, creating a contextual learning environment. There are several characters and objects around the office that the player can interact with. These people have been created to be relatable and charming, generating a pleasant and friendly atmosphere. As in the hospital, a minigame is included to promote engagement. If the player is able to complete the minigame, she is awarded a light bulb to help her against the mayor. There is also a light bulb hidden in this location that awards the curious players later in the game.

SCENE 6 and 7. Outside the City Hall

When leaving the building, the user exits out into the dark evening and is told that the mayor's meeting is about to start. When the player reaches the city hall, she realizes that she has no way of getting inside. She must search for a means to gain access, and by glancing around the area, she will be able to find an access key to be used with an access code, i.e. the step count from the wearable scenario.

Fig. 3. Representation of the IT business as the player sees it

Game Elements. This scene is not associate to any learning goal, but it is meant as an engaging and fun element providing a break to the player. (Although it is not specifically mentioned, the scene could be relevant to security aspects of technology as it depicts the player using a lost keycard to gain access to a location.) This scene is a puzzle where the player needs to find an object. In this scene, the unfamiliar task of solving a puzzle presents the player with a new challenge, increasing motivation and interest.

SCENE 8. Debate
In the final scene, the player interrupts the mayor's presentation about prohibiting technology from the city. This starts a debate between the two where the player must decide how to argue against the mayor's allegations and claims.

Learning Goal. In the previous scenes, the focus is on collecting new information and gaining an understanding of how technology is created and used. In the final debate, the player must use this information to present her argumentation. The level is designed to make the player contemplate the information that has already been presented and see it in a new context when hearing the mayor's side. The discussion facilitates reflection and it is an opportunity to hear the other side of technology and understand the possible trade-offs.

Game Elements. Repetition of information from the game is utilized in the argument to help reinforcing the user's understanding, a strategy that is widely used to boosts learning outcomes. Moreover, the player is able to select the argument she wants to use, drawing on the concept of consequential play and providing her with the opportunity to learn more about what she finds most important. The information she has previously learned will then be repeated in the conversation, resulting in an enhanced learning experience. Because of the reflective nature of this scene, the level contains few other engagement elements, other than a scorekeeper. The score allows the player to pay attention to her answers to see if she is doing better than the mayor.

CITY is built on Phaser3, an HTML game engine for creating two-dimensional games, with support for both Canvas and WebGL rendering, and is JavaScript-based. Images used in the game are designed by illustrators for Freepik.com.

4 Evaluation

The prototype has gone through four iterations, from a paper-based to a fully functional prototype. The intermediate prototypes have been improved through interviews with stakeholders and experts. These intermediate evaluations have been used to improve the game concepts, its playability, and relevance. Here we report only the evaluation of the last prototype, as described in Sect. 3, with focus on the evaluation of the overall concept and the use of a serious game to promote awareness about IT. The main evaluation was done through interviews with the target group and experts, including a group interviews with three lower secondary female students, a group interview with four upper secondary school female students, an two individual interviews with one game design expert and one recruitment expert working in an initiative at the university level to recruit girls for STEM related study programs. Secondary school students were recruited to evaluate the game as possible recipients, share their insight on how the target group would assess the game and supply the researcher with an understanding of how well the game mechanics work to increase the player's awareness. The evaluation with the game design expert aimed at evaluating the game based on her expertise in game design and provide insight into how well the game mechanics work to raise awareness of the topic presented. The evaluation with the recruitment expert aimed at evaluating the game based on her expertise from working with recruiting girl to technology studies and share her knowledge of what younger girls find interesting with IT. Interviews lasted approximately one hour. They all started with a brief introduction to the study and to the game, as well as information about ethical issues. Before the game session started, it was made clear that this was not a usability test. The game is a concept demonstrator, and the goal of the evaluation was to assess its potential, not its functionality. The introduction was followed by a game session and then the semi-structured interview. Notes were taken during the interviews, but no recording to protect the privacy of the participants.

4.1 Lower Secondary School Students

The students were very positive, and they all liked the idea of using a game to get the information. They mentioned that it could be used at school "*I think our science teacher could have used this*", but also for homework, as a more exciting way of learning than having to search for information on the Internet. They emphasized, "*The information was very well explained. We wouldn't have to browse through tons of irrelevant theory on Wikipedia, for instance. Everything we need is right here.*" They also expressed their appreciation of the design, thinking it was fitting. It was, however, proposed to add a method to go back to earlier levels, in case one forgets the code to the city hall.

The game was evaluated as entertaining. Participants liked the mini-games, actually suggesting adding more. An idea the girls suggested was a minigame where the player would assemble a computer. The minigames were, however, not the most engaging game element, as this was found to be the dialogue choices, or the consequential play element. They explained that being able to choose what to say and what action the character should take empowered them as players. It made them excited to discover what the response would be. They also liked that they were able to click on the characters in the buildings, thus being given the ability to select the person they wanted to talk to, rather than being presented with someone. They viewed the storyline as an essential aspect of the game, always leading them further along. "*It's what the game is based on. It follows you from the start to the end, making it easier to learn as you see the overall context at every step.*"

Even if the participants already knew some of the information presented in the game, they got a new perspective by playing the game. As one participant said, "*I haven't thought about clothes or a pacemaker to be part of technology. Neither to what extent hospitals use it.*" Another stated, "*It's a new way of thinking about technology.*" When queried about how interesting the information was, they said that it was fascinating and easy to follow. "*Many sites and articles on the Internet are so long and have difficult language, but the language here was simple and understandable.*" Furthermore, they explained that the game made them think about technology and programming differently than before. "*You get to see that it's more than just creating computers. The domain is so much more than what people might think.*" They also added that CITY could be a motivator to both teachers and students when starting out exploring technology and programming.

Participants also suggested that, for future extensions, a location not directly linked to technology and programming would be educational. "*Something like a farm. They use a great amount of technology, but no one ever thinks about that.*" A police station was also proposed, with emphasis on that it would be fun to solve a case using some particular type of technology. The girls were also eager about the idea of having a final page with resources to learn more about the presented topics and on how to proceed to learn to program. "*Many people don't know where to start. Even the once who are interested in learning.*"

4.2 Upper Secondary School Students

This group of students provided feedbacks similar to the ones from younger students. They thought the game was engaging and relevant. In their opinion, students at the age of 10–13 would benefit from playing the game, though they would not rule out that this could be used also by older students. They liked the idea of the game being created for girls, without being too "girly". As the younger students, they also suggested it could be targeted toward teachers: "*Many teachers don't know where to start so it could be a great tool they could use as a starting point when introducing technology to us.*" The participants proposed to use it at school, at educational fairs, research days, explaining that it would work as an excellent opening into IT.

They liked the design and aesthetics of the game, particularly mentioning the gradually darkening of the sky as the story progress. They all evaluated the game as entertaining, in particular the minigames. The story was also deemed to be an essential part of the game and a central element in generating motivation. "*Without a clear objective to the game, I see no reason to play it, but in CITY I was like: 'Oh no, the mayor has taken all the technology. I must stop him'.*" The participants explained that there was no wow-experience when reading the information because they had some previous understanding of it. However, they stated that it got them thinking. *"The information made it less scary and foreign, and more interesting."*

Talking to the other characters was considered a good way to learn. "*It's more interesting to hear a doctor say something than reading 'Here at the hospital…'.*" The game's flow and clear connection between the goal and the presented information were mentioned as well and said to be engaging. They felt that they knew more about IT after playing the game, saying that the discussion with the mayor was especially interesting.

The girls thought a third location would be a nice supplement, making the game longer and therefore a more suitable learning tool to be used during class. "*Maybe a farm, or a space station that you travel to.*" The space station idea was however, put aside in favor of an airport because of the unrealistic scenario it would present.

4.3 Game Expert

The game expert's first comment after playing the game was "*It's very engaging. This is a feeling you can count on to emerge in the target group.*" She emphasized that the game made her reflect on technology in a way she had not previously done and that it made her stop and think. She evaluated the game to be appropriate for students in both lower and upper secondary school students. "*The upper grades can get a glimpse of what they can choose to study, while the younger students can have their interest in technology kickstarted.*" She was of the opinion that the game would go well with both girls and boys, but that it was particularly accommodating toward girls. She pointed to the use of many female characters and the female-specific information such as examples of using technology in fashion and health. When discussing the game design, the game specialist found the design elegant and easy to navigate.

When asked about her opinion on the game's level of difficulty, she answered that she thought it to be suitable. She declared that it was easy at this point but that it was more important that the game made the students stop and think than have them struggle to complete the game. If it was desirable to raise the challenge level, more difficult questions could be included, or the dialogue choices could be made harder.

She evaluated the dialog options as a good way to promote learning. She also found the storyline and minigames engaging elements that are useful in classroom settings. The game expert believed the game to be a nice supplement in a school class, pointing to research on how games often are used to stimulate discussions afterward. She therefore suggested creating a teacher's guide to facilitate further discussions on the topic of technology and programming. Video interviews with real people were also proposed, as well as having resources to guide interested players in the right direction for learning more.

4.4 Recruitment Expert

The recruitment expert thought the game to be a pleasant way of learning about IT, including a good variety of areas within IT with the potential for expanding it further in the future. In her opinion the game is better targeting students in lower secondary schools, maybe even primary schools. However, with some changes to make the information more complex it could become more relevant also for upper secondary school students. She suggested to use the game in school, at events, and coding clubs.

The expert evaluated the game as engaging: "*The concept was captivating, and I thought the minigames were a good way of maintaining the motivation during the play. There could be even more of them.*" Despite the fact that she enjoyed the minigames, she found clicking on objects and the characters to be the most engaging game mechanics. She also mentioned choosing what to say as part of the debate among the best engagement elements.

In the expert's opinion, the game provides a good mixture of relevant information that girls would find interesting. "*It covers a broad aspect of technology in a short time, demonstrating that it can be so much more than just programming and websites.*" To make the game more engaging, she suggested making the information a more significant part of the minigames. Moreover, she mentioned that much of the information in CITY was related to what her project uses to promote interest in IT, confirming the relevance of the game. She added that the game could include supplementary examples on why we need women/gender-balance in technology fields.

The learning element she found to be most effective in increasing the player's awareness was the conversations with the characters, as well as the debate against the mayor. "*It was fun to be able to use what I had learned during the game.*" When asked if a quiz should be included at the end of the game to test the player's new knowledge, it was said that this would ruin the flow of the game. "*The battle with the mayor is an essential part of the game, but if the quiz was prior to the end discussion, as a challenge the player would have to face before the final 'boss,' then I think it could work.*"

When asked about possible improvements, the expert pointed at the role of programming. She liked how programming was presented as something everybody could learn, but she missed being able to try it out while playing. It was therefore proposed to implement a short code assignment, in form of a minigame, to boost the player's confidence in regard to programming. Sub-quests were also suggested, having the player help characters solve their problems.

5 Conclusions

The paper presents CITY, a game to provide information about IT and improve awareness about IT and IT careers. The work is motivated by the lack of information about IT that is identified in the literature as one of the factors behind the gender gap in IT.

The proposed game is a proof of concept and provides a framework that can be extended to add more detailed learning objectives. The evaluation of the game with different stakeholders was very positive, with the game evaluated as an engaging way to get information and help reflecting on the role of IT in society. Players appreciated the possibility to engage with different characters to get information, to be able to choose different objects and characters, and to play minigames. On the overall they gave a positive evaluation of both the storyline and the aesthetics of the game.

The work is now proceeding in two main directions. First, and following some of the feedbacks received by the evaluators, we are working on an extension of the game to provide more information, for example adding new places to visit and mini-games.

Second, we are researching on ways to capitalize on the interest triggered by the game and help the players to move forward in the path of developing relevant knowledge, e.g. how one could go ahead and learn something about programming.

Acknowledgements. The research is co-funded by Excited, the Norwegian Center for Excellent IT Education (https://www.ntnu.edu/excited). We warmly thank the people who participated to the research and provided valuable feedbacks.

References

1. Ali, A., et al.: Raising awareness on hydroponics via an educational video game using an indirect teaching method. In: 9th IEEE-GCC Conference and Exhibition (GCCCE), pp. 1–6 (2017)
2. Bach, D.: Study examines why some STEM fields have fewer women than others (2016). https://phys.org/news/2016-10-stem-fields-women.html
3. Baranyi, R., et al.: NutritionRush - a serious game to support people with the awareness of their nutrition intake. In: IEEE SeGAH. IEEE, pp. 1–8 (2017)
4. Beede, D.N., et al.: Women in STEM: A Gender Gap to Innovation. SSRN Electron. J. (2011). ISSN: 1556-5068. http://www.ssrn.com/abstract=1964782
5. Boller, S.: How Much Story Does a Serious Game Need? (2014). http://www.theknowledgeguru.com/much-story-serious-game-need/
6. de Castell, S., Bryson, M.: "Retooling play: dystopia, dysphoria, and difference. In: From Barbie to Mortal Kombat, pp. 232–261. MIT Press (1998)
7. Cheryan, S., et al.: Why are some STEM fields more gender balanced than others? Psychol. Bull. **143**(1), 1–35 (2017). https://doi.org/10.1037/bul0000052
8. Cosma, G., et al.: PROCEE: a PROstate Cancer Evaluation and Education serious game for African Caribbean men. J. Assistive Technol. **10**(4), 199–210 (2016)
9. Csikszentmihalyi, M.: Beyond Boredom and Anxiety. Jossey-Bass Publish- ers (1975). (1990). Flow: The Psychology of Optimal Experience
10. Girard, C., Ecalle, J., Magnan, A.: Serious games as new educational tools: how effective are they? A meta analysis of recent studies. J. Comput. Assist. Learn. **29**(3), 207–219 (2013)
11. Hevner, A.R., et al.: Design science in information systems research. Manage. Inf. Syst. Quart. **28**(1), 75–105 (2004)
12. Kafai, Y.V.: Video game designs by girls and boys: variability and consistency of gender differences. In: From Barbie to Mortal Kombat. MIT Press, pp. 90–114 (1998)
13. Kampa, A., Haake, S., Burelli, P.: Storytelling in Serious Games. In: Dörner, R., Göbel, S., Kickmeier-Rust, M., Masuch, M., Zweig, K. (eds.) Entertainment Computing and Serious Games. LNCS, vol. 9970, pp. 521–539. Springer, Cham (2016). https://doi.org/10.1007/978-3-319-46152-6_19
14. Miltenburg, C.V.: Games for Good - Research into the use of serious games to raise awareness for charitable organizations (2014). http://arno.uvt.nl/show.cgi?fid=134760
15. Mortara, M., et al.: Learning cultural heritage by serious games. J. Cult. Heritage **15**(3), 318–325 (2014)

16. Rubin, A., et al.: What Kind of Educational Computer Games Would Girls Like?. AERA presentation (1997). https://www.researchgate.net/publication/265269338_What_Kind_of_Educational_Computer_Games_Would_Girls_Like
17. Wattanasoontorn, V., et al.: Serious games for health. Entertainment Comput. **4**(4), 231–247 (2013)
18. Wouters, P., et al.: A meta-analysis of the cognitive and motivational effects of serious games. J. Educ. Psychol. **105**(2), 249–265 (2013)

Computer Science Problem Solving in the Escape Game "Room-X"

Alexander Hacke(✉)

Didaktik der Informatik, University of Potsdam,
August-Bebel-Str. 89, 14482 Potsdam, Germany
ahacke@uni-potsdam.de

Abstract. Problem solving is a key element of computer science. It is also a research topic within computer science education examining topics like processes, tasks and attitudes with regard to computer scientific approaches and contents. Our computer science escape game "Room-X" offers learners an insight into computer science and enables them to practice problem solving in an attractive and motivating environment. From a research perspective, Room-X allows us to observe learners of computer science while solving problems and to analyze their strategies involved. Video analyses are used to analyze behavioral patterns and to draw conclusions in order to promote problem solving skills in computer science and to further develop Room-X.

Keywords: Computer science problem solving · Escape game · Out-of-school learning experience

1 Introduction

Problem solving is a key element of computer science and forms links with each of its sub-disciplines. In order to obtain a solid foundation for computer science education, secondary school and university students are required to deal explicitly with problem solving. However, little research is available on this topic. Consequently, little is known about how computer science problem solving can be taught in a purposeful manner. Nevertheless, problem solving is an inherent part of the German educational standards for computer science [2] and, in the form of computational thinking, of the K-12 CS standards [8]. Since computer scientific problem solving in German secondary schools is often treated in a rather theoretical manner, the topic is of little interest to many students. Often it is even taught implicitly, which does not do justice to the importance of the topic. Our approach to motivate secondary school students for it and to practice problem solving strategies is the computer science-based escape game Room-X. It was specifically designed with computer science problem solving in mind. Room-X serves as a showcase for computer science (CS) and shows that CS education can also be helpful in a playful environment. In the first part of this paper, there will be a theoretical account of CS problem solving. Afterwards, a

S. N. Pozdniakov and V. Dagienė (Eds.): ISSEP 2019, LNCS 11913, pp. 281–292, 2019.
https://doi.org/10.1007/978-3-030-33759-9_22

video analysis currently being conducted within the framework of Room-X will be described with the aim of finding out which major hurdles play a role in CS problem solving. At a later stage, this allows conclusions to be drawn as to which areas should play a significant role in teaching CS problem solving.

2 Computer Science Problem Solving

In cognitive psychology, *problem solving is described as the attempt to move from an initial state past a barrier to a target state* [9]. Problem solving requires a number of cognitive abilities which, according to Bloom, can be classified into six categories, with the top three ("Analyzing", "Evaluating", "Creating") being higher-order thinking and presupposing the lower three ("Remembering", "Understanding", "Applying") [1]. The processing of simple tasks can usually be represented by the lower three categories. Hence, it is necessary to understand the task (Understanding), to retrieve appropriate information and procedures from the long-term memory (Remembering) and apply them in the given context (Applying). Problem solving also requires higher-order thinking skills. It is important to analyze the problem, distinguishing important from unimportant details and revealing hidden aspects (Analyzing). Based on the analysis, a target-oriented strategy must be generated using appropriate heuristics, which, depending on the case, links known elementary procedures with new contexts (Creating). During the problem-solving process, this strategy must be constantly monitored for effectiveness and, if necessary, reconsidered (Evaluating).

The difference between a task and a problem lies in the fact that tasks require "only the use of known means in a known way to achieve a clearly defined goal", thus requiring only reproductive thinking. Problems, however, can only be solved with productive thinking. So a new or at least a modified solution has to be devised [4]. Whether it is a task or a problem depends on prior knowledge and is therefore not a fixed property.

In order to be successful in problem solving, it is necessary to have confidence in one's own abilities. Also, the attitudes to the specific problem and towards problem solving in general are largely responsible for how effectively a problem solver can use the means at his or her disposal (cf. [12]). The term "problem" needs to be narrowed down in terms of problem solving. A psychology-based definition states that *a problem exists when, in a situation where a particular goal is to be achieved, an obstacle or barrier prevents it* [9]. Problems can be categorized in many ways. For example, they can be differentiated by how clearly a target state to be reached is defined, or by classifying them as so-called *simple* or *complex* problems. In the case of *complex* problems, the surrounding conditions change during the course of the solution attempt, which requires a continuous reassessment of the solution approach. In addition, a large number of variables come into play, with many of them being interdependent. *Complex* problems include situations like managing a business or managing a global crisis. *Simple* problems, on the other hand, have stable conditions and comparatively less relevant variables. However, other than the name suggests, they are not easy to solve, either. Problems within a computer scientific context usually fall into the category of *simple* problems. This means that the general conditions do not change or change only slightly during the solution attempt and the number of variables to be considered is within manageable limits. Of course, embedded in a real-world situation, they can also be part of a *complex* problem. In the context here, however, the focus will be on *simple* problems, since otherwise it is no longer clear whether the problem is of computer scientific or other nature.

> **Definition:** A computer science problem exists when, in a situation with stable conditions, an obstacle or barrier prevents a particular goal requiring a computer science-based solution approach from being achieved.

Computer Science Methods. It now has to be clarified which methods are to be attributed to computer science and which are not. Various attempts have been made in the past to characterize the nature of CS, as demonstrated by Grillenberger [5]. Thus, the theoretical-argumentative and the empirical approach stand opposite to each other. Depending on the focus in terms of subject area and perspective, quite different models or catalogs arise as to what is attributed to computer science. Irrespective of the methodology, the computer science method used for problem solving should be found at least in one of the widely accepted approaches, be it in the Fundamental Ideas of computer science by Schwill [13] or in the Great Principles of Computing by Denning [3]. If, for example, one sticks to the theoretical-argumentative point of view of the catalog of Fundamental Ideas as a description of the essence of CS, then it must be possible to trace computer science problem solving back to at least one of these ideas. This means, for example, that the use of an algorithmic paradigm such as Divide and Conquer or the use of the tree representation can be counted among the computer science methods, since they can be found in the list of Fundamental Ideas.

The question then arises as to whether the problem at hand is of a computer scientific nature or only the problem-solving process chosen or whether both parts may be attributable to computer science. Similar to the approach by Humbert and Puhlmann subdividing computer science phenomena into three categories [6], problems can also be classified according to their relation to computer science:

1. *The problem is not of computer science nature.* Problems of a purely philosophical nature where a computer scientific approach is not appropriate or out of place.
2. *The problem is indirectly of a computer science nature.* Problems that have a real-world character but are inherently computer scientific and can therefore be solved by a CS problem-solving strategy.
3. *The problem is directly of a computer science nature.* Problems that require a problem-solving strategy with computer-scientific principles.

By classifying problems in this way, it becomes obvious that a problem of the third category like finding the closest pair of points that can be solved using the divide-and-conquer algorithm, can certainly also be part of category two, namely as a computer-scientific part of a real world problem. For example, a problem involving the distribution of tasks to employees or vehicle scheduling in suburban traffic systems is often an integer programming problem that can be solved with the branch-and-bound algorithm of computer science. The problem space of such a problem then consists not only of the computer science problem, but also of the fact that the computer-scientific character must first be recognized. However, problems of category two may also be solved in a non-computer-scientific manner. For example, depending on the scenario, in the case of a distribution problem either CS optimization might be necessary or a simple random distribution might suffice. It also becomes apparent that the initial situation of the problem provides information about the likelihood of an involvement of computer science in the problem-solving process.

2.1 Problem Solving Versus Computational Thinking

One of the concepts that seem similar to computer science problem solving at first glance is *Computational Thinking (CT)*. In 2006, Jeannette Wing's term came into play to describe a particular way of thinking.

Wing characterizes CT as problem-solving, system design and the understanding of human behavior through the use of fundamental computer science concepts. It contains mental tools that reflect the breadth of computer science [14]. Since there is no precise definition of Computational Thinking, ISTE and CSTA have sought to narrow down what *CT* is, based on the feedback from people involved in computer science education. *CT* is characterized as a problem-solving process with at least the following properties:

- formulate problems in such a way that we can solve them with the help of computers.
- logical organization and analysis of data.
- Representation of data by means of abstraction (e.g. models, simulations).
- automation of problem solving through algorithmic thinking (sequence of ordered steps).
- identify, analyze and implement possible solutions with the goal of using the most efficient and effective combinations of steps and resources possible.
- generalization and transfer of the problem solving process to a multitude of other problems [7].

The list of properties of Computational Thinking is based on the assumption that a problem from another science should be solved by means of computer science and that this solution should be implemented and automated. CS problem solving plays a role in this process, of course. However, the focus of CS problem solving, as described in this document, is not on the implementation and automation of a solution, but on the previous step, i.e. thinking through CS problems and creating structured solutions. This process does not necessarily require the computer, nor does the automation of problem solving and the generalization and transfer of the problem-solving process take center stage.

3 Problem Solving in Escape Games

Escape rooms (also known as live escape games, exit rooms, and other similar terms) are a special kind of escape game in which players as a team are locked inside a room. With the help of clues and puzzles inside they try to escape the room in a limited time. In most cases, there is also a mission to fulfill, such as disarming a bomb, solving a criminal case or stealing an object. The topics for such games are extremely diverse and are based on exciting settings, e.g. chemical laboratories, prison tracts or agent offices. Escape games also provide incentives for educational contexts. For example, Nicholson [10] describes the benefits of using such games in the classroom as a welcome change from working on the computer, the need for team collaboration, and motivational aspects as the basis for active learning and social constructivism. Escape games provide a great opportunity to train problem-solving skills. The concept of such games incorporates the essential features of a *simple* problem and thus makes the players problem solvers. Within a certain period of time, they have to move from an initial state (the room and the hints provided) to a destination state (usually: to leave the room). This is not possible without further ado because one or more obstacles (riddles, the door cannot be opened easily, etc.) are put in the way. Therefore, they must use heuristic procedures (for example, formation of sub goals, search space limitation, visualization), creatively plan a solution strategy and constantly check this strategy for meaningfulness during execution. In addition, escape games are well-suited as their playful adventure character helps to keep the motivation of the participants high and to mask any negative attitudes to problem solving that may exist. Possibly the contained problem solving will not even be perceived as such.

Group Effects. In addition to the usual hurdles of a problem solver, according to Rosenstiel [11] team interaction creates various additional obstacles. For example, the so-called group think may play a role. The opinion of the majority then becomes the binding factor and deviating ideas are suppressed. A further influence is possible through the effect that a very talkative person might have on the group. The latter is granted a higher influence on group decisions. He or she may therefore consciously or unconsciously lead the group, as long as he is not recognized as a "busybody". Furthermore, the decision-making quality does not increase proportionally with the size of the group. On the contrary, it even decreases with group sizes of ten or more participants due to constraints in communication and interaction. [11] Even though Room-X does not allow for more than six participants, the group effect may affect the result. There are also known negative group effects when the team cohesion is disturbed. The individual may then not exhaust his full potential but rather orient himself towards the maximum performance of the group. He or she does not want to be the only one, who works, if the others do not participate. Nobody really feels responsible and certain team members may choose not to work at all and still profit from the work of the others. However, the group also has positive effects.

Usually there is communication, i.e. the observation of the processes is simplified, which is essential to gain knowledge about problem solving situations. In groups, the participants are usually less inhibited and motivation is higher. Also, the performance of the individual participants can be increased by the team feeling.

4 Room-X: An Escape Game for Computer Science Lessons

The escape game Room-X was set up at our university to give students in a limited time frame a motivating insight into various topics of computer science and to promote the institute of computer science. In this context, groups of students who would like to play the game come to visit us regularly. This gives us the opportunity to observe them while solving problems. Their mission is to spy on the tasks of the next computer science exam, which is stored on a password-protected tablet in the classroom of Mr. Schroeder. The exam must be photographed, otherwise the mission is not completely fulfilled and is considered as failed. The password can be found using the items in the room. In addition, the teacher has activated the alarm system of the classroom door. In order to escape unnoticed, the team must find out the numerical code of the key vault containing the remote control of the alarm system. The team in Room-X is monitored throughout the session by a camera inside the room, so they can be helped if necessary by the game supervisor passing tips into the room. The game lasts 60 min. When the time expires, the alarm system triggers. Opening the door prematurely also triggers the alarm system and leads to disqualification and abortion of the mission. First, the team get all the information about the scenario, the processes and the rules of Room-X in a separate room. The use of the whiteboard and notepads and pens in the room is explicitly permitted. The teams are advised that the game supervisor can contact people in the room during the game. Then the team is led into Room-X, the timer is started, the door is closed and the alarm system is activated. By recognizing and solving characteristic CS tasks and skillfully combining the clues found, it is finally possible to unlock the tablet, open the key vault and deactivate the alarm system. The team members then have the opportunity to discuss their experiences with each other and to learn backgrounds and solutions to the individual puzzles in the room.

In order to prevent the dissemination of the solution for the room, only a rough description of the puzzles is given here:

- The tablet is secured with a password and has a sticky note on it with the words "PW: Holidays! (HexHex)" → What's that supposed to mean?
- On the wall is a piece of paper with a cryptic message: "zpcyidyqr rmbyw dccjq jgic y pmai gl kw qrmkyaf." → What does that mean?
- On the teacher's desk there is an SD card with the inscription *SECRET*. If you insert it into a digital camera lying around, you will see photos of different

objects (for example, a huge device with the inscription *Z3* and a strangely colored map) → Are there any decisive hints in the pictures?

5 Room-X and Computer Science Problem Solving

Aiming at observing the students' approach to solving computer science problems in Room-X, it will first be examined to what extent the game demands or requires computer science problem solving. For this purpose, the room with its associated tasks and puzzles is analyzed below with reference to the definitions and thinking skills mentioned above. In a subsequent video analysis, the strategies of the participants are identified and analyzed with regard to the properties that lead to success to derive conclusions for fostering problem-solving strategies.

5.1 Description of Problem and Problem Solving in Room-X

The starting situation faced by the participants corresponds to a *simple* problem according to the above-mentioned problem definition, because the following characteristics can be found: At the beginning of the game the team is in the initial state, which consists of the room with its hidden clues and the hints given by the game supervisor. The group cannot easily proceed to the target state, because of various obstacles (door code, tablet password). The surrounding conditions do not change during the search in the problem space, if time pressure is disregarded. Also, the number of variables that must be handled in the course of the game is manageable and the inter-dependencies between them are low. Accordingly, the problem is not part of the *complex* category. Examining the path through Room-X reveals that it includes many elements that only need lower-order thinking skills. That is, there are a number of *tasks* to be solved in the room. For the most part it is not possible to establish the connection between the tasks, or to recognize what the solution of a task might be good for in order to progress in the game. This has less to do with the complexity of the strategy to be found than with the fact that the proposed solution is in some places too artificial. Connections do not always follow a recognizable pattern and are thus not predictable. So, the way to the target state often requires brute force, teamwork and luck.

5.2 Computer Science in Room-X

The problem to be solved in Room-X is not computer scientific in itself. However, the path through the problem space contains a number of *tasks* of a computer science nature. The individual tasks on the topics of encryption, logic and automata theory require computer-scientific and general sub-strategies for problem solving, such as following a path, reproducing algorithms, representation and recognition of a model, verification and purposeful combination of results as well as continuous documentation. Room-X therefore does not contain an overarching CS problem-solving strategy, but sufficient sub-strategies in order to allow conclusions to be drawn as to how well the students are prepared for CS problem solving.

5.3 Applied Problem-Solving Strategies in Room-X

In a qualitative video analysis, we aim to examine whether the sub-strategies mentioned above can be observed and whether an influence on the success of problem solving can be derived. This raises the following questions for the video analysis:

RQ1. What typical behavioral patterns can be observed during a problem-solving process in Room-X?
RQ2. What impact do observed behavioral patterns have on success in problem solving in Room-X?

Regarding the questions, the following assumptions can be deduced based on the considerations and definitions in Sect. 2 as well as the properties of Room-X: It is assumed that the teams will search the objects in the room for clues of all kinds. The team will split up according to their preferences or prior knowledge according to the tasks. They will try to solve the individual tasks, use the whiteboard and notepads as a means of visualizing or representing the findings, communicate with each other and evaluate findings in the team. It is assumed that the following behavioral patterns lead to success: systematic search for clues, correct solution of the individual tasks, visualization and representation of the hints and results, involvement of all team members and evaluation and combination of hints and results.

5.4 Conducting the Video Analysis

For the video analysis, video material of 38 groups of five to six people each is available, which corresponds to about 200 participants. The material is high-definition video with sound from a surveillance camera on the ceiling of the room. This monitoring is usually used by the game supervisor to control the game. The video footage was examined for the participants' success in problem solving. The following behaviors were isolated in advance and operationalized (deductive approach):

1. Correct solution of the individual tasks: One or more team members solve one of the tasks and find a correct solution.
2. Involvement of all team members: All participants are focused on the problem, that is, looking for clues, giving advice, helping others, solving tasks.
3. Systematic search for clues: The room is thoroughly examined for clues from one end to the other, ideally independently by several people.
4. Visualization and representation of hints and results: The board or a notepad is used to record intermediate results, hints, findings and questions as soon as they are available.
5. Evaluation and combination of hints and results with each other: results are mutually checked; they are related to each other verbally or in writing on the whiteboard.

Observed Behavioral Patterns. After qualitative evaluation of approx. 70% of the video material, tendencies regarding the first question can be identified. Every group begins by applying a brute-force heuristic strategy: all team members swarm out, scatter in the room, leaf through books, etc. This corresponds to the expected search of the objects in the room for clues. Speed and thoroughness of this process vary greatly. The fast teams need about 13 min, the slow teams up to 30 min (average: 19 min). During the search, various tasks are discovered and usually immediately attempted to be solved. Tasks that seem too difficult for one person are left behind or someone else is consulted. For example, this happens when a conversion to another number system must be carried out. Finding the correct solutions to the CS tasks varies from eight to 31 min (average: 18 min). There are also a number of teams that cannot solve all the tasks.

The whiteboard is used to document individual results. However, the documentation of found hints is often sparse and visualization is rare. Every now and then hints get lost in the communication process of the team members and then have to be rediscovered.

In addition, behavioral patterns become visible that suggest that individual team members are demotivated, which means that sometimes there are participants who often look out of the window or stand around indifferently.

Promising Behavioral Patterns for Solving Problems. The assumptions regarding promising behavioral patterns can also be largely confirmed by the video material: Teams that use the whiteboard in a more structured fashion are usually more successful. For example, dashes for the number of digits of the password were written on the board, which can be seen as a meaningful representation of a sub goal. Teams without recognizable structured sketches on the whiteboard could still be successful, provided they still wrote down a lot in their notepads or kept the results circulating verbally. There was little use of computer scientific graphical aids, e.g. trees or graphs, but that was to be expected. More successful teams also have at least two structured task solvers. These do not jump from task to task but remain focused on one task and use paper and pencil.

Group behavior. The analysis of the video material also revealed that teams work very differently. There are teams whose members communicate a lot with each other, those in which the members seem to be relatively indifferent, and sometimes even teams that work destructively. Certainly, there are group effects involved as described in Sect. 3. The following role types were identified during the analysis: *the leader* (someone who distributes tasks to others), *the coordinator* (someone who writes down intermediate results and ensures that information is passed on, but does not distribute tasks), *the loner* (someone who works alone on tasks for a longer period of time), *the inactive* (someone who is idle for a longer period of time), *the follower* (someone who essentially only follows and watches other team members), *the worker* (someone who gets to work and tries to solve tasks) and *the supporter* (someone who, for example, assists a worker and helps him to solve tasks). These types are not disjoint and there are also role changes. Also, not all types are present in every team. It seems to be more effective to have a coordinator rather than a leader on the team. In fact, at least five teams with a leader present could not finish the game successfully. On the other hand, the fastest team is one with two coordinators. It can also be seen that unsuccessful teams usually have one to five followers or inactive members. Successful teams consist exclusively of coordinators, supporters and workers. It can already be seen that behavior suggesting convergent or divergent thinking is not tied to a specific role. The evaluation must still show whether a certain way of thinking is more likely to belong to a certain role type or not.

Aspects Hampering Success. The game contains some wrong tracks, which all in all lead quite effectively to the group losing sight of the essentials and thus increase the problem space. In addition to these deliberate measures, there were several other hurdles for the participants. An often-recurring phenomenon is the lack of meaningful documentation of intermediate results and the lack of communication within the team. As a result, interim results are lost and it can happen that the notes on the whiteboard, which are mostly lacking any explanation and are usually written by different team members, cause additional confusion. In this regard, there is a tendency not to pursue all hints consistently. More than half of the teams leave at least one discovered item unused for minutes or do not use it thoroughly. Another point is the lack of evaluation of results. Results that appear cryptic are accepted without cross-checking and lead to avoidable errors for at least six teams. Furthermore, the CS tasks lead to failure for approx. 20% of the teams. The reasons are manifold. There are at least two teams that are unwilling to do the tasks. Several teams lack the basic knowledge, which is why they need a very long time to familiarize themselves with the matter. In addition, hints attached to the tasks are often ignored, which leads to incorrect results.

6 Analysis of Behavioral Patterns in Room-X

Known behavioral patterns from research about problem solving (cf. [4]) apparently also become visible in Room-X, as far as the ongoing evaluation of the data shows.

Convergent and Divergent Thinking. Teams that are able to combine convergent thinking with divergent thinking are more efficient. It also seems to be helpful if there are team members who are focused on solving the computer science tasks and those who are able to recombine the results with other details. However, it is not very effective to switch frequently between the individual tasks. (Data shows, that teams with more than two convergent thinkers are usually successful. However, teams with a chaotic approach are usually unsuccessful.)

Convenience. Room-X is not a *complex* problem, but the presence of the team members and the different puzzles require some mental work to keep the overview and to recognize what the structure of the overall problem and its solution looks like. It is therefore a matter of gaining "system knowledge". Teams with good coordination, communication and documentation have an advantage here as described in Sect. 5.4, since the thinking capacities of the team members are tied up in tasks and can only partially deal with the overall view.

Overstraining. The cognitive system reacts to tasks that seem too complicated by preferring other, simpler tasks, even if they seem less relevant or even when the importance of the difficult task is recognized. This effect can also be observed in Room-X. There are teams who postpone or ignore computer science tasks to the end, but instead complete all simple search tasks very quickly. In Room-X this is especially visible for teams with little CS background knowledge.

Protection of the Sense of Competence. It is also not uncommon to observe actions in which participants ignore clues they have found if these did not fit into the solution strategy they had devised. This effect apparently protects the problem solver from getting into a feeling of inability to act if a hint does not fit into the plan. Thus, the hint is rather put aside, than that it ruins the solution plan.

7 Threats of Validity

As the video analysis is still in progress, there are shortcomings in the area of test validity. The objectivity of implementation can be assumed since the situation as an escape game has no direct test character and is carried out independently and without the influence of the researcher. Due to the number of runs, effects that can occur due to irregular external conditions are reduced. Evaluation and interpretation still require analysis by at least one other person in order to achieve a certain degree of objectivity. The same therefore also applies to the reliability of the evaluation and interpretation of the video material. The operationalized characteristics and behaviors must be made available to the second analyst as a manual and interpreted according to fixed rules in order to achieve the highest possible degree of validity.

8 Conclusion and Perspective

Room-X is an escape game with computer scientific tasks that requires general problem-solving strategies. An advantage of the current concept is that no prior knowledge of specific problem-solving procedures is required. Thus, it can address a broad audience as it only expects skills most tenth-grade learners already have. With regard to the individual tasks, it is advantageous that even teams with little or no prior knowledge can be given a motivating insight into ideas of computer science.

In order to be able to adjust the computer science content according to prior knowledge and skills of the visiting groups, the development of interchangeable modules is planned, which emphasize the usefulness of the computer scientific ideas and the meaning of computer science methods.

First indications for the promotion of problem-solving skills can be derived from the results of the video analysis. As for RQ1, many typical basic problem-solving strategies such as systematic search, team collaboration, documentation could be observed as predicted. As for RQ2, the successful teams are more motivated and determined and are better at documentation and communication. They search more thoroughly and work on the tasks more concentrated. In short, they work in a more structured way. In terms of documentation, the low tendency of the teams towards structured representation is particularly noticeable. The causes for this must therefore be examined more closely.

Ideally, problem solvers should use a cleverly chosen strategy to move purposefully through the problem space. The video analysis showed, however, that no planning phase takes place, but instead participants start with the search for clues, since the current concept does not require a planning phase. In order to strengthen the problem-solving aspect in the future, the current procedure must be replaced. One possible approach is to examine computer science concepts in terms of their structure and integrate them as a (sub) strategy.

References

1. Anderson, L.W., Krathwohl, D.R.: A Taxonomy for Learning, Teaching, and Assessing: A Revision of Bloom's Taxonomy of Educational Objectives. Longman, New York (2001)
2. Arbeitskreis Bildungsstandards SII: Bildungsstandards Informatik für die Sekundarstufe II. Supplement to LOG IN 183/184 (2016)
3. Denning, P.J.: Great principles of computing. Commun. ACM **46**(11), 15–20 (2003)
4. Dörner, D., Kreuzig, H.W., Reither, F., Stäudel, T.: Lohhausen: vom Umgang mit Unbestimmtheit und Komplexität. Huber (1983)
5. Grillenberger, A.: Von Datenmanagement zu Data Literacy: Informatikdidaktische Aufarbeitung des Gegenstandsbereichs Daten für den allgemeinbildenden Schulunterricht. Dissertation, Freie Universität Berlin (2019)
6. Humbert, L., Puhlmann, H.: Essential ingredients of literacy in informatics. In: Magenheim, J., Schubert, S. (eds.) Informatics and Student Assessment - Concepts of Empirical Research and Standardisation of Measurement in the Area of Didactics of Informatics. LNI Seminars, vol. 1, pp. 65–76. GI, Bonn (2004)
7. International Society for Technology in Education (ISTE): Operational definition of computational thinking for K-12 education (2011)
8. K-12 Computer Science Framework Steering Committee: K-12 Computer Science Framework. Technical report, Association for Computing Machinery, Code.org, Computer Science Teachers Association, Cyber Innovation Center, and National Math and Science Initiative, New York, NY, USA (2016)
9. Müsseler, J., Rieger, M.: Allgemeine Psychologie, 3rd edn. Springer, Heidelberg (2017). https://doi.org/10.1007/978-3-642-53898-8
10. Nicholson, S.: Creating engaging escape rooms for the classroom. Child. Educ. **94**(1), 44–49 (2018)
11. Rosenstiel, L.: Grundlagen der Organisationspsychologie: Basiswissen und Anwendungshinweise, 7th edn. Schäffer-Poeschel, Stuttgart (2011)
12. Schoenfeld, A.H.: Reflections on problem solving theory and practice. Math. Enthusiast **10**(1), 9–34 (2013)
13. Schwill, A.: Fundamentale Ideen der Informatik. Zentralblatt für Didaktik der Mathematik **25**(1), 20–31 (1993)
14. Wing, J.M.: Computational thinking. Commun. ACM **49**(3), 33–35 (2006)

PrivaCity

A Chatbot Game to Raise Privacy Awareness Among Teenagers

Erlend Berger, Torjus H. Sæthre, and Monica Divitini(✉)

Department of Computer Science, Norwegian University of Science and Technology, Trondheim, Norway
divitini@ntnu.no

Abstract. Privacy is a well-known concern connected to teenagers' use of e.g., social media, mobile apps, and wearables. An increasing number of schools are looking for ways to integrate this topic in their activities, as part of informatics subjects or integrated in other subjects as part of basic digital competences. This paper explores how chatbot serious games, i.e. games that evolves as a conversation between a player and a software agent, can be used as a tool to raise privacy awareness. We present PrivaCity, a chatbot game to raise privacy awareness in smart cities. Focus on smart cities is motivated by a predominant focus in existing games on what to share and not to share on social networks. Little is done to learn about the risks of the digital footprints, when data is collected about the citizens across a multitude of devices, digital services, and ubiquitous digital sensors. The paper presents the game design, implementation, and evaluation.

Keywords: Chatbot games · Privacy awareness · Smart cities

1 Introduction

Privacy is an ever-growing concern. With the technological development and increase in use of connected devices, data is being collected everywhere, leaving people unaware of what data they share, with whom and what it is used for. Teenagers are a user group for which concerns are higher As a consequence, schools are looking for ways to integrate this topic in their curriculum, as part of informatics subjects or integrated in other subjects aiming at developing basic digital competences. For example, Stobert et al. [22] present the development of curriculum modules related to authentication for Swiss schools. An NSF-sponsored project between the International Computer Science Institute and the University of California-Berkeley has developed an extensive set of material for supporting teachers in addressing privacy in K-12 education[1]. Serious games have recently emerged as a way to learn about sharing of personal data and privacy in an engaging and evoking way. Just to mention a few examples of privacy related serious games (hereafter simply games):

[1] https://teachingprivacy.org/.

S. N. Pozdniakov and V. Dagienė (Eds.): ISSEP 2019, LNCS 11913, pp. 293–304, 2019.
https://doi.org/10.1007/978-3-030-33759-9_23

- *Friend Inspector*, described in [5], aims to raise the privacy awareness of Social Network Sites (SNS) users, like Facebook. The conceptual design of the game focuses on the discrepancies between perceived and actual visibility of shared items.
- *Master F.I.N.D.*, described in [23], focuses on awareness about privacy risks in SNSs. The game is a fake SNS to be played individually by teenagers.
- *Google's Interland* [12] aims at educating children in four areas of internet security: Cyber bullying, phishing, password creation and sharing awareness.

Within this line of research, we present PrivaCity, a chatbot game to increase privacy awareness about Smart Cities, intended as a collection of vehicles, buildings and other physical devices that exchange data with the same information grid, and use this data to create safer, cleaner, more sustainable and efficient cities [16]. Focus on Smart Cities is due to a predominant focus in existing games, and in general in the available teaching material, on what to share and not to share on social networks. Little is done to learn about the risks of the digital foot-prints left by simply using digital services [25].

The research presented in this paper has an explorative nature, aiming at studying how to promote privacy awareness using a chatbot narrative game, i.e. a game where the player assumes the role of a protagonist in an interactive story driven by exploration and puzzle-solving through a conversation with a chatbot, i.e. a software agent. In particular, we aim at understanding which game elements promote learning and engagement. It is important here to underline that the goal of the game is to promote awareness. PrivaCity does not have the ambition to change the behavior of the players. This would be a long-term endeavor, particularly challenging when it comes to privacy [4]. PrivaCity is not a silver bullet, but rather aims at providing an additional tool to teacher to help them discussing about privacy with their students in an engaging way.

In the next section, we present motivations and background information, justifying the choice of a chatbot game and the conceptualization of privacy in the game. We then present the design of PrivaCity and its evaluation with teenagers in 5 different schools.

2 Background

Privacy is a complex concept that has evolved throughout the years, mostly responding to emerging challenges connected to an increasingly digitalized world [9]. Early conceptualizations of privacy explain *privacy as control* [24], mainly connecting it to the capability of controlling the flow and use of personal data. Especially relevant for serious games is the concept of *contextual integrity* [18], which is frequently used to understand privacy concerns related to voluntary sharing of information. Contextual integrity is about respecting the social norms of the situation. In this perspective, privacy concerns arise when the information is shared outside its context. Another interesting concept related to privacy is the *privacy calculus* [14]. In this perspective, the user weighs the risks and benefits of a decision, for instance whether or not to share a photo or current geo-location. Therefore, the decision to share information or not becomes a matter of weighing the trade-offs.

PrivaCity looks at privacy in terms of Contextual Integrity and Privacy Calculus. The decisions of the player can be seen as a result of the privacy calculus, whereas whether the privacy of the user has been violated or not can be viewed in the light of the concept of Contextual Integrity. In this perspective, the game refuses an over-simplifying classification of right or wrong behaviors, but rather aims at raising the awareness of teenagers of potential risks and consequences of their actions and the need to reflect carefully before taking any decision. To achieve this learning objective, a chatbot game seems a promising approach since it allows to involve the player with a conversational agent that can support reflection and privacy calculus.

Chatbot serious games have recently grown in popularity. For example, CiboPoliBot [11] is an educational chatbot game specialized in teaching children about a healthy lifestyle. CuCoMag [19] is designed for the training of customer complaint management in electronic shops. Communicate! [13] is a serious game for practicing communication skills for healthcare professionals, such as doctors or psychologists. While in the mentioned examples the game itself is a chatbot, other games integrate chatbots as non-playable characters to improve the playing experience. For example, in Solis Curse [17] the chatbot plays the role of a narrator. In general, a chatbot can be accessed on multiple channels on several platforms, without restricting the player. Chatbots have a very simple User Interface [11]. Advances in Natural Language Processing, machine learning and big data have contributed to making chatbots better and easier to develop [15], without requiring the high cost of developing the graphics of more traditional video games. This simplicity is not paid in terms of learning since a number of studies, see e.g. [20], have shown that players do not require audio-visually rich games to be effective learning tools.

3 PrivaCity Game Design

PrivaCity is a chatbot serious game for teenagers. The progression of the game is mainly conversationally driven, only including a limited number of buttons and lists to guide the player. The game can be played in a web-browser. The game requires the player to have a persistent Internet connection. Expected time to complete the game is 20–45 min. The conversation is in English.

The game is an adventure game, i.e. a game where the player assumes an active role in an interactive story driven by exploration and puzzle-solving [23]. The adventure genre is one of the most common types of serious games and has been studied to a great extent [8]. The choice of an adventure game was grounded in a series of co-design workshops to understand the type of privacy games interesting for the target group [3].

The game takes place in a fictional city *Metropolis*, that has been a smart city for a few years. A lot of information is being collected to improve the environment, safety, and economy of the city. However, a new party, E.N.D. Privacy, gets control of the city and might try to mis-use the collected information, not respecting the privacy of Metropolis' citizens. The player is challenged with helping to solve the situation. The general idea is that at the beginning of the game the player will be presented with the positive sides of a smart city. As the game progresses, more and more privacy issues and concerns emerge. After having seen both positive and negative sides of a smart city, the player puts his knowledge to use in quizzes and in the conversation.

The player advances the story by completing levels. Each level is located in a different area, starting from a hotel room (where the player gets the context) to the server room (Level 6). At Level 4, the player can choose between two paths (Fig. 1), either to try to sneak into the server room (Level 4.1) or to infiltrate the organization by getting employed (Level 4.2).

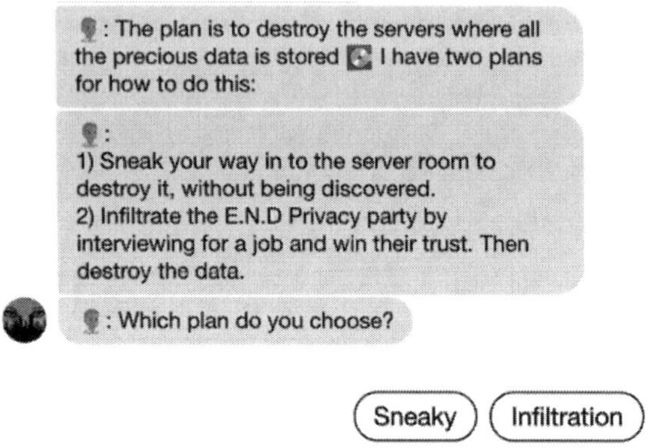

Fig. 1. Choosing between the infiltration or the sneaky path

Both paths, when completed successfully, take the player to the server room. Here the player can weigh risks and benefits of data sharing and decide whether to destroy the server or leave it untouched (Fig. 2). At the end of the game, the player receives a short summary of the game session to promote reflection (Level Sum).

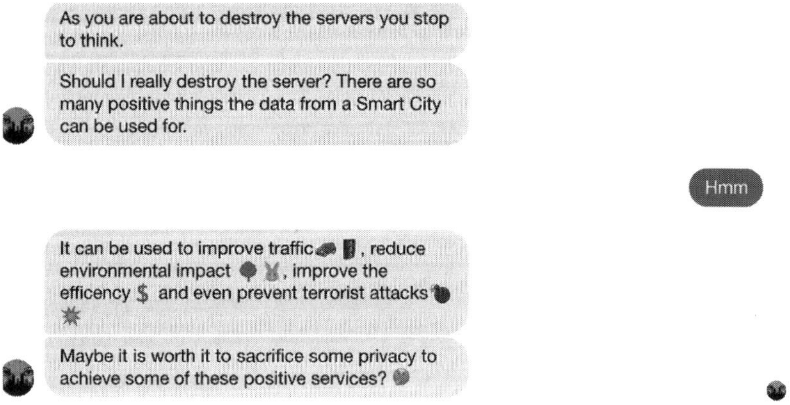

Fig. 2. Reflecting on the final decision, destroying or keeping the server

At the beginning of the game (Level 0), while in its hotel room, the player is presented with the positive sides of a smart city. As the game progresses, more and more privacy issues and concerns are introduced. The main learning goal of the first level is to give a basic introduction to the topic of smart cities. Basic concepts include how a smart city works, as well as how data is gathered and used. Additionally, the player should learn how the smart city can benefit society with improved efficiency, environment, safety and economy. This level also plays an important role in letting the player familiarize with game mechanics, learning how to control the player and interact with objects using the chat only.

In the Hallway (Level 1), the player is made aware of possible problems with smart cities. A secondary learning goal of this level is to teach the player that privacy is often a trade-off, and that one sometimes pays with personal information to receive a reward - such as a monetary reward for sharing location for the rest of the day. Level 2 (the hotel lobby), has the same learning objective and the knowledge of the player is tested with a quiz on privacy. Some questions are general, e.g. Do all mobile apps have access to your position? Others are more specific to smart cities, e.g. How is data collected in a smart city?

When moving to Level 3, a cafe' of the city, the player is made aware about how information in a smart city can be abused by the people with access to it. Additionally, that information collected for one purpose can later be (ab)used for another purpose. The player can also learn about the Facebook and Cambridge Analytica scandal by overhearing the conversation on another table.

At this point the player can choose between two paths. If he decides to break into the server room (Level 4.1), the player is presented with more information about the dangerous misuse of smart city personal data, in form of a quiz based on real-life examples and scenarios. For example, the player has to evaluate if smart street lights that adjusts to natural lighting and people nearby might represent a privacy violation. This level is then followed by a level that is mainly focusing on fun rather than learning.

If the player decides to infiltrate the organization by getting employed (Level 5.1), he is pushed to see things from an attacker perspective and imagine ways that personal information from a smart city can be used. In this way, the game is designed to make the player more aware of privacy trade-offs and understand better the value of the information. At Level 5.2, after being employed, by gaining access to a lot of personal information of the citizens through the audio recordings, the player will get a sense of what information is too personal to be shared online.

Level 6 is the final level, and common for the two paths, aims at underlining the complexity of privacy related decisions. The goal of the player for the majority of the game has been to destroy the data server. However, when the player actually reaches the goal he is once again presented with the positive sides of a smart city, and all the good things collection of information can be used for for example reduce environmental impact, improve traffic and even for counter-terrorism. As in real life, this is a privacy decision with trade-offs that needs to be carefully considered.

Table 1 presents an overview of the game elements used at the different levels. Some of the learning elements are consistently present in most levels of the game, such as *Provide Information*. Others are only present in some of the levels, such as using a *Real Life Scenario*.

Table 1. Game elements to promote learning in each level of the game

Level	Provide info	Consequential play	Repetition	Quiz	Emotions points	Attacker POV	Real scenario	After-action report
0	X							
1	X	X						
2	X		X	X	X X			
3	X	X					X	
4.1	X			X	X		X	
4.2	X		X					
5.1			X	X		X		
5.2	X			X	X	X	X	
6	X	X	X					
Sum			X					X

Table 2 summarizes the game elements used to engage the player. The novelty of interacting with a chatbot is an engagement element that is persistent throughout the game, though likely most effective in the earlier levels of the game and more effective if the player has little experience with chatbots. One of the main ways to engage players in the game is curiosity to explore each level as well as progressing with the narrative. Curiosity is a typical intrinsic motivation [7]. To increase extrinsic motivation, PrivaCity also uses rewards and points for answering quizzes correctly. To promote flow, it is important to balance the difficulty of the task with the ability of the player [6]. For this reason, in the initial levels, when the ability of the player is low, the difficulty to complete the level is low. The player also receives more hints. As the game progresses, the difficulty increases.

Table 2. Game elements to promote engagement in each level of the game

Level	Chatbot novelty	Curiosity	Reward	Points	Consequential play	Funny	Role-play	Character
0	X	X						
1	X	X	X		X			
2	X	X	X	X		X		X
3	X	X			X	X		X
4.1		X		X		X		
4.2		X						
5.1						X	X	X
5.2				X		X	X	X
6					X			

Consequential play, i.e. seeing the consequences of own's actions in the game, is an element that is used to promote both learning and engagement.

PrivaCity was developed using Microsoft Bot Framework and Microsoft LUIS[2] for language understanding; Facebook Messenger and Web-Chat as chat-platforms. Figure 3 provides an overview of the system architecture.

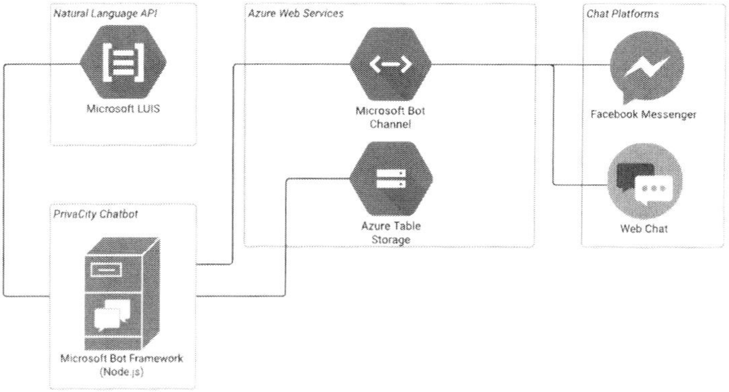

Fig. 3. System architecture

4 Evaluation

A first pilot evaluation of the game was conducted to evaluate the usability of the game and to discover unwanted game behavior, where the game does not respond, freezes, crashes, or provides the wrong response. Running a pilot test helped evaluating which utterances the bot interprets correctly or utterances that are not yet covered by the game and subsequently train the bot. After this first pilot, outside the scope of this paper, PrivaCity was evaluated with teenagers in 5 classes (Table 3).

With this evaluation we want to evaluate if the game indeed promotes awareness of privacy issues in a smart city. More specifically, we aim to evaluate the game in terms of learning and engagement, understanding how different game elements in the game design are perceived by the players.

Table 3. Overview of participants in the evaluation

Class	Time allowed	No. players	No. finishers	Age
A	51 min	30	21	13–14
B	29 min	18	12	16–17
C	25 min	15	2	18–19
D	36 min	25	22	16–17
F	46 min	16	13	14–15

[2] For more information on Microsoft Bot Framework see https://dev.botframework.com/ and for Microsoft LUIS https://www.luis.ai/home.

The evaluation was conducted as part of regular school activities, administered individually by the teachers. The teachers were recruited via e-mail. 4 teachers participated in the evaluation of the game with a total of 104 students, non-native English speakers. (Class C and D had the same teacher.) The classes B, C, and D are from upper secondary schools; A and F from lower secondary schools. The authors were not present during testing but monitored the server logs in case of technical problems. A questionnaire was designed to collect data from students (on a Likert scale 1–5). Some feedbacks from the teachers were also collected via email. The students were given the URL to the game by their teacher, played individually on their own device, and as they reached the final level of the game, they were given a unique ID and a link to the questionnaire. Playing the game was a mandatory classroom activity but answering the questionnaire was voluntary. No sensitive personal data was collected.

Out of the 104 participants, 70 finished the game reaching the final level and 45 of the ones who completed also answered the questionnaire. The low numbers are not completely unexpected. As the game was played individually, it was not possible for the researchers or the teachers to have control on what students were actually doing. Also, it should be noted that in Class C only 2 students completed the game. This was mainly due to some difficulties connected to playing the game on mobile phones. Though it is possible to play, the experience is not optimal. For none of the other players we detected any error or system crash, except for one of the students who made his game session freeze by interrupting the chatbot too many times.

Out of the two paths, 33 participants chose to play the *sneaky* path, and 37 played *infiltration* (out of the 70 participants who finished the game). For the sneaky path of the game, based on the questionnaire's results, there is a gradual increase of perceived difficulty as the game progresses, whereas for the infiltration path the difficulty is constantly around 2 (Easy) to 3 (Medium). Regarding fun, the levels consistently scored between 3 (Medium) and 4 (Fun). There is little difference in the entertainment of the two paths of the game, but sneaky scores slightly higher.

To evaluate if the game raises privacy awareness, the questionnaire included three 5-point scale agreement questions Fig. 4.

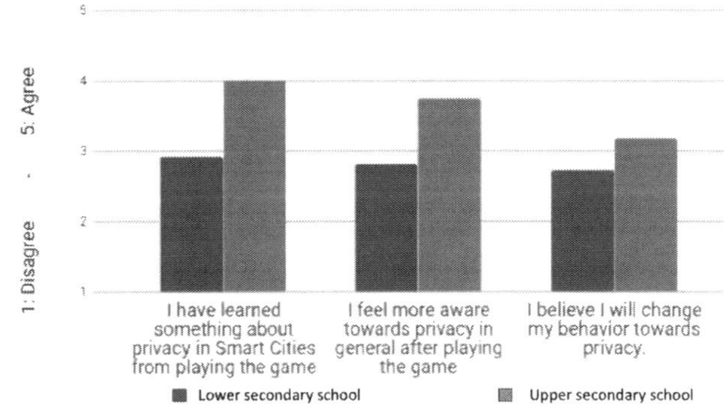

Fig. 4. Privacy awareness, lower versus upper secondary school

Respondents reported a higher agreement on the questions regarding learning outcome and raised awareness, as compared to whether they would change their behavior. This is consistent with multiple studies that discuss the difficulties of achieving behavioral change with a serious game, e.g. [4, 23]. When studying the data grouped by educational stage, there is a significant difference across all three statements, with students from upper secondary schools scoring between 0.5 (p = 0.2360) and 1.1 (p = 0,0133) points higher.

It is also interesting to note that players spending more time playing video games report significantly lower scores on all three questions in comparison to players with little video game time per week (Fig. 5).

Fig. 5. Privacy awareness grouped by hours spent playing video games per week.

One possible reason for this outcome might be that gamers bring different expectations to the game. One participant with 20+ h/week, the one who managed to freeze the game session, commented that the game "*still had a few bugs to iron out*" and provided suggestions to improve the game experience. In comparison, another participant with 0–1 h/week stated that PrivaCity was a "*great game, made me think about how much information the companies Facebook, Snapchat and others know about me and how they can use it*". This feedback is very different from that of the gamer, focusing more on the educational part of the game. This is in line with similar results reported in the literature [11].

The participants were asked to identify the game elements they believe to have helped raise their privacy awareness, with multiple answers allowed (Fig. 6). Quiz is the game element scoring highest. The general idea behind a quiz works well in a chatbot game, where the dialog goes back and forth between the bot asking questions, the player responding, and the bot revealing the correct answer. However, as emerged during the pilot test, it is important to provide an explanation for the answer, even when the player answers correctly. The second most popular learning element is Real life examples. This can be combined with the quiz game element, where when explaining the correct answer, one can use an example from real life. Seeing consequences of actions was also perceived as a good way to learn and raise awareness. It is however very important that the player actually gets to see how actions impact the game, which is the foundation for Consequential Play [2]. Additional research and evaluation are needed to understand how to design the other elements to exploit more their learning potential.

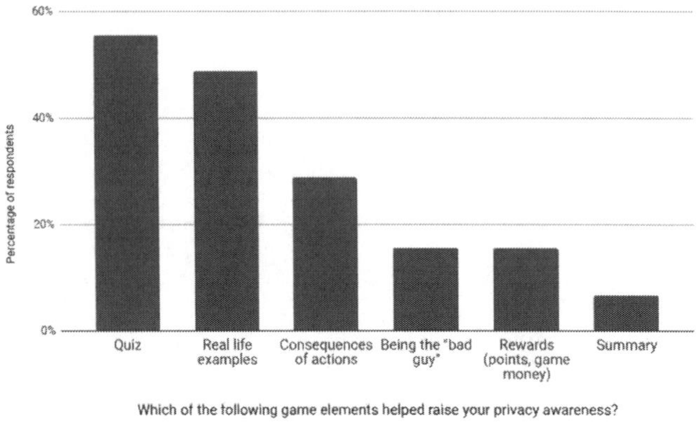

Fig. 6. Evaluation of learning elements

When relating the perceived fun of the game levels with the engagement mechanisms used at that level, the levels relying on *curiosity* seem to be more entertaining than the ones based on extrinsic motivation (rewards, points, etc.). Seeing consequences of actions, which many of the players rated to work well as a learning element, is also a good way to engage the player.

Regarding difficulty, the most difficult level of the game, Level 4.2, is also considered the most entertaining one. This might indicate that increasing the overall difficulty of the game will increase the entertainment value. While an overall increased difficulty of the game might make it more entertaining, the observations from the teachers who were present during the testing indicate that the game was more than challenging enough for some of the students. Therefore, an increased difficulty would probably have led to even fewer students being able to finish the game.

5 Conclusions

The paper presented PrivaCity, a chatbot serious game to promote privacy awareness among teenagers about data sharing in smart cities. The game is a short adventure game where players have to prevent that a malicious organization misuses the data that is collected to provide services to the city's inhabitants. The game aims at promoting awareness about the tradeoffs that are involved in data collection for digital services and make players more aware of the consequences of their choices. The game was evaluated with teenagers of 5 school classes, pointing out strengths and limitations. On the overall, the evaluation was positive. Players reported that their awareness has increased, both in general about privacy and specifically about privacy in smart cities. However, their intention to change behavior was rather low. This is not surprising and calls for a holistic approach to privacy teaching, where the game is seen as one of the tools for a continuous discussion and engagement. This is an approach similar to the one of Google Interland, where the game is used to motivate and interest students, while additional learning material is provided for deepening the understanding of relevant issues. It should also be noted that the results are higher for upper secondary schools. This requires further investigation, but we expect this to be connected to the complexity of the topic and the use of a foreign language for interaction. Students who play less video games also reported higher raised awareness from playing the game. This might imply that the simple text-based interaction becomes boring for experienced gamers. This is another element that requires further investigation.

An important element to promote engagement as well as learning proved to be consequential play. Players enjoyed feeling like they shape the narrative of the game. They also evaluated this to be a successful way to learn about how actions have consequences. This game element may be especially relevant in a serious game trying to raise awareness that all privacy decisions are a trade-off and that choices have consequences for future privacy.

Quizzes also were evaluated as a good game element for promoting learning. In our design experience, the chatbot should provide a brief explanation of the answer, even when it is correct. The explanations that contained real-life examples were considered successful. Even though quiz is a good game element to raise the awareness of the player, we don't believe an entire game based on a quiz is a good idea for a chatbot serious game. That would become too repetitive, and thus quiz is much better suited as a game element in a bigger adventure game.

As part of our future work we aim at conducting a more detailed evaluation of the game, including observations and post-game interviews. We also plan to extend the game using the concept of nudging [1] to research how different ways of presenting information and path choices might influence players.

Acknowledgements. The research is co-funded by the NFR IKTPLUSS project ALerT, #270969. We thank the students and teachers who joined the evaluation.

References

1. Acquisti, A., et al.: Nudges for privacy and security. ACM Comput. Survey **50**(3), 1–41 (2017)
2. Barab, S.A., Gresalfi, M., Ingram-Goble, A.: Transformational play: using games to position person, content, and context. Educ. Res. **39**(7), 525–536 (2010)
3. Bergen, E., Solberg, D.F., Sæthre, T.H., Divitini, M.: Supporting the co-design of games for privacy awareness. In: Auer, M.E., Tsiatsos, T. (eds.) ICL 2018. AISC, vol. 916, pp. 888–899. Springer, Cham (2020). https://doi.org/10.1007/978-3-030-11932-4_82
4. Blythe, J.M., Coventry, L.: Cyber security games: a new line of risk. In: Herrlich, M., Malaka, R., Masuch, M. (eds.) ICEC 2012. LNCS, vol. 7522, pp. 600–603. Springer, Heidelberg (2012). https://doi.org/10.1007/978-3-642-33542-6_80
5. Cetto, A., Netter, M., Pernul, G., Richthammer, C., Riesner, M., Roth, C., Sänger, J.: Friend Inspector: A Serious Game to Enhance Privacy Awareness in Social Networks (2014)
6. Chen, J.: Flow in games (and everything else). Commun. ACM **50**(4), 31–34 (2007)

7. Cherry, K.: Extrinsic vs. Intrinsic Motivation: What's the Difference? Very well Mind (2019). https://www.verywellmind.com/differences-between-extrinsic-and-intrinsic-motivation-2795384. Accessed Aug 2019
8. Connolly, T.M., et al.: A systematic literature review of empirical evidence on computer games and serious games. Comput. Educ. **59**(2), 661–686 (2012)
9. Crabtree, A., Tolmie, P., Knight, W.: Repacking 'Privacy' for a networked world. Comput. Support. Coop. Work. (CSCW) **26**(4-6), 453–488 (2017)
10. Dickey, M.D.: Murder on Grimm Isle: the impact of game narrative design in an educational game-based learning environment. Br. J. Educ. Technol. **42**(3), 456–469 (2011)
11. Fadhil, A., Villafiorita, A.: An adaptive learning with gamification & conversational UIs: the rise of CiboPoliBot. In: Adjunct Publication of UMAP 2017, pp. 408–412. ACM (2017)
12. Interland - Be Internet Awesome. https://beinternetawesome.withgoogle.com/. Accessed Aug 2019
13. Jeuring, J., et al.: Communicate! — a serious game for communication skills —. In: Conole, G., Klobučar, T., Rensing, C., Konert, J., Lavoué, É. (eds.) EC-TEL 2015. LNCS, vol. 9307, pp. 513–517. Springer, Cham (2015). https://doi.org/10.1007/978-3-319-24258-3_49
14. Laufer, R.S., Wolfe, M.: Privacy as a concept and a social issue: a multidimensional developmental theory. J. Soc. Issues **33**(3), 22–42 (1977)
15. Lebeuf, C., Storey, M.A., Zagalsky, A.: Software bots. IEEE Soft. **35**(1), 18–23 (2018). ISSN: 0740-7459
16. McLaren, D., Agyeman, J.: Sharing Cities: A Case for Truly Smart and Sustainable Cities. Urban and Industrial Environments. MIT Press, Cambridge (2015)
17. Neto, J.N., et al.: Solis'Curse - a cultural heritage game using voice interaction with a virtual agent. In: 2011 Third International Conference on Games and Virtual Worlds for Serious Applications, pp. 164–167 (2011)
18. Nissenbaum, H.: Privacy in Context: Technology, Policy, and the Integrity of Social Life. Stanford University Press, Stanford (2009)
19. Othlinghaus, J., Hoppe, H.U.: Supporting group reflection in a virtual role-playing environment. In: Poppe, R., Meyer, J.-J., Veltkamp, R., Dastani, M. (eds.) INTETAIN 2016 2016. LNICST, vol. 178, pp. 292–298. Springer, Cham (2017). https://doi.org/10.1007/978-3-319-49616-0_30
20. Ravyse, W.S., et al.: Success factors for serious games to enhance learning: a systematic review. Virtual Real. **21**(1), 31–58 (2017)
21. Rollings, A., Adams, E.: Andrew Rollings and Ernest Adams on Game Design. NRG Series. New Riders, Indianapolis (2003)
22. Stobert, E., et al.: Teaching authentication as a life skill. IEEE Secur. Priv. **16**(5), 82–85 (2018). https://doi.org/10.1109/MSP.2018.3761712
23. Vanderhoven, E., Schellens, T., Valcke, M.: Educating Teens about the risks on social network sites. Huelva **22**(43), 123–131 (2014)
24. Westin, A.F.: Privacy and freedom. Wash. Lee Law Rev. **25**(1), 166 (1968)
25. van Zoonen, L.: Privacy concerns in smart cities. Gov. Inf. Q. **33**(3), 472–480 (2016). Open and Smart Governments: Strategies, Tools, and Experiences

Author Index

Druck:
Customized Business Services GmbH
im Auftrag der KNV-Gruppe
Ferdinand-Jühlke-Str. 7
99095 Erfurt